The Viennese Minor-Key Symphony
the Age of Haydn and Mozart

The Viennese Minor-Key Symphony in the Age of Haydn and Mozart

Matthew Riley

OXFORD
UNIVERSITY PRESS

OXFORD

UNIVERSITY PRESS

Oxford University Press is a department of the University of
Oxford. It furthers the University's objective of excellence in research,
scholarship, and education by publishing worldwide.

Oxford   New York
Auckland   Cape Town   Dar es Salaam   Hong Kong   Karachi
Kuala Lumpur   Madrid   Melbourne   Mexico City   Nairobi
New Delhi   Shanghai   Taipei   Toronto

With offices in
Argentina   Austria   Brazil   Chile   Czech Republic   France   Greece
Guatemala   Hungary   Italy   Japan   Poland   Portugal   Singapore
South Korea   Switzerland   Thailand   Turkey   Ukraine   Vietnam

Oxford is a registered trademark of Oxford University Press
in the UK and certain other countries.

Published in the United States of America by
Oxford University Press
198 Madison Avenue, New York, NY 10016

© Oxford University Press 2014

Library of Congress Cataloging-in-Publication Data

Riley, Matthew, 1975–, author.
The Viennese minor-key symphony in the age of Haydn and Mozart / Matthew Riley.
pages cm
Includes bibliographical references and index.
ISBN 978–0–19–934967–8 (hardback) — ISBN 978–0–19–934968–5 (electronic text) —
ISBN 978–0–19–934969–2 (online content)   1. Symphony—Austria—Vienna—
18th century   I. Title.
ML1255.R55 2014
784.2'1840943613—dc23
2013039927

1 3 5 7 9 8 6 4 2
Printed in the United States of America
on acid-free paper

{ CONTENTS }

{TABLES, FIGURES, AND MUSIC EXAMPLES}

Tables

Figures

Examples

The Viennese Minor-Key Symphony
in the Age of Haydn and Mozart

The Viennese Minor-Key Symphony

A very small proportion of eighteenth-century symphonies are in minor keys: perhaps no more than 2 percent.[1] Yet they include some of the most dramatic and best-known works of the symphonic repertoire, such as Haydn's "Farewell" Symphony and Mozart's Symphony in G minor, K. 550. In Vienna and the surrounding Habsburg territories over fifty minor-key symphonies by at least eleven composers were written in the late eighteenth century, and they account for some of the finest instrumental works of Haydn and Mozart's contemporaries. Their scarcity in comparison with the thousands of eighteenth-century symphonies in major keys and their distinctive stormy character, nervous energy, and intense pathos make them a unique phenomenon of eighteenth-century instrumental music. A decision to commission, write, or perform a symphony in a minor key was significant. In the mid-eighteenth century, symphonies were usually functional pieces that opened concerts, theatrical performances, and church services, and provided background music at social functions and civic or state occasions. They preceded the main event or discreetly accompanied it. Eighteenth-century critical writings and press reviews mentioned symphonies only occasionally and never discussed them in detail.[2] The symphony was not what mattered. Not all major-key symphonies fit this mold, of course, but minor-key symphonies break it time and again with

---

[1] This often quoted figure is given by eighteenth-century symphony expert Jan LaRue and reported by H. C. Robbins Landon, "La crise romantique dans la musique autrichienne vers 1770. Quelques précurseurs inconnus de la Symphonie en sol mineur (KV 183) de Mozart," in *Les influences étrangers dans l'oeuvre de W. A. Mozart*, ed. André Verchaly (Paris: Centre nationale de la récherche scientifique, 1958), 27–47 (p. 31). About 4 percent of the almost 2000 symphonies listed in the sales catalogs of the publisher Breitkopf between 1762 and 1787 are in minor. R. M. Longyear, "The Minor Mode in the Classic Period," *Music Review* 32, no. 1 (1971): 27–35 (p. 28). LaRue's own Union Thematic Catalogue of eighteenth-century symphonies lists 1075 symphonies in minor keys out of a total of 16,558, thus 6.5 percent, but this is an overestimate, as a symphony is listed as minor if it begins with a slow introduction in minor, even if it turns to major thereafter. The catalog contains opera overtures as well as concert symphonies. See also Jan LaRue, *A Catalogue of 18th-Century Symphonies*, vol.1, *Thematic Identifier* (Bloomington: Indiana University Press, 1988), chap. 2, n. 28.

[2] Neal Zaslaw, "Meanings for Mozart's Symphonies," chap. 12 in *Mozart's Symphonies: Context, Performance Reception* (Oxford: Clarendon, 1989), 510–44.

unusual compositional strategies and forceful emotional expression that demand close attention and participation from the listener.

It is unsurprising that the minor-key symphonies of Haydn and Mozart have generated anecdotes, acquired descriptive titles, and, in the case of Mozart K. 550, attracted an enormous body of criticism, analysis, and philosophical commentary. These works seem to pose questions of meaning and invite interpretation with special urgency. Yet firm conclusions are difficult to establish. The eighteenth-century symphony, after all, is a problematic research field. As its pioneer Jan LaRue put it, "The condition of sources of the 18th-century symphony challenges one's command of pessimistic adjectives."[3] Most Viennese symphonies—aside from those of Haydn and Mozart—are preserved not in autograph but in professionally hand-copied, undated sets of orchestral parts. These sources are scattered far and wide across European archives, and it is often impossible to establish a hierarchy amongst them. Even identifying the composer is not always straightforward, as copyists, publishers, and contemporaneous catalogs sometimes listed works under the wrong name (not always by mistake). The repertory is thus beset by basic problems of authorship, textual authenticity, dating, and chronology, many of which will probably never be resolved. Moreover, the aesthetics and poetics of the Viennese minor-key symphony are obscure. It is hard to reconstruct a prevailing climate of critical opinion in Vienna. There was no regular season of public concerts, and the city lacked a "Republic of Letters" akin to those of Paris, London, Hamburg, or Berlin. There were no discursive newspaper reviews of performances or printed music, and only a patchy legacy of concert advertisements and programs survives. Whatever the opinions of patrons and connoisseurs, they did not communicate them to a regular readership through the medium of print. Practicing musicians did not write treatises for publication, and there was no Viennese tradition of speculative music aesthetics in the form of books or pamphlets. Very few letters by Haydn survive from the period around 1770 when he worked on minor-key symphonies, and Mozart's correspondence is silent as regards his two. The reasons why Haydn suddenly stopped writing minor-key symphonies at the end of 1772 or why Mozart wrote K. 183 on his return to Salzburg from Vienna in 1773 or K. 550 and the other two great symphonies from the summer of 1788 remain subjects of musicological debate. Given the dearth of information, it is unsurprising that critics have tried to explain the phenomenon of the minor-key symphony through biographical anecdotes and loose analogies with the north German literary *Sturm und Drang*.

Luckily the picture is not altogether bleak. Over the decades musicologists have gradually assembled catalogs and published editions of the music of the many so-called *Kleinmeister* working in Vienna and the Habsburg territories whose activities form the backdrop to the familiar works of Haydn and Mozart. They

---

[3] Jan LaRue, "Major and Minor Mysteries of Identification in the 18th-Century Symphony," *Journal of Musicology* 18, no. 2 (2001): 249–67 (p. 249). For a more recent account of the "challenges" facing the scholar, see Mary Sue Morrow, "Reclaiming the Eighteenth-Century Symphony," in *The Symphonic Repertoire*, vol. 2, *The Eighteenth-Century Symphony*, ed. Mary Sue Morrow and Bathia Churgin (Bloomington and Indianapolis: Indiana University Press, 2012), 3–17 (pp. 5–9).

include Georg Christoph Wagenseil, who introduced the "galant style" to the capital, and, from the next generation, Florian Leopold Gassmann, Carl Ditters von Dittersdorf, Michael Haydn, Karl von Ordonez, Leopold Hofmann, and Johann Baptist Vaňhal. Although the quality of their work is uneven, at their best the *Kleinmeister* are fully deserving of modern performance. All wrote minor-key symphonies, many of which are now available in recordings on modern or historical instruments. Meanwhile working chronologies have been established and existing ones revised, including that of Haydn's symphonies to 1774. Although the best scholarship has always recognized that Haydn and Mozart did not compose in a vacuum, never before has the evidence for this fact been so readily available.[4]

A second development in musicology makes the study of minor-key symphonies a timely project. North American music theory has recently turned new attention to conventions and form in late eighteenth-century music. William E. Caplin (*Classical Form*, 1998) has successfully revived nineteenth-century *Formenlehre*—once thought dead—as a theory of formal functions for the instrumental music of Haydn, Mozart, and Beethoven.[5] His concepts are central to this study, although his theory as a whole best describes the music of those three composers between about 1780 and 1800. Many of the symphonies composed in the 1760s and 1770s do not display all the features of the highly consolidated "Classical" syntax that Caplin convincingly describes. James Hepokoski and Warren Darcy (*Elements of Sonata Theory*, 2006) have developed a systematic method of analysis for late eighteenth-century sonata movements derived from the literary theory of genre.[6] Their reconstruction of hierarchies of compositional default options at various stages of a sonata movement helps us understand compositions as individual musical utterances unfolding against a background of conventions. It is now easier to identify when a certain convention or cliché was being called on, when tacitly rejected, and when elaborately transformed or alluded to in passing. The present book pays attention to the conventions specific to the sonata-form outer movements of minor-key symphonies, though it recognizes that such conventions are relatively few and are unevenly distributed within a typical movement, that they were more strongly consolidated at some historical moments than at others, and that the composers of sonata movements communicated with their listeners in many other

---

[4] Ever since Guido Adler and his students began publication of *Denkmäler der Tonkunst in Österreich*, some of the most distinguished musicological work of the twentieth century on the Classical period has been devoted to the raising of awareness, or the actual reconstruction, of the Viennese background. See, for instance, Warren Kirkendale, *Fugue and Fugato in Rococo and Classical Chamber Music*, trans. Margaret Bent and the author, rev. ed. (Durham, NC: Duke University Press, 1979); Jens Peter Larsen, *Handel, Haydn, and the Viennese Classical Style* (Ann Arbor: UMI Research Press, 1988); and Daniel Heartz, *Haydn, Mozart and the Viennese School, 1740–1780* (New York and London: W. W. Norton, 1995).

[5] William E. Caplin, *Classical Form: A Theory of Formal Functions for the Instrumental Music of Haydn, Mozart and Beethoven* (New York: Oxford University Press, 1998).

[6] James Hepokoski and Warren Darcy, *Elements of Sonata Theory: Norms, Types and Deformations in the Late-Eighteenth-Century Sonata* (New York: Oxford University Press, 2006).

ways as well. Robert O. Gjerdingen (*Music in the Galant Style*, 2007) reconstructs the courtly musical "behaviors" of eighteenth-century composers, describing a repertory of shared "schemata" rooted in the eighteenth-century pedagogical tradition of *partimento* exercises, which formed "a musical medium of exchange between court artisans and their patrons."[7] Although, as Gjerdingen admits, almost all his examples are in the major mode, most of the schemata work just as well in minor.[8] The musical language of the Viennese minor-key symphony was essentially an energized minor-mode dialect of the galant style. Given the dearth of written evidence for the meaning of minor-key symphonies and, by contrast, the abundance of compositions that survive, a flexible analytical approach based on these theories seems the most promising way to interpret the sources.

Method

In practice the method adopted in this study is an eclectic combination of criticism, analysis, and historical musicology, which varies according to the composers and works under consideration. At times it is useful to treat the minor-key symphony as a "subgenre," building a picture of the conventions specific to these pieces, their degrees of strength and coherence, and, where possible, their associations and meanings. Around 1770 the sample of works is large enough to establish a sense of the "horizon of expectations" for the Viennese minor-key symphony (although the lack of a precise chronology or any information about performance practices mean that caution is necessary).

The justification for the concept of subgenre is threefold. First, the most salient fact about a minor-key symphony of the late eighteenth century—apart from its identity as a symphony—was its mode. The minor mode in late eighteenth-century music is semiotically "marked."[9] It occurs much less frequently than major and is associated with negative emotional states. Late eighteenth-century writers thought this reflected the artificiality of minor, as they saw it, in comparison with the naturalness of major. According to Jean-Jacques Rousseau in 1768, "the minor mode is not given by Nature; it is discovered only by analogy and inversion."[10] For that very reason, argued Johann Philipp Kirnberger in 1779, music in minor is less complete and settling than music in major, and "is appropriate for the expression of sad, doubtful sentiments, for hesitation and indecision."[11] In 1785 Bernard Germain de

---

[7] Robert O. Gjerdingen, *Music in the Galant Style* (New York: Oxford University Press, 2007), 16.

[8] Ibid., 23.

[9] Robert S. Hatten takes the major-minor opposition as his first example of "markedness" in music. See his *Musical Meaning in Beethoven: Markedness, Correlation and Interpretation* (Bloomington and Indianapolis: Indiana University Press, 1994), 36.

10 Jean-Jacques Rousseau, *Dictionnaire de Musique* (Paris: Duchesne, 1768), 285; cited in Leonard Ratner, *Classic Music: Expression, Form and Style* (New York: Schirmer, 1980), 56.

[11] Johann Philipp Kirnberger, *Die Kunst des reinen Satzes in der Musik*, 2 vols. (Berlin and Königsberg: G.J. Decker, 1776–79), ii, pt. 1, 70; cited in Ratner, *Classic Music*, 56.

Lacépède argued that the minor mode could offer only "impaired consonance" that left the listener dissatisfied and unsettled.[12] Musicians had not always thought this way. About 30 percent of Vivaldi's concertos are in the minor, and are often based on figuration similar to that found in his major-key concertos. Thematic material in major can be immediately repeated in the minor version of the same key as an effect of local color. Early eighteenth-century cycles through the twenty-four major and minor keys such as Bach's *Das wohltemperierte Clavier* imply theoretical equality of major and minor, while Rameau in his *Traité de l'harmonie* (1722) derived both major and minor triads directly from the resonance of the *corps sonore*.[13]

The second justification is the existence of conventions in Viennese minor-key symphonies that seldom appear in contemporaneous symphonies in major keys. In addition to the well-known rhetoric of the *Sturm und Drang* style—driving rhythms, syncopations, wide leaps, unison opening gestures, dramatic pauses—they include a formal convention of fast sonata-form expositions (the "mediant tutti"), counterpoint—sometimes even canon—in minuet movements, and an "untimely rhetoric" of pre-galant idioms (fugato, imitative textures, canon, species counterpoint textures, ritornello gestures, Corellian trio-sonata textures, fast-moving basslines). The minor-key symphony can thus be placed on an equal footing with subgenres such as the Viennese C major "trumpet symphony" and the "sonata da chiesa" symphony with slow first movement.[14] ("Major-key symphony," by contrast, cannot designate a subgenre; indeed, in generic terms the phrase is meaningless as "major" is unmarked in this context.) The first step towards understanding the significance of a minor-key symphony is to compare it with other works of the subgenre. Minor-key symphonies of course allude to other kinds of contemporaneous music, such as operatic rage arias, infernal scenes and storm scenes, contrapuntal chamber music of the imperial court, and Passion music. Some present a mixture of conventional "topics." All these factors are important for critical interpretation. However, the shared melodic figures of the galant style, characteristic scoring and figuration for

---

[12] Bernard Germain de Lacépède, *La poétique de la musique*, 2 vols. (Paris, 1785; repr., Geneva: Slatkine, 1970), 1:189; trans. in Peter Le Huray and James Day, *Music and Aesthetics in the Eighteenth and Early-Nineteenth Centuries* (Cambridge: Cambridge University Press, 1981), 184; cited in Floyd Grave, "Recuperation, Transformation and the Transcendence of Major over Minor in the Finale of Haydn's String Quartet Op. 76 No. 1," *Eighteenth-Century Music* 5, no. 1 (2008): 27–50 (pp. 27–28). An updated version of this view based on compositional practice is proposed by Charles Rosen. "In eighteenth-century tonality a major chord still had less tension than a minor one, and gave a more satisfactory resolution. Haydn's abandonment of minor endings in his later work is not an outbreak of cheerfulness in middle age, but a development of the classical taste for resolution.... On the rare occasions when Mozart chose to end in minor—that is, with some of the harmonic tension still echoing in the mind when the music is over—he always compensated for this by an added simplicity of phrasing and articulation." *The Classical Style: Haydn, Mozart, Beethoven*, new ed. (London: Faber, 1997), 276.

[13] Grave, "Recuperation, Transformation and Transcendence," 27–34.

[14] A. Peter Brown uses the term "subgenre" for the trumpet symphony in: "The Trumpet Overture and Sinfonia in Vienna (1715–1822): Rise, Decline and Reformulation," in *Music in Eighteenth-Century Austria*, ed. David Wyn Jones (Cambridge: Cambridge University Press, 1996), 13–69 (p. 13).

string instruments, the phrase structures and movement-level sonata forms typical of the concert symphony, and the three- or four-movement layout are fundamental to this repertory. The works remain first and foremost late eighteenth-century symphonies in the minor mode, not fragments or arrangements of music from other genres prefaced with the title "symphony."

The final justification for treating the Viennese minor-key symphony as a subgenre is negative. These compositions consistently feature what Hepokoski and Darcy call "deformation": "a stretching or distortion of a norm beyond its understood limits; a pointed overriding of a standard option."[15] The very fact that an eighteenth-century symphony is in the minor mode cues the listener that the ensuing experience will be extraordinary, and, time and again, that cue finds a response in extraordinary compositional choices by composers, communicated with rhetorical force, regardless of whether the specific means employed—contrapuntal textures are the obvious example—can sometimes be located in major-key symphonies too. To take some examples from early in the period, the massive, stylistically retrospective opening gestures of Wagenseil G5 and G6 and Gassmann H83 (see chapter 2) instantly differentiate those pieces from the numerous major-key symphonies the composers were writing in the 1760s, not just in terms of technical procedures, but in the way they propose an alternative musical aesthetic and alternative late eighteenth-century values (probably the values cultivated within the music room of the imperial court). The slow first movement of Haydn 49 with its somber Lenten atmosphere and hushed opening in the rare key of F minor is unique amongst eighteenth-century symphonies. Haydn 45 is deformational in numerous ways (choice of tonic key—the even rarer F♯ minor—bipartite finale, conspicuous inter-movement connections, triple meter in the first movement, v as secondary key, minuet in the development). Haydn 44/iv and 52/iv modify the composer's usual sonata-form recapitulation in ways that he never again attempted in symphonies, string quartets, or piano trios to the end of his life. As later chapters show, the list could continue.

Genre is understood here not as a rigid system of classification but, as for Hepokoski and Darcy, a "regulative principle."[16] What is shared objectively by Viennese minor-key symphonies is a loose constellation of features that includes local syntax, large-scale formal procedures, textures associated with specific movement types, and untimely rhetoric. Not every minor-key symphony displays all these features—far from it—and some conventions were better defined than others, or were well defined only at certain times. In first movements a wide range of tempi, moods, and textures are found. A stormy opening to a minor-key symphony was common but by no means inevitable. Thus the generic approach does not yield equal insight into all minor-key symphonies. The analyses in chapters 4, 5, and 6 acknowledge varying degrees of subgeneric definition and its tendency to dissolve in the 1780s. By that time, composers faced the choice of whether to

---

[15] Hepokoski and Darcy, *Elements of Sonata Theory*, 11.

[16] Ibid., 605.

reestablish dialogue with a lapsed Viennese tradition. Chapter 7 describes contrasting strategies found in the first movements of Haydn 78 and 83. Although they start from similar premises, the former firmly reestablishes that dialogue, while the latter largely abandons it by the time the recapitulation is reached, thereby turning itself into a different type of movement. It is difficult to understand the first and third movements of Mozart K. 550 without recognizing the establishment in the late 1760s and the later dissolution of minor-key subgeneric conventions. While Mozart's symphony is highly original in many ways and was recognized as "modern" in its own time, it also refers conspicuously to minor-key procedures that by the late 1780s had largely died out. This can be interpreted as a distinctive aesthetic/ideological move on Mozart's part.

In addition to this fluidity and changing focus, there were two distinctive strands within the Viennese minor-key symphony, discussed in the first three chapters of this book, which in the 1760s overlapped only occasionally. One is represented by the composers employed by or associated with the Habsburg imperial court (Wagenseil, Gassmann, Ordonez), and the other by "outsiders" such as Haydn, Vaňhal, and Dittersdorf. The former took up something of the style of the contrapuntal chamber music written for the imperial court at the time, which reflected the self-consciously old-fashioned taste of Joseph II. They seldom evince the "stormy style" that we readily associate with minor-key symphonies around 1770: that is found in the second strand.

At first glance it might seem dubious to assert an indigenous Viennese development within the minor-key subgenre (even if taking the term "Viennese" broadly to include the Hapsburg monarchy as a whole). By the late eighteenth century, after all, music and musicians moved freely and rapidly across Europe. But the evidence does support such an argument. Although some "stormy" features (repeated notes, driving rhythms) were relatively common in non-Viennese minor-key symphonies, other subgeneric conventions were not. For instance, a trawl through the minor-key symphonies by Giovanni Battista Sammartini, Franz Xaver Richter, Christian Cannabich, Franz Beck, Johann Christian Bach, Johann Christoph Friedrich Bach, Luigi Boccherini, Francesco Antonio Rosetti, and Joseph Martin Kraus—to take a sample of relatively well-known works from different decades—throws up not a single contrapuntal minuet (these non-Viennese symphonies usually have only three movements), only one "stormy finale" (by J. C. Bach), and only a few mediant tuttis (Beck, op. 3, no. 3/i; J. C. Bach, op. 5, no. 6/iii; Rosetti, A42/i and iv). The latter tend to be less clearly articulated than in most Viennese works. The most obvious is the one in the Bach finale, a movement that seems closer to the Viennese minor-key traditions than any other by a composer working outside the Habsburg monarchy. The mediant tutti and the contrapuntal minuet in Mozart K. 550 strongly suggest that Mozart, for all his stylistic cosmopolitanism, rhetorically evokes past Viennese traditions just as he does in K. 551 with respect to the C-major "trumpet symphony." The two strongly articulated mediant tuttis in the outer movements of Koželuch's G minor Symphony (1787) likewise stand out: there is nothing like them in non-Viennese minor-key symphonies of the time. All of this makes sense insofar as composers educated or based in Vienna maintained a relatively close network defined by pedagogical, professional, and social relationships.[17]

Parts of this book are necessarily descriptive, especially in the first half. This approach helps to establish the background of generic norms and introduces readers to unfamiliar composers and works in an accessible way, giving a sense of the repertory beyond Haydn and Mozart. It is also a suitable method for testing the new theories of form on a wider range of eighteenth-century composers than has hitherto been attempted. On the other hand, the book does not offer a work-by-work survey or pretend to pay equal attention to all symphonies. The movements vary in interest, and some *Kleinmeister* symphonies are limited by the composer's imperfect technique, imagination, or orchestral resources. Thus a balance must be struck between value-free, blow-by-blow description and canon-reaffirming selectivity. I regard Vaňhal as the best composer of instrumental music who inhabited Vienna day-to-day in the 1760s and 1770s. He is an attractive figure, who rose from serfdom to international renown through his own efforts and the merits of his compositions, yet he has received little analytical or critical attention in musicology. So two whole chapters are devoted to Vaňhal, whereas, for instance, the three composers associated with the imperial court, Wagenseil, Gassmann, and Ordonez, are covered in a single chapter. The existing literature on minor-key symphonies focuses heavily on Haydn's great works from the 1760s and early 1770s. Symphony No. 45 ("Farewell") has been the subject of a 400-page monograph.[18] I pay more attention to No. 44 ("Trauersymphonie"), which I regard as a work of equal quality, and to a neglected masterpiece, No. 52.

The book deals mainly with fast, outer movements and with the minuets proper of minuet movements. Internal slow movements of Viennese minor-key symphonies at this time are in major with only one exception (Vaňhal c2/ii is in F minor). Minor-key slow movements are found more frequently in non-Viennese minor-key symphonies (J. C. Bach, Symphony in G minor, op. 6, no. 6; Boccherini, Symphony in D minor, op. 12, no. 4). Moreover, the Viennese slow movements are usually relatively unambitious in invention and emotional range, despite notable exceptions such as Haydn 44/iii, Haydn 45/ii, Haydn 52/ii, and Mozart K. 550/ii.[19] They are stylistically interchangeable with the slow movements of major-key symphonies and are thus not specific to the subgenre. It would seem that most composers did not expect their audiences to pay the same kind of attention to slow movements

---

[17] See John Irving, "The Viennese Symphony 1750–1827," in *The Cambridge Companion to the Symphony*, ed. Julian Horton (Cambridge: Cambridge University Press, 2013), 15–28 (p. 23). "In such a close-knit environment, it is understandable that the generic hallmarks of the Viennese symphony might to a large extent have been determined internally, in a progressive, influential dialogue between professionals working with the materials of their symphonic craft and defining the genre constructionally from within."

[18] James Webster, *Haydn's "Farewell" Symphony and the Idea of Classical Style: Through-Composition and Cyclic Integration in His Instrumental Music* (Cambridge: Cambridge University Press, 1991).

[19] On Haydn 52/ii, see W. Dean Sutcliffe, "Expressive Ambivalence in Haydn's Symphonic Slow Movements of the 1770s," *Journal of Musicology 27*, no. 1 (2010): 84–134 (pp. 98–110).

as to outer movements or even minuets (with the exception of "sonata da chiesa" symphonies in which the slow movement comes first). Presumably for most slow movements the listeners, depending on their sophistication, either took a mental break, or reverted to the exercise of good taste and fine discrimination that is invited by galant-style music in major.[20] Perhaps the presence of minuet movements in Viennese symphonies, which, at least in the 1760s and 1770s, were always in minor and often quite stern in mood, meant that slow movements had to be lighter. Trios of minuet movements likewise do not show any consistent features that are not shared with trios of major-key symphonies, although they may relate to their framing minor-key minuets in interesting ways.

The Symphonies

Table 1.1 shows the symphonies considered in this study. The list includes concert symphonies only (not pieces originally written for the theater). In accordance with conventional usage, any symphony whose first movement "proper" begins in minor is regarded as a minor-key work. If, therefore, only the slow introduction to the first movement is in minor, as in Haydn's Symphonies Nos. 98, 101, and 104, the symphony is not on the list, but works that turn to the tonic major later in the course of the three- or four-movement cycle, even during an opening sonata-Allegro, such as Haydn's Symphonies Nos. 78, 80, 83, and 95, are included. Table 1.1 lists only symphonies with fairly certain attribution. Anonymous works or those once erroneously attributed to one of the listed composers are omitted. Lost works alluded to with attribution by an eighteenth-century source are given in Table 1.2. Ordonez F12, a "sinfonia a 4" that could have been performed by string quartet, is included, but not the pieces by Wagenseil sometimes entitled "Sinfonia" in the sources that are in practice string trios in both scoring and style.[21] Dates are from the modern catalogs of *Kleinmeister* and from Sonia Gerlach's revised chronology of Haydn's symphonies to 1774.[22] Symphonies likely to have been composed after 1800 are omitted. Dating in this format is problematic because musicologists' manner of presenting information and degree of caution vary. Therefore the symphonies are listed not by date, but by (1) composer surname, (2) composer first name, (3) letter name of key, and (4) thematic catalog number. This has the disadvantage of not showing a chronological sweep, but an attempt to arrange the works in chronologically

---

[20] Gjerdingen, *Music in the Galant Style*, 4.

[21] John Kucaba, "The Symphonies of Georg Christoph Wagenseil" (PhD diss., Boston University, 1967), 7–8. Several "symphonies" by Paul Wranicky are actually chamber music, composed at a time when the distinction was relatively clear. They are omitted here. See Nos. 13 and 29 in Milan Poštolka, "Thematisches Verzeichnis der Sinfonien Pavel Vranickýs," *Miscellanea musicologica* 20 (1967): 101–27.

[22] Sonia Gerlach, "Joseph Haydns Sinfonien bis 1774: Studien zur Chronologie," *Haydn-Studien* 7, no. 1–2 (1996): 1–287. Gerlach's chronology is not universally accepted, but it seems to make good sense when the numerous paraphrases of Haydn by Vaňhal are taken into account. (See chapters 3 and 6 in the present text).

TABLE 1.1 Viennese minor-key symphonies c. 1760–90 studied for this book

1	Key	Catalog No.	Date
Dittersdorf, C.	a	Grave a1	1782–85?
	a	Grave a2	–1779
	d	Grave d1	1773–79?
	e	Grave e1	–1766, 1763?
	g	Grave g1	–1768
Gassmann, F. L.	b	Hill 83	1769
	c	Hill 23	1765
	g	Hill 45	1767
Haydn, F. J.	c	Mandyczewski 52	1771
	c	Mandyczewski 78	1782?
	c	Mandyczewski 95	1791
	d	Mandyczewski 26	1768
	d	Mandyczewski 34	1763
	d	Mandyczewski 80	1783/84
	e	Mandyczewski 44	1770–71
	f	Mandyczewski 49	1768
	f♯	Mandyczewski 45	1772
	g	Mandyczewski 39	1765
	g	Mandyczewski 83	1785
Hoffmeister, F. A.	e	Hickman e1	–1778
Koželuch, L.	g	Poštolka I:5	–1787
Mozart, W. A.	g	Köchel 183	1773
	g	Köchel 550	1788
Ordonez, K.	b	Brown B1	1770s?
	c	Brown C14	–1775
	f	Brown F12	–1775
	g	Brown G7	–1780?
	g	Brown G8	–1775
Swieten, G. B.	c	Schmid 7	–1779
Vaňhal, J. B.	a	Bryan a1	1773–74?
	a	Bryan a2	1769–71?
	c	Bryan c2	1764–67?
	c	Bryan c3	1762–64?
	d	Bryan d1	1767–68?
	d	Bryan d2	1773–74?
	e	Bryan e1	1764–67?
	e	Bryan e2	1771–72?
	e	Bryan e3	1760–62?
	f	Bryan f1	1773–74?
	g	Bryan g1	1767–68?
	g	Bryan g2	1764–67?
Wagenseil, G. C.	g	Kucaba G5	–1766
	g	Kucaba G6	–1762
	g	Kucaba G4	–1764

TABLE 1.1 (Continued)

1	Key	Catalog No.	Date
Wranitzky, P.	c	Poštolka 10	1790s?
	c	Poštolka 11	–1791
	c	Poštolka 12	1797
	d	Poštolka 30	–1795
	g	Poštolka 42	1790s?
	g	Poštolka 43	–1790

TABLE 1.2 Viennese minor-key symphonies c. 1760–90 with attribution but not surviving in source

Hoffmeister, F. A.	g	Hickman g1	–1785?
Hofmann, L.	g	Kimball g1	–1775
Ordonez, K.	g	Brown G6	–1766
Swieten, G. B.	g	Schmidt 7	–1799

would involve arbitrary decisions or a very complex method of presentation and might well prove misleading. It is better to deal with chronology discursively.

These symphonies are by composers working within the Habsburg monarchy with close connections to Vienna if not permanently resident there. Those employed at aristocratic courts joined the seasonal moves between city and country estate. There are inevitable ambiguities on account of the complex political arrangements of central Europe in the eighteenth century. Salzburg was not under direct Habsburg jurisdiction, and the Symphony in D minor attributed to Michael Haydn and presumably composed there has not been included. On the other hand, Mozart's Symphony in G minor, K. 183, composed in Salzburg in 1773, is included on the grounds that it was composed directly after Mozart's return from a visit to Vienna during which he had absorbed and even begun to practice himself the latest trends in Viennese instrumental music. The decisive factor is stylistic. The Mozart symphony shows certain similarities with the minor-key symphonies being written at the time by Haydn and Vaňhal, and has melodic figures that recall minor-key music by Gassmann. The one by Michael Haydn does not have such resemblances. For three listed works there is currently no known source; in other words, they are known only from eighteenth-century catalog references.

All the symphonies in Table 1.1 have been consulted in modern edition if one exists. The exceptions are Gassmann 45, Hoffmeister e1, Swieten 7, Vaňhal c3 and f1, Wagenseil G4 and G5, and Wranitzky 10, 42, and 43. The Hoffmeister and Swieten symphonies exist in eighteenth-century editions; the others have been studied in reproductions of manuscript copies of parts. Both eighteenth-century and modern editions are often imperfect. The latter do not always carry critical notes and may be based on just one source out of many alternatives in different archives. For this study it would be impractical to try to smooth out these imperfections; they must be accepted. All the symphonies in modern editions are available on commercial recordings, except for Dittersdorf a1, Gassmann 83 and 23, and Ordonez C14 and F12. Appendix 1 gives details of the sources used and the catalogs and other publications from which the information in Table 1.1 has been gleaned.

Table 1.1 contains much material for reflection, before one even opens a score. For a start it provides evidence of many more Viennese minor-key symphonies than critical or analytical studies of Haydn and Mozart have ever acknowledged. While a few bars of Vaňhal or Ordonez have occasionally been cited as context for the works of the two great masters, it is now clear that the selection must have been haphazard. Secondly, the table confirms a long-held suspicion of musicologists working in this area that the traditional textbook account of a discrete *Sturm und Drang* period around 1770—usually involving a sudden minor-key "crisis" in the instrumental music of one or more Austrian composers followed by an equally sudden abandonment of the minor mode—must be questioned. Although the years around 1770 were certainly the heyday of the minor-key symphony in Vienna, such works were produced at a more consistent rate than the "crisis" theory would allow, covering approximately the thirty years from 1760 to 1790. We should not be surprised that the numbers are lower in the 1780s and 1790s, as by then the overall rate of production of symphonies in the Habsburg territories was falling. Although the symphonies by Haydn and Mozart that are best known today were composed after 1785, by that time the heyday of the symphony in the Habsburg monarchy was past. Mozart wrote only six symphonies after his arrival in Vienna in 1781, and most of Haydn's last thirty were not for home consumption but were written to fulfill foreign commissions or engagements. Finally, the evidence here suggests that the *Kleinmeister* were not merely following the lead of Haydn, as has sometimes been claimed. At least five minor-key symphonies had been written by others in Vienna in the years immediately before Haydn produced his first minor-key symphony with a fast first movement (No. 39, 1765). Although that piece was almost certainly a model for subsequent symphonies, by Haydn himself and others, earlier practices too remained a point of reference for later works.

A Subgeneric Convention: The "Mediant Tutti"

The analytical method and the kind of insights it yields can be illustrated through an examination of one particularly well-consolidated subgeneric convention. The "mediant tutti," as I call it, occurs at an early stage in fast, minor-key sonata-form movements. Thus it is confined to outer movements in the symphony cycle (it is not relevant to slow movements or minuet movements).[23] The large majority of minor-key fast movements in the familiar "stormy" style of the late 1760s and early 1770s allude to it. By contrast, it does not occur in Dittersdorf's or Vaňhal's minor-key symphonies of the early 1760s or in any of the symphonies of the imperial-court composers with the exception of Ordonez C14/i (closely related

---

[23] An exception is Haydn 49/ii—a special case as it is from the only minor-key "da chiesa" symphony of the time that does not turn to the tonic major after the opening slow movement.

to—perhaps even an imitation of—the style of Vaňhal, and rather unlike Ordonez's other four surviving minor-key symphonies). Haydn's Symphony No. 39 (1765) stands at the head of the tradition, with mediant tuttis in both of its outer movements. The mediant tutti does not appear in major-key movements, and it gives rise to exposition structures and, consequently, recapitulation strategies and expressive outcomes that are unique to minor-key sonata-form movements.[24]

The mediant tutti occurs at (or, occasionally, very soon after) the start of the second main paragraph of a minor-key fast movement, often (though not always) after a phase of dwindling energy, repeated figures or chords, a phase of motivic liquidation, or a pause. The final harmony of the preceding (first) paragraph is usually V/i. A loud, energetic gesture is then made, starting on a chord of the mediant. Although it is not always a literal tutti, it often comes as a sudden shock, and emphasizes the harmonic *non sequitur*. The new paragraph begins in the mediant key, without modulation, and normally remains there for the rest of the exposition. The tutti usually expresses the formal function of "initiation" more strongly than "continuation" or "concluding" (Caplin's terms); in other words, it sounds clearly like the start of a new section. It also re-establishes rhythmic continuity and regular phrase rhythm if they have been disrupted. The harmonic progression calls up associations with certain early eighteenth-century music, in particular the link between a slow movement of an instrumental cycle that ends with a half cadence in minor with a "Phrygian" semitone step in the bass before a fast movement begins in the relative major. (Relative to the key of the fast movement the progression is V/iv–I).[25] However, the mediant tutti can also be understood as a rhetorical heightening of a current, non-archaic technique. Many mid-eighteenth-century minor-key pieces, vocal and instrumental, move directly to the relative major without modulation, though most do not articulate the move strongly. (The late eighteenth-century theorist Heinrich Christoph Koch assumes that all modulation in the major mode will occur within a rhythmically continuous phrase, whereas in minor the music may move straight to the relative major following a half cadence.)[26]

The mediant tutti is related to a particular type of "medial caesura" (Hepokoski and Darcy) found in contemporaneous major-key sonata movements: the tonic half-cadence type.[27] This is encountered, for instance, in the symphonies of the

---

[24] The mediant tutti has been noticed by several scholars but seldom isolated for discussion. See Robert S. Winter, "The Bifocal Close and the Evolution of the Viennese Classical Style," *Journal of the American Musicological Society* 42, no. 2 (1989): 318–19; Heartz, *Haydn, Mozart and the Viennese School*, 291, 457; and Hepokoski and Darcy, *Elements of Sonata Theory*, 27 and (the best discussion) 111–12. See also R. M. Longyear, "The Minor Mode in Eighteenth-Century Sonata Form," *Journal of Music Theory* 15, no. 1–2 (1971): 182–229 (p. 198).

[25] Jan LaRue, "Bifocal Tonality: An Explanation for Ambiguous Baroque Cadences," in *Essays on Music in Honor of Archibald Thompson Davison* (Cambridge, MA: Department of Music, Harvard University, 1957), 173–84.

[26] Winter, "Bifocal Close," 279–80. Heinrich Christoph Koch, *Versuch einer Anleitung zur Komposition*, 3 vols. (Leipzig: Adam F. Böhme, 1782–93; repr. Hildesheim: Olms, 1969), 3:345.

[27] On the medial caesura and its harmonic types, see Hepokoski and Darcy, *Elements of Sonata Theory*, 24–29.

first generation of Mannheim composers and in Mozart's early symphonies. The cadence and caesura are followed directly by the subordinate theme, without modulation.[28] In the case of both mediant tutti and tonic half-cadence medial caesura, a tonic half cadence is followed by the tonic chord of the subordinate key. There is obviously a crucial difference between the two: in the first case the final cadential dominant and the new tonic are the same chord and the change of key is relatively seamless; in the second they are not. In major-key sonata movements a tonic half-cadence medial caesura tends to occur relatively early in an exposition (earlier, in general, than other medial caesura options), just like the mediant tutti in minor-key movements.

The mediant tutti follows a main theme rather than a transition, so the analogy with the medial caesura is not exact.[29] In some minor-key movements, indeed, the mediant tutti will itself behave like a transition, working to a second caesura after a half cadence in the relative major that is followed by a subordinate theme with characteristic rhetoric (low dynamic level, lyricism). The exposition is then divided into three main parts (Fig. 1.1). If this is to be regarded as a transition, though, it is one not acknowledged by textbooks, for when it begins it is already in the subordinate key. (The existence of non-modulating transitions is well known, but it is usually thought that they begin and end in the tonic.) On the other hand, the section beginning with the mediant tutti will sometimes extend all the way to the perfect authentic cadence in the relative major at the end of the exposition, thus dividing the exposition into only two main parts, neither modulating, the second longer and more loosely organized than the first, the overall harmonic scheme being i: i–V; III: I–I (Fig. 1.1). Viewed in retrospect from the end of the exposition, in this type of movement the mediant tutti does resemble a medial caesura, even if an independent transition is lacking. The second part can then be regarded as a subordinate theme. Its vigorous character and the material it often shares with the main theme should not bar it from subordinate-theme status, as these qualities are relatively common in subordinate themes, especially in Haydn. From the point of view of Caplin's functional theory, it presents the correct succession of formal functions (initiating–medial–closing), it begins and ends in the correct key (the subordinate key), it ends with the correct cadence (perfect authentic), and its organization is appropriately loose.

	Two-part			Three-part		
Section	I	II		I	II	III
Harmony	i: i–V	III: I–I		i: i–V	III: I–V	III: I–I

FIGURE 1.1 Minor-key outer-movement expositions with mediant tutti: two types.

---

[28] Winter, "Bifocal Close," 295–310.

[29] Hepokoski and Darcy claim that the tonic half-cadence medial caesura is rare in minor, which, strictly speaking, may be true, although they appear unaware of the plentiful examples of the mediant tutti considered here. See *Elements of Sonata Theory*, 26–27.

The mediant tutti is the pivotal moment in a common pattern of energy transfer in fast minor-key symphony expositions. Although the phrase *Sturm und Drang* in music usually implies driving energy, the highest levels of energy are seldom sustained from start to finish of a movement. Indeed, the subtle handling of decreases in energy—including caesuras, rhythmic hesitancy, and reductions in texture—is a central compositional strategy of the subgenre. The main theme, stated at the opening in the tonic, often loses energy—rhythmic, dynamic, or both—or seems to falter towards its end. Rather than an authentic cadence it usually ends with a half cadence and a phase of "standing on the dominant." In Classical sonata expositions, the pointed articulation of a half cadence would be reserved for the end of the transition; indeed, main themes that end with a half cadence are uncommon by the 1780s. In contrast to the typical main theme of later Classical sonata style, the main themes of minor-key symphonies around 1770 are often relatively loosely organized. That might mean repetition of the continuation and cadential units (the typical "galant" abb or abb' structures favored especially by Vaňhal for main themes), extension of the dominant harmony of the half cadence, or other techniques that result in asymmetrical phrase structures or the inefficient expression of formal functions. The hesitancy of the main theme's conclusion is swept away by the mediant tutti, which leads to what is often a relatively long paragraph entirely in the mediant key. The gain in energy at this point is far more sudden than one would normally find in sonata-form expositions of the late eighteenth century.

There are no constraints on what motivic material appears at the mediant tutti. Sometimes the tutti will reuse material from the basic idea of the main theme or from its continuation, in similar or altered guise. Sometimes the material will be entirely new. The mediant tutti may use altogether conventional motivic material such as scales or other passagework in keeping with the tendency of fast minor-key symphony movements to foreground energy at the expense of the presentation of characteristic motivic material. Whatever the case, however, the mediant tutti almost always projects the formal function of initiation, regardless of whether its motivic material is new or old, characteristic or conventional, and it will do so even when it is not preceded by actual silence. In a sense the mediant tutti contradicts what has gone before: it is not just a second start but a new start for the movement as a whole, in a different tonal direction.

The first symphony composed in the Habsburg monarchy to use the mediant tutti was probably Haydn 39, where it occurs in both outer movements. The first movement is the likely model for the convention of energy loss. Other examples of the late 1760s and early 1770s include Haydn 26/i, 44/i, 49/ii and iv; Vaňhal g1/i and iv, g2/i and iv, e1/i and iv, d1/iv, a2/iv, and e2/i; and Mozart K. 183/i. A short modulating transition occurs before the tutti in Vaňhal a2/iv, e2/i, and Haydn 44/i, while in Haydn 49/ii the main theme ends with a perfect authentic cadence rather than a half cadence. Less fully articulated examples from the same period include Vaňhal c2/i and iv. The mediant tutti is alluded to distantly in Vaňhal d2/i, Haydn 44/iv, and Haydn 52/i. Exx. 1.1–1.5 give examples from three G-minor symphonies, which have been selected partly because they have been cited in the past as evidence of influence amongst composers of minor-key sym-phonies.[30] Studying them in the light of the mediant tutti brings a new perspective to this discussion. Paradoxically, given its likely convention-defining status, Haydn 39/i (Ex. 1.1) is a little unusual in bringing back the presentation phrase of the main theme between the dominant caesura (bars 11–12) and the mediant tutti (bar 17). This is what Hepokoski and Darcy call a "grand antecedent / dissolving consequent" strategy.[31] Nevertheless, the hesitant C♯ appoggiaturas and unaccompanied repetitions of bars 10–11 were a model for later movements that move straight from the dominant pro-longation to the tutti. In any case, bar 16 re-establishes dominant harmony. The tutti reuses part of the basic idea of the main theme, but instead of "exact repetition" of the basic idea, such as occurs in the presentation phrase of the main theme (compare the statement of the basic idea in bars 13–14 with that in bars 15–16), the tutti features the "Romanesca" schema (only the first two bars shown in Ex. 1.1).[32] This gives the tutti something of the character of a continuation, even though presentation function is expressed too. In Haydn 39/iv (Ex. 1.2), the phase of standing on the dominant at the end of the main theme occupies five bars, the last three of which (from the drop to *piano*) are shown. The tutti uses new, and largely conventional, material, save for the figure in thirds in the oboes. The corresponding standing on the dominant in Vaňhal g1/i (Ex. 1.3) suggests a debt to one or both of the Haydn movements. As in Haydn 39/i, the main theme features exact repetition of its basic idea and at the mediant tutti that basic idea reappears but is drawn into a Romanesca, a similarity that is hard to attribute to chance. At the tutti the original violin figuration is smoothed out, the rests eliminated, and the intervals of the melody expanded, revealing an underlying affinity with the wide leaps at the start of Haydn 39/iv. In Vaňhal g1/iv (Ex. 1.4), the mediant tutti reuses the basic idea of the main theme in almost unaltered form, with the same kind of repetition ("exact"), but with the melody transferred to the bass (Vaňhal used the latter technique also in the finales of g2, d1, and e1). In Mozart 183/i (Ex. 1.5), a longer-than-usual initial section in the tonic—more than just a "main theme"—ends with a stereotypical standing on the dominant with a decrescendo marking and *pp* final chords. This amounts to an exaggeration of the convention of dwindling energy, especially in the context of the stormy opening bars and the preceding doleful repeti-tion of the theme by the oboe. (Exaggeration of minor-key conventions is rather typi-cal of this movement.)[33] The motivic material used for the mediant tutti is entirely new and includes a Lombardic figure that is familiar from countless major-key works in the galant style: a sharp contrast to what has gone before and a new beginning in a new idiom. Of the five movements considered here, Haydn 39/i, Vaňhal g1/i, and Mozart

---

[30] H. C. Robbins Landon, "La crise romantique," 37–41; Landon, *Haydn: Chronicle and Works*, vol. 2, *Haydn at Eszterháza, 1766–1790* (London: Thames and Hudson, 1978), 380–82, 390–93; see also Winter, "Bifocal Close," 318–19, which mentions Vaňhal g2 as well.

[31] Hepokoski and Darcy, *Elements of Sonata Theory*, 77–80.

[32] Gjerdingen, *Galant Style*, 25–34.

[33] A. Peter Brown, "Haydn and Mozart's Stay in Vienna: Weeding a Musicological Garden," *Journal of Musicology* 10, no. 2 (1992): 192–230 (p. 223).

Ex. 1.1 Haydn 39/i, bars 9–18

183/i make a dominant half-cadence medial caesura later in the exposition and move to a separate subordinate theme in the mediant (three-part exposition type), while Haydn 39/iv and Vaňhal g1/iv make no subsequent medial caesura in the exposition (two-part exposition type). On this evidence one might suspect that three-part expositions with mediant tuttis are characteristic of first movements, two-part expositions of finales, but in fact that is not the case. In Vaňhal e1, for instance, the reverse applies.

The highly dramatic effect of the mediant tutti and its swift stereotyping in Haydn and Vaňhal made it readily available for ironic treatment. In Haydn 49/ii, the stormy opening with typical wide leaps, running passagework, and syncopations ends with loud, repeated dominant chords. After a caesura the music begins again on III, but softly, strings alone, with scurrying figures in imitation. Both outer movements of Dittersdorf g1 parody the convention. The main theme of the first movement begins forcefully, but its continuation is based on jerky staccato eighth notes and trills in octaves, implying nothing more than a tonic–dominant alternation (bars 9–14). After the half-cadence caesura, at the moment when a mediant tutti is to be expected, the jerky phrases begin again on III, but *pp* instead of *forte*. This is a repetitive duet between first and second violins, a comic touch, but one at first based on a voice-leading pattern reminiscent of a "Corelli leapfrog," an untimely gesture that evokes grandeur and seriousness. There are several layers of humor here: the seriousness of the opening and the Corelli allusion contrast with the jerky phrases,

Ex. 1.2 Haydn 39/iv, bars 11–17

Ex. 1.3 Vaňhal g1/i, bars 14–19

Ex. 1.4 Vaňhal g1/iv, bars 12–16

Ex. 1.5 Mozart K. 183/i, bars 25–32

which, rather incongruously, are made to express an initiating function based on a complex voice-leading pattern and substitute for the expected grand tutti. If this example is relatively subtle, the treatment of the mediant tutti in the finale of the same symphony is an unmistakable burlesque (Ex. 1.6). The stormy main theme is constructed from obviously shop-worn material—descending arpeggio eighth notes—while the continuation phrase (bars 17–29) is subjected to exaggerated dramatization and extension. The half-cadential dominant is prolonged first through melodic flourishes and alternations with the tonic, then through soft repetitions of the dominant note separated by rests, as if in hushed anticipation. After the caesura there is a soft beginning on III, just as in the first movement. The passage that follows evokes opera buffa by means of a crescendo and increasing density of motivic repetition that could accompany a mad "patter" sequence in a typical "buffa aria" for a male comic character (bars 30–37).[34] An opera buffa allusion is entirely out of place at this point in a minor-key symphony. Occasionally, buffa-style material might appear later in an exposition (in a subordinate theme), but its presence here defeats the purpose of the mediant tutti. There is no doubt about the humorous intent: such effects were no less characteristic of Dittersdorf than of Haydn.

Generic analysis after the manner of Hepokoski and Darcy finds significance in the compositional decision to make a merely oblique or passing allusion to a well-established convention or indeed to omit it altogether. The mediant tutti was well enough established by 1770 to allow such interpretative moves. In Dittersdorf a1/i and a2/i, both probably composed rather later than most of the symphonies discussed hitherto, the possibility of a mediant tutti is opened by means of a dominant prolongation, but the tutti itself is merely hinted at or avoided altogether (a1/i, bars 16–17, 32–33; a2/i, bars 32–33). This technique is akin to the strategy that Hepokoski and Darcy call "medial caesura declined."[35] Haydn 45/i makes a gesture towards a mediant tutti—oblique but unmistakable—before going on to establish the unusual v rather than III as the exposition's subordinate key. This is the only movement amongst all the works listed in Table 1.1 to practice tonal deception by means of a feint towards a mediant tutti, and the return to minor mode after the taste of major contributes to the obsessive, driven quality of the movement's exposition.

The spate of mediant tuttis in fast minor-key movements subsided after the early 1770s. The pattern is not even hinted at in fast movements of the later 1770s and early 1780s such as Vaňhal a2/i, a1/i, a1/iii, d2/iii, e2/iv, f1/i, or f1/iii, Hoffmeister i, van Swieten 7/i or 7/iii, or Haydn 78/i. It reappears in Haydn 95/i, while 80/i and 83/i evoke distant memories. (The later Haydn finales are either not sonata forms or are in the major mode, so the question does not arise for them.) By the 1780s, to write a clearly articulated mediant tutti was to make an unambiguous statement: it meant a return to a conception of the minor-key symphony that had once been commonplace but had since been superseded. Koželuch I:5/i and I:5/iii (1787) fall into this category. Mozart K. 550/i (1788) alludes to the convention (bar 28), but combines several techniques encountered in earlier symphonies in a new way. The six-bar dominant prolongation (bars 16–21) and the $c\sharp^3$–d^3 progression in the melody are

---

[34] James Webster, "The Analysis of Mozart's Arias," in *Mozart Studies*, ed. Cliff Eisen (Oxford: Clarendon Press, 1991), 101–99 (p. 108).

[35] Hepokoski and Darcy, *Elements of Sonata Theory*, 45–47.

Ex. 1.6 Dittersdorf g1/iv, bars 17–38

Ex. 1.6 (Continued)

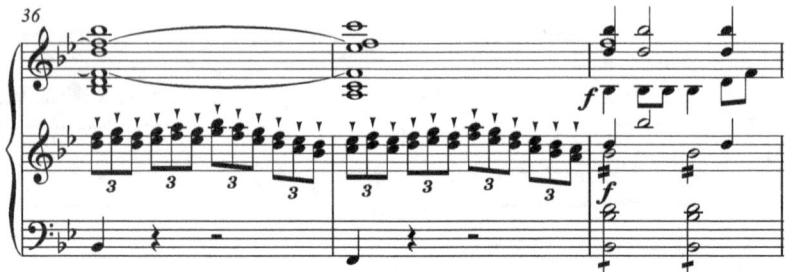

familiar gestures, and even the repeated alternation of dominant and augmented sixth chords had been used by Vaňhal in a G-minor symphony (Ex. 1.3). By bringing back the opening bars of the main theme in the tonic after the caesura, however, Mozart draws the mediant tutti into a grand antecedent / dissolving consequent strategy that had not been heard in the Viennese minor-key symphony since Haydn 39/i (Ex. 1.1).[36] Those bars form a short modulating transition similar to those found in Vaňhal a2/iv and e2/i and Haydn 44/i. However, the hesitancy of the dominant prolongation preceding the mediant tutti of Haydn 39/i and the sparse textures characteristic of it and of several symphonies that followed it are absent. The hypermeter is comparatively regular, the surface rhythm consistent and the caesura filled with a retransition-like descending phrase. The sharp disjunction created by earlier mediant tuttis is avoided. Mozart's strategies in this movement in relation to minor-key conventions are discussed in detail in chapter 8.

To modern ears attuned to minor-key music post-1780, especially that of Beethoven, the mediant tutti may sound problematic. The sudden turn to a positive gesture expressing an initiating function in the major mode so early and with such vigor may seem anticlimactic or may even appear to trivialize the pathos of the preceding minor-mode music. Celebration, one might feel, should not follow suffering so easily: it ought to be more hard-won. Beethoven practiced writing a mediant-tutti gesture in the first movement of the "Kurfürsten" Sonata in F minor WoO 47, no. 2 (1783), but he never used it thereafter. To view minor-key symphonies of the 1760s and 1770s through a post-Beethoven lens, though, is anachronistic—at least, if it implies negative aesthetic judgments. It should not be assumed that around 1770 an energetic turn to major carried the redemptive associations it would acquire in the nineteenth century. (In the strong Counter-Reformation Catholic culture of eighteenth-century Austria, after all, redemption was a gift of divine grace, not something achieved through human struggle.) Though it is certainly rhetorically exaggerated, the mediant tutti is just one of many strategies for handling the transfer of energy in this subgenre. It would be better to compare it with the heightened rhetoric of music for the Viennese stage of the 1760s, where the representation of

---

[36] K. 550 is in fact Hepokoski and Darcy's example of a "grand antecedent." See *Elements of Sonata Theory*, 78–79.

an individual's faltering courage and, conversely, growing resolution in the face of destiny was often vividly portrayed.[37] We should try, then, as far as possible, not to hear the mediant tutti through a nineteenth-century filter. Nevertheless, it is quite possible that, through its frequent use, the convention began to seem hackneyed even at the time, as the ironic treatments in Dittersdorf g1/i and g1/iv and its relative neglect in the later 1770s and 1780s suggest.

The mediant tutti is crucial to the understanding of the status of the minor mode in these symphonies, its relation to major, and the expressive profile of each movement. At the mediant tutti, the initial premise of the movement is contradicted, and the more common, and, in late eighteenth-century terms, more "natural" major bursts in, almost as if to recommence the movement on the terms of a festive, major-key symphony. Central to the overall strategy of minor-key symphony movements with mediant tuttis is that in the recapitulation this surging major-key energy—along with whatever galant-style gestures might follow in the course of the subordinate key area—is not eliminated but is drawn into the minor, a modal reversal that may be articulated through further dramatization of the tutti itself (now in tonic minor), greater continuity, the extension of the main theme's continuation phrase, or a lessening of its hesitancy. While some movements of the 1770s and 1780s turn to the tonic major at some point in the recapitulation, occasionally even at the beginning, movements that clearly articulate a mediant tutti in their exposition almost always conclude in minor.

This account of the mediant tutti and its associated strategies owes something to Hepokoski and Darcy's understanding of late eighteenth-century sonata movements in minor, though with caveats. They maintain, with a nod to the aesthetics of the era, that the minor mode signifies an imperfect and troubled condition that seeks "emancipation," "escape," or "liberation" in the more optimistic and natural major. The minor-mode sonata movement tries to normalize itself (on semiotic terms, to dissolve its own "markedness"). Expositions that modulate to III—the large majority—present an opposition not just of tonal regions, as in major, but of mode. The modulation allows a release from the minor mode into the major, although outside the tonic. Thus the exposition constitutes a "structure of promise."[38] Only a move to the tonic major at some point in the recapitulation can fulfill the promise and effect a "'truer' liberation." The achievement or failure of that liberation results in optimistic or pessimistic scenarios. Therefore, if the tonic major is not established in the recapitulation, "the

---

[37] Examples can be found in several numbers from Gluck's *Don Juan* (1761) marked "risoluto," all of them, ironically, containing moments of unmistakable irresolution. In "Ombre, larve, compagne di morte" from Gluck's *Alceste* (1767), the heroine recoils in horror at the fate decreed by the gods, but then discovers her will to contest it. The "Intrada" to Act I of *Alceste*, a powerful minor-key sonata movement, contains a kind of mediant tutti. This is admittedly a different type of piece from the concert symphonies considered in this book. The mediant tutti occurs relatively late in the first part of the form, only after the modulation to the subordinate key (in this case, v) has taken place (thus the key of the tutti is VII relative to the overall tonic), and it is repeated in the recapitulation in III.

[38] Hepokoski and Darcy, *Elements of Sonata Theory*, 311.

emancipatory paradigm has been unfulfilled, and for this reason we may speak of one type of sonata-process failure."[39] Hepokoski and Darcy's understanding, however, works best for a relatively restricted repertory of music composed in the last quarter of the eighteenth century.[40] In the mid-eighteenth century it is highly unusual for any instrumental movement that begins in minor to end in major. In Viennese minor-key symphonies of the 1760s, the option of a turn to major during the recapitulation of a sonata movement was almost never taken. There is only one exception: Haydn 26/i (1768).[41] It proves the rule insofar as it is a semi-programmatic movement from a work entitled in the earliest source "Passio e Lamentatio," probably intended for performance during Holy Week. Its mediant tutti paragraph is uniquely based on an old church melody borrowed from a medieval Passion drama that could hardly be transformed into a minor version without impiety (see chapter 5). Around 1770, then, any "structure of promise" in a minor-key-symphony outer movement is established by the events of the exposition alone, not by precedent. Hepokoski and Darcy's vocabulary is unhelpful here, as the "emancipatory paradigm" is almost always "unfulfilled," and minor-key "sonata-process failure" is the norm.

Interpretations: *Sturm und Drang*, "Crisis," "Reform"

Twentieth-century research progressed more quickly on Haydn and Mozart than on their Viennese contemporaries. In the absence of accurate dating, Viennese critical writings, or published scores of the other composers, musicologists' attempts to make sense of minor-key symphonies were speculative. There was a biographical interpretation ("romantic crisis"), a link with the German literary *Sturm und Drang*, a theory of a collective "Austrian musical crisis," and the idea of a "reform movement" in Austrian instrumental music.

---

[39] Ibid., 313.

[40] As regards Haydn they appear to have concentrated on minor-key sonata movements composed after 1780, as they say that he "is usually eager to get to the major mode quickly within these recapitulations—sometimes at the earliest available opportunity," and that the "few notable cases" in which the minor mode persists well into the recapitulation, or even to the end of the movement, are "less common." As James Webster pointed out fifteen years earlier, this does not apply to most of Haydn's music pre-1780, and not to his movements in sharp-side minor keys at any time. See Webster, *Haydn's "Farewell" Symphony*, 221–24. For Beethoven, Hepokoski and Darcy's model works especially well for fast sonata movements in C minor, which almost always modulate to III in the exposition and at least touch on I in the recapitulation, even if i is reasserted thereafter. See also Joseph Kerman, "Beethoven's Minority," in *Write All These Down: Essays on Music* (Berkeley and London: University of California Press, 1994), 217–37.

[41] Vaňhal a2/iv, probably composed around 1770, is the next example. Gassmann 23/iv (1765) is a long binary movement that turns to the tonic major near the end, but the form is so unconventional that it is moot whether one can speak of a recapitulation at all.

The phrase *Sturm und Drang* was introduced to musicology by Théodore de Wyzewa in an article on the centenary of Haydn's death (1909).[42] Wyzewa conjectured that Haydn, provoked by the death of an unknown woman, suffered a "romantic crisis" in 1772 that manifested itself in minor-key works such as Symphonies Nos. 44, 45, and 49, and the Keyboard Sonata in C minor, Hob. XVI/20. Unfortunately, Wyzewa had no evidence for this interpretation, and in fact his theory was little more than a theme of contemporary Beethoven biography (the "immortal beloved") transferred wholesale to Haydn.[43] In any case, Wyzewa went on to point out similar stylistic traits in contemporaneous works by Gluck, Mozart, C.P.E. Bach, Vaňhal, and Dittersdorf, suggesting that they reflected a general *Zeitgeist*. This mood did not last for long, however. It was a sudden "paroxysm," which, like the literary *Sturm und Drang*, flared up suddenly and then fizzled out. The label *Sturm und Drang* is handy and has persisted in textbooks, although there is little consensus as to whether it applies only to minor-key works, to all Haydn's works around 1770, to Austrian music in general, or to a Europe-wide movement. Its defects are well known. Wyzewa's chronology was awry: later studies showed that most of the Austrian minor-key symphonies he listed were composed well before the German literary *Sturm und Drang* had begun.[44] As sociological phenomena, the musical and literary movements were quite distinct. The German writers were young, Protestant, bourgeois, educated but frustrated; Viennese composers were seldom bourgeois in origin and sometimes had little education beyond music; their symphonies were performed at aristocratic courts and wealthy monasteries. In recent decades, growing sensitivity to these cultural differences has meant that the idea of a pan-European *Zeitgeist* has lost its appeal.[45] *Sturm und Drang* as a discrete period in the history of compositional style has likewise fallen into disrepute, even if restricted to minor-key works. Sammartini composed stormy minor-key symphonies in the 1740s; the minor-key sonatas and quartets of Haydn and Vaňhal of the 1770s are in a different style from their symphonies; only one of Ordonez's five surviving minor-key symphonies fits the pattern, and his minor-key quartets are heterogeneous in style.[46] *Sturm und Drang* is a useful label for individual

[42] Théodore de Wyzewa, "Apropos du centenaire de la mort de Joseph Haydn," *Revue des deux mondes* 79 (June 15, 1909): 935–46.

[43] Mark Evan Bonds, "Haydn's 'Cours complet de la composition' and the *Sturm und Drang*," in *Haydn Studies*, ed. W. Dean Sutcliffe (Cambridge: Cambridge University Press, 1998), 152–76 (p. 152).

[44] H. C. Robbins Landon, *Chronicle*, vol. 2, 266–67.

[45] But see Barry S. Brook, "*Sturm und Drang* and the Romantic Period in Music," *Studies in Romanticism* 9 (1970): 269–84; and Abigail Chantler "The *Sturm und Drang* Style Revisited," *International Review of the Aesthetics and Sociology of Music* 34, no. 1 (2003): 17–31. Brook's approach is self-consciously old-fashioned, even for 1970; it all but accepts the principle of a *Zeitgeist* and argues that a "Commonwealth of Art" could be said to exist in 1770 (pp. 278, 283).

[46] Bathia Churgin, "Stormy Interlude: Sammartini's Middle Symphonies and Overtures in Minor," in *Giovanni Battista Sammartini and His Musical Environment*, ed. Anna Cattoretti (Turnhout: Brepols, 2004), 37–62 (p. 38); David Wyn Jones, "The String Quartets of Vanhal," 3 vols. (PhD diss., University of Wales, 1977), 1:95–97, 175; David Wyn Jones, Introduction to Johann Baptist Vaňhal, *Six Quartets: An Edition and Commentary* (Cardiff: University College Cardiff Press, 1980), 14; A. Peter Brown, "The Symphonies of Carlo d'Ordonez," *Haydn Yearbook* 12 (1981): 5–121 (pp. 42–45); A. Peter Brown,

movements by various composers, for a set of recurrent characteristics (minor mode, driving rhythms, syncopations, wide leaps, unison opening gestures, dramatic pauses), and for a conventional "topic" that could be invoked in almost any piece, but not for a historical period.

Most writings that use the phrase have adapted it to an Austrian/Viennese context, usually by establishing the theatrical origins of the stormy or emotional minor-key style, thus dating it well before the literary movement. Antecedents have been found in Hasse's penultimate Viennese opera *Piramo e Tisbe* (1768); in Gluck's reform operas and the ballet *Don Juan* (1761); in the parallel operatic reforms of Jomelli and Traetta; in Haydn's own operas; and in his non-operatic theater music.[47] However, the most cogent reformulation of the *Sturm und Drang* theory as regards Viennese instrumental music is the combined work of two eminent Haydn scholars, Jens Peter Larsen and H. C. Robbins Landon. One provided the theory, the other evidence and interpretation. Their arguments deserve some attention, as the concept of the minor-key subgenre developed in this book takes them as a starting point.

In the mid-twentieth century, Larsen conducted a critique of conventional thinking about eighteenth-century music history, especially historians' understanding of what he called the "mid-century style" (a somewhat obscure concept) and its relation to the "great composers" from the early and late eighteenth century (the "Baroque" masters Bach and Handel, the "Classical" composers Haydn and Mozart). He rejected the application of evolutionary theories to music history that led to the search for a "missing link" in the midcentury in favor of a dialectical model.[48] Larsen proposed 1770 rather than 1780 as the onset of Viennese Classicism, arguing that the new style that emerged at the time was not a development of the midcentury style that would lead gradually onward to "high" Classicism but a sharp reaction against that style and a return to Baroque traditions. This is not a Baroque defined by Bach and Handel, but a specifically Viennese Baroque with Italian and Catholic associations,

---

"The Chamber Music with Strings of Carlos d'Ordoñez: A Bibliographic and Stylistic Study," *Acta Musicologica 46*, no. 2 (1974): 222–72, 222n2.

[47] Ernest Harriss, "Johan Adolf Hasse and the *Sturm und Drang* in Vienna," *Revista de Musicologia* 16, no. 5 (1993): 10–21; Landon, *Chronicle*, 2:267, 280; Joel Kolk, "*Sturm und Drang* and Haydn's Opera," in *Haydn Studies*, ed. Jens Peter Larsen, Howard Serwer, and James Webster (New York: W. W. Norton, 1981), 440–45; Elaine Sisman, "Haydn's Theater Symphonies," *Journal of the American Musicological Society* 43, no. 2 (1990): 292–352; see also Daniel Heartz, "Sturm und Drang im Musikdrama," in *Bericht über den internationalen Musikwissenschaftlichen Kongress, Bonn, 1970*, ed. Carl Dahlhaus et al. (Kassel: Bärenreiter, 1971), 432–35.

[48] Jens Peter Larsen, "Traditional Prejudices in Connection with Viennese Classical Music," chap. 22 in *Handel, Haydn*, 281–99 (p. 285). First published in *Symbolae historiae musicae: Hellmut Federhofer zum 60 Geburtstag*, ed. Friedrich W. Riedel and Hubert Unverricht (Mainz: Schott, 1971), 194–203. See also the other essays in the section "Viennese Classical Style," in *Handel, Haydn*; and "The Viennese Classical School: A Challenge to Musicology," *Current Musicology* 9 (1969): 105–12.

epitomized by Johann Joseph Fux and Antonio Caldara.[49] Larsen was taking a stand against German nationalist historiography that traced stories linking one great German master to the next. For Larsen, the midcentury trend towards small-scale, easygoing music for performance by and entertainment of dilettantes was replaced by a return to strong emotions, large forms, and the demand for professional standards of performance. As the midcentury style was itself a reaction against the Baroque, the new movement was a reaction to a reaction. It was a "reform" movement in Austrian instrumental music to match that of Gluck in opera, and was underpinned by a streak of conservatism in Viennese composers that had already ensured that the midcentury style never laid deep roots.[50] "[Haydn] did not to go through a 'Romantic crisis', but he simply realized his artistic will to overcome the intermediate style, and to a great extent resorted to the style conception and in part to the stylistic means of Baroque music."[51] This theory retained Wyzewa's original notion of a turn to seriousness and a sudden break, but loosened the music from both biography and literature, finding purely musical reasons for a collective change of style within an Italian-Viennese tradition. Mozart's Symphony in G minor, K. 183, for instance, was not a "self-confession" or the expression of the composer's depression.

> Mozart's choice of this key was hardly the result of a personal conflict, but due simply to his acquaintance with Haydn's series of symphonies in minor keys written about this time, and more particularly with the G minor Symphony, No. 39.... It is quite obvious that Mozart's concern with symphonic problems during those years must, in any case, have forced him to try his hand at a symphony in a minor key.[52]

Landon's first essay on the subject, entitled "La crise romantique dans la musique autrichienne vers 1770," was written before most of Larsen's had been published, but did not go so far, even though it favored the idea of a reform movement over purely biographical explanation. Landon retained something of the idea of a *Zeitgeist*, speaking of a "violent spiritual revolution" in both German literature and Austrian music, and a general revolutionary atmosphere in Europe and the American colonies.[53] In this reform movement the composer's aim was no longer merely to entertain, but to reflect intellectual and moral problems. In line

---

[49] Larsen, "Some Observations on the Development and Characteristics of Viennese Classical Music," chap. 18 in *Handel, Haydn*, 227–61 (p. 233). First published in *Studia musicologica Academiae scientarium Hungaricae* 9, no. 1 (1967): 115–39.

[50] Ibid., 236.

[51] "Traditional Prejudices," 286. See also "Some Observations," 239. "What happened was most likely that Haydn at last got tired of the worn-out style of midcentury music, and realized how much more expansive force was to be found in the traditions of Baroque music."

[52] Jens Peter Larsen, "The Symphonies," in *The Mozart Companion*, ed. H. C. Robbins Landon and Donald Mitchell (London: Rockliff, 1956), 156–99 (p. 173). Interestingly (see text below) the editors added a dissenting footnote.

[53] Landon, "La crise romantique," 29, 32.

with Larsen's view, it marked "the dawn of the great classical era."[54] In particular, composers of symphonies were in reaction against the shallowness of the Italian opera *sinfonia*. Landon kept in touch with Wyzewa's idea of romantic crisis, but adapted it as "a curious sort of collective emotional crisis that was not limited to a single composer."[55] The essay was published in a book on Mozart, and Landon's aim was to show that, although K. 183 was isolated in Mozart's output, it was not isolated in Viennese music and did not require biographical explanation. He drew comparisons between three G-minor symphonies—Haydn 39, Vaňhal g1, and Mozart K. 183—and quoted from them abundantly. The lasting contribution of the essay was the identification of the composers who participated in the reform (Haydn, Mozart, Vaňhal, Ordonez, and Gassmann) along with characteristics of their shared style: minor keys, the reappearance of counterpoint, syncopations, tremolando effects, wide melodic leaps, themes stated in unison, and weightier finales that become more like first movements in duration, meter, and character. Landon found these characteristics not just in symphonies but in keyboard music and chamber music as well.[56]

In his later compendious Haydn "Chronicle," Landon returned to the concept of a collective "Austrian musical crisis." He now maintained that it ran in parallel with the crisis in German literature but was independent of it, following a purely musical logic.[57] The Austrians were led by Haydn; the other composers were his "seguaci," including, at that stage, Mozart. Dissatisfied by "Tafelmusik," they set out to reform Austrian music by drawing on their indigenous contrapuntal tradition, the severe style of C.P.E. Bach, opera seria, and, in the case of Haydn, Gregorian chant and folksong. Landon now cited Gassmann b1 and Vaňhal g1 and d1 along with Haydn Nos. 49 and 52 as revolutionary works in their respective composers' oeuvres. Like the literary *Sturm und Drang*, the new passionate style in music soon burned itself out, and was collectively abandoned by its composers as suddenly as it had arisen. "[B]oth movements were extremely similar in their essential message, in their language and structure, in their relatively short span of life, and not least in the fact that the leading members of both schools later repudiated (either in fact or in word, or both) their *Sturm und Drang* period."[58] Haydn's String Quartets op. 20 or his Symphonies Nos. 45 and 49 amount to "a grand cul-de-sac." With this literary analogy Landon modified Larsen's purely musical approach.

Larsen and Landon's idea of a reform movement in Austrian instrumental music is appealing. By the mid-eighteenth century, demand for instrumental music was intense from both the aristocracy and the middle classes. In Europe's large cities, music publishing and subscription concerts were opening new markets, and

---

[54] Ibid., 46.

[55] Ibid., 32.

[56] Ibid., 33.

[57] Landon, "Crisis Years: *Sturm und Drang* and the Austrian Musical Crisis," vol. 2, chap. 4 in *Chronicle* (see esp. pp. 266–84).

[58] Landon, *Chronicle*, 2:267.

production could hardly keep up. Symphonies in particular were needed by publishers, theaters, concert promoters, noble patrons, ecclesiastical bodies, and civic organizations. The midcentury styles—for want of a better term—especially the Italian opera *sinfonia*, lent themselves to rapid and voluminous production. The sheer number of symphonies turned out is astonishing: the Union Thematic Catalogue for the eighteenth-century symphony lists 16,558.[59] A single composer often wrote over 100. As Jan LaRue points out, in the eighteenth century "the printing and playing of symphonies...approaches mass production."[60] Of course, there was no mechanized production line, and most symphonies circulated in sets of parts copied by hand. But Italian composers of opera prided themselves on their ability to turn out an aria or *sinfonia* at top speed. The latter were usually noisy and relied on highly conventionalized material. In the theater, the audience would have talked through them. Dittersdorf satirized the results with the deliberately empty and repetitious second movement ("Italiano") of his *Sinfonia nationale nel gusto di cinque nazioni* (–1766). Yet Dittersdorf himself wrote over 120 symphonies, and perhaps as many as 200, most of them in the 1760s.[61] Not only were these pieces quick and easy to write, they were quick and easy to learn and play, and were ideally suited to a culture in which rehearsal time was minimal or nonexistent. Many symphonies composed for the ensembles of small courts—this is true even of Vaňhal—required professional standards of performance only on the first violin part. Other orchestra members would likely have been amateur musicians who were principally employed in administrative roles. In Vienna countless new symphonies and concertos (especially for violin) were performed in public from the late 1750s, pushing older music off the programs, even that of famous names. As the leading solo violinist in Vienna in the early 1760s, Dittersdorf maintained that in Vienna the music of Tartini and Locatelli was considered suitable only for practice, not public performance.[62]

These forms of musical production and performance unsurprisingly found their correlate in reception. The inattention of some eighteenth-century audiences has been abundantly documented.[63] A painting of 1766 shows the ten-year-old Mozart playing at the salon of Prince Conti while aristocrats display their nonchalance by drinking tea and holding conversations.[64] In the 1780s even the playing of the famous Mannheim orchestra accompanied card games. A satirical drawing of 1785 shows chamber music in a Viennese salon being ignored by the chatting company. In an account of his travels through Germany and Austria, Friedrich Nicolai

---

[59] LaRue, *A Catalogue of 18th-Century Symphonies*.

[60] La Rue, "Major and Minor Mysteries," 251.

[61] Eva Badura-Skoda, Introduction to Karl Ditters von Dittersdorf, *Six Symphonies*, Series B, vol. 1 of *The Symphony, 1720–1840* (New York and London: Garland, 1985), xxvii–xxviii.

[62] Heartz, *Haydn, Mozart and the Viennese School*, 52, 57.

[63] See esp. James H. Johnson, *Listening in Paris: A Cultural History* (Berkeley and Los Angeles: University of California Press, 1995).

[64] Michel Barthélemy Ollivier, *Le Thé à l'anglaise dans le salon des quatre glaces au Temple, avec toute la cour du prince de Conti, écoutant le jeune Mozart* (1766).

observed that the Viennese expected refreshments and gambling at their concerts, in contrast to the public at home in Berlin.[65] When he visited the Burgtheater in Vienna in 1781 he reported "I paid close attention not only to the operas but also to the symphonies played between the acts, to which the auditors usually pay so little heed."[66] They included pieces by Haydn and Vaňhal. North German writers of music criticism and theory became preoccupied by problems of attention and distraction.[67]

Deep fault lines in musical life emerged at this time as reaction against the new practices set in. Upholders of traditional musical values complained a lack of education and judgment in the large, "anonymous" audiences that attended modern concerts. They maintained that the musical public was dominated by untutored listeners who were swayed by sensational effects. At some public concerts, inexpert listeners apparently outnumbered experts by a wide margin.[68] Composers were acutely aware of these circumstances, as witnessed, for instance, by the Mozarts' correspondence, and discussed the problem of what kind of compromise might be justifiable.[69] C.P.E. Bach told a young composer, "In works that are to be printed, and therefore are for everyone, be less artful and give more sugar."[70] In pieces written for his own enjoyment and his small circle of expert colleagues, however, Bach was much more ambitious. Criticism of contemporaneous musical culture often ran in parallel with a new awareness of the musical past and an interest in the new subject of music history, which challenged the reigning preference to contemporaneous musical production and the belief that music dated quickly.[71] The music historians Johann Nikolaus Forkel and John Hawkins and the diplomat and patron Baron Gottfried van Swieten disliked contemporary music and harked back to an earlier golden age of fine compositional craft. Even the emperor Joseph II took this view and attempted to foster the traditional ways. In France, after the political crisis of the early 1750s and the *Querelle des bouffons*, a "dichotomy of taste" emerged between "la musique moderne" and "la musique ancienne" or "la musique française"—the official style of Lully that still dominated the *Opéra* and recalled

---

[65] Heartz, *Haydn, Mozart and the Viennese School*, 59, 58.

[66] Friedrich Nicolai, *Beschreibung einer Reise durch Deutschland und die Schweiz*, 4 vols. (Berlin: Stettin, 1784); cited in Heartz, *Haydn, Mozart and the Viennese School*, 62.

[67] Matthew Riley, *Musical Listening in the German Enlightenment: Attention, Wonder and Astonishment* (Aldershot: Ashgate, 2004).

[68] For statistics, see Riley, *Musical Listening*, 110n6.

[69] See Leopold Mozart's letters to his son (urging him not to make his music too difficult for the majority of listeners) of May 6, 1778, August 13, 1778, and December 11, 1780, and Wolfgang's letter to his father on December 28, 1782, in Emily Anderson, ed. and trans., *The Letters of Mozart and His Family*, 3rd ed. (London and Houndsmills: Macmillan, 1985), 536, 599, 685, and 833.

[70] C.P.E. Bach, letter to Johann Christoph Kühnau, August 31, 1784, quoted and translated in Stephen L. Clarke, ed. and trans., *The Letters of C.P.E. Bach* (Oxford: Clarendon Press, 1997).

[71] William Weber, "The Contemporaneity of Eighteenth-Century Musical Taste," *Musical Quarterly* 70, no. 2 (1984): 175–94.

the glorious reign of Louis XIV.[72] This marked an early phase in the opening of the "great divide" between popular and elite production so characteristic of modern Western musical culture. The old literary quarrel of the ancients and the moderns found its way into music, and in England, France, and Germany notions of "ancient music" and "musical classics" appeared for the first time, with academies and concerts to support them. The experts may have been outnumbered, but they formed a significant and articulate minority, whose views influenced the compositional choices of composers.

The low numbers of minor-key symphonies may reflect the taste of the growing number of dilettantes who wanted to play and listen to instrumental music and who expected undemanding entertainment. A telling statistic from the sales catalogs of the Leipzig publisher Breitkopf has the proportion of string quartets in minor keys slowly but steadily increasing between 1767 and 1787, but the proportion of violin concertos and keyboard concertos in minor, which was almost 17 percent in 1762, dropping to almost nothing in the late 1760s and remaining there for the next twenty years.[73] At this time the string quartet was developing from a divertimento to a genre for small gatherings of musical experts; the concerto, by contrast, was a public genre aimed at an untutored audience. Minor-key symphonies may reflect the desire of traditionally minded patrons to cultivate fine musical craftsmanship and encourage attentive listening, objectives that would help to account for the contrapuntal idioms often encountered in these works. Several of Haydn's minor-key symphonies were probably composed for performance in church during Holy Week and allude to Jesus' Passion. Their audience would presumably have listened with the attitude of sobriety and spiritual self-discipline practiced during Lent in Catholic countries. The music theorist Joseph Riepel remarked in 1765 that "today most music lovers are no longer pleased to listen to sad things, except in church."[74] Some of the Viennese minor-key symphonies invited them to transfer the attitude they brought to their worship to abstract instrumental music normally played at concerts. Of course, none of this should be taken to imply that major-mode music was inevitably shallow or that it could not be equally finely crafted. That would be palpably untrue, and is not the point at issue.

This interpretation of the minor-key symphony helps to account for the otherwise curious combination in the subgenre of what was, for its time, exceptionally subjective (stormy passion) and exceptionally objective (conspicuous counterpoint). The apparent paradox is resolved if the subgenre is understood—after the fashion of Larsen and Landon—as a mode of resistance to the contemporary practices of compositional overproduction and distracted listening, in short, a decline

---

[72] William Weber, "*La musique ancienne* in the Waning of the Ancien Régime," *Journal of Modern History* 56, no. 1 (1984): 58–88 (p. 82).

[73] Longyear, "The Minor Mode in the Classic Period," 29–30.

[74] Joseph Riepel, *Anfangsgründe zur musikalischen Setzkunst* (1752–68), vol. 4 (Augsburg: Lotter, 1765), 32; cited in W. Dean Sutcliffe, "Expressive Ambivalence in Haydn's Symphonic Slow Movements of the 1770s," *Journal of Musicology* 27, no. 1 (2010): 84–134 (p. 89).

in the quality of musical experience. When in 1788 the old-fashioned Hawkins complained that "We hear no more the solemn and pathetic Adagio, the artful and well-studied Fugue, or the sweet modulation of the keys with the minor third," the characteristic features of the subgenre are linked in a single sentence: pathos, the minor mode, traditional compositional craft, counterpoint, and solemnity.[75] In Vienna there was a strong tradition of music for imperial public ceremony until the death of Charles VI (1740), in which counterpoint was consciously cultivated. This repertory, dominated by Johann Joseph Fux and Antonio Caldara, remained in living memory for decades and was preserved in the imperial archive and maintained in practice in chamber-music composition for Joseph II's private salon. The pedagogical tradition established by Fux flourished in Vienna throughout the century despite the deviation of contemporary practice from the style of Palestrina that Fux took as his teaching model. If, as one source reported, Joseph II was a "lover of the music of pathos,"[76] then we find the same coupling of pathos and counterpoint as in Hawkins.

But the concept of reform needs refinement. Ironically, Landon's own weapons—improved chronology and evidence of Austrian music beyond Haydn and Mozart—undermine his own case. He and Larsen based their arguments on too small a sample of compositions. Landon's claim that the characteristics he found in minor-key symphonies appear consistently in other genres can be discounted. As regards the symphony, the information in Table 1.1 has already shown that the notion of a sudden flare-up that quickly blew itself out is too simple. Despite the vogue circa 1770, Viennese minor-key symphonies are distributed more widely in time than is often thought, while, on the other hand, at no stage did they outnumber major-key symphonies in the production of any composer, even around 1770. The most recent chronology for Haydn's symphonies suggests that his main minor-key phase lasted at least seven years (1765 to 1772), and more if Symphony No. 34 (1763) is counted, the first movement of which is in minor. To grant Haydn undisputed leadership of the movement is questionable, as Wagenseil, Dittersdorf, and Vaňhal had written minor-key symphonies in the early 1760s (it is possible that Gassmann and Ordonez had contributed too). And, as more recent research has made clear, Vaňhal g1 and d1 were not "revolutionary" works within his oeuvre. They were not his earliest minor-key symphonies, and others, composed both before and after those two, are no less powerful or interesting, and arguably more so.[77] Further minor-key symphonies were written in the later 1770s and the 1780s.

---

[75] From Hawkins's introduction to William Boyce, *Cathedral Music*, 2nd ed. (London: John Ashley, 1788); cited in Percy Young, *A History of British Music* (London: Benn, 1963), 343, and in Daniel Heartz, *Music in European Capitals: The Galant Style, 1720–1780* (New York: W. W. Norton, 2003), 905.

[76] *Musikalische Korrespondenz* 1 (Speyer, 1790): cols. 27–30. Quoted in Kirkendale, *Fugue and Fugato*, 38–39 (translation adapted). Original given in the German edition. "Der Kaiser war Liebhaber vom Pathetischem…." Warren Kirkendale, *Fuge und Fugato in der Kammermusik des Rokoko und der Klassik* (Tutzing: Hans Schneider, 1966), 88.

[77] Paul Bryan, *Johann Wanhal, Viennese Symphonist: His Life and His Musical Environment* (Stuyvesant, NY: Pendragon Press, 1997). See Table 1.1 for works and Bryan's provisional dating.

The numbers were smaller, but statistically that is hardly surprising, as the overall number of symphonies composed in Austria fell significantly in the 1780s. The continuities in mood and syntax evident in some of these later works show that there was still much to say with the resources available. One advantage of understanding the minor-key symphony as a subgenre is that it reminds us—as Larsen himself realized—that the music need not be understood on the terms that the literary *Sturm und Drang* invented for itself: the pouring forth of powerful "nature" unmediated by reason or civilization, which might start or stop inexplicably. Minor-key symphonies were just as bound up with conventions as any other pieces: they did not appear *sui generis* through an irrational urge.

The study of influence amongst the composers around 1770 can now be executed more precisely than was possible for Landon. It has long been known that Vaňhal, Ordonez, and Gassmann wrote minor-key symphonies at the same time as Haydn and Mozart. But until Paul Bryan's thematic catalog (1997), it was unclear exactly how many Vaňhal had written and when, and the influence cited was just a similarity of restless, driving, energetic minor-key music.[78] Landon's coupling of G minor symphonies by Haydn, Mozart, and Vaňhal obscures the fact that many features shared by these three works, such as the mediant tutti (Exx. 1.1–1.5), appear in other minor-key symphonies by Haydn and Vaňhal, in keys other than G minor. In this light, it is the differences between the various movements that show up clearly: the main theme of Vaňhal g1/i, for instance, uses the common galant abb' structure that he favored strongly for the main themes of outer movements in his symphonies of the late 1760s, but which Haydn and Mozart hardly ever used. Moreover, as will become clear in chapter 3, there are far more obvious examples of Vaňhal modeling his work on Haydn, to the point of paraphrase. As far as minor-key symphonies are concerned, Ordonez can hardly be regarded as a follower of Haydn: four of his surviving five are in a very different style and the one *Sturm und Drang* piece follows Vaňhal more closely than Haydn. Only in the thorough rewriting of the recapitulation of Ordonez G7/i can the influence of Haydn be felt, and that technique of Haydn's was hardly confined to minor-key movements (see chapter 2). Mozart K. 183, though it follows the example of Haydn and Vaňhal in important ways, is also indebted to the music of Gassmann, as A. Peter Brown has pointed out.[79]

Finally, the unity of the reform movement should not be taken for granted. Even when certain obvious features of style were shared, such as *Sturm und Drang* topic, the mediant tutti, and contrapuntal techniques, they could be deployed in markedly different ways. Recent theoretical work such as that of Hepokoski and Darcy makes us more alert to these differences in strategy than traditional histories of musical style that enumerate common features such as wide intervals and syncopations. Differences in compositional strategy may reflect differences in technique,

---

[78] Bryan, *Johann Wanhal.*

[79] Brown, "Haydn and Mozart's Stay in Vienna," 223–29.

patronage, audience, and orchestral resources, but also deep-seated issues in aesthetics and musical ideology. Professional rivalry may have played a role too. The presence of shared techniques and vocabulary might reflect a desire to improve on the work of another composer as much as benign influence. It may be necessary to conceive of competing versions of reform and extend the concept beyond the minds and intentions of composers to include the reform of musical patronage (the taste, values, and aims of Joseph II or Nikolaus Esterhazy, for example).

This book takes up a dialogue—sometimes tacit, sometimes explicit—with Larsen and Landon, drawing on recent work in music theory to refine and update their basic insights. In doing so, it tends to bypass developments in North American historical musicology of the last few decades that paint a less differentiated picture of the late eighteenth century. This work has focused on communication, rhetoric (music as an oration in tones), comedy and entertainment, and has largely set itself against the alleged anachronism of "Romantic/Modernist" perspectives of a previous generation of musicologists.[80] (Those perspectives are said to have valued originality over convention, tragedy over comedy, and integrity over communication.) To be sure, the literature on conventional "topics" in eighteenth-century music that has emerged along with this way of thinking is important and informs much analytical work in the present study.[81] But the sensitivity of today's musicologists to potential anachronism in their own viewpoint means that they downplay the diversity of eighteenth-century musical life. One sometimes gets the impression of an Edenic oneness of eighteenth-century composer and listener under the heading of "rhetoric," which is shattered in the nineteenth century by a fall into Romantic solipsism on the one hand and the objectified "work" on the other. That dichotomy

---

[80] For statements of this position, see Wye J. Allanbrook, "Mozart's Tunes and the Comedy of Closure," in *On Mozart*, ed. James M. Morris (Cambridge: Woodrow Wilson Center Press and Cambridge University Press, 1994), 169–86; and James Webster, "Haydn's Symphonies between *Sturm und Drang* and 'Classical Style': Art and Entertainment," in *Haydn Studies*, ed. W. Dean Sutcliffe (Cambridge: Cambridge University Press, 1998), 218–45. Larger studies along these lines include Elaine Sisman, *Haydn and the Classical Variation* (Cambridge, MA: Harvard University Press, 1993); Mary Hunter, *The Culture of Opera Buffa in Mozart's Vienna: A Poetics of Entertainment* (Princeton, NJ: Princeton University Press, 1999); and Melanie Lowe, *Pleasure and Meaning in the Classical Symphony* (Bloomington: Indiana University Press, 2007).

[81] This work was pioneered by Leonard G. Ratner. See *Classic Music: Expression, Form and Style*. See also Wye J. Allanbrook, *Rhythmic Gesture in Mozart: "Le nozze di Figaro" and "Don Giovanni"* (Chicago: University of Chicago Press, 1983); and a large subsequent literature. It should be pointed out that the eighteenth century hardly had consensus on the matter: by far the most influential aesthetic position on music of the midcentury—that of the *encyclopédistes*—held that music was distinctive among the fine arts precisely because it was wholly independent of social conventions and imitated the animal cries of passion. It seems inevitable that Mozart for one, who lodged in Paris at the home of Baron Grimm, was aware of that theory. In fact mid-eighteenth-century theories of the fine arts in general tended to attribute to the aesthetic medium the illusion that conventions are dissolved and replaced by direct, "natural" communication. See David Wellbury, *Lessing's "Laocoon": Semiotics and Aesthetics in the Age of Reason* (Cambridge: Cambridge University Press, 1984). Although eighteenth-century writers enumerated various musical styles, there was no formal theorizing of anything like the late twentieth-century notion of musical topic (an "arbitrary sign"). Charles Rosen is the only major writer on the music of this period to grasp this point. See *The Classical Style*, xvii.

is said to be inherited by twentieth-century scholarship, which the contemporary musicologist then seeks to overcome.[82] This is to smooth over uneven terrain. Already in their lifetimes the music of C.P.E. Bach and Mozart was regarded as complex and difficult, and more so than other composers'. Mozart is notable for his frequent failure to communicate effectively with his audiences. As we can now discern from Gjerdingen's analyses, Mozart's application of the schemata of the galant style in his major works was intricate and eccentric and demanded a mode of listening rather different from the customary exercise of good taste and discernment.[83] And although the technical terminology of classical oratory abounds in eighteenth-century treatises and critical writings, published theoretical and oral pedagogical traditions were independent. As aspirant "men of taste," Haydn and Mozart would likely have dismissed many published treatises as "pedantry": a term just as common in the eighteenth-century lexicon of abuse as was "rhetoric" in music theory.[84] There were, moreover, cultural divisions between north and south Germans. The Berliners Johann Philip Kirnberger, Johann Abraham Peter Schulz, and Johan Georg Sulzer left a voluminous legacy of musical writings, but the historian should be wary of interpreting Viennese music on the terms they set out, convenient though it might be (no such writings appeared in Vienna itself). Haydn's music offended their basic aesthetic principles and he suffered a poor reception in Berlin for decades.[85] The best insights of today's music theorists such as Caplin, Hepokoski and Darcy, and Gjerdingen, whose knowledge of the Viennese repertory is vastly wider and deeper than that of any eighteenth-century treatise writer, are a more reliable guide. Meanwhile, the celebration of the entertainment character of music and the aristocratic values that supported it tends to reduce late eighteenth-century music and theater to the image that the *ancien régime* itself wanted to promote: an unchanging world in which each social class had its place and shared conventions were manipulated and combined but not transformed or replaced. The metaphors here are the spheres on their eternal cosmic paths and the aristocratic ballroom with its fixed repertory of dances and gestures. Mozart's music is said to convey "overarching communal hierarchy" and "confidence in the

---

[82] See especially Mark Evan Bonds, *Wordless Rhetoric: Musical Form and the Metaphor of the Oration* (Cambridge, MA: Harvard University Press, 1991). For a more recent version, see Danuta Mirka and Kofi Agawu, eds., Introduction to *Communication in Eighteenth-Century Music* (Cambridge: Cambridge University Press, 2008).

[83] Gjerdingen, *Music in the Galant Style*, 19, 436–37.

[84] Music theorists and lexicographers had their own systems of value and prestige and some simply copied one another rather than responding to contemporary music. Heinrich Christoph Koch, a ubiquitous presence in musicological studies of this period since the 1980s, was a resourceful theorist, but he spent his entire professional life at the tiny provincial court at Rudolstadt and in his oft-quoted treatise *Versuch einer Anleitung zur Komposition* (1782–93) took most of his examples from composers such Georg Benda, Carl Heinrich Graun, Johann Adam Hiller, Ignaz Holzbauer, Franz Anton Rösler, Christian Gotthelf Scheinpflug (his insignificant predecessor at Rudolstadt), Anton Schweitzer, and himself.

[85] Even Koch criticized Haydn severely on one occasion. Felix Diergarten, "'Auch Homere schlafen bisweilen': Heinrich Christoph Kochs Polemik gegen Joseph Haydn," *Haydn-Studien* 10 (2010): 78–92.

social equilibrium."[86] In fact, in music history just as in society this was an excit-
ing era of turbulent change, asynchronous phenomena, contrasted and contested
styles, and clashing views. Music could engage with reality, express the thoughts
and feelings of the individual, and propose alternatives to the present settlement.
To insist on this point is not to indulge in anachronism, but to recognize that musicians of the late eighteenth century were part of the same Western modernity—in
an earlier phase—that we too inhabit.

A Revised Interpretation and Two Plots

The chapters of this book will tell the following story about the data assembled in
Table 1.1. There are, roughly speaking, two different types of symphony within this
repertory, which were written by composers working, respectively, within or outside
the influence of the imperial court. Wagenseil, Gassmann, and, to a lesser extent,
Ordonez were insiders; Haydn, Vaňhal, and Dittersdorf were not. Mozart's position was ambiguous. Some cross-fertilization took place between the two types. The
earliest Viennese minor-key symphonies were probably composed by Wagenseil in
the early 1760s. In contrast to his major-key symphonies, which, almost without
exception, epitomize the galant style, they contain fugato, ritornello-like gestures,
trio-sonata textures, and fast-moving basslines. "Untimely rhetoric," my collective term for these features, avoids the evolutionary framework that mars much
historical work on mid-eighteenth-century instrumental music. These symphonies
do not represent a lapse into conservatism or a failure to keep up with the times,
but an active compositional decision to evoke a still current but unfashionable
idiom.[87] Wagenseil's untimely rhetoric helped to define the subgenre: later Viennese
minor-key symphonies frequently adopt it, even when the actual techniques and
the manner of their application differ from his. Wagenseil's preference for G
minor over other minor keys was also shared by his Viennese successors, though
not by eighteenth-century composers in general.[88] (As in almost all later Viennese
G-minor symphonies, Wagenseil's slow movements are in Eb major.) Gassmann's
three minor-key symphonies and various movements by Ordonez belong to this
type. Most of these works were composed in the 1760s.

The first minor-key symphonies by composers outside the imperial court
appeared also in the early 1760s; they were probably Dittersdorf e1 and Vaňhal

---

[86] Allanbrook, "Comedy of Closure," 176, 186.

[87] One should avoid the implication that there was a "correct" style for any given "period," especially if the judgment is made with the benefit of hindsight. Most of the studies of *Kleinmeister* by
American musicologists that have made this book possible with their catalogs, editions, and stylistic
studies, are informed by evolutionary thinking, covert or overt, deliberate or involuntary. The text of
this book occasionally alludes to these matters, but to unpick their arguments systematically would
take too much space.

[88] Almost 38 percent of the works in Tables 1.1 and 1.2 are in G minor. This issue is further discussed in chapter 2.

e3, which share certain traits. The minor-key canonic minuet (see chapter 4) begins here (Vaňhal e3/iii), not with Haydn. In 1765, however, Haydn 39 brought a new kind of energy to the outer movements of the minor-key symphony. Its nervous rhythms, driving energy, sudden pauses, and the wide melodic leaps of the finale were new to Austrian instrumental music. The outer movements, as noted earlier, contain the first examples of the mediant tutti. In short, this is the first Viennese *Sturm und Drang* symphony. In the late 1760s and early 1770s a succession of symphonies were composed on this model by Haydn and others. In contrast to the early Dittersdorf and Vaňhal minor-key symphonies, works of this type typically do not turn to the tonic major near the end of the finale or the first movement, and almost always use III as the subordinate key of their outer movements rather than v. The only gesture in the direction of this new type of symphony by an imperial court composer is Ordonez C14.

When Haydn's development of the minor-key symphony after No. 39 is viewed against the background of the others being composed in Austria at the time, his originality and ceaseless inventiveness are confirmed yet again. Haydn plays with the conventions established by himself and Vaňhal, yet builds on the solemn mood established by the imperial court composers, taking their untimely allusions much further and realizing the latent religious associations of the subgenre. In the later 1770s and in the 1780s, however, Haydn, Vaňhal, and Dittersdorf explored other ways of writing minor-key symphonies that departed from the models of the 1760s in relatively consistent ways. Now the stormy style appears less frequently, and when it does it may be treated ironically by close juxtaposition with cheerful major-key music, galant gestures, or allusions to the language of opera buffa. The mediant tutti and the contrapuntal minuet likewise seldom occur. In the works of all three composers, outer movements tend to turn to the major by the end; sometimes the entire finale is in the major. Vaňhal sometimes returns to the choice of v instead of III as the subordinate key for outer movements, and adopts "monothematicism." These developments may indicate openness on the part of all three composers to rationalist aesthetics from beyond the Habsburg territories and perhaps a sense that the stormy minor-key symphony had become a fashion and was now outmoded.

One work of the 1780s—Mozart's Symphony No. 40 in G minor, K. 550 (1788)—stands out as a rare throwback to the models of the late 1760s, though also a further stage of reform. Rather than extending recent developments in the minor-key symphony, Mozart took the old type (which as a multi-movement form he had tried just once before, fifteen years earlier) in quite new directions. Uniquely for the 1780s, he retains traces of both the mediant tutti and the contrapuntal minuet, and remains in the minor mode to the end of both outer movements. Yet in terms of topic, rhythm, phrase structure, tonality, and, above all, scoring and timbre, K. 550 is original. It can be compared with only one other Viennese minor-key symphony of its time: Koželuch I:5 (1787), also in G minor. Although not as great a work, the Koželuch symphony likewise conducts a dialogue with the old type of minor-key symphony. An understanding of its strategies helps to bring those of K. 550 into clearer focus, confirming it as a "triumph of modern music" that nevertheless draws deeply on eighteenth-century traditions.[89]

Both types of symphony within the subgenre make use of the same untimely rhetoric. In the second type, its devices typically appear less frequently and do not form the basis for the general syntax, which is "modern" (homophonic texture, slow harmonic rhythm, short, regular phrases). That does not make their appearances less significant, however. Often they are drawn into movement-level compositional strategies, playing an important role in an unfolding narrative. In movements that modulate to III in the exposition but end in minor, untimely rhetoric is often heightened in recapitulations and even in codas, coinciding with the elimination of the major mode as a significant force in the movement. The recapitulation conveys a fateful quality; the extension of the emotionally negative domain of minor to the subordinate-key material is coordinated with signals that de-emphasize subjective expression (melody and homophony) in favor of objectivity and law (counterpoint) or uniformity (unison ritornello gestures). By contrast, movements of the 1770s and 1780s that move to the tonic major during the recapitulation (usually for the subordinate theme(s)) and remain there to the end tend to downplay untimely rhetoric after the modal reversal; the turn to major is accompanied by a decisive confirmation of modern syntax. These were the two basic "plots"—tragic and comic—that offered themselves to the composer of a minor-key symphony, who faced a decision about which of them to realize and how strongly. In Symphony No. 44, Haydn took the first option in both outer movements. The austere character of the work is underlined by the presence of a canonic minuet as the second movement. He did so again—and for the last time—in 78/i. Thereafter Haydn turns to major during the recapitulation of fast minor-key movements, although he adds a characteristic twist, feinting toward heightened untimely rhetoric in the development or the early, minor-mode part of the recapitulation before abandoning both it and the minor mode. Mozart consistently favored the tragic plot in fast minor-key instrumental music. It is found in K. 183/i, K. 183/iv, K. 550/i, and the first movements of the Piano Quintet in G minor, K. 478, and the String Quintet in G minor, K. 516.

---

[89] Peter Gülke, *"Triumph der neuen Tonkunst": Mozarts späte Sinfonien und ihr Umfelt* (Kassel and Stuttgart: Metzler-Bärenreiter, 1998); the title borrows a phrase applied to the finale of the "Jupiter" Symphony by the nineteenth-century composer and theorist Johann Christian Lobe; and A. Peter Brown, "Eighteenth-Century Traditions and Mozart's 'Jupiter' Symphony K. 551," *Journal of Musicology 20*, no. 2 (2003): 157–95.

{ 2 }

Imperial Court Composers: Wagenseil, Gassmann, Ordonez

The minor-key symphonies of the three composers studied in this chapter make up the first of the two types within the subgenre. If these composers are mentioned at all in the literature on the musical *Sturm und Drang*, then it is in one breath with Vaňhal, as fellow contemporaries of Haydn, who collectively demonstrate that the phenomenon cannot be ascribed solely to a personal crisis on Haydn's part. But the nature of their contribution has not been assessed. Landon, for instance, mentions just one symphony by Gassmann,[1] which had been published in the 1930s, and though he refers to several by Ordonez, he quotes only from Ordonez's overture to his parody opera after Gluck's *Alceste* (1775).[2] That piece is in a style quite different from most of Ordonez's minor-key symphonies, and when coupled with extracts from Vaňhal g1/iv and d1/i, gives the misleading impression that both composers wrote minor-key orchestral music in a loud, stormy style that was less sophisticated than Haydn's. It is now possible to piece together a fuller picture. Three minor-key symphonies survive by Wagenseil, three by Gassmann, and five by Ordonez (see Table 1.1). One symphony by Ordonez has been lost (see Table 1.2). One of the symphonies by Gassmann and two by Wagenseil remain unpublished. One by Wagenseil and three by Ordonez are currently available on commercial recordings. These minor-key symphonies collectively stand out from those of Haydn, Vaňhal, Dittersdorf, and Mozart as a separate type. The imperial court composers almost never use the stormy style or the mediant tutti. The one exception is Ordonez C14/i, probably modeled on the style of Vaňhal and rather different from the rest of Ordonez's minor-key symphonies. Yet the two types of symphony share certain strategies and vocabulary that were uncharacteristic of the major-key symphonies of any of these composers. Some movements by Haydn and Mozart, most notably Haydn 44/iv and Mozart K. 183/iv, evoke the imperial type of minor-key symphony quite explicitly, so it is necessary to understand this repertory in order to envisage

---

[1] Landon, *Chronicle*, 2:282.

[2] Ibid., 2:389–92.

the horizon of expectations against which those pieces unfold and to decode their meaning. This chapter provides an introductory critical survey of the repertory and descriptions of compositional style. The imperial composers are of interest in their own right, especially Ordonez, but the main function of the chapter is preliminary: it sets up the context for the study of generic norms in chapter 4 and for the more conceptually and methodologically sophisticated analyses in chapters 5, 7, and 8.

The composers associated with the imperial court in Vienna, no less than their counterparts across Europe, registered an overall change of style around midcentury that favored homophonic textures, short, regular phrases, and slower harmonic rhythm. But these changes initially faced resistance, and gathered momentum only in the 1750s, while traces of traditional practices remained alive for decades. Musical practice at the court of Charles VI (d. 1740) cast a long shadow. Like his forebears and successors, the Emperor was musically educated and himself a composer. Central to his policy was the absolute solidarity of the house of Habsburg with the Roman Catholic Church. The need for clear and constant public demonstration of this identity of temporal sovereignty and religion led to a program of lavish display and court ceremonial. It was the main purpose of the *Hofkapelle* to contribute the musical dimension. Oratorios, cantatas, and even operas by Johann Joseph Fux and Antonio Caldara served this objective: they were brilliant, festive or solemn, and met the taste for counterpoint of Charles VI (shared with successive Habsburg monarchs).[3] Hofkapellmeister Fux held to the timeless value of "ancient music"—the style of Palestrina—and he attempted to conserve what remained of the dying art (as he saw it) of sacred composition in the face of modern trends. The glorious music of the Roman Counter-Reformation (Palestrina) was wholly fitting, after all, for the Holy Roman Emperor. After the death of Charles VI, the Austrian monarchy faced financial and political crises, and his daughter Maria Theresa could not afford extravagant musical festivities. Charles's expensive *Hofkapelle* had to be scaled back and went into long-term decline. The center of musical patronage in Vienna shifted from the imperial court to the aristocracy, and, to a lesser extent, the middle class. Nevertheless, the court traditions were not forgotten. They were preserved partly in the theory of Fux, whose treatise *Gradus ad Parnassum* (1725), dedicated to Charles VI, was used as staple teaching material in Viennese musical pedagogy long after the rise of the galant style. The old ways were also continued here and there in compositional practice, notably in a tradition of contrapuntal chamber music for strings, encouraged by Habsburg monarchs, that stretched to the end of the eighteenth century.

That extensive chamber repertory has been documented by Warren Kirkendale. In addition to the three composers considered in this chapter, its contributors include Johann Georg Hintereder, Gregor Joseph Werner, Franz Tuma, Georg Reutter, Ignaz Holzbauer, Karl Kohaut, Joseph Pirlinger, Christoph Sonnleithner,

---

[3] Susan Wollenberg, "Vienna under Joseph I and Charles VI," in *The Late Baroque Era: From the 1680s to 1740*, ed. George J. Buelow (Englewood Cliffs, NJ: Prentice Hall, 1994), 324–54.

Johann Georg Albrechtsberger, and Wenzel Pichl.[4] The roots of the tradition lie in the sonata da chiesa, which was commonly performed in church services in Austria in the first half of the century, but by the time of Joseph II (1765–90) and Francis II (1792–1806), whose private collection of chamber music was built up from the 1780s, that practice had long ceased. Chamber music in contrapuntal style was now performed for the emperor in his private rooms, and some was withheld from wider dissemination. In Joseph II's private afternoon concerts the significance of the strict style had changed too, as, unlike his grandfather, Joseph's outlook was secular and he sought to curtail the power and independence of the Catholic Church within the monarchy. His policies led to the near-elimination of instrumental music in church. The imperial taste for counterpoint now simply registered the dynasty's commitment to tradition and historical continuity in an age of revolution.[5] According to Kirkendale the chamber-music contrapuntists were insiders. "For the Viennese composers, a link with the imperial household can nearly always be traced.... No fugues for strings were found among the works of other composers active in Austria at the time. Fugue-writers thus form a special group."[6]

When these same composers wrote symphonies, they usually did so in a modern style. The argument of this chapter, however, is that their few symphonies in minor keys consistently feature an untimely rhetoric that parallels the contrapuntal idiom of imperial chamber music. According to one report, as well as counterpoint Joseph II was a "lover of the music of pathos."[7] If so, then two of his tastes converge in these minor-key symphonies. (In the chamber music itself, minor keys are slightly more common than in the symphonies, although there is plenty of contrapuntal writing in major-key pieces too.) The minor-key symphonies of Wagenseil and Gassmann are unlikely to be performed today, with the exception of Wagenseil G6. Ordonez, however, was good at both counterpoint and composition. All his minor-key symphonies deserve a hearing.

The imperial composers and their contrapuntal chamber music were not always warmly regarded beyond the court. These musicians enjoyed privileges that incurred the envy and indignation of outsiders. The subject of counterpoint aroused strong feelings in the second half of the eighteenth century, both for and against. While some held it up as the expression of universal law, timeless values, and a criterion of compositional mastery, others decried it as pedantic, tedious, unnatural, or "gothic." A report from 1790 is contemptuous of Joseph II's afternoon chamber-music concerts, which, it is implied, were rigged by the second-rate insiders who were taking part (the imperial chamber musicians Strack and Kreibich) and packed with their

---

[4] Warren Kirkendale, *Fugue and Fugato in Rococo and Classical Chamber Music*, trans. Margaret Bent and the author, rev. ed. (Durham, NC: Duke University Press, 1979), 278–98.

[5] Ibid., 4, 29, 33–42.

[6] Ibid., 30. It is not quite clear what Kirkendale means by "at the time," but he is obviously excluding Haydn and Mozart.

[7] *Musikalische Korrespondenz*, vol. 1 (Speyer, 1790), cols. 27–30. Quoted in Kirkendale, 38–39 (trans. adapted). "Der Kaiser war Liebhaber vom Pathetischem...." Kirkendale, *Fuge und Fugato*, 88.

own music. Quartets were seldom played, and, when they were, the music of the best composers (including Haydn and Mozart) was deliberately excluded so the emperor could not tell what he was missing.[8] In 1777 Mozart had a conversation with the composer Ignaz von Beecke in which they agreed on the emperor's poor taste in music. Beecke had once performed for him and decided to play "fugues and such childishness, and all the time I played I was laughing up my sleeve." They agreed that "in the Emperor's apartment music is performed that would drive the dogs away." Mozart said that "whenever I hear that kind of music and can't escape from it, it gives me a headache."[9] In a conversation book of 1823—precisely the time he was writing fugues intensively himself—Beethoven entered a fugue subject with a long penultimate note and a trill. Schindler recorded that "Beethoven is ridiculing the stereotyped manner of those he called the 'old imperial composers'."[10]

The scheming of second-rate imperial court musicians is a theme of romantic Mozart biography. Leopold Mozart himself was convinced that Viennese court musicians (with the exception of Wagenseil) were set against his son's advancement during their stay in Vienna in 1767–68, and that they sabotaged the production of Wolfgang's opera *La finta semplice*.[11] Haydn had a difficult relationship with the Viennese musical establishment until he moved permanently to the city in the 1790s.[12] Indeed, Haydn and Mozart seem for a long time to have been in disfavor with the Habsburg monarchs, or perhaps were simply unknown to them. In 1771 Maria Theresa warned her son Archduke Ferdinand not to employ Mozart or his father,[13] and in 1772, when she explained her tastes in music to her daughter-in-law, she mentioned instrumental music last, and gave it just one sentence. "Pour les instruments il y a un certain Haydn qui a des idées particulières, mais cela ne fait que commencer."[14] However one reads this remark, it does not suggest close familiarity with Haydn's already astonishing output of the previous twelve years. Joseph II, despite his regular afternoon concerts and his cultivation of chamber music, appears to have shown no interest in Haydn's music. As regards Mozart, to be sure,

---

[8] Ibid. Kirkendale thinks this judgment unjust.

[9] Mozart to his father, November 13, 1777. Anderson, *The Letters of Mozart and His Family*, 369. Trans. from Kirkendale, *Fugue and Fugato*, 157. Again (see n. 8) Kirkendale regards this judgment as unjust, as Mozart had never attended an imperial concert.

[10] Quoted in Kirkendale, *Fugue and Fugato*, 94.

[11] See the letters from Leopold Mozart to Lorenz Hagenauer, January 30, February 3, 1768, and July 30, 1768, in *The Letters of Mozart and His Family*, 80–83, 87–91.

[12] David Wyn Jones, *The Life of Haydn* (Cambridge: Cambridge University Press, 2009), 114–15. Haydn appears to have regarded his well-connected fellow symphonist Leopold Hofmann, Kapellmeister at St. Stephen's Cathedral, as a rival. See the letter from Haydn to the publisher Artaria, July 20, 1780, cited in Heartz, *Haydn, Mozart and the Viennese School*, 472. Hofmann came from a family of Viennese courtiers, was a pupil of Wagenseil, succeeded him as Hofklaviermeister, and held the positions of Kapellmeister at the Peterskirche and both positions at St. Stephen's cathedral.

[13] December 12, 1771. Alfred Ritter von Arneth, ed., *Briefe der Kaiserin Maria Theresia an ihre Kinder und Freunde*, 4 vols. (Vienna: Wilhelm Braumüller, 1881), 1:93.

[14] November 12, 1772. Ibid., 3:149

the romantic picture is too one-sided. In the 1780s Mozart's operas were performed in the Burgtheater; in 1787 he was appointed imperial *Kammermusicus*, a position that for him was practically a sinecure; and at the end of his life he was in line to succeed Leopold Hofmann as *Kapellmeister* of St. Stephen's Cathedral. Nevertheless, it may be the case that some of the court musicians were in place by virtue of their administrative or teaching abilities, their personal connections, or their skills at pulling the levers of patronage, rather than their ability at composition.

Wagenseil

Georg Christoph Wagenseil (1715–77) was the leading imperial court composer of instrumental music in the middle decades of the century, and a pivotal figure in the history of Viennese instrumental music. He is remembered chiefly as the musician who introduced the galant style to Vienna, which thereafter gained much ground. Born in Vienna to a family in imperial service, he had enjoyed close connections with the Habsburg family since childhood, singing as a boy in the private chapel of Empress Amalie Wihelmine. He studied with the court organist Gottlieb Muffat and was a favored pupil of Fux, who wrote him excellent references. Wagenseil was appointed court scholar in composition in 1735 and court and chamber music composer in 1739. For the rest of his career he enjoyed the unstinting support of the imperial family. On the death of Charles VI (1740), Wagenseil became organist in the private chapel of the widowed Empress Elizabeth Christine until her death in 1750. An excellent keyboard player, in 1749 he became *Hofklaviermeister* to Maria Theresa and the four young archduchesses, succeeding Muffat, and devoted much time to teaching them. At this point he turned to the production of instrumental music, including many keyboard pieces but also symphonies and concertos. Wagenseil's output was large. Many of his works were published outside Austria, and his name was well known throughout Europe. Wagenseil retired as *Hofklaviermeister* in 1769 due to ill health, but continued to hold his other posts and draw his salary. He had many pupils who seem to have held him in great respect. Haydn adopted his style in his early keyboard divertimenti. Mozart met Wagenseil on his first visit to Vienna in 1762 and played one of his keyboard concertos.

Wagenseil was a man with the right talents at the right time, a melodist who excelled in small-scale, elegant, courtly pieces more than in heroic arias or high drama.[15] The galant style was in fashion and suited the straightened circumstances of the monarchy. But Wagenseil was also a contradictory figure who embodied the split between musical theory and practice that emerged in the eighteenth century. In a reference letter of 1738 Fux said that he was "more diligent than others in writing according to the basic rules of counterpoint," and that through him

---

[15] Heartz, *Haydn, Mozart and the Viennese School*, 90, 92.

"orderly composition could be upheld in the face of the current licentious style."[16] Indeed, Wagenseil's early keyboard suites (1740) are in a traditional, contrapuntal style. He was well known for improvising fugues at the keyboard, and the themes of his notated fugues display knowledge of Bach's *Das wohltemperierte Clavier*.[17] Wagenseil was the chief mediator of the pedagogical legacy of Fux in Vienna. But had Fux lived longer, in practice he would have seen his hopes dashed, as by 1750 Wagenseil had turned almost entirely to the "current licentious style" and was perfecting it. In the preface to the first of Wagenseil's four books of *Divertimenti da Cimbalo* (1753), each of which was composed for and dedicated to one of the four archduchesses, he says that he avoided the ties used by "the best composers" (suspensions, thus implying contrapuntal textures), so as not to tire the patience of amateur players.[18] His pupil Johann Baptist Schenk, who began to study with Wagenseil in 1774, recorded that his teaching was based on Fux's *Gradus ad Parnassum*, and that he gave the pupil the preludes and fugues of Bach and keyboard studies of Handel to practice. But after that, "My wise teacher guided me to the art of composing in a freer style. His intentions seemed to have been to wean me from the dry movement and to direct me toward a beautifully blossoming melody."[19] Handel still loomed large, but now Hasse and Galuppi were models too.

Over 120 surviving symphonies carry attributions to Wagenseil. He probably wrote around fifty symphonies, mainly in the 1750s and early 1760s (discounting the small-scale, more delicate works sometimes entitled "sinfonia," but sometimes "sonata" or "trio").[20] Wagenseil's symphonies achieved remarkable international success: they were printed in Paris and London by many competing firms, and were also published in Amsterdam, The Hague, Lyons, Leipzig, and Vienna. They are mentioned favorably in reviews.[21] In Vienna, Wagenseil's were the most abundant of the many new symphonies played at the 1758 season of Lenten concerts at the Burgtheater, and his popularity continued into later seasons.[22] Sixteen were originally opera overtures, most of which he composed in the 1740s. They are shorter than the later concert symphonies, are scored for larger forces, are less sophisticated in structure, use less characteristic material, and usually have no repeated

---

[16] Ludwig Ritter von Köchel, *Johann Joseph Fux: Hofcompositor und Hofkapellmeister der Kaiser Leopold I., Josef I. und Karl VI. von 1698 bis 1740* (Vienna: A Hölder, 1872; repr., Hildesheim: Georg Olms, 1974), 450; quoted in Kirkendale, *Fugue and Fugato*, 7 (trans. altered).

[17] Kirkendale, *Fugue and Fugato*, 7; Helga Michelitsch, Das Klavierwerk von Georg Christoph Wagenseil: Thematischer Katalog (Vienna: Böhlau, 1966), 110–42.

[18] Heartz, *Haydn, Mozart and the Viennese School*, 103.

[19] Johann Baptist Schenk, "Autobiography," in *Forgotten Musicians*, ed. and trans. Paul Nettl (New York: Philosophical Library, 1951), 267–68. Quoted in Heartz, *Haydn, Mozart and the Viennese School*, 113–14.

[20] John Kucaba, "The Symphonies of Georg Christoph Wagenseil" (PhD diss., Boston University, 1967), 7–8; and Introduction to Georg Christoph Wagenseil, *Fifteen Symphonies*, series B, vol. 3 of *The Symphony, 1720–1840* (New York and London: Garland, 1981), xxi.

[21] Kucaba, "Symphonies," 2–3.

[22] Heartz, *Haydn, Mozart and the Viennese School*, 52, 54.

sections in the outer movements.[23] In his concert symphonies Wagenseil stuck to the three-movement scheme derived from the Italian overture, rather than adopting the four-movement plan more characteristic of Viennese symphonies. All the movements are in binary forms with repeats. In the 1750s Wagenseil favored duple or triple meter rather than quadruple, although the latter appeared a little more often in the 1760s. Slow movements are generally in minor keys, but they are in the galant style, their mood lightly melancholic rather than tragic.[24] The concert symphonies are scored for strings, sometimes alone (à 4), sometimes with the standard oboes and horns, occasionally replaced by flutes or clarini (with timpani).[25] The texture is almost always homophonic; even the second violins seldom carry the melody; there is even less independence for the violas and the wind instruments.[26] At their best, Wagenseil's symphonies achieve a galant ideal: elegant and playful, they offer a diverse stream of attractive ideas. For the Wagenseil scholar John Kucaba, "most arresting of all is the novel sprightliness, amiability, and suppleness that now replace the opera *sinfonia*'s predominantly four-square pomposity, bustle, and sweep."[27]

The three symphonies in minor keys contrast sharply with these general trends. They are from the second half of Wagenseil's phase of symphonic production, G6 (–1762) probably being a little earlier than G4 (–1764) and G5 (–1766). All three are in G minor and are scored for strings and a pair of oboes. G minor had already been favored by Sammartini for minor-key symphonies, and in Vienna it would continue to be the most frequent choice for decades to come, a tendency that is not reflected across Europe as a whole, where D minor and C minor were more common.[28] The second movements are all in the submediant (E♭), again a choice that would apply to almost all later Viennese G-minor symphonies, but not to all minor-key symphonies in general, in Vienna or elsewhere. The outer movements of Wagenseil's minor-key symphonies stand out for their unusual style. In G5 and G6 Kucaba notes "hammerstroke openings, long passages containing undifferentiated rhythms, running bass patterns, frequent tutti/solo alternation [akin to a Baroque concerto], fast chordal rhythm,… typically Baroque snap-off phrase endings,"[29] and "interplay between the violins."[30] In the first movement of G4, "there is again

---

[23] Kucaba, "Symphonies," 97–100.

[24] Wagenseil likewise often turned to the minor mode as an inflection in the subordinate-key area of his first-movement expositions.

[25] Ibid., 89–90.

[26] Ibid., 90–92.

[27] Kucaba, Introduction, xxi.

[28] Vienna: g 38%, c 19%, d 13%; Europe: g 22%, c 25%, d 30%. The data for Europe as a whole, compiled from LaRue, *A Catalogue of 18th-Century Symphonies,* is imperfect: the catalog includes opera overtures, and LaRue's research assistants in Europe may not have been reliable or consistent. For instance, two symphonies listed as F♯ minor are in fact in D major. Webster, *Haydn's "Farewell" Symphony,* 3n8. Haydn's Symphony No. 98 in B♭ is listed as B♭ minor, but only the slow introduction to the first movement is in B♭ minor.

[29] Kucaba, Introduction, xxii.

[30] Kucaba, "Symphonies," 89.

much alternation between light and heavy textures."[31] In his evolutionary vocabulary, Kucaba calls these traits "conservati[ve]"[32] and even "retrogressive."[33] The finale of G6, by contrast, which has homophonic textures, regular phrase rhythm, and slow harmonic rhythm, displays "progressive" features.[34] These outer movements would be better understood as countergeneric, employing a deliberately untimely rhetoric.

G6, very likely the first of the three to be composed, was also one of the most widely disseminated of all Wagenseil's symphonies. Manuscript copies are found in nine archives in central Europe, the symphony was published by Huberty in Paris, and it is listed in four eighteenth-century catalogs.[35] A modern edition of G6 was published in 1972 by Universal Edition, and the work has since been recorded. (G4 and G5 survive in four and three copies respectively, and there are no eighteenth-century or modern editions or recordings.) The first movement, in an elaborately subdivided 4/4 meter, alludes to certain features of early eighteenth-century concertos, as noted by Kucaba (see above). The first six bars function like a concerto ritornello; in the third the music moves into a phase of "spinning out,"[36] and idiomatic compound melody emerges from the passagework (Ex. 2.1). Bar 8 could be compared with the first solo section of a double violin concerto. There is a melody based around a chromatic descent (bars 23–26) of a kind that is almost never found in major-key symphonies of the time. The movement is a sonata form, with the "double return" of opening material and tonic key at bar 53, most of the material of the first section returning thereafter in the tonic. The early eighteenth-century concerto idioms therefore remain on the level of rhetorical allusions: Wagenseil does not observe the principles or exploit the subtle expressive strategies associated with true ritornello form.[37]

Like G6/i, G4/i opens with a unison gesture in a sprightly triple meter that more distantly suggests a ritornello. The first violin part features the "tied notes" that Wagenseil avoided in his divertimenti for the archduchesses. The economical treatment of thematic material in the exposition of G4/i, which contrasts with Wagenseil's usual emphasis on variety, gives rise to an unusual form for the movement as a whole. It is an exaggeration to maintain, as Kucaba does, that the exposition is

---

[31] Ibid.

[32] Ibid.

[33] Kucaba, Introduction, xxii. See, likewise, Allan Badley, "Georg Christoph Wagensil," in *The Symphonic Repertoire*, vol. 2, *The Eighteenth-Century Symphony*, ed. Mary Sue Morrow and Bathia Churgin (Bloomington and Indianapolis: Indiana University Press, 2012), 472–82.

[34] Kucaba, "Symphonies," 89.

[35] Breitkopf (1766), Goettweig 8 (1762), Lambach 325, Singmaringen. Kucaba, Introduction, xliv.

[36] Wilhelm Fischer, "Zur Entwicklungsgeschichte des Wiener klassischen Stils," *Studien zur Musikwissenschaft* 3 (1915): 25–84 (pp. 29–33).

[37] For an introduction to these principles and strategies, see Simon McVeigh and Jehoash Hirschberg, *The Italian Solo Concerto, 1700–1760: Rhetorical Strategies and Style History* (Woodbridge: Boydell Press, 2004), 6–26.

Ex. 2.1 Wagenseil G6/i, bars 1–9

"monomotivic," but it is certainly the case that the second half of the exposition (in the relative major) draws its material from the first, aside from a minuet cadence figure (bars 26^3–28^1 and 30^3–32^1)—a gesture that keeps the work in touch with the vocabulary of the galant style. The second section of the movement begins with a striking gesture of untimely rhetoric: conjunct running eighth notes in the bass against slower-moving upper parts that strongly recalls a trio-sonata texture. This material is completely new in the movement, as is the whole of the "development" section: something very unusual for Wagenseil.[38] In G4/i Kucaba finds "continuous expansions" in "one unarticulated sweep," which he regards as an attempt to avoid the "over-exposure" of material that has already been intensively used in the exposition.[39] The finale of this symphony is a kind of rondo, although still with unison sixteenth-note textures, spinning out and implied solo/tutti contrasts.

The outer movements of G5 are the weightiest of the three works. G5/i, like G6/i, is in a subdivided 4/4 meter. Its opening is massive, and the running sixteenth-note octaves and compound melody again refer to the style of a concerto ritornello. The movement likewise evokes solo-tutti contrasts, but its two-part form is sonata-like, with double return of opening theme and tonic midway through the second part and return of subordinate material in the tonic thereafter. The exposition and recapitulation end with ritornello-like returns of the opening in octave sixteenth notes. The finale is of special interest as it resembles a common type of fugato movement

---

[38] According to Kucaba, the large majority of "development sections" (as he freely terms them) in Wagenseil's approximately fifty symphony first movements begin with all or part of the opening theme in the dominant. Of the nine that do not, only one other is based, like this one, on entirely new material. Kucaba, "Symphonies," 116.

[39] Ibid., 117.

Ex. 2.2 Wagenseil G5/iii, bars 1–12. Staatsbibliothek zu Berlin—Preußischer Kulturbesitz, Musikabteilung mit Mendelssohn-Archiv D Bds KHM 5547

in the chamber repertory described by Kirkendale. Such movements are in binary form, with each of the two sections beginning with two entries in the upper parts as a *dux-comes* pair, before the contrapuntal textures disintegrate and the movement proceeds homophonically. G5/iii is a sonata form, and in terms of meter, tempo, and gesture resembles a conventional "tempo di menuetto" finale. The imitative entries, however, are in even quarter notes, and stand outside the minuet topic. There is a pair at the start of the exposition (Ex. 2.2), two pairs at the start of the development, and, in this case, the original two again at the start of the recapitulation. The answer is always in stretto at the subdominant.

In the twentieth century Wagenseil became a pawn in a scholarly battle between Hugo Riemann and Guido Adler and his students at the University of Vienna over the genealogy of the Viennese Classical style.[40] The Adler party, which held to an internal Viennese development independent of the court of Mannheim, maintained that Wagenseil was the precursor of Haydn and Mozart as regards the symphony and sonata form in general. As regards Wagenseil's minor-key symphonies, this is true in a paradoxical way. Wagenseil was probably the first composer working in the Habsburg monarchy to treat minor-key symphonies as extraordinary, as locations for "deformation," and the first consistently to use untimely idioms—the unfashionableness of which he had helped to bring about—in these works. The practices of breaking the mold and returning to the past for rhetorical effect would later flourish and help to define the subgenre.

---

[40] For a summary see Kucaba, "Symphonies," 3–7.

Gassmann

Florian Leopold Gassmann (1729–74) was born in Brüx (Most) in northwest Bohemia.[41] The details of his early life are unclear, but it seems that as a teenager he ran away from his parents' house and lived for more than two decades in Venice. Between 1757 and 1763 he composed operas in Venice until he was summoned to Vienna in 1763 to replace Gluck as a composer of ballet music. Soon Joseph II made him *Hof- und Kammercompositor* and for five years he wrote an opera annually for Vienna. Gassmann was a good administrator. On his appointment to the position of *Hofkapellmeister* in 1772 he reorganized the *Hofkapelle* and halted its long decline under his predecessor, Georg Reutter. It was through Gassmann that the Tonkünstler-Societät was founded in 1771 to raise money for the widows and children of deceased musicians, and he became its leader the following year. He also began to catalog the collection of the imperial music library, which, when he took Burney to see it, was in chaos.[42] But Gassmann died in 1774, not yet forty-five, from the effects of a fall from a carriage. Gassmann was the perfect court insider. He led Joseph II's chamber music afternoons, which took place three times a week,[43] and became a friend of the emperor. As a consequence he turned out a large quantity of chamber music, including approximately seven duos, fifty-seven trios, seventy-two quartets, and thirty-four quintets, many of them including contrapuntal movements or organized in the manner of a sonata da chiesa with slow first movement and fugal second movement.[44] Gassmann's compositions continued to be performed for decades after his death.[45] Viennese legends that the emperor kept many of Gassmann's compositions for his own use and prevented their public dissemination appear to be confirmed by the sources.

Gassmann wrote about forty-four concert symphonies, of which thirty-two survive in source, while the rest are known only by incipits in thematic catalogs.[46] They are easy to distinguish from his opera overtures and quartets. Twenty-four of the symphonies survive in holograph (manuscript full scores in what is almost certainly the composer's hand, but unsigned and undated).[47] These twenty-four are bound together in four

---

[41] For details of Gassmann's life, see Eve R. Meyer, ed., Introduction to Florian Leopold Gassmann, *Selected Divertimenti a tre and a quattro* (Madison, WI: A-R Editions, 1983); and George R. Hill, "The Concert Symphonies of Florian Leopold Gassmann (1729–1774)" (PhD diss., New York University, 1975), chap. 1, pp. 1–22.

[42] Hill, "Concert Symphonies," 18–19.

[43] Ibid., 10.

[44] George R. Hill, *A Thematic Catalogue of the Instrumental Music of Florian Leopold Gassmann* (Hackensack: Boonin, 1976).

[45] Hill, "Concert Symphonies," 21–2.

[46] George R. Hill, Introduction to Florian Leopold Gassmann, *Seven Symphonies*, series B, vol. 10 of *The Symphony 1720–1840* (New York and London: Garland Publishing, 1981). It appears that Hill had earlier thought there was another symphony by Gassmann. "Concert Symphonies," 23.

[47] Hill, "Concert Symphonies," 23. Much of the following information is also related in Hill, Introduction.

groups of six, dated on the covers 1765, 1767, 1768, and 1769. The Gassmann scholar George R. Hill suggests that the consistent placement of three-movement works at the beginning and end of these groups, with four-movement works between them, and the organization of the keys by sequences of thirds or fifths, may reflect a penchant for orderliness on Gassmann's part.[48] None of the other sources bears a date, but it is likely that most of Gassmann's symphonies were written after his appointment as *Hof- und Kammercompositor* in 1764 or 1765, but before he left for a trip to Italy in 1769. The stories of the emperor's jealous guarding of Gassmann's compositions may well apply to the symphonies, as very few manuscript copies of parts for these works exist aside from the collection held by the Österreichische Nationalbibliothek, which almost undoubtedly originated in the old Hofkapelle-Archiv. Of the twenty-four dated symphonies in that collection, seventeen have the word "secreta" written in the lower right-hand corner of the cover. These symphonies correspond very closely with the holographs dated 1767, 1768, and 1769,[49] and they appear to have been frequently used for performance. Hill believes that the composer may have agreed on his appointment as *Hof- und Kammercompositor* that his symphonies would be reserved for the exclusive use of the court.[50] Not a single symphony by Gassmann was published until the twentieth century, in contrast to his chamber music, of which twenty-nine works were printed by 1810.[51]

Opinions differ as to the quality of Gassmann's instrumental music. Burney praised the quartets Gassmann gave him to take back to England. "I have had these pieces tried, and have found them excellent: there is pleasing melody, free from caprice and affectation; sound harmony, and the contrivances and imitation are ingenious, without the least confusion. In short, the style is sober and sedate, without dullness; and masterly, without pedantry."[52] Still, Burney did not mention Gassmann in his list of active Viennese composers distinguished for their instrumental music around 1770: Hofmann, Haydn, Dittersdorf, Vaňhal, and Huber. Several modern musicologists are skeptical. Daniel Heartz dislikes the finale of Gassmann's Symphony in E♭, H26 (1765), in which

> the themes have so little profile that it scarcely matters in what order they occur. A monotonous rhythmic sameness pervades this finale, which operates on a two-measure module throughout. No wonder Gassmann's symphonies were admired only by the circle around Joseph II.[53]

(The last sentence is somewhat beside the point, as almost half the symphonies were probably unknown beyond that circle.) The opening theme of another Symphony in E♭,

---

[48] Hill, "Concert Symphonies," 85–87.

[49] Ibid., 54.

[50] Ibid., 56.

[51] Ibid., 53.

[52] Charles Burney, *The Present State of Music in Germany, the Netherlands and the United Provinces,* 2 vols. (London: T. Beckett and Co., 1773), 1:361–62; quoted in Kirkendale, *Fugue and Fugato,* 10.

[53] Heartz, *Haydn, Mozart and the Viennese School,* 411.

H85 (1769), is "particularly insipid."[54] Gassmann's was the single most substantial contribution to the contrapuntal chamber music repertory that Kirkendale documents, and, for the most part, defends against potential criticism. But he has to admit that

> Gassmann, notwithstanding his reputation in his own time, betrays more abject poverty of invention than many other "Kleinmester" of a period which delighted naively in an excess of broken tonic and dominant triads. For all his formal conservatism (retention of the church-sonata form) he was, to a greater extent than his contemporaries, the composer who introduced modern, periodized cantabile melody into the fugue.[55]

On the basis of his three minor-key symphonies alone, Gassmann seems to have suffered from limitations, perhaps limitations on his time as well as his technique and imagination. It is important to grasp these in order to recognize what talented "outsiders" might have made of his music.

Gassmann's concert symphonies are mostly scored for strings (often in five parts), oboes (usually just doubling the violins), and horns. Gassmann's movements tend to be longer than Wagenseil's, especially finales, and he favored a four-movement rather than three-movement scheme. Five of Gassmann's symphonies have slow introductions before the first movement, something that Wagenseil avoided, although it was favored around this time by his pupil Leopold Hofmann. Gassmann's first-movement forms are strikingly diverse, especially as regards the recapitulation. Hill makes a valiant attempt to classify the formal types of the first movements of the surviving major-key symphonies as follows: (a) "sonata form" (10 movements); (b) "bifocal recapitulation" (eight movements) with the opening material returning in either IV or vi in the second half of the movement and the subordinate material in I; (c) "differentiated binary" (four movements), avoiding restatement of the opening material in the second half of the movement (except possibly at the very end), though allowing for an area of tonal stability on ii or iii; (d) types sharing binary and bifocal recapitulation characteristics (six movements); and (e) others (two movements).[56]

Gassmann's three minor-key symphonies show some of the traits of Wagenseil's in heightened and more dramatic form. They too are scored for strings and oboes only (by contrast, only four of Gassmann's major-key symphonies lack horn parts).[57] H45 and H83 contain contrapuntal devices, ritornello gestures, and fast, running basses. Counterpoint is not entirely absent from the major-key symphonies, but it is relatively rare, and is overwhelmingly outweighed by homophonic textures.[58] As

---

[54] Ibid.

[55] Kirkendale, *Fugue and Fugato*, 11.

[56] Hill, "Concert Symphonies," 146, and the lengthy ensuing discussion. It may be that one of the two "others" under (e) is not by Gassmann at all, and Hill appears to have reached that conclusion by the time the Gassmann volume in the Garland series, *The Symphony*, was published (1981). See n. 46 above.

[57] Hill, "Concert Symphonies," 65.

[58] Hill cites just one example of an "extended contrapuntal fabric" in a major-key symphony movement. Ibid., 219–21.

regards first-movement form, the three minor-key symphonies follow a consistent pattern. In all three the second section of the binary form is about twice as long as the first, and a return of the opening material occurs halfway through it, but not in the tonic. A different tonal area is stabilized instead at this point, v in bars 23 and 45, VI in bar 83, akin to the "bifocal recapitulation" in eight of the major-key first movements. The opening material returns again at the end of the movement, now in i, a technique also used in sixteen major-key first movements.[59] There are too few minor-key symphonies by Gassmann to call this a strong default. Still, as Hill points out, the return of the opening material in a non-tonic key in the middle of the movement and in the tonic at the end is reminiscent of early eighteenth-century concertos. Hill does not provide statistics for Gassmann's finales.[60]

The first of the holograph sets of symphonies (1765) includes H23 (C minor). The first movement's untimely features include the ritornello-like construction (the opening material makes a clearly articulated return in v halfway through the second half, and returns in i near the end); a running bass in eighth notes against quarter and half notes in the upper parts (Ex. 2.3); and, in the final bars (following the tonic reprise), dotted rhythms in the manner of a French overture and a phrase in octaves to end. The latter are new ideas, and conclude the movement with a rhetorical flourish. Like the ending of Wagenseil G5/i they sound like a closing ritornello or perhaps even the final bars of a fugue. H23 was published in 1981, and subsequently attracted adverse criticism. For Heartz it typifies the "rhythmic monotony" of Gassmann's outer movements.[61] Hill admits that this movement relies excessively on two-bar units.[62] Moreover, the texture is unimaginative: the movement remains in four parts almost throughout as though it were an exercise in four-part harmony. There is little idiomatic writing for strings or exploration of the full range of the instruments. In the first four bars the inner parts are fussy and purposeless, and distract attention from the first violin melody (bars 2–4). The other movements of H23 display similar faults and are of minimal interest. Perhaps this symphony is better regarded as an ensemble etude than a work of art, aimed at dilettantes who wanted their music practice to be a sociable occasion. At Joseph II's "concerts" there was often no audience; they were really sight-reading sessions, in which he too might take part.[63] Gassmann gives the participants something interesting but not too difficult to play; the regularity of the two-bar units makes it easy to stay together; no

---

[59] Ibid., 144–45.

[60] Ibid., 145.

[61] Heartz, *Haydn, Mozart and the Viennese School*, 410. "Its exposition of sixty measures never strays from the initial two-measure modules. The main idea is motivic rather than thematic, and is given a bass accompaniment in quarter notes, which are then divided into eighth notes upon repetition, to a rather schoolmasterly effect, as if demonstrating species counterpoint. The other motifs have scarcely enough profile of their own to be remembered. Gassmann scrambles these ideas in the brief reprise, the first being saved for last. It matters little in what order they come because they resemble one another and are all equally unmemorable."

[62] Hill, Introduction, xx.

[63] Hill, "Concert Symphonies," 10.

Ex. 2.3 Gassmann H23/i, bars 1–14

one has the unflattering tedium of playing *Trommelbass*; there is a faintly "learned" air to the music, and the whole movement might come together in one afternoon's practice.

H45 (G minor) from the second holograph set (1767) is a much more interesting symphony. It is the only Viennese minor-key symphony with a slow introduction to the first movement before Paul Wranitzky's symphonies of the 1790s, and the introduction contains some unusual progressions of chromatic harmony.[64] A remarkable aspect of the work is that all three movements in minor mode—the outer movements (disregarding the slow introduction) and the minuet—begin with contrapuntal textures (Exx. 2.4(i), 2.5(i), and 2.6(i)). All three allude to Fuxian models, with fairly regular note durations in the upper part or parts (equivalent to the *cantus firmus*) and faster notes in the "added" part or parts beneath. The opening of the first movement piles up the allusions to strict style, with a figure of instrumental rather than vocal origin that is reminiscent of the opening of Wagenseil G4/i (Ex. 2.4(i), bars 27–28[1], viola)—perhaps a handy tag for "old-fashioned concerto"— and a four-note descending phrase that links a half cadence with the opening of the next subject entry, likewise something of a cliché (Ex. 2.4(i), bars 33[2]–33[3], first violin). The first movement and minuet both display three traits that Kirkendale identified in binary movements in Viennese contrapuntal chamber music (and that surfaced also in Wagenseil G5/iii): imitation at the unison or octave between the two upper parts; a parallel contrapuntal opening for the second part of the binary form

---

[64] Ibid., 213.

Ex. 2.4 Gassmann 45/i, strings. Moravské zemské muzeum, Brno. CZ Bm A 16 700a

(i) bars 26–33

(ii) bars 58–65

(iii) bars 82–89

(Exx. 2.4(iii), 2.5(ii)); and an early switch to homophonic textures thereafter. In the first movement, counterpoint returns also midway through the exposition on a dominant pedal in III (Ex. 2.4(ii)). The "subject" here is indirectly related to the one at the start of the movement by inversion. As in H23/i, the first movement's reprise of the opening material is on v; but it comes back again on i at the end, with another of Gassmann's octave conclusions. This deferral of the tonic return of the opening material until the very end seems derived from ritornello form. There is another octave/unison ending in the finale, again invoking a closing ritornello (Ex. 2.6(ii)).

Ex. 2.5 Gassmann 45/iii. Moravské zemské muzeum, Brno. CZ Bm A 16 700a

(i) bars 1–8

(ii) bars 17 -24

Ex. 2.6 Gassmann 45/iv. Moravské zemské muzeum, Brno. CZ Bm A 16 700a

(i) bars 1–12

[Allegro]

(ii) bars 181–89

H83, from the fourth and final holograph set (1769), was published in 1933, edited by the Haydn biographer Karl Geiringer, and so has been alluded to in the literature on *Sturm und Drang*.[65] It is one of only two concert symphonies in B minor composed in the Habsburg monarchy in the late eighteenth century, and is the best of Gassmann's minor-key symphonies. There is evidence that Gassmann was now aware of the developments in minor-key symphony writing that had been taking place beyond the imperial court in the later 1760s (Haydn and Vaňhal, also perhaps Leopold Hofmann). In the first movement (Ex. 2.7), the accompaniment *Trommelbass* and tremolandi in bars 9–12 and the wide melodic leaps over diminished seventh harmony of bar 15 allude to the stormy style. The outer movements display precisely the qualities—character, contrast, energy, drama, rhetoric—that are missing in H23 and, to a lesser extent, H45. Neither, interestingly, employs fugato, although other aspects of untimely rhetoric are much in evidence. The main theme of H83/i has a sharp internal contrast: a loud, vigorous dotted figure suggestive of the opening of a French overture is followed by a chain of suspensions, marked *p* (Ex. 2.7). Hill finds this opening "particularly unusual" as its four bars are divided into 1+3 rather than Gassmann's customary 2+2.[66] Thereafter "a two-bar rhythmic habit pervades the movement as a whole,"[67] established first at bar 9, although subsequently broken up by several elisions. The exposition is heterogeneous in texture, including plaintive snatches of melody over a pedal and with an odd thirty-second-note accompaniment in the second violins (bars 17–20) and a running sixteenth-note bass with slower notes in the upper parts (bars 23–31; yet another untimely element). These different textures are directly juxtaposed, an approach familiar from the practice of mixing "topics" so familiar in later Viennese instrumental music.

The finale is also dramatic, and its main theme too has an internal contrast. A unison gesture that resembles the bass of a Romanesca schema is followed by a phrase with faster surface rhythm that uses tied notes that call to mind suspensions, although the first two are not (Ex. 2.8). Much of the rest of the exposition consists of a running bass in eighth or sixteenth notes with slower notes above, often with ties, whether suspensions or not, reminiscent of a Fuxian exercise in fourth-species counterpoint. The second half of this section typifies certain aspects of Gassmann's approach to composition (Ex. 2.9). Small units are continually repeated, although literal sequences are avoided; tied notes in one or two parts are used consistently, regardless of whether they form suspensions. The relationship between unity and variety in this passage is different from that in most of the late eighteenth-century Viennese instrumental music with which modern listeners are familiar. Constant changes occur, but there is no development of ideas, fragmentation of units, or

---

[65] Landon, *Chronicle*, 2:282.

[66] Ibid., 106.

[67] Ibid., 107.

Ex. 2.7 Gassmann 83/i, bars 1–16

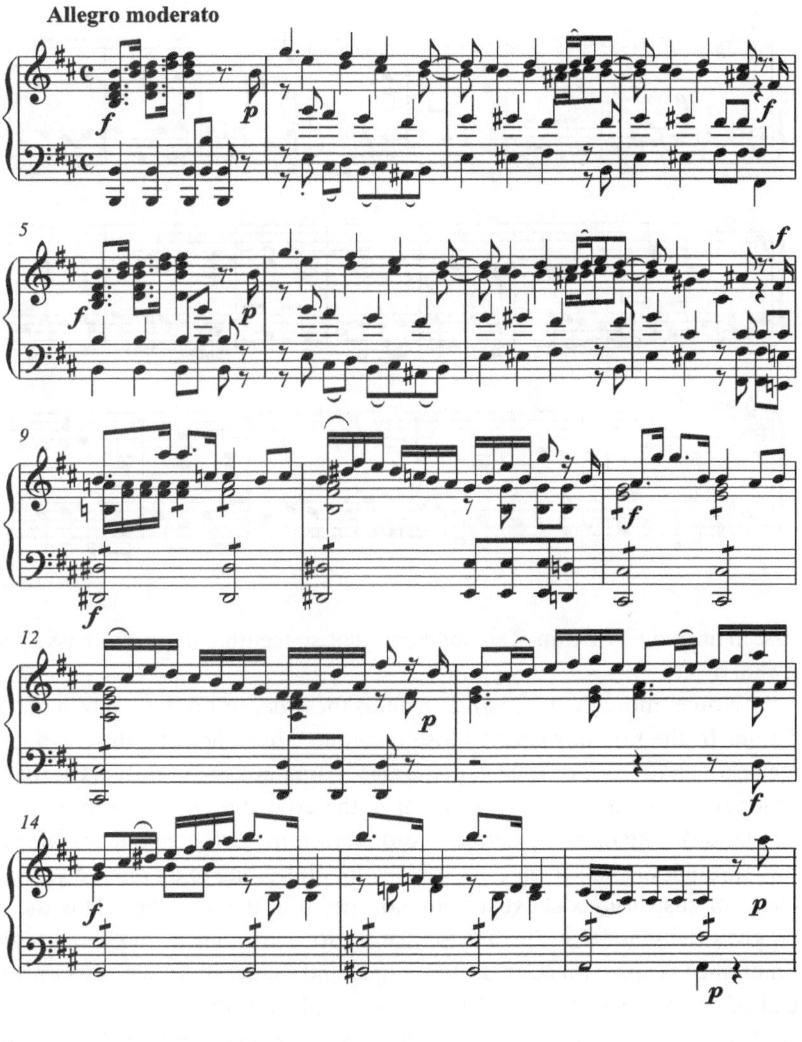
Allegro moderato
f
p
f
5
f
p
f
9
f
f
12
p
f
14
f
p
p

Ex. 2.8 Gassmann 83/iv, strings, bars 1–9[1]

Allegro assai
f

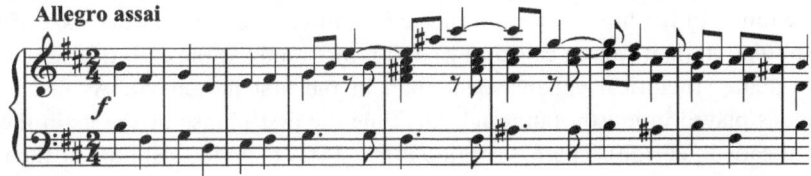

Ex. 2.9 Gassmann 83/iv, strings, bars 33–52

increase in harmonic rhythm. The positioning of sixteenth notes in the bass appears somewhat arbitrary.

In both outer movements Gassmann alters the order of his materials in the recapitulation. In the first movement those materials are sufficiently differentiated in character that a reversal of their order is also a dramatic reversal. It is coordinated with the reversal of modes (minor–major in the exposition to major–minor in the recapitulation). The opening dotted chords return in bar 58, about two-thirds of the way through the movement, but initially in VI, leading to an altered version of the chain of suspensions above a dominant pedal in the tonic key. This thematic return gives the sense that the "recapitulatory rotation" has begun,[68] but without the simultaneous appearance of dotted chords and tonic key. That occurs only near the end of the movement (Ex. 2.10), and is varied so as to emphasize closure: the chain of suspensions ends with a perfect authentic cadence rather than, as in the exposition, a half cadence, and is repeated immediately, with no return to the dotted figure. The first four bars of the subordinate theme (bars 46–49) appear in the development (in VI), but are missing from the recapitulation, and never appear in the tonic. In the finale the main theme is omitted altogether at the start of the recapitulation (if it can be called that) and returns only at the end, this time with even greater rhetorical enhancement than in the first movement. As usual the theme is played in unison (although this time the first phrase of the main theme was already in unison). There is a pause in bar 168, before the last note of the previous phrase is repeated softly, and another pause precedes the final flourish. This

---

[68] Hepokoski and Darcy, *Elements of Sonata Theory*, 231.

Ex. 2.10 Gassmann 83/i, bars 79–90

kind of fragmentation and rhetorical hesitation is rare in Gassmann, and is very effective here.

Gassmann's minor-key symphonies helped to define and consolidate the sub-genre, even if H45 and H83 may not have been known beyond the imperial court. At their best, they heighten the tendencies found in Wagenseil and exploit the rhetorical possibilities of invoking untimely idioms within the form of a modern symphony. Gassmann's approach to instrumental counterpoint is entirely differ-ent from that found in, say, Haydn's Symphonies Nos. 3/iv (1761), 38/iv, 44/i and iv (1770–71), or String Quartets op. 20, nos. 2/iv, 5/iv, and 6/iv (1771). Fugue is invoked, but its principle is seldom carried through for long; when it is (H45/iv), the result is unsuccessful. There are often "lazy parts" that merely fill out the texture or seem directionless, as though inked in as an afterthought. This much is not atypical of the Viennese tradition of contrapuntal instrumental music.[69] With Gassmann, though, the use of *cantus firmus* models combined with the lack of interest in har-monic progression, suggest a too-direct synthesis of Fuxian theory and instrumen-tal practice.

---

[69] Kirkendale, *Fugue and Fugato*, 74–75.

Ordonez

Karl von Ordonez (1734–86)[70] was not a salaried court musician until relatively late in his life (1779), when he was appointed to the Hofkapelle as a chamber musician on a modest 250 gulden per year, evidently a part-time post.[71] Already in 1766, however, a report on the imperial chapel and chamber music listed him as a court chamber-music violinist, so there may have been an informal relationship stretching back for over a decade.[72] His twenty-seven string quartets, many of them, like those of Gassmann, containing fugues or with the order of movements of a sonata da chiesa,[73] were assiduously collected by Joseph II, who was still having them performed in the 1780s,[74] and suggest substantial imperial patronage. The son of an infantry lieutenant and member of the lowest order of nobility, seemingly without estate, Ordonez spent his whole life in Vienna.[75] He pursued a dual career as a civil servant in the administration of Lower Austria (1758–83) and as a musician. The latter was probably not regarded as an appropriate sole profession for a man of his social rank.[76] Nothing is known of his musical education. He is recorded as playing the violin at the salons of the aristocracy, and as leading the second violins in the orchestra of the *Tonkünstler-Societät* in 1784, although he had probably been playing for the society since its first concert season in 1772.[77] Ordonez's wife died in 1780, in 1783 he was forced out of his administrative position and out of the Hofkapelle on grounds of illness,[78] and his last three years were spent in poverty. Given his official position and performing activities, Ordonez was an extraordinarily prolific composer: aside from his quartets and much other chamber music, his output includes about seventy-three symphonies, a parody opera on Gluck's *Alceste* (1775), and a *Singspiel, Diesmal hat der Mann den Willen* (1778).

---

[70] There are variant spellings of the composer's name, but this is the one used by Ordonez himself. David Young, "The Symphonies of Karl von Ordonez (1734–1786): A Biographical, Bibliographical and Stylistic Study" (PhD diss., University of Liverpool, 1980), vi. On Ordonez's life, see also David Young, "Karl von Ordonez (1734–1786): A Biographical Study," *Royal Musical Association Research Chronicle* 19 (1983–85): 31–56.

[71] Young, "The Symphonies of Karl von Ordonez," 11.

[72] Johann Adam Hiller, "Von dem dermaligen Etat der kaiserl. königl. Hof- und Kammermusik," *Anmerkungen die Musik betreffend* 13 (September 23, 1766); reproduced in Heartz, *Haydn, Mozart and the Viennese School*, app. 1, 725. Haydn's name appears on the same list, so its significance may be limited.

[73] Brown, "The Chamber Music with Strings of Carlos d'Ordóñez," 233–34; *Carlo d'Ordonez, String Quartets, Opus 1*, ed. A. Peter Brown (Madison, WI: A-R Editions, 1980).

[74] *Musikalische Korrespondenz*, vol. 1 (Speyer, 1790), cols. 27–30. Quoted in Kirkendale, 38–39.

[75] Young, "The Symphonies of Karl von Ordonez," 7.

[76] Ibid., 8.

[77] Ibid., 12–13.

[78] Ibid., 9.

Ordonez probably composed symphonies from the mid-1750s until about 1780.[79] Dating most of them accurately is difficult.[80] During the late 1750s and the 1760s a number gained wide distribution across Europe, although only five were printed.[81] Ordonez excelled in the galant style, especially in the amiable, courtly idiom pioneered in Vienna by Wagenseil. Throughout his career Ordonez favored Wagenseil's three-movement scheme over the four movements that became standard for Viennese symphonies after about 1770. But Ordonez was also a capable contrapuntist, willing and able to draw on Fuxian species models and freer, instrumental types of counterpoint for rhetorical effect. Most of his later symphonies evoke "strict style" at some point, and it seems likely that at least some of them were composed for the Hofkapelle.[82] Unlike his quartets, however, twenty-one of which contain complete fugal movements (out of a total of twenty-seven works), contrapuntal textures in the symphonies are usually brief, intermittent, or both. There are only two complete fugues. Ordonez, however, had only one foot within the court and the sphere of imperial patronage; he was versatile and open to influences from outside. He was a good orchestrator,[83] and his symphonies are interesting for their varied timbres and textures; they often feature concertante writing, in particular for solo viola. He was clearly familiar with a range of past and present musical styles, dances, and rhetorical gestures. In his symphonies of the 1770s one can detect the influences of Vaňhal and Haydn, the latter especially as regards his tendency to reconceive the recapitulation of sonata-form movements. The quartets and the symphonies may have been aimed at different patrons. The imperial music collection contained every one of Ordonez's string quartets but only six of his symphonies, and the other large collections of the chamber music do not include any of the symphonies. Conversely, the archives that hold large numbers of the symphonies—derived from the collections of great aristocratic families and monasteries—lack quartets.[84]

Ordonez composed six symphonies in minor keys, of which one is known only from an incipit in an eighteenth-century catalog (see Table 1.2). Catalogs provide a terminus ad quem of 1775 for C14, F12, and G8, and 1766 for the lost G6, but there are few clues for B1 or G7. The attempts at dating the symphonies by A. Peter Brown and David Young suggest that F12 and G8 are from the 1760s or

---

[79] On the symphonies, see Young, "The Symphonies of Karl von Ordonez"; A. Peter Brown: "The Symphonies of Carlo d'Ordonez: A Contribution to the History of Viennese Instrumental Music during the Second Half of the Eighteenth Century," *Haydn Yearbook* 12 (1981): 5–121; A. Peter Brown, Introduction to Carlo d'Ordondez, *Seven Symphonies,* series B, vol. 3 of *The Symphony 1720–1840* (New York and London: Garland, 1981); Heartz, *Haydn, Mozart and the Viennese School*, 473–74.

[80] Brown's dating of the symphonies relies on an elaborate system of rectangular boxes of various dimensions. "The Symphonies of Carlo d'Ordonez," 41. For an alternative approach, see also Young, "The Symphonies of Karl von Ordonez," 54–62.

[81] Brown, "The Symphonies of Carlo d'Ordonez," 10.

[82] Young, "The Symphonies of Karl von Ordonez," 63.

[83] Ibid., 64–71.

[84] Brown, "The Symphonies of Carlo d'Ordonez," 13–14.

perhaps even the late 1750s, C14 is from the early 1770s, and B1 and G7 are among Ordonez's last symphonies, perhaps composed late in the 1770s. The scoring and style of the works suggest that these conclusions are reasonable.[85]

The outer movements and minuet movements of Ordonez's minor-key symphonies—that is, those movements that are actually in the minor mode—are diverse in style. Brown points out that, although Ordonez's name has often appeared when claims are made for a brief, discrete *Sturm und Drang* period around 1770, these works in fact furnish little evidence for it. His dating of the symphonies suggested that they were widely distributed across Ordonez's career. Furthermore, many of the movements do not display the characteristic traits of the *Sturm und Drang* style as Brown understands them (syncopations, wide leaps, sharp contrasts of texture and dynamics, weighty finales). Some movements are highly emotional, but not all. Brown considers only the outer movements of C14 a "truly convincing tour de force of the *Sturm und Drang* concept," although he thinks that the best examples in Ordonez's work are not concert symphonies at all but the two sinfonias in his parody of *Alceste*.[86] Considered alongside the minor-key symphonies of Wagenseil and Gassmann, those of Ordonez do not always consolidate the emerging subgenre. F12/i and G8/i, B1/i, and B1/iii (the finale) are in what Floyd Grave has termed (in Haydn) a "galant minor."[87] B1/iii is a gavotte in a sectional form, marked "Rondeau non troppo presto." These movements always feature contrapuntal textures at some stage, but that does not in itself distinguish them from Ordonez's symphonies in major keys. At the opening of the development section of G8/i, for instance, the parts move quite independently, with the melody of the main theme transferred to the bass, but there is no sense of ecclesiastical associations or display of compositional learning, and the passage lacks nothing in elegance. F12/i begins like a minuet, soon introducing dotted figures that indicate the "aristocratic" type of minuet. These are occasionally transferred to the bass, rather in the manner of a French overture, yet in rhetorical terms none of this seems to come from outside the movement's normal language. B1 probably dates from the 1770s, thus postdating most of minor-key symphonies of Vaňhal and Haydn and several of Dittersdorf's, yet it registers no trace of their existence.

One relatively consistent feature—shared by four of the five symphonies—is a sonata-form finale in fast *alla breve* time, something that will later become a recognizable Viennese minor-key type (see chapter 4). In the two early minor-key symphonies, F12 and G8 (Ex. 2.11), the finale is contrapuntal throughout—unusual

---

[85] B1 and G7 are the only of Ordonez's minor-key symphonies to call for horns, and as they are crooked in the mediant they are not likely to have been composed before the mid-1760s, unless they are highly unusual for a minor-key symphony.

[86] Brown, "The Symphonies of Carlo d'Ordonez," 44, 45. Brown's discussion on pp. 43–45 is unfortunately rather unclear, and it appears that he confuses his own numbering for the symphonies in G minor. An extract from one of the minor-key orchestral movements from *Alceste* is given by Landon (*Chronicle*, 2:391–92).

[87] Floyd Grave, "Galant Style, Enlightenment, and the Paths from Minor to Major in Later Instrumental Works by Haydn," *Ad Parnassum* 7 (2009): 9–41 (pp. 11–12).

Ex. 2.11 Ordonez G8/iii, bars 1–23

for an Ordonez symphony movement—though not fugal, and with much variety of texture. These two movements are almost different versions of the same piece, or different ways of composing a movement on the same idea: the openings are extremely similar. Their energy is unrelenting, and anticipates the stormy finales of Haydn and Vaňhal. F12/iv touches on ritornello technique at the very end, introducing completely new material for the final four-bar codetta (bars 98–101), as though placing the rest of the movement inside a frame. This recalls a number of minor-key movements by Wagenseil and Gassmann.

C14, probably the next minor-key symphony in the Ordonez chronology, is the odd one out. It is a paradox that, even though he cites Ordonez's work to dispute the existence of a *Sturm und Drang* stylistic period, Brown chose to publish precisely the one that best illustrates it, calling it "an unusually strong work."[88] He admitted that "this particular symphony provides powerful ammunition for those who believe in this aesthetic period" (i.e., the *Sturm und Drang*), noting the outer movements' rhythmic drive, syncopations, sudden contrasts, *sforzandi*, and contrapuntal textures, and pointing to the weight of the finale.[89] Indeed, the work

[88] Brown, Introduction, xvi.

[89] Ibid.

is strikingly different from Ordonez's other four surviving minor-key symphonies, and it is also one of only two minor-key symphonies by professional composers before the 1790s to call for clarini and timpani (the other is Vaňhal c2). Today, thirty years after Brown's work on the Ordonez symphonies, and following the publication of Ordonez's other four and most of Vaňhal's, we can see clearly that in C14 Ordonez approaches the minor-key style that Vaňhal was cultivating in the late 1760s (see chapter 3). The first four bars of C14/i (Ex. 2.12), for instance, are based on the "Do-Re-Mi" schema (Gjerdingen's term; $\hat{1}$–$\hat{2}$–$\hat{3}$ above $\hat{1}$–$\hat{7}$–$\hat{1}$)[90] that also opens Vaňhal e3/i, e1/i, and c2/i, including Vaňhal's characteristic drop to $\hat{5}(g^1)$ and eighth-note *Trommelbass* accompaniment (compare with Exx. 3.2, 3.3, and 3.5). The triple meter was also favored by Vaňhal for this type of movement (e1/i, c2/i, g2/i, a2/i). At the end of the main theme, dominant harmony is prolonged for four bars, and a gesture akin to a mediant tutti follows in bar 13. Elsewhere, Ordonez moves directly to III from V/i at this point in a movement (as do many eighteenth-century minor-key pieces), for instance in G8/i, bars 14–15, and G8/iii, bars 14–15,[91] but in C14/i the join is more clearly articulated than in any of the other concert symphonies (there is a clear mediant tutti in one of the sinfonias from *Alceste*).[92] In this respect it resembles those movements that take Haydn 39/i as their model, especially as the horns (in E♭) enter at this point, as they do at the mediant tutti in Haydn, Vaňhal, and Mozart. The exposition is more tightly organized than those of Ordonez's other minor-key symphonies, lasting only twenty-five bars, and contrapuntal textures are avoided in favor of a continuous rhythmic drive and urgent repetitions such as those at bars 5–8, 10–11, and 17–20. The characteristic ascending octave leap from a strong beat that closes the exposition and the recapitulation is shared with Vaňhal c2/i. The decisive stylistic factor in C14/i is the combination of relatively fast surface rhythm in the bass (*Trommelbass*) with relatively slow harmonic rhythm: this is at the core of Vaňhal's dynamic but homophonic conception of the minor-key fast movement. Yet something of the fine finish typical of Ordonez is still in evidence. The trills on the first beats of bars 1, 2, 3, and 4 are an elegant touch almost never encountered in this context in Vaňhal, who, moreover, would not have drawn attention away from the melody with the descending scale in the second violins in bar 2. The third-movement minuet and the *alla breve* finale of C14 may be indebted to Vaňhal too, as well as Haydn (see chapter 4).

The fact that C14 is the easiest symphony by Ordonez to assimilate to a *Sturm und Drang* stylistic period does not in itself make it an "unusually strong" work. Indeed, Brown's aesthetic judgment now seems questionable. Ordonez's galant minor-key first movements, such as F12/i, G8/i, and B1/i, are less stormy than C14/i but in some ways more subtle in expression and more sophisticated in their part-writing. C14 matches neither the nervous energy, broad melody, nor large-scale formal

---

[90] Gjerdingen, *Music in the Galant Style*, 77.

[91] Young, "The Symphonies of Karl von Ordonez," 85.

[92] Score extract provided in Landon, *Chronicle*, 2:391–92.

Ex. 2.12 Ordonez C14/i, bars 1–15

sweep of the best symphonies of the type by Haydn and Vaňhal. This was not quite Ordonez's sphere, but C14 does show that, alone amongst the imperial court composers, he was willing to follow the trend set in aristocratic salons beyond the Hofburg and test himself in open competition with the best instrumental composers of the day.

G7 is a remarkable work. It is probably one of Ordonez's last symphonies, and Young regards it as one of his finest in either mode.[93] As with C14 some prominent

---

[93] Young, "The Symphonies of Karl von Ordonez," 101.

features distinguish it sharply from most of Ordonez's major-key symphonies, but the features themselves are rather different in G7. This is not a stormy work in the manner of Haydn or Vaňhal around 1770, and there is no *Trommelbass* or mediant tutti in the outer movements. Instead, the symphony looks back (from the late 1770s or perhaps even 1780) to the type of minor-key symphony composed by Wagenseil and Gassmann in the early and mid-1760s, taking the characteristic strategies of those works a stage further. One might speculate that the composition of G7 had something to do with Ordonez's formal appointment as a court musician in 1779, although that cannot be confirmed. Whatever the case, it revives the practice of transferring certain techniques of contrapuntal chamber music into symphonies in minor keys. All three movements conspicuously evoke "strict style" in a way seldom found in Ordonez's symphonies.

G7/i is a sonata form of unusual dimensions, packed with fugato-like procedures (series of imitative entries of a short motive or motives, though not necessarily in tonic–dominant order) in up to four parts, along with sequences; a long dominant pedal point; hemiolas and dotted rhythms at some cadences; and, at the very end (bars 158–64), a sequence of descending sevenths in octaves that recalls, once again, a closing ritornello. The imitative entries at the start suggest the lineage of the fugato binary movements from midcentury Viennese chamber music, although here there are four entries rather than the usual two in the upper voices (Ex. 2.13). Indeed, the opening motive d^2–bb^2 followed by an answer at the subdominant strikingly recalls the opening of Wagenseil G5/iii (Ex. 2.2). The key and meter are the same, although Ordonez sustains the contrapuntal texture longer. Despite the intensive counterpoint, the exposition's four paragraphs are relatively short, the conclusion of each being clearly articulated with a cadence and sometimes a caesura (a half cadence for the first three, then a perfect authentic cadence).[94] This pattern continues through the brief development section. The movement thus moves through the cycle of initiating, medial, and concluding functions rather frequently, and almost every phase of initiation draws on the rhetoric of fugato.

The recapitulation is different. It is longer than the exposition and development put together,[95] and combines these broader dimensions with heightened untimely rhetoric. Young points out that Ordonez often substantially rewrites his recapitulation, sometimes lengthening or shortening it, extending or shortening sections within it, omitting material that has appeared frequently in the development (as in G7/iii), reordering the events of the exposition, or interrupting it for a further passage of development.[96] This last technique tends to appear in later works and may indicate the influence of Haydn.[97] After its short first paragraph, the recapitulation

---

[94] Unfortunately, the second paragraph is not well written: it seems aimless and unshaped. The first violins get stuck on bb^2 and a^2. Young notes that Ordonez had a weakness in modulation, and seldom wrote good transitions in his expositions. Ibid., 84–86.

[95] The movement is 164 bars in total; the exposition ends at bar 45 (not counting the four-bar transition for the exposition repeat), and the development at bar 81.

[96] Young, "The Symphonies of Karl von Ordonez," 86–88.

[97] Young speculates that Ordonez was influenced by Haydn 45/i. Ibid., 107–8.

Ex. 2.13 Ordonez G7/i, bars 1–19

of G7/i tonicizes vii (F minor; bars 86–87), VI (E♭ major; bars 89–95), and ♭II (A♭ major; bars 96–99). Charles Rosen would call this passage the "secondary develop-ment," which typically features modulation to the subdominant or more distant flat-key regions.[98] When the tonic key returns, the cadence is delayed by a long dominant pedal (bars 107–24), a procedure that evokes the grandeur of a formal fugue. Then, after a cadence (bars 131–33), the recapitulation picks up from bar 20 of the exposition and parallels the exposition to the end, before the ritornello-like codetta is added. In other words, the recapitulation replaces the exposition's second paragraph, thirteen bars in length, with one of fifty-one bars (see Fig. 2.1; compare paragraphs 2 and 9).[99]

G7/ii shares with the first movement a combination of contrapuntal and homophonic writing, the latter articulating the rather frequent section boundar-ies. This movement is an odd hybrid, a G-major Andante in 2/4 in which serene trio-sonata-like textures with abundant suspensions stand cheek-by-jowl with fussy galant violin figures over homophonic, repeated-note accompaniments. G7/iii like-wise brings together old and new styles in an unusual way. It takes up the fast *alla breve* meter of F12/iii, G8/iii, and C14/iii, a meter not used for a finale by Wagenseil or Gassmann except for the contrapuntal Gassmann 45/iv. At 151 bars it is almost as long as the first movement (itself substantial). Like the other two movements of G7, and unlike its predecessor finales by Ordonez, it evokes learned style rather self-consciously, and, moreover, it is quite clear when the music switches back to a modern style. The tempo direction keeps the latter in mind: "Allegro non troppo

---

[98] Charles Rosen, *Sonata Forms*, rev. ed. (New York: Norton, 1988), 289–95.

[99] This recapitulation is also analyzed by Young ("The Symphonies of Karl von Ordonez," 88).

Paragraph	1	2	3	4	codetta
bars	1–6	7–19	20–28	29–37	38–45
no. of bars	**6**	**13**	**9**	**9**	**8**

Development

Paragraph	5	6	7
bars	50–58	59–67	68–79
no. of bars	**9**	**9**	**12**

Recapitulation

Paragraph	8 (≈1)	9 (replaces 2)	10 (≈3)	11 (≈4)	codetta	"closing ritornello"
bars	80–85	86–133	133–141	142–150	151–8	158–64
no. of bars	**6**	**51**	**9**	**9**	**8**	**7**

FIGURE. 2.1 Ordonez G7/i, length of paragraphs

Ex. 2.14 Ordonez G7/iii, bars 1–17

Allegro non troppo con garbo

con garbo." "Con garbo" was a favorite marking of Ordonez, but strict style is conventionally associated with the church and with compositional learning, not social graces. The unisons gesture at the opening (Ex. 2.14) recalls other minor-key pieces composed around 1770; Brown compares it with the opening of Haydn 44/i.[100] The movement is full of trio-sonata textures: a fast, running bass in eighth notes and a pair of upper parts that often consist only of half notes or whole notes with suspensions. There are obvious concerto-like solo/tutti contrasts (see bars 23, 47, and 87). Nevertheless, the exposition gradually drifts away from its untimely beginning to a more modern idiom. A two-bar melodic figure with one of Ordonez's trademark trills (Ex. 2.14, bars 11–12) takes over and is repeated frequently as the texture simplifies. This music is galant in several senses: elegant in gesture as well as homophonic and constructed with short phrases. The movement as a whole ends in this vein; there is nothing to suggest a closing ritornello, not even the opening unison figure; the final phrase features the trill figure, and there are no quick repeated "hammer blows" at the end in the fashion of Vaňhal or Haydn around 1770.

For Young, G7/iii, along with the D5/vii, is "Ordonez's most complete and successful integration of counterpoint with the symphonic style,"[101] although in a sense it is the lack of seamless integration that makes the movement, and the symphony as a whole, so effective. G7 adapts and enhances rhetorical strategies of the minor-key symphonies of the 1760s by Wagenseil and Gassmann. More than theirs, however, it presents itself as syntactically heterogeneous. In the contrasts between its homophonic and polyphonic passages the listener hears the gap between the musically "ancient" and "modern" and, by extension, between competing musical value-systems of the later eighteenth century. Ordonez's unique professional position partly inside, partly outside the imperial court may have helped him along this path, but, as subsequent chapters will show, he was far from the only Viennese composer to take it in the 1770s and 1780s.

---

100 Brown, "The Symphonies of Carlo d"Ordonez," 44.
101 Young, "The Symphonies of Karl von Ordonez," 100.

{ 3 }

Vaňhal to 1771: Five First Movements

Johann Baptist Vaňhal (1739–1813) has a central role in the story of the Viennese minor-key symphony. His symphonies, which probably total almost eighty,[1] were popular in the 1760s and 1770s within the Habsburg monarchy and far beyond. In some cases multiple manuscript copies—sometimes more than a dozen—survive in European archives. More than thirty symphonies by Vaňhal were printed in the eighteenth-century, sometimes in several editions, and his most popular pieces appeared in keyboard arrangements. References to Vaňhal in the press and in music periodicals and dictionaries were generally favorable.[2] When Charles Burney visited Vienna in 1772 to gather material for *The Present State of Music in Germany, the Netherlands and the United Provinces* (1773) he took pains to search out Vaňhal. From humble origins in the small town of Nechanice (then Nechanicz) in east Bohemia, Vaňhal took advantage of the Viennese fashion for symphonies in the 1760s, a time when aristocrats maintained private orchestras and new and old nobility vied with one another for status as patrons of the latest instrumental music. Vaňhal wrote more symphonies in minor keys (twelve) than any other composer of the eighteenth century—more, for that matter, than almost any composer since. Today most of them—though still not all—are published and recorded.

Vaňhal and Haydn dominated the vogue for minor-key symphonies in the late 1760s and early 1770s, and together they defined the styles of the stormy fast movement and the contrapuntal minuet. When other composers adopted the stormy style or revived it in later years, it was to Vaňhal as much as to Haydn that they alluded. Vaňhal himself knew Haydn's compositions well and often took them as models. Haydn knew some of Vaňhal's symphonies, although direct influence in that direction is more difficult to pin down. Unlike Haydn, Vaňhal had no permanent employment as Kapellmeister and could not count on a virtuoso orchestra to perform his compositions. On the other hand, he was permanently resident in Vienna and was not tied to a court, so he could take advantage of individual commissions as a freelancer. Vaňhal largely avoided the ritornello gestures and—in his

---

[1] Bryan, *Johann Wanhal*, 41.

[2] Ibid., 26–30.

outer movements—the contrapuntal procedures found in the minor-key symphonies of the imperial court composers.[3] Many of his fast movements are built around a demanding and expressive first violin part. The other parts could have been played by amateurs or semi-amateurs such as made up the numbers in hastily assembled aristocrats' orchestras of the day. Within these constraints Vaňhal's minor-key symphonies maximize their dramatic impact. Perhaps to the commissioner it seemed as though something of the passion and drama of the operatic stage had been brought inside his own salon, at minimal cost.

Sources of information on Vaňhal's music and his life are scarce and their reliability uncertain. Only one autograph of a Vaňhal symphony survives, and that is an atypical, single-movement work.[4] The identity of the commissioner of a Vaňhal symphony, if there was one, is usually unknown. Exact dating of the works is extremely difficult, and the information in Table 1.1 (from Paul Bryan's thematic catalog of the symphonies) is approximate. No letters to or from Vaňhal survive and only two people who met him (Burney and Gottfried Johann Dlabacž) left significant records of him, so only the rough outlines of his biography can be established.[5] Almost no trace survives from which to reconstruct the world of feverish musical activity in aristocratic households of the 1760s in which Vaňhal's career blossomed. What remains in abundance are manuscript copies and prints of the symphonies themselves.

As a promising young musician Vaňhal arrived in Vienna around 1760 at the behest of his local overlords, the Schaffgotsch family. There he studied with their *Klaviermeister* Matthäus Schlöger, although according to Dlabacž, Vaňhal was dissatisfied with this teaching and "began to study the scores of the greatest masters on his own."[6] Later one Baron Riesch identified Vaňhal as a potential *Kapellmeister* for the musical establishment he planned for his palace in Dresden. He paid for Vaňhal to undertake a tour of Italy in preparation for the job, which lasted from May 1769 to September 1771. Vaňhal visited Venice, Bologna, Florence, and Rome, met Gluck, and assisted Gassmann by providing numbers for Gassmann's Roman operas. Unfortunately, this trip was to culminate in what was perhaps the fateful moment in his life. On his return to Vienna Vaňhal suffered a mental breakdown, possibly a heightened form of an existing instability. He recovered, but did not take up the position of *Kapellmeister* at Baron Riesch's court. Instead, he lived in Vienna for another forty-two years, dying in 1813 at the age of seventy-four, having outlived all the other composers whose symphonies are discussed in this book. But Vaňhal wrote his last works in the genre in the 1770s. His later career took a different path. He eventually ceased to write the string quartets that had been almost as successful as his symphonies, and turned to sacred music, undemanding but widely

---

[4] Ibid., 41, 263.

[5] Burney, *The Present State of Music in Germany*, 1:351–54; Gottfried Johann Dlabacž, *Allgemeines historisches Künstler-Lexicon für Böhmen und zum Theil auch für Mähren und Schlesien*, 3 vols. (Prague: Gottlieb Haase, 1815). Both reproduced in Bryan, *Johann Wanhal*, 4–6.

[6] Dlabacž, *Künstler-Lexicon*, 325; cited in Bryan, *Johann Wanhal*, 5.

published instrumental pieces for amateurs, and teaching. In the 1790s Vaňhal damaged his reputation in the eyes of some educated musicians by composing "characteristic" (programmatic) pieces such as *Die Schlacht bei Würzburg* (1796), *Die grosse Seeschlacht bei Abukir* (1800), and *Die Seeschlacht bei Trafalgar* (1806). Some critics, starting with Burney, have expressed disappointment with Vaňhal's music after his return to Vienna from Italy, but the reasons for his change of direction are debatable. This chapter deals only with the first movements of minor-key symphonies Vaňhal composed before or during his Italian trip, deferring the controversies surrounding his later style, and discussion of his last four minor-key symphonies, to chapter 5.

Despite the popularity of Vaňhal's symphonies, few contemporary writers referred to them specifically. Burney, in his Rousseauian vein, called them "spirited, natural and unaffected," and said that they preceded those of Haydn in England (arriving about 1771), and excited more attention there than any foreign music for a long time. The English were even more impressed than they had been by the symphonies of the Mannheim school. Burney said that the symphonies "deserve a place among the first productions, in which unity of melody [again a phrase of Rousseau's], pleasing harmony, and a free manly style are constantly preserved."[7] Vaňhal's "compositions for violins"—presumably his symphonies or quartets—Burney called "wild" and "new" (in context, these are clearly compliments).[8] In his lexicon of musicians (1792) Ernst Ludwig Gerber remarked that the early symphonies contained "fire, combined with beautiful singing melodies, and liveliness."[9] Burney and Gerber, however (the latter possibly paraphrasing the former), criticized a falling away in Vaňhal's later compositions, calling them "cold" and "common."

From today's perspective Vaňhal stands out as the best composer of instrumental music permanently resident in Vienna in the 1760s and the 1770s. His symphonies are neither as technically sophisticated nor as boldly original as those of Haydn, but in fast minor-key movements his handling of the dynamic ebb and flow is just as effective. These pieces are idiomatic instrumental music, obviously composed by a violinist. Even when making allowances for amateur players on some parts, they make better use of the instrumental resources than the minor-key symphonies of Wagenseil or Gassmann. Furthermore, in Vaňhal it is easy to recognize an understanding of formal function comparable to that of Haydn, Mozart,

---

[7] Charles Burney, *A General History of Music from the Earliest Ages to the Present Period*, 4 vols. (London: Payne and Son, 1776–89), 4:599; article "VAŇHALL," in *The Cyclopaedia; or Universal Dictionary of Arts, Sciences, and Literature*, ed. Abraham Rees, 39 vols. (Longman, Hurst, Rees Orme and Brown: London, 1802–19), vol.39, pages unnumbered. Most of this information is shared by the two sources, although some details are found only in the *Cyclopaedia* article. Both are reproduced in Bryan, *Johann Wanhal*, 1, 2.

[8] Burney, *The Present State of Music in Germany*, 1:352; Bryan, *Johann Wanhal*, 4.

[9] "…das mit dem schönen Gesange verbundene Feuer und die Lebhaftigkeit." Ernst Ludwig Gerber, *Historisch-biographisches Lexicon der Tonkünstler*, 2 vols. (Leipzig: Breitkopf, 1790–92), 2:767.

and Beethoven. Vaňhal knew how to write a beginning, a middle, and an end of a musical paragraph, how to write a tight-knit and a loosely organized paragraph, how to expand a paragraph from within, extend it, and so on, all the while delaying the expected cadence and sustaining tension. He did not piece together his symphony movements as a mosaic of small, functionally undifferentiated, interchangeable fragments, like some of the Mannheim composers and, often, Gassmann.[10] Thus, although his fast movements may be relatively short in terms of clock time, they seem broad in trajectory. This sense of a large-scale dynamic curve is what really gives his minor-key symphonies of the 1760s their "fire," notwithstanding such details as accents, wide leaps, and syncopations. The analyses in this chapter lay emphasis on Vaňhal's handling of formal function and phrase rhythm with the aim of revealing his work as strangely familiar, albeit with its own idiosyncrasies. Finally, to complement his dynamic qualities Vaňhal had a lyrical gift, doubtless derived from his violin playing, and perhaps from the school of Tartini that was strong in Bohemia at the time. His minor-key music harbors moments of tenderness that, when placed in juxtaposition with forceful tutti passages, lift the music out of the sphere of aristocratic entertainment and give it a narrative quality and a human dimension. Like the best of his Viennese contemporaries, Vaňhal did not mind mixing these different styles or topics in a single movement. To this extent Burney's comment about "manly style" seems to miss the point.[11] Gerber was on the right track: the juxtaposition of fire and beautiful melody is at the heart of Vaňhal's best music.

An Early First Movement: e3/i

Vaňhal's first minor-key symphony is probably e3 (the catalog numbers of the symphonies do not reflect the chronology of composition). This is an impressive debut; the first movement in particular rivals Haydn's later minor-key first movements in its dynamic energy, and well illustrates Gerber's judgment. Although one might consider E minor an unusual choice of key in the late eighteenth century, Vaňhal wrote three symphonies in this key (his most in any minor key), and there are six in total by Viennese composers from the period, all composed before 1780 (see Table 1.1). (From an earlier Viennese generation, Georg Matthias Monn has a symphony in E minor, probably his only one in a minor key.)[12] Paul Bryan dates e3 to the years 1760–62, slightly favoring 1760. He thinks that e3 is one of the

---

[10] Eugene K. Wolf, *The Symphonies of Johann Stamitz: A Study in the Formation of the Classic Style* (Utrecht and Antwerp: Bohn, Scheltma & Holkema, 1981), 103–6, 134n36. See the discussion of Gassmann's music in chapter 2 above.

[11] In comparison with Haydn's style of the same period, Heartz finds that Vaňhal B♭1, with its sighing chromatic appoggiaturas, is "a little lacking in virility." *Haydn, Mozart and the Viennese School*, 457.

[12] Kenneth E. Rudolf, ed., *Georg Matthias Monn, Five Symphonies,* series B, vol.1 of *The Symphony, 1720–1840* (New York and London: Garland, 1985), lxxxvi.

first nine symphonies that Vaňhal composed, soon after his arrival in Vienna. Seven of these are found in the collection of the Waldstein family that was once held at the castle at Doksy in north Bohemia. They clearly form a group: all seven are copied in the same wide format and by the same two copyists.[13] These symphonies are found in relatively few sources; the only other one for e3 is from the archive of the former monastery at Neuberg in Styria.[14] Bryan's dates for these symphonies are based largely on grounds of style. However, he does not take into account the fact that Vaňhal appears to have modeled many aspects of e3 on Dittersdorf e1, a work which Margaret Grave, in her catalog of Dittersdorf's symphonies, dates to 1763, though it could conceivably have been written as early as 1760.[15] Dittersdorf claimed in his autobiography, seemingly in earnest, that Vaňhal had been his pupil.[16] Vaňhal appears not to have mentioned the connection to Dlabacz, and, since he and Dittersdorf were born in the same year, it seems very unlikely that this was a conventional pedagogical relationship. Still, as a native of Vienna and the leading virtuoso violinist there Dittersdorf might have acted as a role model to Vaňhal.[17] As Bryan himself points out, the encounter could only have taken place while Dittersdorf was in Vienna in 1762–63.[18] So it seems likely that e3 was written no earlier than 1762–63 (Bryan tends to date Vaňhal's symphonies too early).

Vaňhal e3 and Dittersdorf e1 are both in four movements, with the minuet third. Both second movements are in the tonic major, both trios are in the relative major and feature duets for woodwind instruments, and both finales turn to the tonic major at the end and conclude softly. The subordinate key of both first-movement expositions is v rather than the more common III. Both finales are in the style of a "Contradanse": fast 2/4 meter with eighth-note upbeat, sectional form with each short section repeated. A notable feature of both finales is the turn to the relative major for a new section after one ending with a perfect authentic cadence in the tonic. This type of finale to a minor-key symphony became very rare after the mid-1760s. Dittersdorf's finale is marked "Presto"; Vaňhal's is marked "Contratantz" in the Doksy parts and "Presto" in those from Neuberg.[19] The opening four bars of the respective first movements are octave unison gestures in strings with a note or two from the horns to punctuate them. Both phrases descend through the E minor tonic triad from b^1 to e^1, touch on the descending third c^2–a^1,

---

[13] Bryan, *Johann Wanhal*, 85.

[14] Bryan, *Johann Wanhal*, 303.

[15] Eva Badura-Skoda argues for the possibility of this earlier date. See her Introduction to Karl Ditters von Dittersdorf, *Six Symphonies*, ed. Eva Badura-Skoda, thematic index by Margaret Grave, series B, vol. 1 of *The Symphony, 1720–1840* (New York and London: Garland, 1985), xxiv, xxix–xxx.

[16] Carl Ditters von Dittersdorf, *Lebensbeschreibung, seinem Sohne in die Feder diktiert* (Regensburg: Gustav Bosse, 1940 [1801]), 191.

[17] Bryan, *Johann Wanhal*, 16–17.

[18] Bryan, *Johann Wanhal*, 16.

[19] Paul Bryan, "Foreword" to AE290, v.

Ex. 3.1 Openings of E minor symphonies by Dittersdorf and Vaňhal c. 1762–63

(i) Dittersdorf e1, bars 1–4

Allegro molto

(ii) Vaňhal e3/i, bars 1–4

Allegro (molto)

and end with the descending fifth b¹ to e¹ (Ex. 3.1 (i) and (ii)).[20] When the turn to tonic major occurs near the end of the finales, in both cases an eight-bar repeated phrase begins with the first violins on e¹, before they descend to b at the start of the fifth bar, rise to a¹ and then fall back to f♯¹ (Ex. 7.3 and Ex. 7.4). In both phrases the harmony features a 5/3–6/4–5/3 pattern over a tonic pedal.

Nevertheless, on this evidence Dittersdorf's claim that Vaňhal was his pupil can only be regarded as conceited. Assuming that the modeling was undertaken on the part of Vaňhal rather than Dittersdorf—and his tendency to do this even in later years makes it seem more likely than not—then by 1762 at the age of twenty-three Vaňhal was well ahead of his "teacher," despite the disadvantages of a provincial background, a non-German-speaking home and a lack of good instruction. The two composers' treatment and continuation of their similar opening ideas are very different. Dittersdorf's is relatively stable and symmetrical. He immediately repeats his first four-bar phrase in the violins (now marked *piano*) with violas and cellos adding harmonic accompaniment. He ends both statements of the phrase on root-position tonic harmony with the tonic note in the melody, and he begins the third phrase also on root-position tonic harmony. The latter turns out to be a much longer, modulating phrase that eventually cadences in the dominant at the end of the first part of the form, but it continues to rely on the motives of the first two phrases and on octave unisons in the strings.

Vaňhal's conception is more dynamic and unstable in terms of melodic figures, melodic processes, and tonality (Ex. 3.2). His first phrase consists only of quarter notes, and functions like a motto. His fifth bar introduces a completely new idea with distinct melody, texture, and scoring and clear differentiation amongst the parts (the first violins have the melody, the seconds a tremolando, the viola and cello the *Trommelbass*). At this point there is a distinct echo of a ritornello / solo contrast: a hint of untimely rhetoric. The new phrase brings a sudden increase in energy and breaks the symmetry of the opening unison phrase, reiterating its motive as though stammering, and repeating part of its 1̂–2̂–3̂–ascent (bars 7² to 9¹). It seems plausible to hear that nervous repetition as a substitution for an implied

---

[20] Bryan's edition has the tempo of the first movement of e3 as "Allegro (molto)." He does not explain the meaning of the parentheses. It may be that "molto" appears in only one of the two sources.

Ex. 3.2 Vaňhal e3/i, bars 5–16[2]

but unrealized continuation through $\hat{4}$ to $\hat{5}$ (b[2]). The energy reaches its apex at bar 12 (the start of a cadential progression): the length of the melodic units is halved, the harmonic rhythm doubles in pace, and the surface rhythm increases sharply with a half-bar "spinning" idea built from dotted and trill motives. The cadential progression, the various forms of rhythmic acceleration, and the following caesura in the upper parts articulate a section boundary. But this first cadence is already in the subordinate key (bars 12–14[1]). The ten-bar unit thus projects a sense of headlong energy: its melodic figures are nervous, its melodic processes disconnected, and it does not even have time, as it were, to confirm its own tonic key before modulating.

There is no let up before the very end of the exposition. To be sure, after bar 14[2] some sense of stability is conveyed by the prolongation of tonic harmony and the repetition of a two-bar unit in a symmetrical phrase projecting an initiating function (presentation). But there is a sense of medial function (continuation) here too, given the second inversion harmony at the start of the phrase (bar 14[2]). The faster harmonic rhythm of half notes continues from the cadence phrase, and the duetting of first and second violins produces piquant dissonances, crossing of parts, and rhythmic complexity. Tension is heightened in bar 19 as characteristic material is abandoned for tremolandos in both violin parts, rising stepwise in the first violins. The climax on chord iv and a dramatic caesura—highly characteristic of Vaňhal in the second halves of his expositions—of three quarter notes follows, strongly implying an energetic continuation despite the silence. Headlong momentum is sustained to the final chords of the exposition.

Vaňhal demands less of the players—aside from the first violinists—than Dittersdorf. One result of this is the relatively slow harmonic rhythm. The violas and cellos contribute energy through the repeated notes of their *Trommelbass*, but they are not asked to articulate figuration of any complexity. Vaňhal compensates for this limitation with subtle melodic and harmonic processes. His "fire," as Gerber would have called it, is a function not just of the minor mode, fast tempo and tremolandi, but of form. From bar 5 until the final bar of the first section (bar 29) the music is never stabilized; it leaves the tonic almost before that tonic is established, and its momentum does not flag. When energy is reduced in one parameter, another sustains it. After the motto, the whole exposition is a single trajectory.

Four Lyrical, Triple-Meter First Movements: e1, c2, g2, a2

After e3 and (probably) c3,[21] Vaňhal wrote six more minor-key symphonies before undertaking his trip to Italy (1769–71). These works contain some of the best minor-key fast movements of the time. In the literature on the musical *Sturm und Drang* the two most often cited are g1 and d1, probably because of their publication and wide dissemination in the eighteenth century rather than any intrinsic qualities. Théodore de Wyzewa and Georges de Saint-Foix suggested that d1 was an influence on Mozart K. 183. H.C. Robbins Landon added g1 as a likely precursor to Mozart K. 183, while citing both g1 and d1 as examples of Vaňhal's debt to Haydn.[22] The two symphonies do share one notable feature with Haydn 39 and Mozart K. 183: they call for two horns crooked in the tonic key and two in the mediant. But they are not the finest of the six minor-key symphonies Vaňhal wrote in the later 1760s: the other four—e1, c2, g2, and a2—are more subtle and expressive. Those four share certain distinctive traits, notably their quiet, lyrical openings, which are otherwise extremely rare for minor-key symphonies of the time, and the triple meter of their first movements, which was seldom found in fast minor-key outer movements. Moreover, these four movements yield especially interesting results when studied with an eye to formal function and generic conventions.[23] They appear to have been almost as popular in the eighteenth century as g1 and d1, as they survive in many manuscript copies. One (c2) was published under Haydn's name by Forster, while a2 was published by André, Bailleux, and Hummel. The handsomely copied sets of six symphonies that Bryan calls the "Presentation" symphonies include e1, which might indicate that Vaňhal himself valued it highly.[24] On the other hand, g2,

---

[21] On the difficulties of dating c3, see chapter 4.

[22] Théodor de Wyzewa and Georges de Saint-Foix, *W.-A. Mozart: sa vie musicale et son œuvre de l'enfance à la pleine maturité (1756-1777): essai de biographie critique, suivi d'un nouveau catalogue chronologique de l'œuvre complète du maitre*, 5 vols. (Paris: Perrin, 1912), 2:121–22; Landon, "La crise romantique," 37. Landon couples Haydn 39, Vaňhal d1 and g1, and Mozart K. 183 in *Chronicle*, 2:380–93 (see also p. 282).

[23] Bryan notes some of the connections between the four works. *Johann Wanhal*, 203, 213.

[24] Ibid., 89–91.

in some respects an exceptional work, given its chromatic, contrapuntal opening, was neither published nor included in the Presentation set.[25]

Dating these works precisely is difficult. Bryan suggests 1764–67 for e1, c2, and g2, and 1769–71 (Vaňhal's Italian period) for a2. The first three are found in one group of five Vaňhal symphonies in the music collection of the Clam Gallas family (the largest single collection of his symphonies). All five works in the group were produced by the same Viennese copy shop and the same team of copyists, using paper with the same watermark.[26] The later date for the other symphony, a2, makes sense in terms of its style. The first three are especially close in several respects,[27] but a2 displays some different traits, of which Vaňhal made further use in later minor-key symphonies (post-1771).

All four first movements are in triple time, marked "Allegro moderato," and begin with a song-like, legato theme played by violins. Two (e1 and a2) begin with an upbeat, something of a Vaňhal hallmark in first movements at the time. The expositions share certain galant schemata, and the main themes of e1, c2, and a2 use versions of the galant abb' phrase structure, in which a contains a repeated idea like the presentation phrase of the Classical sentence, and b behaves like a continuation phrase. The varied repetition of b (as b') results in a looser organization than in most Classical main themes, which are normally tight-knit. The abb' pattern is another favorite of Vaňhal's, especially for the main themes of symphony outer movements (in either major or minor). All four of these symphonies have four movements, the first, third, and finale in the tonic (minor), the slow second movement in a related key. All use non-tonic crooks for at least some of the brass instruments: e1 has two horns in E and two in G; c2 has two clarini in C and two horns in E♭; g2 has two horns in B♭; and a2 appears to require two horns in A and two in C, although the many manuscript copies of the symphony vary, reflecting the different orchestras that played it.[28] As one might expect, given this scoring, the mediant tutti is found in almost all the outer movements (the exception is a2/i), and all have III as the subordinate key (in contrast to e3/i). All eight outer movements rely heavily on *Trommelbass* accompaniment and relatively slow harmonic rhythm. All the finales are stormy, in *alla breve* time, and are in sonata form, unlike the more lightweight, contradance finale of e3. Seven of the eight outer movements end in the tonic minor; only the finale of a2 turns to the major. None has a major-key coda like the outer movements of e3. All four minuets are in the tonic minor, but none of them is significantly contrapuntal (as will be shown in chapter 4, the minuet movements of Vaňhal's early-1760s minor-key symphonies, e3 and c3, are both canonic).

Many of these features probably reflect Vaňhal's new knowledge of Haydn 39 (1765). The latter is the first Viennese minor-key symphony to use horns crooked in different keys (G and B♭); its first movement has a soft opening paragraph (though the

---

[25] Ibid., 264–65, 300–301, 328–29, 340–41.

[26] Ibid., 69.

[27] Ibid., 213.

[28] Ibid., 340–1.

theme is neither legato nor lyrical); both outer movements have a mediant tutti and use III as the subordinate key; and both outer movements begin with *Trommelbass* figuration (even if not in the bass register). The halting approach to the caesura that precedes the mediant tutti in Haydn 39/i is echoed at the parallel moments in e1/i and g2/i. Indeed Vaňhal directly paraphrases several passages from Haydn 39 in these (and two other) symphonies.[29] Although the dating of all these works is disputable, it seems very unlikely that the influence was in the other direction. Haydn would surely not have copied passages from four different Vaňhal symphony movements in one work of his own, especially a work of such originality as Symphony No. 39; it is far more likely that Vaňhal knew this one work and modeled passages in several of his movements on it. After all, as he told Dlabacž, the imperfect instruction he had received meant he had to teach himself by studying the scores of the "best masters." Indeed, Vaňhal did not stop with Haydn 39. The idiosyncratic opening paragraph of g2/i is modeled on the equally unusual opening of Haydn's Symphony No. 16/i (1763), and later the movement even quotes 16/i briefly; there is no doubt in this case that Haydn's symphony was written earlier. Vaňhal also paraphrased music by Haydn in his string quartets.[30] This evidence, taken collectively, all but rules out 1764 as the date of composition for e1, c2, or g2.

Bryan's dating was probably decided before Gerlach's revised chronology of Haydn's symphonies to 1774 was published.[31] One of Gerlach's most interesting results, given the symphony's centrality to the literature on *Sturm und Drang* and its probable influence on other composers, was the dating of No. 39 to 1765 rather than 1768 or 1770, as previously believed. But in any case Bryan (from a generation of musicologists for whom "originality" was a decisive mark of historical significance) is at pains to assert Vaňhal's absolute independence from Haydn. He is stung by Landon's description of Vaňhal as Haydn's "seguace," and insists (unconvincingly) that "there is little similarity between the symphonies Wanhal [*sic*] composed during the period ca. 1760–1780 and Haydn's symphonies nos. I: 1–70, composed at about the same time," and that there is no evidence Vaňhal ever heard Haydn 39/i.[32]

---

[29] Compare Vaňhal e1/iv, bars 69–75, with Haydn 39/i, bars 61–67; Vaňhal G8/iv, bars 1–8, and Vaňhal d1/iv, bars 1–7, with Haydn 39/iv, bars 1–8 (see chapter 4); Vaňhal g2/iv, bars 24–31, with Haydn 39/i, bars 40–45. In each case the positions and functions within the two fast sonata form movements are identical (respectively, development section, opening of finale (twice), continuation phrase of subordinate theme). There are other close relationships. See the text below for the unusual strategy at the start of the first-movement recapitulations of Vaňhal e1/i and Haydn 39/i. See chapter 1 and the text below for a comparison of Vaňhal's mediant tuttis with those of Haydn 39/i and iv.

[30] Compare Vaňhal String Quartet E2/ii, bars 1–4 with Haydn Symphony 44/ii, bars 1–4; both movements are canonic minuets placed second in a four-movement cycle, one in E minor, the other in E major (see chapter 4); compare the entire exposition of Vaňhal String Quartet g3/i with that of Haydn op. 20, no. 3/i (both in G minor). For the Vaňhal extracts see Jones, "The String Quartets of Vanhal," 3:40 and 2:192–96.

[31] Gerlach, "Joseph Haydns Sinfonien bis 1774."

[32] Bryan, *Johann Wanhal*, xxii, 37–38. See also Paul Bryan, "Johann Baptist Wanhal," in *The Symphonic Repertoire*, vol. 2, *The Eighteenth-Century Symphony*, ed. Mary Sue Morrow and Bathia Churgin (Bloomington and Indianapolis: Indiana University Press, 2012), 529–41 (p. 539); and Landon, *Chronicle*, 2:380–89. Heartz strikes the right note. "If Vaňhal told Dlabacž in 1795 that he 'began to

The psychology of Vaňhal's paraphrasing of Haydn is discussed in chapter 6. But, whatever the reasons for it, there is no question of Vaňhal being a second-rate Haydn. He was a quite different kind of composer. While he might imitate Haydn in brief passages, he never truly emulated him, and could not have done so had he tried—he did not have the Esterhazy orchestra at his disposal, and in any case he simply did not possess Haydn's technique. In terms of their overall formal strategies, the first movements of e1, c2, g2, and a2 are determined by their initial lyricism, where the main influence is probably Italian violin music. The Italian opera overture is doubtless the source for much of Vaňhal's fast violin figuration. In terms of process he comes closest to Haydn in finales, where the debt to operatic rage arias and the stage representation of "furies" is shared. More concretely, Haydn's fast minor-key first movements, unlike Vaňhal's, never have lyrical openings, and, apart from the exceptional and non-lyrical 45/i, are never in triple time before the 1780s. Vaňhal's minor-key symphonies do not display Haydn's flashes of humor, penchant for irregularity and surprise, contrapuntal fluency, textural inventiveness, or dense processes of motivic derivation.[33]

In the first movements of e1, c2, g2, and a2, the lyrical openings are decisive for the movement's expressive trajectory. The key to understanding these movements usually lies in the relationship of the overall energetic shape of the recapitulation to that of the exposition, in particular what is often the combination of an increase in formal continuity and a change of mode for the material first presented in the relative major. In the expositions, the lyrical, minor-key main themes tend to falter and dissolve into fragmentary gestures or a caesura. That hesitancy is swept away by the mediant tutti and its energetic music in the relative major. In the recapitulation the discontinuities of the exposition are reduced and the music after the mediant tutti, no less energetic than before, returns in the tonic minor. The recapitulation is a more continuous flow of energy centered firmly in the tonic minor.

Lyricism (1): e1/i

Vaňhal's second symphony in E minor, e1, is one of his finest works. The first movement begins in a lyrical vein, yet even within the main theme that initial assurance is disrupted by discontinuity and hesitation. As often in Haydn, the rest of the movement can be interpreted as a response or a working-through of the "problem" set up at the beginning. This response encompasses the minor-mode recapitulation, resulting in an intriguing movement-level strategy. As with e3/i, the intense

---

study the scores of the greatest masters on his own', we have no difficulty in believing, on the basis of his own works, that these included the scores of Joseph Haydn." *Haydn, Mozart and the Viennese School*, 460.

[33] When Vaňhal paraphrases the contrapuntal sequences from the development section of Haydn 39/i in the development of e1/iv (see n. 29), he eliminates Haydn's motivic connections with other parts of his movement (violas and oboes) but provides no equivalent of his own; there is nothing that specifies this passage as belonging to e1.

expression of this movement can be attributed not just to surface rhythmic activity and negative minor-mode emotional content, but to larger formal processes. Ex. 3.3 gives the exposition.

The main theme, which contains the problematic and significant disruption, follows Vaňhal's favorite abb' pattern. The a-phrase (bars 1–4) resembles the presentation unit of a Classical sentence, with statement-response repetition of the basic idea. The b-phrase (bars 5–8) in turn is somewhat continuation-like: although there is no increase in harmonic rhythm or surface rhythm, it features a reduction in the

Ex. 3.3 Vaňhal e1/i, bars 1–47

Ex. 3.3 (Continued)

length of the units (from two bars to one), and an incipient cadential progression in the bass. The first violins leave the A and E strings and move down to the D string as the melody dips to f♯¹, and, in the b¹-phrase, to e¹. In music conceived primarily in terms of a lyrical first violin part, a move to a lower string may be of great expressive significance. In the b-phrase this descending gesture is followed by an end to the long melodic line, which fragments into nervous figures that foreground augmented fourths (within an Italian augmented sixth chord), semitones, and caesuras (bars 12–15). This jerky approach to the final half cadence of the main theme extends the theme further than would normally be expected, either in the Classical style or even in the 1760s. For a galant abb' theme, especially in Vaňhal's style of the 1760s, a tonic chord at bar 12 would have been standard: this would also have produced another galant stereotype: the cadential bass pattern $\hat{3}$–$\hat{4}$–$\hat{5}$–$\hat{6}$; $\hat{3}$–$\hat{4}$–$\hat{5}$–$\hat{1}$ (bars 5–12).[34] The first movement of Haydn's Symphony No. 39, to be sure, uses a similar technique, and the similarity between Vaňhal e1/i, bars 12–15, and Haydn 39/i, bars 7–11 (compare Ex. 3.3 with Ex. 1.1) suggests a debt on Vaňhal's part. But Haydn's opening phrase is already nervous and edgy, and it avoids the sighing appoggiaturas of Vaňhal's, so the fragmentation at the approach to the cadence is not such a contrast to the opening. In several ways the main theme of e1/i is reminiscent of that of Vaňhal's own e3: the key, the register of the melody, the Do-Re-Mi schema for the a-phrase, and the melodic descent from bar 5 (compare Ex. 3.3 with Ex. 3.2). But the almost immediate instability of e3/i is avoided: in e1 the disorder that disrupts the melody comes later and is, as it were, more insidious. In e1/i the heightened contrast of lyricism and discontinuity, mediated by the expressive descent to the D string, stands out and invites an interpretation of the rest of the movement as a response.

That invitation is immediately taken up by the mediant tutti paragraph, which parallels the main theme in a new version rather than, as usual for minor-key fast movements, proposing a new start for the movement as a different kind of piece. The mediant tutti of bar 16, although unmistakable, is understated by the general standard of minor-key fast movements of the time. It is a louder echo of the start of the main theme, using the same basic idea, harmony, and statement-response repetition. It is marked *f*, and oboes join the pair of horns (now the horns crooked in G rather than those in E, which are silent; this is not a literal tutti).[35] A little energy is supplied by the syncopated accompaniment in second violins, and the texture is more widely spread than at the opening of the movement. The scoring of this passage is warmer owing to the presence of the third of the local tonic chord in the second horn part (b). This is hardly a brand new start for the movement. As in e3/i, the rising melodic line of the opening bars of the theme, which had been cut short by the descent of bars 5–8, is realized here, with the melody moving from g^2 through a^2 to b^2, albeit all in the mediant key rather than the tonic. The new section likewise follows the main theme in the $\hat{3}$–$\hat{4}$–$\hat{5}$–$\hat{6}$ bass pattern used for the continuation phrase (bars 20–23), here more typically continuation-like on account of the

---

[34] Howard Brofsky, "The Symphonies of Padre Martini," *Musical Quarterly* 51, no. 4 (1965): 649–73 (pp. 656–57); Roger Kamien, "Style Change in the Mid-18th-Century Keyboard Sonata," *Journal of the American Musicological Society* 19, no. 1 (1966): 37–58 (p. 46); Wolf, *The Symphonies of Johann Stamitz*, 108. Heinrich Christoph Koch mentions this kind of thematic construction: Koch, *Versuch*, 2:351–52; see Leonard Ratner, "Eighteenth-Century Theories of Musical Period Structure," *Musical Quarterly* 42, no. 4 (1956): 439–54 (p. 441). See also Heartz, *Haydn, Mozart and the Viennese School*, 91, 97, 457–58.

[35] In this symphony the E-horns and G-horns never play together, even though the players must have been different: there would not be time for two players to switch between E and G crooks. See Bryan, *Johann Vaňhal*, 164.

increase in surface rhythm. All these factors make the second paragraph sound like a reconception of the first.

This interpretation is strengthened when the mediant tutti paragraph turns out not be transition-like. In other words, this exposition with mediant tutti is of the "two-part" type (see Fig. 1.1). At bar 24 it sounds as though there might be a move to a D major chord, the dominant of the local tonic G major, for a half-cadence medial caesura at bar 25 or shortly thereafter, but the caesura is avoided in a fashion that Hepokoski and Darcy would call "bait-and-switch."[36] No cadential phrase ensues either, so the phase of continuation function following the original presentation of bars 15–18 is resumed and the whole paragraph is extended. A cadence in fact does not occur until the end of the exposition. Given that the exposition falls into two parts that run in parallel in significant ways, the events of the second half of the former might reasonably be understood as responses to the "crisis" at the end of the latter.

The responses are in fact rather direct. The second paragraph, in short, rehearses the original melodic descent and symbolically "saves" it. Bars 27–28 reopen the lower register of the first violin melody and use the D-string for the first time (bar the odd eighth note) since bar 14. In bar 27 there is a sharp melodic descent, and the first violins in bar 28 echo the original 4–3 appoggiaturas of bars 12 and 14 with the same melody notes ($f\sharp^1$–e^1) over the same cello c^1. Now the dynamic falls to p and the music gets stuck on a one-bar melodic figure over dominant seventh harmony (alternating second and third inversions); these repetitions recapture something of the stuttering effect of bars 12–15, even though they are much smoother: the melody is conjunct, and the augmented fourths, semitones, rests, and Italian sixth chord are absent. A caesura occurs midway through the long continuation phrase (bar 33)—a common technique in the second half of Vaňhal's first movement expositions (compare e3/i, bar 21). But in the context of this movement the convention carries a special significance, for it follows, and thus echoes, the pauses of bars 12–15. The events of the first paragraph's continuation phrase are therefore presented here in the same order, though with a less disruptive effect. In bar 34 an energetic tutti gesture opens the final phase of the continuation that will lead to the cadence and the end of the exposition. Yet there is a final twist to the exposition: a third descent by the first violins to their low register, the D string, and the $f\sharp^1$–e^1 appoggiatura, once again played above a c^1 in the cellos. This time these events are even less problematic: there is no repetition and no caesura, the low register is quitted swiftly, and the event is integrated into the continuity of the tutti and its drive to the perfect authentic cadence.

Against the background of typical mediant-tutti minor-key expositions, that of e1/i stands out. The fragmentation and discontinuity at the end of the main theme

---

[36] Hepokoski and Darcy, *Elements of Sonata Theory*, 54–55. This interpretation is supported, retrospectively, by the fact that the melodic idea of bars 25–26 is used for the exposition's codetta and subsequently to prolong the final cadential harmonies of both development "subrotations" and that at the end of the recapitulation.

is typical of such expositions, yet the sharpness of its contrast with the evenly flow-
ing lyricism of the opening bars is unusual. The first and second paragraphs of the
exposition parallel one another more closely than usual, so the melodic descents
and caesuras of the second, more loosely organized, paragraph can be understood
as corrections or normalizations of those of the first, bringing them into the orbit
of the major mode, integrating them into regular phrase structures, continuous
melodic processes, and a broader span.

The second half of the movement—development plus recapitulation—is characterized by longer paragraphs and greater continuity, with a special twist at the start
of the recapitulation, where the a-phrase of the main theme is withheld. Vaňhal
tends not to write dense development sections, but the development of e1/i is one
of his longest and most dramatic. It contains two "developmental rotations," as
Hepokoski and Darcy might term them,[37] presenting similar materials in the same
order, sustaining an increase in energy and a progressively rising melodic line, and
driving to a half cadence and a caesura. The first rotation begins in III (G major,
the subordinate key of the exposition) and ends on V/VI, while the second begins in
VI and ends on V/i. The main difference between the two lies in the greater density
of alternations in the second between lyrical music and energetic tuttis. Halfway
through this second developmental rotation the a-phrase of the main theme appears
in the tonic (Ex. 3.4, bars 85–88), anticipating what is expected at the start of the
recapitulation. Tonal instability continues briefly, however, before the movement's
most expressive gesture (bar 96). The recapitulation begins not with the a-phrase
again (given in the tonic a few bars earlier), and not even with root-position tonic
harmony, but with the b-phrase, with its first inversion tonic harmony and its crucial dip down to the D string, on this occasion reaching $d\sharp^1$ (bar 103), the first
violins' lowest note of the movement, and especially striking as it is approached
from the high b^2 that ended the preceding dominant prolongation (bar 95). Unlike
in the exposition, there is no b'-phrase and no fragmentation, hesitation, or caesura. Instead, the end of the b-phrase is elided with a new, energetic continuation,
based motivically on the codetta figure, but recalling the contours of the a-phrase
(and, incidentally, the main theme of e3/i). In fact, there is no presentation phrase
anywhere in the recapitulation (if we count it as beginning at the upbeat to bar 96,
after the half cadence and dominant prolongation). Neither is there a cadence until
the very end of the movement. The exposition's first "response" to the main theme's
descent is paralleled in the recapitulation, the melody again descending lower than
in the exposition (and again to $d\sharp^1$; bars 109–11), but the second response is absent.

One should not be surprised to encounter an increase in continuity in the recapitulation of a fast movement of a minor-key symphony, especially one that features a mediant tutti. The interest here lies in the way the strategy is accomplished
and in its relation to the path taken by the exposition. The increase in continuity
is far-reaching in e1/i. Not only are there fewer paragraphs in the recapitulation
than in the exposition, but the recapitulation as a whole is not itself a complete

---

[37] Ibid., 206–7.

Ex. 3.4 Vaňhal e1/i, bars 83–106

paragraph, for it lacks a phrase unambiguously expressing initiating function. The allusion to the main theme's a-phrase during the development is integrated into the modulating sequences, and does not sound like the beginning of a new paragraph. For a clear initiating function one must go back to bar 73, the start of the second developmental rotation. By the same token, the half cadence at the end of the development (bars 92–95) is, retrospectively, not treated as a true concluding function. If this is accepted, then the movement can be divided into four paragraphs, as illustrated in Fig. 3.1. Their increasing dimensions are striking. Thus by the recapitulation the movement has symbolically resolved the problem of discontinuity that disrupted its initial lyric continuity. Just as in the exposition's second paragraph, the

Paragraph	1	2	3	4
Bars	1–15	16–47	49–72	73–121
No. of bars	**15**	**32**	**24**	**49**
Formal section	main theme	mediant tutti to end of exp.	devt. rotation 1	devt. rotation 2 plus recap.

FIGURE 3.1 Vaňhal e1/i, length of paragraphs

recapitulation makes two responses to the initial melodic descent and fragmentation (the first being the return of the b-phrase itself), and in both cases those features are normalized, integrated within more regular and continuous melodic and harmonic processes. The differences between the responses of exposition and recapitulation lie in the degree of formal continuity and of course the tonality, above all the change to minor mode. Thus the recapitulation does not merely reinterpret the exposition as a whole; rather, by transforming the response of the exposition's second, major-mode paragraph, it has the effect of a response to a response. The "saving" gestures are now absorbed into an even broader span of music, characterized by minor-mode lyricism and controlled energy. The minor-mode recapitulation, in other words, is not straightforwardly tragic: its transformation of the exposition does not cut short the surging energy unleashed by the major-mode mediant tutti. Rather, it draws that energy into its own sphere, casting it in new, more somber, colors. Although this is a typical strategy for minor-key outer movements with mediant tuttis, the problem set up by the crisis of lyricism in the main theme gives the movement a unique profile.

It seems likely, given his other borrowings from Haydn 39/i, that that movement was also Vaňhal's source for the unusual opening of the recapitulation (following a caesura on dominant harmony by the main theme's b-phrase and absorbing the tonic statement of the a-phrase back into sequences within the development section). In Haydn 39/i the main theme's presentation phrase appears as the last two of six rising sequential repetitions of its basic idea (bars 74–85) at the end of the development. It is not articulated as the start of the recapitulation, and is followed, not preceded, by a caesura on dominant harmony. Only when the continuation phrase is heard, also in the tonic, does it become clear, retrospectively, that the recapitulation has already begun. However, the different "initial conditions" of the two movements, including the quite different characters of the two main themes, and Vaňhal's unique strategies earlier in e1/i, mean that he does not run up a heavy debt to Haydn. This is one of several point of convergence between two movements that deploy shared conventions in contrasting ways.

Untimely Returns (1): c2/i

A number of features are shared by c2/i and e1/i, making it convenient to think of them as a pair. But from the outset c2/i displays more consistent formal continuity than e1/i—there is no disruption within the main theme—so the movement's expressive strategies must be sought less in details than in architectonics. Just as in

Ex. 3.5 Vaňhal c2/i, bars 1–15

e1/i, the exposition of c2/i is of the two-part mediant-tutti type, the recapitulation is more continuous than the exposition, and the main theme is in abb' form. Its melody shows remarkable similarities with that of e1/i in both a- and b-phrases (Ex. 3.5). The "Do-Re-Mi" schema and statement-response repetition (repeated basic idea over I–V; V–I)[38] are used for the a-phrases of both themes and similar bass patterns for the b- and b'-phrases (in e1/i $\hat{3}$–$\hat{4}$–$\hat{5}$–$\hat{6}$; $\hat{3}$–$\hat{4}$–$\hat{5}$–$\hat{1}$ in c2/i $\hat{3}$–$\hat{4}$–$\hat{5}$–$\hat{1}$ for both phrases). Just as in e1/i, the mediant tutti of c2/i is underplayed. In this case it is preceded by an earlier tutti section in the tonic (bar 12), with which the mediant tutti shares material, and this lessens its impact when it finally arrives (bar 27). On the other hand, the main theme of c2/i is far more tightly organized than that of e1/i; there is less contrast between a- and b-phrases; the b-phrase does not dissolve or fragment; and chromaticism is avoided. There are no caesuras in the mediant tutti paragraph. This greater continuity means that the exposition has a more even flow of energy than that of e1/i, more so in fact than most first-movement minor-key expositions with mediant tuttis.

This greater continuity may reflect a difference in scoring. Most unusually for a minor-key symphony of the late 1760s, c2 calls for two clarini (in C) and timpani (C and G), along with the more standard pair of horns in E♭. This scoring is unique amongst Vaňhal's minor-key symphonies, and almost unique amongst Viennese minor-key symphonies in general before the 1790s, which normally employ no more than strings, oboes, and horns. On the evidence of the surviving sources, the only

---

[38] Caplin, *Classical Form*, 39.

exceptions are Ordonez C14 and Swieten 7. Haydn used clarini and timpani only once in a minor-key symphony: No. 95 (1791), composed for Salomon's orchestra in London. Paul Wranitzky's minor-key symphonies of the 1790s also use these instruments. Their presence in c2, along with the fact that the horns are crooked in E♭, means that passages in the tonic and the mediant can be given quite different timbres. The "warm" major third degree of the mediant chord is available to the second horn at the mediant tutti (bar 27), whereas the second clarino always has to play the tonic and dominant notes in C minor. The broad spans of c2/i maximize the impact of these differences in orchestral color without (as usual) making significant demands on the players.

The second half of the movement—specifically the recapitulation, as the development section is short—increases the continuity and introduces untimely rhetoric, achieving a stern grandeur quite unlike anything in e1 and uncharacteristic of Vaňhal in general.[39] This is Vaňhal's clearest realization of the tragic plot (see chapter 1) in a minor-key movement. Its strategy anticipates that of Ordonez G7/i, probably composed about a decade later (see chapter 2; compare Fig. 2.1 and Fig. 3.2). There are no caesuras or sudden, loud tuttis, as in the exposition. Indeed, the main theme, although still marked *p*, is now accompanied by clarini and timpani, and so any sense of solo / tutti contrast is lessened. Instead, the movement gradually builds momentum over a broad span, all centered on the tonic minor. The recapitulation is forty-three bars in length to the exposition's fifty-two, but there is only one paragraph instead of three, and it is the longest of the movement (Fig. 3.2). Whereas the exposition goes through three phases of initiating function (bars 1–4, 12–19, and 27–34), followed each time by medial and concluding functions, the recapitulation "initiates" only once (bars 73–76; see Ex. 3.6), and even there the statement-response repetition of the presentation phrase is disrupted by incipient continuation on the final beat of bar 76. The recapitulation features a variety of techniques of phrase extension and the general loosening of the formal organization. Yet, despite the emphasis on medial functionality (continuation), the main theme's b-phrase itself appears nowhere in the recapitulation. The a-phrase is repeated twice, tonicizing first A♭ (VI) and then F minor (iv), before its initial motive is drawn into a descending sequence that leads back to the tonic (Ex. 3.6). Charles Rosen would call this passage the "secondary development."[40] The roles of the two

Paragraph	1	2	3	4	5
Bars	1–12	12–26	27–52	53–72	73–115
No. of bars	**12**	**15**	**26**	**20**	**43**
Formal section	main theme (i)	tonic tutti paragraph (i–V/i)	mediant tutti paragraph (III)	development (III–V/i)	recapitulation (i)

FIGURE 3.2 Vaňhal c2/i, length of paragraphs

---

[39] It is worth noting that in the first movements of his string quartets Vaňhal is more likely to recompose the recapitulation if the mode is minor than if it is major. Jones, "The String Quartets of Vanhal," 1:179–80.

[40] Rosen, *Sonata Forms*, 289–95.

violin parts are exchanged for each repetition, again turning the focus to process as
much as the presentation of ideas. The use of the wind instruments changes tellingly in the recapitulation. For the first time in the movement, clarini and horns are
used in rapid alternation, sometimes even in overlapping phrases (bars 89–92 and
97–99; see Ex. 3.6). If the sequences and dominant pedal recall the closing section
of a grand fugue, then this use of clarini and timpani distantly recalls the old C

Ex. 3.6 Vaňhal c2/i, bars 73–103

Ex. 3.6 (Continued)

major symphony style of Fux and Caldara, a style not wholly forgotten in Vienna in midcentury, as witnessed by Ordonez's Symphonies C9 and C10.[41] By contrast, the exposition of c2/i is more typically "modern" in its organization. Its phrases are short and are arranged fairly symmetrically; galant schemata appear such as the "Do-Re-Mi" and the ubiquitous "Prinner riposte" (bars 36–42);[42] and there are equally galant "sigh" figures (bars 36, 38, and 40). The coordination of untimely rhetoric with the turn to the minor mode in the recapitulation is here brought off in grand style.

The fateful quality of the recapitulation is heightened by the way its single moment of recognizably "modern" syntax is conspicuously brushed aside. Back in the exposition, as the eighth-note and sixteenth-note passagework of the third

[41] Brown, "The Trumpet Overture and Sinfonia in Vienna," 50.

[42] Gjerdingen, *Galant Style*, 45–60.

paragraph seems to be approaching a cadence, the dynamic falls to *p*, wind instruments fall silent, and a stereotypical minuet cadence phrase enters in a lyrical, legato style. On its final tonic chord it is elided with a codetta that brings back the *f* dynamic, the wind instruments, and the passagework. Despite the continuing *Trommelbass*, this is a rare moment of calm within an otherwise steady dynamic flow. In the recapitulation version of this passage, the short and symmetrical phrase structure is overridden, and the Prinner and the sigh figures are absent. The only modern idiom left is the minuet cadence. It recurs dramatically, again functioning as the cadential phrase for a whole paragraph, but now transposed to the minor mode. This hushed and poignant phrase is the only moment in the recapitulation when the strings play alone (in the exposition there was no wind accompaniment for the main theme either) and the only temporary abatement of the recapitulation's momentum. The return of the minuet cadence is typical of the free mixing of topics in late eighteenth-century Viennese instrumental music. The untimely allusions of the recapitulation, then, are rhetorical; modern idioms are still (just) available and the two can be combined to create the effect of narrative. The intimate character of the minuet phrase is swept away by the recapitulation's inexorable drive.

Vaňhal c2 is the only Viennese minor-key symphony of the period to have an internal slow movement in minor. It preserves something of the mood of the tragic first movement, with its dotted rhythms, chromatic harmonies, heavy appoggiaturas, and descending chain of suspensions over a long dominant pedal in the second half (a direct parallel with the dominant pedal in the recapitulation of the first movement). Its F minor tonic was regarded in the eighteenth century as the darkest of minor keys, and was associated with the Passion and Lamentation (see chapter 5). This combination of keys and moods means that, as a multi-movement cycle, c2 is the most somber of Vaňhal's minor-key symphonies.

Untimely Return (2): g2/i

The very opening of g2/i amounts to what Hepokoski and Darcy call "deformation," which they describe as "a pointed overriding of a standard option" or "a surprising or innovative departure from the constellation of habitual practices."[43] Untimely rhetoric is here taken to an extreme, with a combination of ostinato, lamento, and fugato. Moreover, the combination of soft dynamic and chromatic harmony distinguish it not only from all of Vaňhal's other symphonies, in either mode, but from all Viennese minor-key symphonies composed to that date. The assignment of the opening phrase to the second violins (the firsts are silent) is also extremely unusual. No eighteenth-century listener could have failed to hear this opening as exceptional.

The movement begins softly with a short motive repeated sequentially above a chromatic descending bass (Ex. 3.7 gives the whole exposition). Since the mid-seventeenth-century the descending bass tetrachord $\hat{8}$–$\hat{7}$–$\hat{6}$–$\hat{5}$ as an ostinato in

---

[43] Hepokoski and Darcy, *Elements of Sonata Theory*, 11.

Ex. 3.7 Vaňhal g2/i, bars 1–66

Allegro moderato

Ex. 3.7 (Continued)

minor had been closely associated with the genre of *lamento* in *opera seria*. The descending tetrachord with chromatic passing notes had been used for settings of the *Lamentations* even earlier.[44] The semantics of this theme are subtle, as the pair of slurred quarter notes on the first two beats suggests a minuet figure of a type that Vaňhal used elsewhere for the charming and witty main theme of a major-key symphony first movement (G11/i). By bar 10 there are conflicting generic signals. On the one hand, the chromatic descending bass continues while the melody is altered and decorated with diminutions (rests and dotted figures in bars 10, 12, and 14) as though the piece were to be constructed on an ostinato ground bass, continuing the *lamento* allusion. On the other, a fugal process develops: the key changes to the dominant and the initial melody is played by the first violins instead of seconds, while the seconds continue with a different strand of melody, rhythmically differentiated from the first like a countersubject. (The presence of a bassline from the outset of the movement does not detract from this allusion; it was common in early eighteenth-century fugues and survived in Viennese contrapuntal chamber music by Monn, Wagenseil, Werner, Birck, Ordonez, and Albrechtsberger.)[45] At bar 19 the chromatic bass drops out of the texture and is replaced by a fugal bass entry, but the ostinato principle is still observed insofar as the phrase structure remains constant and more elaborate figuration appears in the first violins. After this third iteration (the third entry in the fugal exposition) the pattern is broken. Now the movement reestablishes dialogue with the formal conventions of the minor-key subgenre as they stood in the late 1760s. The music stands on the dominant; its motives foreground chromatic lower appoggiaturas, downward staccato octave leaps, and a $c\#^2$–d^2–d^1 figure (bars 28–31), all features that call to mind the parallel bars of Haydn 39/i (Ex. 1.1, bars 7–11), which is also of course in G minor. A mediant tutti follows, marked f (all the preceding music has been quiet), with the horns, both in B♭, entering for the first time.

As noted above, Vaňhal's primary model—notwithstanding the allusion to Haydn 39/i just before the mediant tutti—is the opening of Haydn 16/i. Both movements have two-flat key signatures and are in 3/4 meter; both openings are in two-part counterpoint, later to be inverted; in both cases one part is in even eighth notes, the other mainly quarter notes; both use two-bar units, repeated sequentially with the bass descending chromatically; at the end of bar 6 in both pieces a quarter note in one part is suspended across the barline; both present three entries like a fugal exposition in the order tonic–dominant–tonic; both lead to a loud tutti on a chord of B♭ in sudden contrast to the previous, soft music; and both expositions later feature a dotted-eighth-note–sixteenth-note pattern followed by four eighth notes. In bars 53–56 of Vaňhal g2/i the first violins actually quote the opening four bars of Haydn 16/i (cello part), with identical slurring and dynamics, and in the same key (B♭ major). However, just as in the case of the "convergence" at the end of the development

---

[44] Ellen Rosand, "The Descending Tetrachord: An Emblem of Lament," *Musical Quarterly* 65, no. 3 (1979): 346–59; Peter Williams, *The Chromatic Fourth during Four Centuries of Music* (Oxford: Clarendon, 1997), see esp. "Sacred Music," 19–21, and chap. 3, "Laments and Operas," 50–76.

[45] Kirkendale, *Fugue and Fugato*, 60.

sections of Vaňhal e1/i and Haydn 39/i, the similarities disguise essentially different compositional strategies. For a start, by the early 1760s (Symphony No. 16 dates from 1763) Haydn was already an accomplished contrapuntist, whereas it is reasonable to infer from the evidence that Vaňhal was not. In his instrumental music of the 1760s and 1770s counterpoint of any complexity is very rare, and when it does appear it is usually within a paraphrase. Two of his canonic minuets are closely related to pieces by Gassmann and Haydn; a contrapuntal passage from the development section of e1/iv is based on one from the development of Haydn 39/i (see note 29). It would be easy to pick holes in the counterpoint of g2/i, although Vaňhal's later sacred music shows that he eventually acquired a workable contrapuntal technique.

Whatever its technical limitations, the semantics of g2/i are richer than its model. Unlike Haydn 16/i its allusions to strict style are complemented by the *lamento* topos, linking the Viennese contrapuntal tradition with its imperial / ecclesiastical associations specifically to musical idioms associated with the Passion. The opening of g2/i would have been recognized by Joseph II as "the music of pathos." The combination of minor key and diminished intervals to open an orchestral piece in a manner that subverts generic expectations would later be used by Haydn (78/i) and Mozart (Piano Concerto in C minor, K. 491/i). Unique to g2/i, however, is the brooding atmosphere and perhaps faint air of menace contributed by the *Trommelbass*—qualities that anticipate the mood of Mozart's D minor music. The exposition is highly dramatic even for a minor-key symphony, and in this respect can be compared with the expositions of Haydn 26/i and Mozart K. 183/i.

Mediant tuttis of minor-key symphonies typically give the impression of starting the movement anew, sweeping away what had gone before. In g2/i that impression is unmistakable, although because motivic materials, phrases, and textures are shared, the emphasis is on transformation. The second half of the exposition contrasts sharply with the ostinato main theme not just in terms of mode, harmony (diatonic rather than chromatic), texture, dynamics, and scoring, but also in its "modern" syntactic organization. Whereas bars 1–31 do not articulate clear distinctions between initiating and medial functions, it is easy to distinguish bars 32–35 as the presentation phrase and bars 36–52 as the continuation phrase of a sentence. The presentation uses statement-response repetition and the "Meyer" schema,[46] while the first half of the continuation uses a melodic sequence built around a Prinner riposte. Later ideas receive exact repetition (bars 43–46) and sequential repetition (bars 53–56): all standard late eighteenth-century fare. The reiterated cadence gestures of the closing section are based on a stereotypical galant descending figure (bar 59), and they alternate with a figure that suggests a stamping dance (bars 60–61, 63–64): an idea as far from the strict-style opening as could be. Only bars 53–56 (the quotation of Haydn 16/i) give a reminder of the untimely opening. In the minor-key symphonies of the imperial court composers the opposition of modern and untimely idioms had already been put to rhetorical effect. The exposition of Vaňhal g2/i invests heavily in this rhetoric. It lines up a series of

---

[46] Gjerdingen, *Galant Style*, 111–16.

binary oppositions: untimely / timely; sacred / secular; chromaticism / diatonicism; lamentation / joy; *Fortspinnungstypus* / *Liedtypus*; and, from an aesthetic point of view, cyclical time (ostinato) / unidirectional time (the functional order initiating–medial–concluding). All of these it maps onto the fundamental binary opposition of mode—minor / major—and articulates them temporally by the caesura at bar 31 and the mediant tutti. The one element that is out of alignment, and that saves the exposition from being schematic, is the minuet rhythm. (The dark ironies of contrapuntal minor-key minuets are discussed in chapter 4.)

The recapitulation, entirely in the tonic minor, is recomposed in ways that increase continuity and grandeur (as in c2/i) and reduce the exposition's dichotomy of untimely / modern. Like the opening of the movement, the development section is deformational: it ends, very unusually, with a perfect authentic cadence in the tonic. If the mediant tutti sounds like the proposal of an alternative beginning, then the start of the recapitulation, following this cadence, is a second new beginning to answer the first. It gives a new version of the movement's opening bars, now with the bass altered and the original fugue subject split between the two upper parts. These changes tilt the meaning of the theme towards ground bass and *lamento* rather than fugue and indeed this time there are no further subject entries: the music cuts straight to stuttering figures over dominant harmony and the caesura that, in the exposition, preceded the mediant tutti. The tutti (bar 124) is transposed to the tonic minor, the only occasion on which such a dramatic modal reversal occurs in the four symphonies considered here and a highly significant expressive moment in any minor-key symphony movement.

The continuation phrase of this sentential tutti is subtly altered: the "Prinner riposte" is still the schema, but its upper part appears in the second violins (bars 129–33) beneath an inverted tonic pedal in the firsts, and is more succinctly expressed (one chord per bar, and one chord per schema note, as opposed to two in the exposition), although with a chromatic passing note $c\sharp^2$ in bar 131. This results in several parallels with the recapitulation's statement of the main theme. Both main theme and tutti are more tightly organized than in the exposition (rare for a recapitulation), and the latter echoes the former not just with its new minor mode, but with its $c\sharp^2$, which recalls the chromatic descents of the main theme (the mediant tutti of the exposition, by contrast, contained no harmonic chromaticism). In fact, the real climax of the recapitulation—and of the movement as a whole—is neither the start of the recapitulation nor the entry of the now-minor-mode tutti, but the entry of an embedded sentence within the tutti (bar 133), the goal to which the newly tightened riposte drives. Despite the tighter organization of the themes in the recapitulation, this delaying of the climax suggests a series of dynamic waves of increasing power. As in c2/i, there is a soft but dramatic event near the end of the recapitulation: another alteration relative to the exposition. After the tutti dies down, instead of the Haydn quotation in the tonic minor, there is a second statement of the music from the preceding climax: the presentation phrase of the embedded sentence (bars 143–46). Since this is the first time the phrase has been heard softly, it gives the impression of an after-shock or a traumatic memory.

This is a movement of cycles on the one hand, symbolizing endlessness (ostinati, fugal exposition, sequences, regular phrase rhythm, and harmonic rhythm), and, on the other, sharp discontinuities and oppositions, both syntactic (caesuras, the mediant tutti, the perfect authentic cadence at the end of the development) and semantic (sacred / secular, lamentation / joy). When the movement is restarted for the second time, some of those oppositions are dissolved. The hesitant conclusion of the main theme is downplayed, and the materials of the second half of the exposition are drawn into a single dynamic span in the tonic minor. The minor mode now inflects the modern formal syntax, galant schemata, minuet cadence figures, and stamping rhythms with its fateful, darker colors.

Lyricism (2): a2/i

The last of the group of four symphonies is one of Vaňhal's most copied, published, and recorded works. It survives in nine manuscript copies and three eighteenth-century prints, there are two twentieth-century editions, and, unusually for Vaňhal, the symphony has attracted some critical commentary. It is certainly one of his most immediately appealing works. In several respects a2/i returns to principles of e1/i: the lyrical main theme (as usual in abb' form) has a rising a-phrase using largely conjunct motion and small intervals, but then dips sharply in the b-phrase (Ex. 3.8). The b- and b'-phrases have the standard bass patterns $\hat{3}$–$\hat{4}$–$\hat{5}$–$\hat{6}$; $\hat{3}$–$\hat{4}$–$\hat{5}$–$\hat{1}$. Like e1/i, and unlike c2/i or g2/i, the movement has a long development section that presents the thematic materials of the exposition in roughly the same order as the exposition; it is thus well described as a "rotation." Yet a2/i is also comparable to g2/i, not on account of any contrapuntal writing—there is none—but in its dramatic juxtaposition of soft, lyrical passages and tuttis. This symphony was probably composed a few years later than e1, c2, and g2, and in several respects it strikes out in new directions, ones that Vaňhal was to take again

Ex. 3.8 Vaňhal a2/i, bars 1–15

after his return from Italy and his recovery from illness. For the first time in a minor-key symphony by Vaňhal there are just three movements, and for the first time the finale turns to the tonic major for the whole recapitulation, not just (as in e3/iv) for a coda. In the first movement there is no mediant tutti, and the subordinate theme uses a new basic idea that contrasts in character with that of the main theme: a sweet, Ländler-like rocking tune (the textbook "second subject"). Indeed, the exposition can be analyzed quite comfortably in terms of Classical syntax: the main theme is relatively tight-knit; it ends with a perfect authentic cadence; it is followed by a transition, which begins in the tonic with an allusion to the start of the main theme, before modulating and ending with a half cadence in the subordinate key; and the subordinate theme is more loosely organized than the main theme. The recapitulation is not extensively recomposed.

The formal dynamics of a2/i are also different from those of the other three symphonies. There are greater melodic contrasts and even a sense of dialogue as though between different characters. Heartz hears the whole main theme as a kind of anacrusis; certainly this is true of the a-phrase, which unfolds over a tonic *Trommelbass* pedal. Although replete with sigh figures, the theme therefore conveys a slight air of menace, as though potential energy were about to be unleashed. This effect is seldom found in main themes that are followed by mediant tuttis, as they tend to conclude hesitantly and on dominant harmony rather than driving to a perfect authentic cadence. Heartz also notes that the boundary between a- and b-phrases is blurred by the continuity of the rising melody (a^1 at bar 1^1; c^2 at bar 3^1; e^2 at bar 5^1). Interestingly, this is true of the subordinate theme too (Ex. 3.9; bars 29–30), where, despite the *Ländler* rhythm and the doubling of the melody in octaves (a typically Viennese touch pioneered by Haydn; see chapter 4), it would not be amiss to speak of motivic "linkage" between phrases, a technique associated with Brahms.[47] The continuation phrase is extended by another rocking melody, and then a short cadential phrase bursts in with conventional sixteenth-note figuration. But after a caesura the second rocking melody begins again, as if to begin the b'-phrase in an abb' pattern, even though the b-phrase has already brought a perfect authentic cadence. In Vaňhal's earlier first movements, caesuras in vigorous subordinate key paragraphs occurred during the continuation stage but before a cadential progression had begun, thus carrying the strong implication of further continuation to come within the same paragraph. Here the theme fully articulates the formal function of conclusion by means of its cadential phrase (albeit hurriedly), before beginning all over again from the half-way stage of its continuation. Vaňhal had earlier always avoided this sense of stop-start in favor of broad dynamic spans.

One especially beautiful touch in a2/i is the four-bar retransition at the end of the development (bars 109–12; see Ex. 3.10), which uses two bars of the rocking

---

[47] Heinrich Schenker called this *Knüpftechnik*. See *Harmony*, ed. Oswald Jonas, trans. Elisabeth Mann Borghese (Cambridge, MA: MIT Press, 1973), 9–10. See Walter Frisch, *Brahms and the Principle of Developing Variation* (Berkeley and London: University of California Press, 1984), 15–16.

Ex. 3.9 Vaňhal a2/i, bars 26–42

Ex. 3.10 Vaňhal a2/i, bars 108–14

melody of the subordinate theme (the only occasion where it occurs in the development), and represents the final stage in the development's rotation of exposition materials. By the middle of bar 111 the listener can reasonably predict the moment, about six quarter-note beats in the future, when the recapitulation will begin. Until that point, significance lies not in what occurs or what might occur—that is all but determined—but in how the inevitable will be brought about. In the event the fragment of melody borrowed from the *Ländler* theme, poised above implied dominant harmony, accomplishes its $\hat{5}$–$\hat{1}$ descent, and thus brings about the start of the recapitulation with lyrical grace. It is hard to resist hearing this moment as Mozartian.[48] There is nothing comparable to it in Viennese minor-key symphonies before the retransition of Mozart K. 550/i.

"Vaňhal at his best approaches Mozart the intimate and sometimes melancholy poet of pure beauty," according to Heartz. "Like Mozart, he combined a rich vein of Italianate melody with a fine feeling for thematic contrast."[49] Bryan agrees, favoring the Mozart connection over the one with Haydn.[50] In his expressive handling of formal functions, phrase extension, and cadential delay, of course, Vaňhal resembles both Mozart and Haydn. Another comparison—even if it seems unlikely at first—is with Schubert. The juxtaposition of quiet lyricism and aggressive minor-key energy occurs surprisingly seldom in late eighteenth-century instrumental music. But it can be found in the development section of e1/i, near the end of the recapitulation of c2/i, at the beginning and end of the recapitulation of g2/i, and throughout a2/i. The use of lyrical melodies for both main theme and subordinate theme in a2/i, and the repetition of the main theme in a forceful tutti version, still in the tonic (bar 12), have few parallels in eighteenth-century minor-key sonata movements, but can be found readily in Schubert: for instance, in the String Quartets in A minor, D. 804, and D minor, D. 810, respectively. There is a Romantic tinge to these Vaňhal first movements, perhaps the atmosphere of a ballad, suggesting a dialogue between vulnerable youth and stern fate, or the contrast of a comforting dream with harsh reality. After 1771, as will become clear in chapter 6, Vaňhal did not continue down this path. Whether because of changes in taste, different opportunities, critical judgments, his illness, or (Burney's eccentric view) his all too effective recovery, his last four minor-key symphonies are very different works.

---

[48] On the structure and beauty of Mozart's retransitions, see Roman Ivanovitch, "Mozart's Art of Retransition," *Music Analysis* 30, no. 1 (2011): 1–36.

[49] Heartz, *Haydn, Mozart and the Viennese School*, 463.

[50] Bryan, *Johann Wanhal*, xxii.

Two Subgeneric Conventions

THE CONTRAPUNTAL MINUET, THE STORMY FINALE

In the late 1760s two characteristic types of movement—the contrapuntal minuet and the stormy finale—emerged as conventions of the minor-key subgenre. Both appear infrequently in major. In minor, not all minuet and finale movements fit the respective types, even around 1770, but no other types specific to the subgenre emerged. In other words, the remaining minuets and finales of minor-key symphonies are a miscellany. The two types occurred less frequently after the early 1770s. By the 1780s, to write movements of these types can be interpreted as a significant compositional decision: a demonstration of awareness and valuing of a past practice, a conscious revival of a neglected tradition. Analyses of the contrapuntal minuet and the stormy finale require different approaches. With the former, the characteristic traits are quickly described. Distinctive formal strategies appear in only a few works and are used consistently, thus becoming themselves subgeneric conventions. With the latter the characteristic traits require a lengthier description, while movements that adopt interesting formal strategies are more diverse. For the stormy finale, some discussion of those strategies will be deferred to chapters 5 and 8.

The Contrapuntal Minuet

The contrapuntal minuet is one of the most strongly consolidated subgeneric conventions of the Viennese minor-key symphony. On a reasonable count—the criteria for what is "contrapuntal" are disputable—there are eighteen such movements (Table 4.1): about 60 percent of minor-key minuet movements within the subgenre.[1] This applies only to minuets "proper," as the trios are seldom contrapuntal and in any case are usually in major.[2] By contrast, with regard to the late

---

[1] A few minuet movements in the sample are in major; these are discounted in the calculation.

[2] Canonic trios are found, however, in Haydn 23/iii (symphony in G major, trio in C major) and Mozart's Serenade, K. 388/iii (minuet in C minor, trio in C major). The Haydn may have been the model for Mozart in this case.

eighteenth-century Viennese symphony in general, counterpoint in minuets is countergeneric. Major-key minuets are rarely contrapuntal in any conspicuous way. In particular, canon, while relatively common in minor-key minuets, is almost never found in their major-key counterparts, with the exceptions of Haydn 3/iii and 23/iii. Among Mozart's symphonies the only notably contrapuntal minuet is K. 550/iii, although, tellingly, there is also the "Menuetto al canone" from the Wind Serenade in C minor, K. 388, a four-movement work that can be thought of as a minor-key symphony for wind ensemble.[3] As shown in chapter 2, contrapuntal textures are relatively common in the outer movements of minor-key symphonies. The contrapuntal minuet is a further stage in the transferral of the manner of imperial contrapuntal chamber music to the symphony, although the practice was certainly not confined to composers who enjoyed imperial patronage. Every composer who wrote more than one minor-key symphony wrote at least one contrapuntal minuet, and the most intensively contrapuntal of them are by Vaňhal, Haydn, and Mozart rather than Wagenseil, Gassmann, or Ordonez. In terms of quantity, Haydn (six) and Vaňhal (probably five) contributed most,[4] perhaps unsurprisingly, as they were also the most prolific composers of minor-key symphonies. The best known movement in Table 4.1 is Mozart K. 550/iii. It illustrates the imbalance in the scholarly literature: it has occasioned a significant body of commentary, while only one of the other movements in Table 4.1, Haydn 26/iii, has been singled out for any detailed discussion. The first section of this chapter corrects the imbalance, as well as placing K. 550/iii in compositional context. Like that symphony as a whole, the movement looks back to conventions established in the 1760s that had been largely forgotten by the 1780s, yet it is also an original conception.

In genres other than the symphony, contrapuntal, especially canonic, minuets existed even in major keys. As Kirkendale points out, there is a "broadly based tradition" of canonic minuets in Viennese music from which two famous examples—the third movements of Haydn's D minor Quartet, op. 76, no. 2, and Mozart's C minor Serenade, K. 388, both as it happens in minor keys—emerge. He lists canonic minuets going back to Wenzel Ludwig von Radolt's Partita in F (1701), including chamber music by Wagenseil, Kohaut, Gassmann, Ordonez, Albrechtsberger, and Mozart, along with Haydn's Keyboard Sonata, Hob. XVI:25, Baryton Trio, Hob. XI:94, and Symphonies Nos. 3, 23, and 44, and some non-Viennese music that includes keyboard sonatas by Clementi and Dussek, and a symphony by E.T.A. Hoffmann. The tradition continued in nineteenth-century scherzos from Beethoven's Violin Sonata, op. 30, no. 2 (trio), and Schubert's Piano Trio, op. 100.[5]

---

[3] But usually from "sonata da chiesa" symphonies (i.e., with slow first movement and all movements in the same key), which for Haydn were related to the minor-key symphonies, or are in an overall minor-key symphony (e.g., Haydn 45/iii also has the slurs, but the movement is in a major key, even though the symphony is nominally in minor).

[4] I have doubts about the authorship of the work that Paul Bryan calls Vaňhal c3. See chapter 5.

[5] Kirkendale, *Fugue and Fugato*, 148–49. In addition, see the partially canonic Mozart K. 168/ii and its likely model, Ordonez, op. 1/3/i. Brown, "Weeding a Musicological Garden," 208–9.

TABLE 4.1 Contrapuntal minor-key minuets

Non-canonic	Canonic		
	Canon at Start of All Three Paragraphs	**Canon Only in Second Part of Binary Form**	**Entirely Canonic**
		Dittersdorf a2	
Gassmann 45			
Gassmann 83			
		Haydn 26	
Haydn 39			
			Haydn 44
Haydn 49			
Haydn 52			
Haydn 80			
		Mozart K. 550	
Ordonez C14			
	Vaňhal c3		
Vaňhal d1			
		Vaňhal e1	
		Vaňhal e2	
			Vaňhal e3
	Wagenseil G5		
Wranitzky 43			

It appears that only in the symphony was the use of counterpoint in minuets closely tied to the minor mode.

Contrapuntal minor-key minuets are paradoxical pieces, full of ironies. In its original slow tempo the minuet was the archetypical courtly dance, which, with its formal gestures and noble character, could evoke the ancien régime. At a slightly faster tempo, the elegant and easeful qualities of the minuet made it a suitable vehicle for the new galant style (in the broad definition of the term).[6] The minor mode, of course, was becoming closely connected with pathos and intense subjective expression—not obviously compatible with either formal reserve or easeful elegance. The rhetorical evocation of counterpoint—its use as a "topic" sometimes known as "strict style"—complicates the semantics still further. The ecclesiastical and vocal associations of counterpoint conflict with the dance origins of the minuet and its associations with human gestures, yet contrapuntal objectivity also tempers the potential subjective expression of the minor mode. The composer of a contrapuntal minor-key minuet has the opportunity to stress one aspect or another at certain moments, and to alter the emphasis as the piece unfolds. Whatever strategy is adopted, though, takes place on terms set by the highly conventionalized idiom

---

[6] Judith L. Schwartz, "Periodicity and Passion in the First Movement of Haydn's 'Farewell' Symphony," in *Studies in Musical Sources and Style: Essays in Honor of Jan LaRue*, ed. Eugene K. Wolf and Edward H. Roesner (Madison, WI: A-R Editions, 1990), 293–388 (see esp. 313–16).

of the dance and within the modest dimensions of a small binary form. Given the vast number of minuets turned out in the eighteenth century, through which the composed dance became a kind of musical common currency, it seems reasonable to assume that attentive listeners would have been sensitized to even modest disruptions to the usual patterns, which could thus have acquired considerable expressive significance.

Despite the learned air of counterpoint, the writing of a contrapuntal minuet in the late eighteenth century can be viewed as a tacit intervention in current aesthetic controversies. North German critics objected to the inclusion of minuets in symphonies and more broadly regarded Viennese symphonies as tending to the frivolous. These criticisms came to focus in the late 1760s, just as most of the minor-key canonic minuets were being written. The critics complained that the symphony was a serious genre for which the minuet was too shallow; that a minuet disrupted the unity of the work by making too sharp a contrast with the fast, outer movements; and that it inappropriately evoked the atmosphere of dance and elementary music lessons.[7] (They may have had in mind the fast 3/8 minuets that concluded Italian sinfonias rather than elegant slow minuets.) In the case of Haydn these reservations merged with criticism of his part-writing in the minuet movements of his early string quartets composed around 1760.[8] In these pieces and in some early orchestral music Haydn doubled melodies in octaves or even wrote minuets in two-part counterpoint with both parts doubled. For these and other sins against traditional musical craft Haydn was censured; his octave doublings reminded one critic of the singing of a pair of beggars, father and son.[9] Minuets could thus function as test cases within a typical Enlightenment debate: criteria of rhetorical decorum (matching the style of a piece to its genre) and pre-established compositional rules faced a challenge from the judgment of the musician's ear and the scope of his imagination. A contrapuntal minuet, especially one in a minor key, highlights these issues in a reconfigured form. On the one hand, it is a dance regarded by some as too vulgar for a symphony and contains part-writing that flouts traditional rules. On the other, it adopts an untimely rhetoric, evoking the idioms of strict style and (supposedly) eternal musical truths. Octave doubling appears frequently in the movements listed in Table 4.1, yet sometimes it is, ironically, the two parts in a strict canon that are doubled in octaves in the four string parts (Vaňhal e3/iii, Haydn 26/iii).

---

[7] Zaslaw, *Mozart's Symphonies: Context, Performance Practice, Reception* (Oxford: Clarendon, 1989), 415–16 gives a translation of a negative piece by the Berlin court official Johann Gottlieb Carl Spazier, "Über Menuetten in Sinfonien," *Musikalisches Wochenblatt* (1791–92): 91–92.

[8] Heartz, *Haydn, Mozart and the Viennese School*, 255.

[9] For this debate, see Hubert Unverricht, *Geschichte des Streichtrios* (Tutzing: Hans Schneider, 1969), 156–57, and Heartz, *Haydn, Mozart and the Viennese School*, 256–57. Contributions included: the essay "Abhandlung vom musikalischen Geschmack" published in the *Hamburger Unterhlatungen* in 1766; Carl Ludwig Junker, *Zwanzig Compoinisten, eine Skizze* (Bern: Typographische Gesellschaft, 1776), 67, and *Tonkunst* (Bern: Typographische Gesellschaft, 1777), 61; and Heinrich Bossler in Forkel's *Musikalischer Almanach*, appendices for 1782–84.

The critical disparagement of Haydn's music was far from universal in north Germany, and had limited impact on the public reception of his music.[10] But it was well known, and, to judge by the reactions it drew, was taken seriously enough to cause offense. In 1766 a defense of Haydn's parallel octaves came in the article "Von dem Wienerischen Geschmack in der Musik" in the *Wiener Diarium*, probably authored by Dittersdorf.[11] In a biographical sketch of 1776 Haydn privately expressed his anger about sniping from Berlin critics at some length.[12] By the 1780s, however, Haydn had become a power in modern music, enjoying unprecedented fame, popularity, and (eventually) commercial success in the new musical economy of subscription concerts and competitive publishing. An English writer in 1784 observed that Haydn had beaten his German critics with unknown sounds and "a new species of music."[13] Although the carping continued in the 1780s, in 1790 the north German Ernst Ludwig Gerber admitted in his *Lexicon der Tonkünstler* that Haydn had triumphed.[14] Yet Haydn's responses had been musical rather than literary.

The contrapuntal minuet was only one of a number of ingenious twists that Haydn and other composers put on their minuets at this time, proving that this conventional dance was capable of surprising possibilities.[15] The minuet could be a vehicle of parody and humor: high and low styles could be blended, the latter including folk idioms, Hungarian or gypsy styles, *Ländler* rhythms, and even so-called "Turkish" style. Syncopation, metrical dissonance, and "alla zoppa" effects can be found in Haydn's Symphony No. 58/iii and Symphony No. 65/iii and many of his minuets have irregular phrase lengths that render them undanceable. The popular contemporaneous dice games that enabled musical amateurs to compose minuets by chance combinations were sometimes evoked in pieces by professional composers.[16] The minuet in the banquet scene from Mozart's *Don Giovanni* undergoes a simultaneous combination: two other dances in different meters are added until all three are played at once. The manuscript parts for the minuet of Haydn's Symphony No. 51 contain a joke for the players, the bass part consisting of just three notes, with various clefs indicated in which they must be read in turn. Haydn's minuets

---

[10] Mary Sue Morrow, "Reception: The Netherlands and North Germany," in *Haydn*, ed. David Wyn Jones, Oxford Composer Companions, 2nd ed. (New York: Oxford University Press, 2009), 330–31.

[11] Translated in Landon, *Chronicle*, 2:128–31 (p. 130).

[12] Translated in Ibid., 2:399.

[13] A. Peter Brown, "The Earliest English Biography of Haydn," *Musical Quarterly* 59 (1973): 343; cited in Heartz, *Haydn, Mozart and the Viennese School*, 258.

[14] Gerber, *Lexicon* (1790–92), 1:611, cited in Heartz, *Haydn, Mozart and the Viennese School*, 262–63.

[15] "The minuet fought back with innumerable devices and disguises." Christopher Hogwood, "In Defence of the Minuet and Trio," *Early Music* 30, no. 2 (2002): 237–51 (p. 241).

[16] Leonard G. Ratner, "Ars Combinatoria, Chance and Choice in Eighteenth-Century Music," in *Studies in Eighteenth-Century Music: A Tribute to Karl Geiringer on His Seventieth Birthday*, ed. H. C. Robbins Landon (London: Allen and Unwin, 1970), 343–63.

include mirror patterns (Symphony No. 47/iii, "al roverso," and Sonata in A, Hob. XVI:26/ii, "al rovescio") as well as canon and free counterpoint.[17] In Haydn's Symphony No. 46, material from the minuet movement is quoted in the finale: a type of inter-movement reminiscence that became common in the nineteenth century but for its time was extraordinary. The contrapuntal minuet takes its place on this spectrum of the quirky, the witty, and the combinatorial. In Haydn's case the use of the minor mode and counterpoint together resulted in a distinctive tactical combination in his compositional response to his critics.

Some of the decisions as to which movements to include in Table 4.1 are disputable, not least because an exact line between homophony and counterpoint is impossible to draw. The movements included possess a degree of independence of parts relative to most minuets of the later eighteenth century that can be considered a rhetorical gesture. The inclusion of Haydn 39/iii could be contested. It is perhaps more closely related to those trios of Haydn and Mozart that imitate the construction of an artificial minuet through a dice game. The odd repetitions, short units, and occasional unpredictable longer phrases give the impression of having been generated by inversion and retrograde operations. Moreover, even though 39/iii is certainly not canonic, the short units that suit combinatorial treatment also often appear in canons, so the minuet's melody shares characteristics with those of canonic minuets. Finally, tied notes in a melody were a strong rhetorical indication of "strict style" in the late eighteenth century, and their presence assures 39/iii of a place on the list. The tied dotted half note in the upper voice in the first bar immediately indicates a refusal of conventional homophonic textures with differentiated melody and accompaniment. (This applies also to Haydn 49/iii.) Ordonez C14/iii appears in Table 4.1, but not its likely model, Vaňhal g1/iii. The latter is on the fringes of the contrapuntal minuet, whereas Ordonez C14/iii has more differentiation of parts and alludes to species counterpoint with a *cantus firmus*-like treble and a bass that resembles an added part in fifth species. Ordonez, in other words, heightened the contrapuntal tendencies of his model, realizing a convention only implicit in Vaňhal's minuet. (In chapter 2, links with Vaňhal were detected in the outer movements of C11; the minuet confirms this work as exceptional among Ordonez's minor-key symphonies.) Ordonez F12/iii is another candidate for inclusion, but is omitted on the grounds that the contrapuntal texture is too fleeting. These decisions result in a total of eighteen minuets in minor keys that can be regarded as significantly contrapuntal: a high number, given that it leaves only eleven non-contrapuntal minor-key minuets in the repertory.[18] (There are also seven minuets in major keys in these symphonies, none contrapuntal; the rest lack minuet-and-trio movements altogether.)[19]

---

[17] For these and more examples, see Hogwood, "In Defence of the Minuet and Trio," 241–44.

[18] The non-contrapuntal minor-key minuets are Dittersdorf g1/iii and e1/iii, Gassmann 23/iii, Hoffmeister e1/iii, Mozart 183/iii, Ordonez F12/iii, Haydn 95/iii, Vaňhal c2/iii, g1/iii, and g2/iii, and Wranitzky 11/iii.

[19] The major-key minuets from minor-key symphonies are Haydn 34/iii, 45/iii, 83/iii, and 78/iii, Dittersdorf a1/iii and d1/iii, and Wranitzky P10/iii.

Most contrapuntal minuets were written in the 1760s and early 1770s. At that stage the convention was strongly consolidated; thereafter, the only certain examples are Haydn 80/iii, Mozart K. 550/iii, and, probably, Dittersdorf a2/iii (composed some time before 1779). The decline of the contrapuntal minuet reflects the lower production of symphonies in general from the later 1770s, including those in minor keys; the omission of minuet movements from some minor-key works; and the tendency to write major-key minuets in minor-key symphonies.

Most of the minuets in Table 4.1 are third movements within cycles of four. Only in Haydn 44 does the minuet come second in the cycle. Wagenseil G5/iii is a "tempo di menuetto"-type finale that evokes minuet as a topic, but it is a sonata-form movement and lacks a trio. Haydn 26/iii is a finale within a three-movement cycle, but in minuet-and-trio form. The minuet "proper" of these movements is usually in a rounded binary form with the return of the opening dramatized at some point in the second part. Gassmann 45/iii, Haydn 44/ii, and Haydn 52/iii are non-rounded binary forms. Some movements recall the tradition of Viennese contrapuntal chamber music described in chapter 2, introducing contrapuntal textures at the start of certain sections before quickly dissolving into homophony. The counterpoint may appear at the start of the A and B sections only (Gassmann 45/iii, which evokes Fuxian species counterpoint; see Ex. 2.5 (i) and (ii)); at the start of A, B, and A' (Wagenseil G5/iii, Vaňhal c3/iii), or at the start of the A and A' sections only (Ordonez C14/iii). In Vaňhal e1/iii each of the A, B, and A' sections begins contrapuntally, but in different ways (inexact imitation in A and A', canon in B). In contrast to the standard pattern of imperial chamber music, each phase of contrapuntal texture in e1/iii is relatively long, homophony appearing only near the end of each paragraph.

The well-known contrapuntal minor-key minuets in genres other than the symphony (Haydn, op. 76, no. 2/iii; Mozart K. 388/iii) are strictly canonic. Those in symphonies may be intermittently canonic or just freely contrapuntal, with no canon at all. The latter are listed in the first column of Table 4.1. Those listed in the first two columns of the second group ("canonic") may also contain free counterpoint, although often the canonic sections are the only significantly contrapuntal ones, and thus carry particular rhetorical force. Among intermittently canonic movements, five introduce canon only in the second half of the binary form, whereas only two introduce it in the first half (compare the first two columns under the heading "canonic" in Table 4.1). Those two are relatively early pieces from the early or mid-1760s and represent a strategy typical of imperial chamber music that was later avoided in symphonic minuets. Two minuets, Vaňhal e3/iii and Haydn 44/ii, are entirely canonic. In this case "entirely" does not mean that a single phase of imitation lasts the entire movement. Instead, the texture becomes homophonic at the cadences that occur at the end of sections. But each main section of the form is canonic; in other words, new imitative entries begin immediately after each cadence. No symphony minuet goes as far as Mozart K. 388/iii, in which both minuet and trio are entirely canonic, and the latter, in major, is a double canon by inversion.

The canons are usually at the octave, though the counterpoint is not always invertible. In Vaňhal e3/iii it is invertible, and the inversion of the parts occurs in

Ex. 4.1 Vaňhal e3/iii, bars 1–16 (string parts)

the A' section (Ex. 4.1). The B section has another canon, this one over a dominant pedal. The answer in the short fugato of Wagenseil G5/iii is at the subdominant. In Vaňhal e1/iii the second voice in the canon enters a seventh below the first; this canon is actually an altered "Corelli leapfrog" pattern—a canon at the second. The witty Dittersdorf a2/iii (Ex. 4.2) presents its chirpy theme first in unison, then, in the second part of the binary form, in canon at the fourth (bars 9–14), then at the fourth again but with inexact imitation (bars 19–23), and finally at the fifth (bars 27–31). The eccentricity of this piece is underlined by its modulation to VI at the end of its first part (bar 8) rather than the usual III.[20] In Mozart K. 550/iii the canon is at the fourth, but the counterpoint is invertible and the parts are doubled at one or more octaves.

The key of E minor seems favored for canon. There are four minor-key canonic minuets in E minor, including all three of Vaňhal's in that key (out of his total of twelve; E minor was the only minor key in which he wrote more than two symphonies). The two entirely canonic minuets, Haydn 44/ii and Vaňhal e3/iii, are both in E minor. In his other nine minor-key symphonies Vaňhal wrote only two other contrapuntal minuets, and only one other with canon. He certainly knew Haydn 44/ii, as he paraphrased it in an E-major minuet in a string quartet. But in symphonies Vaňhal came first with e3/iii and e1/iii.

---

[20] Compare the trio of Haydn's String Quartet, op. 17, no. 2, which also starts in minor and modulates to VI in its first part. See Webster, *Haydn's "Farewell" Symphony*, 161.

Ex. 4.2 Dittersdorf a2/iii, bars 1–34

The decisive step for the contrapuntal minuet in the minor-key symphony seems to have been taken with the entirely canonic Vaňhal e3/iii (1762–63). This minuet introduces the practice of strict counterpoint into the minor-key symphony, as opposed to the homophonic-turning Wagenseil G5/iii, Gassmann 45/iii, and the contemporaneous Vaňhal c3/iii. Vaňhal e3/iii also introduces octave doubling for the first time in a contrapuntal minuet. Although it predates the contrapuntal minuets of Haydn's minor-key symphonies, for the 1760s it is nevertheless distinctively Haydnesque. The rhetoric of strict style is found in many minuets in Haydn's early string quartets.[21] Vaňhal's later contrapuntal minuets do not take the principle any further, or even as far. By contrast, after 39/iii Haydn himself wrote four impressive contrapuntal minor-key minuets between 1768 and 1772. Two of them, 26/iii and 44/ii, are canonic minuets of searing expression, while the other two, the non-canonic 49/iii and 52/iii, are strange and disturbing. All share certain features, however, that distinguish them from contrapuntal minuets by all other composers of the 1760s and 1770s, notably a strategy of increasing expressive intensity, sometimes combined with increasing contrapuntal complexity, in the second half of the binary form. Each of these pieces seems to make an attempt to transform itself and even to escape its destiny as a minuet, attempts that are thwarted and end in frustration. Haydn was establishing his own subset of conventions and detaching the contrapuntal minor-key minuet from the formal procedures of imperial chamber music. Mozart was to follow this path in his own extraordinary fashion in K. 550/iii.

Four Haydn Minuets c. 1770: 26/iii, 44/ii, 49/iii, 52/iii

Haydn 26/iii is a curious piece. Its gestures are ungainly, its textures spare, and its sonorities at times astonishingly harsh for its time. It is the last movement of three, resulting in what for Haydn is an unusual multi-movement cycle. The abrupt, soft ending is certainly a uniquely anticlimactic end to an eighteenth-century symphony, and some twentieth-century scholars have speculated that a finale is missing, although without evidence.[22] The almost grotesque effect of the third movement is especially surprising given the high drama of the first and the serenity of the second, both of which use Gregorian chant melodies borrowed from a Passion drama of the late Middle Ages that was printed and still performed in the eighteenth

---

[21] Conspicuously imitative textures are found in the minuets (or trios) op. 1, no. 1/iv; and op. 1, no. 4/iv. Species counterpoint textures occur in op. 1, no. 3/iv; op. 9, no. 3/ii; op. 9, no. 3/ii; op. 17, no. 1/ii; and op. 17, no. 4/ii. A brief canon occurs in op. 3, no. 2/ii.

[22] Landon, *The Symphonies of Joseph Haydn* (London: Universal Edition and Rockliff, 1955), 285. According to Landon, the manuscript held at Melk abbey contains only the first two movements, but the minuet is found in a separate collection of Haydn pieces (ibid., 291). Landon thinks the copyist must have omitted the movement on his own initiative, although it was normal to omit the minuet of a symphony when it was performed in church. On this movement see also Webster, *Haydn's "Farewell" Symphony*, 243–44, and Reiner Leister, *Das Finale in der Sinfonik Joseph Haydns* (Stuttgart: Ibidem-Verlag, 1999), 126–38.

century. The melodies were destined for the representation of the events of the Passion and the Lamentation respectively. In one source the symphony is entitled "Passio e Lamentatio" (in others simply "Lamentatione"),[23] but if anything this deepens the puzzle. It is unclear what the finale could represent that would follow the Passion and the Lamentation. The symphony was presumably played during Holy Week. In this light the humorous codetta to the first part of the minuet and the clumsiness suggested by the metrical disruption and massive textural contrasts of the trio seem doubly incongruous.

One of the reasons for the awkwardness of this minuet is its failure to establish a clear succession of formal functions in the order initiating–medial–concluding, either in a single key or even in the course of a modulating paragraph. The first two phrases together have sentential characteristics: they are both the standard four bars in length, making an eight-bar unit; the initial two-bar idea is immediately repeated in varied form, as in a presentation phrase; and at bar 5 the surface rhythm slightly increases as though it were the start of a continuation phrase. But this is not a genuine sentence. The melody goes straight to ♭2 in bar 3, and thus the harmony to a Neapolitan sixth chord that strongly implies pre-dominant function in an approaching cadence. The second four-bar unit (bars 5–8) simply prolongs dominant harmony over a pedal: retrospectively it is clear that a harmonic progression of half-cadential content began at the very start of the piece with the opening i6/3 chord. Thus the minuet begins without a clear initiating gesture, even though, in functional terms, this eight-bar section is not a true cadence either (it does not conclude anything).

The second phrase of the minuet's first part likewise eschews an orderly succession of formal functions: it first repeats the iambic idea of the opening in unharmonized octaves before abruptly making a progression of perfect authentic cadential content in III, with the stereotyped minuet cadence figure that has already been encountered in Vaňhal c2/i (chapter 3). The phrase rhythm is irregular: a four-eighth-note pause precedes the phrase, which is five bars in length and is elided with a four-bar codetta that in turn is elided with its own repetition. This chirpy, staccato major-key codetta contrasts sharply with the bleakness of the minor key, Neapolitan harmony, and sighing appoggiaturas of the first eight bars. By the double bar, the minuet has established its awkwardness on two levels: the incongruity that comes from the combination of the vocabulary of suffering and lament with the rhythmic gestures of a minuet, and a clumsiness of melodic gesture that adds a humorous dimension. At this point the movement could be taken in either direction: towards tragedy or humor.

Haydn chooses the first option. The second part begins with the "Monte" schema—a common choice to opening the second part of binary forms in the galant style.[24] The pace of events, harmonic rhythm, and phrase rhythm decelerate,

---

[23] Landon, *Chronicle*, 2:291–95.

[24] Gjerdingen, *Music in the Galant Style*, 89–106.

setting up the main event of the movement: the transformation of the movement's opening at the start of the A' section of the rounded binary form. This is one of the harshest passages in eighteenth-century music, unique in its combination of forceful character, bare, two-part texture, each part doubled in octaves, and the "open" fifths of the harmony, both perfect and diminished, unsoftened by thirds. The falling fifth idea is now presented loudly, in canon at the octave and unison, with both parts doubled at the octave, one bar apart. The diminished fifths that now appear in the melody and that sound between the parts (bars 35^1 and 37^1) are especially harsh and there is even a strong hint of a whole-tone scale as the melody rises through d^2–e^2–$f\sharp^2$–$g\sharp^2$ and touches on $b\flat^2$ as well.

This remarkable passage conveys urgency as well as harshness. The length of the units is halved relative to the preceding section while the canon at the distance of one bar creates a sense of even faster hypermeter. The start of the canon is elided with the four bars of standing on the dominant that end the B section,[25] so that it is only the second voice in the canon that continues the phrase rhythm set up by the Monte. The first voice thus gives the impression of entering prematurely and continually anticipating the hypermetrically "correct" entries, contributing to the sense of pressing onwards.[26] The initial idea is given fourfold, rising sequential repetition, continuing the direction of the Monte, though proceeding at a faster rate and reaching the highest notes of the minuet, c^3 and d^3. The Neapolitan harmony of the opening is avoided (no $\flat2$), so the sense of cadential harmony is absent and the formal function of concluding is no longer expressed; indeed, the continuational character of the Monte is sustained right through this dynamic A' section.

The short codetta that follows the canonic climax of bars 32–41 has the character of an aftershock. There are telling modifications to the codetta in comparison with the A section: the mode, of course, is now minor, destroying the original cheerful character; it is shortened to three bars; it is neither elided nor repeated, but is preceded by a pause; it is marked *pp*, not *p*; and the rising melodic line on dominant harmony is eliminated, making the compass of the melody much narrower, focused closely around the tonic note. The presence of the codetta ensures that the order of presentation of characteristic materials in the second part of the form preserves that of the first—as usual for a binary movement—but it now functions quite differently, behaving not humorously, but like a twitch that records the lingering pain expressed by the canonic passage even after that paragraph has been formally closed by the perfect authentic cadence.

---

[25] This means four bars as an independent function, even though there are five bars of dominant harmony in total: the Monte ends with one bar of dominant harmony (bar 28), but the next four bars, which prolong it and are unified motivically, match the two four-bar phrases of the Monte and continue its hypermeter.

[26] Webster notices the premature entry, but unfortunately describes the harmonic V–i succession here as a "perfect cadence." *Haydn's "Farewell" Symphony*, 243–44. See William E. Caplin, "The Classical Cadence: Conceptions and Misconceptions," *Journal of the American Musicological Society* 57, no. 1 (2004): 51–117 (pp. 81–85).

Haydn 26/iii is an unstable hybrid: a minor-key minuet that makes initial gestures of pathos in a symphony of suffering and lament, before turning briefly cheerful. Its second part could be understood as the movement's attempt to transform itself, as though it were breaking the shackles of minuet topic and form, leading to music of unprecedented harshness. Normally, eighteenth-century minuets do not effect anything like transformation: they remain minuets to the end. Mixture of topics in minuets proper (not trios) is usually confined to the occasional allusion to *Ländler*. Indeed, even in 26/iii the attempted transformation fails.[27] After the pause following the German sixth chord in bars 40–41, the completion of the cadence and the codetta formally reassert the genre and topic of minuet, enclosing the events of the piece within their "proper" frame.

The majestic, entirely canonic Haydn 44/ii likewise undertakes an abortive transformation in its second half. It is less austere in sonority than 26/iii and less obviously irregular in syntax. The texture is fuller; the contrapuntal parts are not doubled at the octave but often in thirds in the wind instruments, giving a warmer sound; the melody is much smoother; and there is less disruption of phrase rhythm. As in 26/iii the first part of the binary form presents material of two different types, although the contrast is less dramatic. At the opening there is a conventional two-bar minuet gesture of a type often encountered at cadences, and indeed it returns at the cadence at the end of the A section. Like 26/iii, then, the movement opens with a gesture of conclusion. Thereafter, however, contrasting material takes over, the melody full of descending phrases with appoggiaturas. In the A section these occur only after the turn to III, but, as in 26/iii, at the double bar the minuet could be taken in either of two directions. In 44/ii a symmetrical second part would underline the movement's minuet character, downplaying the extraordinary modal and contrapuntal aspects, whereas a greater emphasis on the descending phrases when the second part returns to the tonic key and the minor mode would draw out the character of lament that in the first part, given the coordination of descending gestures with major mode, is still latent.

Haydn again takes the negative option. As in 26/iii a phase of standing of the dominant is reached during the second part, although this is not to be a rounded binary form, for the return of tonic harmony in the tonic key is not marked by a return of the opening material. Instead, stereotypical minuet figures are abandoned entirely in favor of a full realization of the rhetoric of lamentation in broad, lyrical phrases replete with descending gestures, melodic chromaticism, and appoggiaturas. Haydn's simple masterstroke in 44/ii is the doubling of the time interval of the canon at this point (bar 32) from one bar to two. Now the harmonic rhythm can be slowed and longer appoggiaturas are available. The new canon begins with sigh figures, *pp*, now without accompanying parts or harmonic filling, but further prolonging the dominant harmony (bars 32–39). At the return to tonic harmony a cry of anguish bursts out in a phrase that leaps to g^2, the violins' highest note

---

[27] As with Hepokoski and Darcy's concept of "sonata failure" (chapter 1), this usage is meant to be non-pejorative.

in the minuet proper, before the melody wearily descends, largely stepwise, all the way to e^1, by way of appoggiaturas, diminished fifths, and augmented seconds, all in two-part canon (bars 40–55), and concludes with a perfect authentic cadence in the tonic. The opening material returns as a codetta, the canon now at the original interval of one bar. The soft dynamic of the codetta recalls 26/iii, and, just as in that piece, the movement's identity as a minuet is reasserted after the emotional outburst. Again there is a sense that in its second part the piece has attempted to break out of its minuet topic and formal framework, realizing the expression of sorrow that was only hinted at in the first part. The attempt is again frustrated. Haydn 44/ii stands alongside Mozart K. 550/iii as one of the two finest minuets in Viennese minor-key symphonies. It is the strictest in its contrapuntal construction and the most forceful in expression.

The mood of Haydn 49/iii is unease tinged with the melancholy of repetition. The piece behaves as though stuck in a loop, continually alternating contrapuntal allusions and minuet gestures. The counterpoint is less conspicuous than in 26/iii or 44/ii. There is no canon or even imitation, but the texture consists of two strands with the strong rhythmical differentiation characteristic of good counterpoint, and as in 39/iii there are conspicuous tied notes in the treble, notably in the first bar. These are clear rhetorical gestures towards counterpoint, although at the same time they sound like sighs. The minuet continually starts phrases with tied notes before moving into more conventional minuet figures in groups of six eighth-notes, often repeated as an echo. This order of materials recurs so often, like a series of "mini-rotations," that it becomes monotonous and obsessive. The final mini-rotation is an intensified version, paralleling, in less dramatic fashion, the events at the equivalent positions in the second parts of 26/iii and 44/ii. At this point, the start of the A' section, the minuet attempts to break out of its loop and gain expressive freedom. The six-eighth-note figure is delayed: the movement's initial dotted-half-note–eighth-notes figure is immediately repeated in varied form, resulting in the first uninterrupted eight-bar phrase of the movement. At last the music takes, as it were, a deeper breath; the phrase sounds like a longer sigh, less constrained than before, though still melancholy rather than impassioned. For the first time the melody starts on the tonic note rather than the dominant, and does not fall immediately after the resolution of the first tied note, instead rising to bb^2 (bar 34^3) the violins' highest note of the movement. A long melodic descent follows, moving through the expressive chromatic passing note $b\natural^2$. The contrapuntal implications of the tied notes are now realized more fully, with three suspensions in the bass across successive barlines. The six-eighth-note figure finally appears at the perfect authentic cadence that ends the phrase, this time without an echo (bars 39–40). So, despite its internal expansion and heightened expression, the phrase does not break out of the pattern of rotations, presenting the same materials in the same order as before.

The strange closing section introduces new motives and a slightly grotesque character, but also strong and conventional signals of closure, recording the failures of the last mini-rotation to escape the rotational pattern and of the movement to transcend its minuet form and topic. The wide leaps of the first codetta, one spanning a diminished twelfth (bar 42), the upbeat figures, and the staccato notes all contrast sharply with the rest of the minuet and distinctly recall the nervous reflexes of the codetta of 26/iii. A conventional minuet cadence concludes the first codetta (bars 47–48). The second codetta reintroduces tied notes, although the initial dotted half note is now the leading note rather than the usual dominant, and the eighth notes are absent, suggesting that this will be the last occurrence of the gesture. The V^7/V chord (bar 49) and the stereotyped minor-key cadence gesture (suspended)—♮– are further strong indications of impending closure. Just as in 26/iii and 44/ii, the closing section reasserts the formal boundaries and restricted dimensions of the minuet movement.

The final minuet in the group, 52/iii, lacks the emotional intensification at the return of the tonic in the second part or indeed the sense of aftershock in its closing section, although it shares other features with the other three. This movement is emotionally understated and has the air of a puzzle, like a combinatorial minuet game or a canon cancrizans. Like 26/iii and 44/ii its opening signals closure in certain ways, in this case by means of a variant of the minor-key cadence idea that concluded 49/iii. (Here, however, scale degree $\hat{3}$ is inserted, producing the unusual pattern $\hat{6}$–$\hat{5}$–$\hat{3}$–♮ $\hat{7}$–$\hat{1}$. There is logic to the presence of this $\hat{3}$, given that the diminished fourth $\hat{3}$–♮$\hat{7}$ appeared with the same pitches (e^1♭–b♮) at the very opening of the first movement of the symphony.) The closing section of the minuet's second part again brings back some features of the opening, and ends softly with the $\hat{6}$–$\hat{5}$–$\hat{3}$♮$\hat{7}$–$\hat{1}$ figure, now in its conventional guise as a concluding gesture. This procedure recalls 44/ii, while the wide intervals in the codetta (bars 30^1–33), used nowhere in the movement to that point, and the appoggiatura-like figures are strikingly similar to those at the start of the first codetta in 49/iii. 52/iii is in two parts almost throughout, each played in unison by two string parts. The texture is built from short overlapping figures that strangely anticipate Webern, especially in the way their treatment follows sentence construction, with the varied repetition of a basic idea followed by a continuation-like section in which the units are lengthened. The tied note at the very end of each of the minuet's two parts gives the impression that some mysterious strict logic is being followed. In fact, this is merely rhetorical: the counterpoint is actually free.

Three of these four Haydn minuets share one further trait. In 26/iii, 49/iii, and 52/iii there are motivic connections between the minuet and the trio, especially the openings of each.[28] The trio can therefore be heard as an alternative treatment of the materials of the minuet and a reinterpretation of them. Each trio begins with a close variant of its minuet's initial idea, but each is in the tonic major and has more regular phrase rhythm, more literal repetition, and a more placid character. The trio of 26/iii, in D major (the tonic major), conveys gentle humor. It begins with the A–D of the opening of the minuet in the same rhythm, but now inverted into a rising fourth. The d^2–c♯^{2} appoggiatura in the trio's second bar recalls the same notes in

---

[28] The descending scale near the start of the trio 44/ii could be linked to its minuet too, but the connection is more tenuous than in the three other movements.

bar 5 of the minuet. The trio is remarkable for its metrical disruption and textural contrasts on the small scale. On the larger scale of phrase rhythm, however, it is more regular than the minuet. The A and A' sections are identical twelve-bar periods, while the B section consists of a four-bar phrase followed by a literal repetition. The trio of 52/iii effects the regularization of the unusual patterns of its minuet: a rhetorical resolution of the minuet's apparent puzzle. It begins with overlapping figures in rhythms identical to the opening of the minuet, but the overlapping is eliminated thereafter. As in the minuet, the bass has short, slurred figures in eighth notes (now mainly iambic), but they match the rhythm of the upper part, and the two articulate the meter unambiguously. Indeed, the repetitions take this articulation to the point of redundancy. Given the nature of the preceding minuet, they amount to a deliberate, ironic banality. While the trios of 26/iii and 52/iii relieve the unease that prevails in their minuets through humor or irony, that of 49/iii sustains it. This trio is extraordinarily static and heightens the minuet's impression of constraint. As well as the opening, it alludes to the strange closing section of the minuet. Again the trio is more regular in phrase rhythm and more literally repetitive than the minuet. The A and A' sections are identical and the B section consists of a single bar played, with the odd embellishment, four times. There is no modulation, and only one accidental. The first violin part moves entirely within the fourth a–d^1, while the harmony remains closely tied to root position tonic chords.

It is hard to resist attributing some special significance to the strategies that Haydn adopted around 1770 in his contrapuntal minor-key minuets. Granted, Haydn's comment near the end of his life to his biographer A. C. Dies that "in instrumental music I generally allowed my purely musical fantasy free play" should not be forgotten.[29] But his fantasy seems not to have been quite free in these pieces, for, given similar starting conditions, it took a similar course on four separate occasions. If it was guided by a concept, then the most likely source is the function of Symphony No. 26, probably No. 49, and possibly the others too as works for Holy Week. Most ecclesiastical institutions did not allow minuets in church. Whether or not Haydn's minor-key symphonies were actually performed in church,[30] the symphonic minuet was potentially inappropriate to the Lenten atmosphere of seriousness and penance. This might help to explain the contrapuntal dimension to the movements. More specifically, the frustration conveyed by these minuets could be taken as an allusion to original sin. The "bound style" (*gebundener Styl*) stands for Adam's bond, and the failure of the minuets' attempts to transform themselves

---

[29] Translated in Vernon Gotwals, *Joseph Haydn: Eighteenth-Century Gentleman and Genius* (Madison: University of Wisconsin Press, 1963), 155 (May 27, 1806).

[30] Instrumental music was supposedly banned in church during Holy Week, although it could have been performed elsewhere at that time, for instance, at a Lenten "Concert spirituel." See Neal Zaslaw, "Mozart, Haydn and the Sinfonia da Chiesa," *Journal of Musicology 1*, no. 1 (1982): 95–124 (p. 115). However, in some liturgical practice Lent was deemed to have ended on the evening of Maundy Thursday. Vaňhal d2 was performed in Regensburg cathedral on Good Friday 1781, according to the Regensburg parts. Bryan, *Johann Wanhal*, 286. Haydn's *Seven Last Words* were composed for a Lenten observance in Cádiz, which most likely took place in Holy Week.

speaks of the human condition in the absence of divine grace. There is no hint of release, of loosening the bond, in the minuets proper. They possess a narrative quality, but the story they tell is not that of Easter itself (Christ's Passion and resurrection) but the fallen state to which those events come as the resolution.

A Memory of the 1760s: Mozart K. 550/iii

Mozart's only contrapuntal minor-key minuet in a symphony, K. 550/iii (1788), stands out from contemporary practice. By the mid-1770s, counterpoint in symphony minuets was rare, and canon even more so. Haydn did not use canon after 44/ii (1771), Vaňhal after e2/iii (1771–72?), where in any case it is only fleeting, or Dittersdorf after a2/iii (composed before 1779). Even non-canonic contrapuntal minuets were scarce, aside from Haydn 80/iii (1783–84). Wranitzky evokes the tradition in 43/iii (pre-1790), although the contrapuntal technique is weak and the piece is unsuccessful.[31] Moreover, while Haydn's contrapuntal minuets may have been conceived partly as an answer to conservative critics, by 1788 his battle for Viennese music was all but won. The significance of K. 550/iii lies instead in the way that Mozart recollects and extends a musical tradition of the previous generation, conducting a dialogue with compositions that had been forgotten by contemporary Viennese society.

The initial conditions of K. 550/iii are rather different from those of the minuets discussed hitherto. In addition to the two oboes and two horns that had been customary in Viennese symphonies composed around 1770 it is scored for flute, two obbligato bassoon parts, and, in the revised version, two clarinets. The wind parts are written for first-rate players (seldom the case in Vaňhal's symphonies). Furthermore, although marked "Menuetto," the minuet character of K. 550/iii is obscured by means of strategies unusual even for the late 1780s. The *Allegretto* marking means that the piece moves at a faster tempo than most late eighteenth-century minuets.[32] The scoring produces thick textures, especially in the lower registers, as well as a good deal of multi-octave doubling, which negate the grace typical of the dance. The opening bars project a generically unprecedented "metrical grouping dissonance" by setting a duple meter in half notes against the triple meter in eighth notes. The hypermetrical dissonance in the first half of the minuet, which sets groups of two and three bars against each other, is likewise unprecedented in minor-key contrapuntal minuets.[33] The upward leaps of a minor seventh followed by downward plunging arpeggios (bars 15–20) and of an augmented sixth

---

[31] The part-writing is fussy and directionless, as though the composer had aimed for independence of parts as an afterthought.

[32] See Claudia Maurer Zenck, *Vom Takt: Untersuchungen zur Theorie und kompositorischen Praxis im ausgehenden 18. und beginnenden 19. Jahrhundert* (Vienna: Böhlau, 2001), 96–103.

[33] On these metrical dissonances in K. 550/iii see Richard Cohn, "Metric and Hypermetric Dissonance in the *Menuetto* of Mozart's Symphony in G Minor, K. 550," *Intégral* 6 (1992): 1–33 (pp. 14–16). Indirect metrical grouping dissonance can often be found as a witty effect in Haydn's and

(bar 25) that later reinforce the metrical dissonance are found nowhere else in the repertory. A characteristic minuet rhythm does not appear until the cadence at the end of the A section (bars 13^1–14^1). In most other bars the three beats are accented more or less evenly, and there is a steady rate of attacks on almost every beat. The chromaticism in vigorous melodic lines is also new in the minor-key contrapuntal minuet; in Haydn 44/ii and 49/iii descending chromatic lines were present but expressed sighs of lamentation. The soft chromatic passage for wind instruments at the end of the minuet (bars 36–39) without string support is unique to K. 550/iii and concludes the minuet with dark, exotic colors.

Nevertheless, despite changes in the technical resources available to Mozart in the seventeen years since Haydn 52/iii, the paradoxical combination of topic, mode, and contrapuntal texture in Mozart K. 550/iii creates unease just as in Haydn's minor-key minuets. Indeed, its dialogue with the generic conventions of the contrapuntal minor-key minuet as they stood around 1770 extends to the overall formal strategy as well, recalling the second-part expressive intensification in Haydn 26/iii, 44/ii, and 49/iii. The first part of K. 550/iii effects a certain regularization, moving from minor to major, from contrapuntal to homophonic texture, from metrical dissonance to consonance, and from evenly stressed beats to more normal minuet gestures with slurs and detached notes combined. At the double barline, as in Haydn 26/iii and 44/ii, the minuet might be taken in several directions in the second part. It might repeat the drift to regularity while remaining in minor or, alternatively, uphold and intensify the connection between minor mode and irregular syntax. In the event, Mozart opts for the second route, through an intensification of the extraordinary qualities of the opening of the first part. At the return to the tonic at the start of the A' section, the movement's opening idea returns in a two-part canon at the fourth, pursuing a succession of wide, overlapping upward leaps and conjunct, falling figures like an exaggerated Corelli leapfrog progression.[34] Duple meter is now expressed by both canonic parts against triple in the bass. And to this metrical dissonance is added a direct triple/duple hypermetrical dissonance (this was present at the opening of the movement in indirect form) that results in a "double hemiola,"[35] an extremely rare phenomenon in the late eighteenth century. This passage of great urgency and contrapuntal intensity reaches its climax with the first violins' highest note of the movement (eb^3), before dissolving into homophony for

---

Mozart's minuets, but seldom direct dissonance, and never at the very opening. Grouping dissonance is not found in any other minor-key contrapuntal minuets listed in Table 4.1. For this terminology see Harald Krebs, *Fantasy Pieces: Metrical Dissonance in the Music of Robert Schumann* (New York and Oxford: Oxford University Press, 1999), 31–33, 45–46. The suspension from the last beat of bar 1 to the first of bar 2 is not unprecedented in the minor-key contrapuntal minuet; tied notes have been encountered across this very barline in Haydn 39/iii and 49/iii. Those began as dotted half notes, however, not as third beat eighth notes as in K. 550/iii. For further metrical analysis see Zenck, *Vom Takt*, 98–103, and the literature given in her n. 241.

[34] There is a resemblance on paper to Wagenseil G5/iii (Ex. 2.2), but it is probably coincidental. Mozart's counterpoint is certainly far more effective.

[35] Cohn, "Metric and Hypermetric Dissonance," 22–24.

the cadence. It is followed by a soft codetta, which, as in the Haydn minuets, has the effect of framing the climax, although conventional minuet syntax is not reasserted as it is, for instance, in Haydn 44/ii. The codetta accomplishes a certain degree of metrical regularization, but even that is ambiguous.[36]

It is possible that in K. 550/iii Mozart took Haydn 26/iii as a model. Both are unusually ungraceful for minuets; both introduce canon at the start of A' with a forceful rising shape and an intensification of the underlying emotional unease. Both precede this passage by standing on the dominant for several bars while alternating dominant harmony with chromatic neighboring chords. Both avoid a literal caesura at that point in favor of onward drive, 26/iii making an elision with the start of the first canonic entry, K. 550/iii filling the caesura with melodic diminutions in the bass. In both movements there is a melodic connection between the openings of the minuet and the trio, the latter being more regular in phrase rhythm, with more literal repetition (although this is also true of Haydn 49/iii and 52/iii). There is circumstantial evidence that Mozart knew Haydn 26. For instance, there is a very similar moment of canon in his Fugue in C minor, K. 426,[37] which he arranged for string quartet while working on K. 550 in the summer of 1788; the metrical irregularities of the trio of Haydn 26/iii caused by wide, triple stopped chords closely anticipate the opening of the second movement of Mozart's String Quintet, K. 516 (another minor-key minuet); and the syncopated opening theme of Haydn 26/i is a precursor to the opening of Mozart K. 183/i.[38] If this thesis is correct, it is remarkable that Mozart should have remembered such an harsh, ungainly piece in one of his grand symphonies of 1788. In K. 550/iii he reestablished connections with all but forgotten conventions and strategies and took them in his own highly original directions.

The Stormy Finale

Finales of Viennese minor-key symphonies often share something of the mood and many of the techniques of first movements, although in general their range of expression is narrower and their formal strategies more straightforward. As with the minor-key contrapuntal minuet, distinctive subgeneric conventions for minor-key finales emerged clearly in the late 1760s. Thereafter, other possibilities, including major-key finales, blur the picture. The characteristic "stormy finale" that arose from these conventions is a fast sonata form in duple or quadruple meter, usually notated as 2/2 (seventeen out of twenty-seven movements in Table 4.2), sometimes

---

[36] Ibid., 26–30.

[37] Landon, *Chronicle*, 2:294.

[38] A. Peter Brown finds parallels also in the syncopated openings of symphonies by Gassmann, but none of these are in minor keys and none uses the "pathotype" figure of K. 183/i. Brown, "Weeding a Musicological Garden," 223.

C. Triple meter is avoided.[39] The stormy finale sustains an almost relentless energy, in particular a fast surface rhythm. There is usually less variation of texture and rhythmic gestures than in first movements and there are fewer dramatic pauses to interrupt the flow. Lightweight finales of the kind commonly found in major-key symphonies of the 1760s and sometimes even in the 1770s—lively dances in meters such as 3/8, 6/8, or 2/4, often in sectional forms rather than sonata forms—are seldom found in the minor mode, at least after Wagenseil. (Many of the minor-key symphonies absent from Table 4.2 have finales in major keys.) Exceptions to this rule amount collectively to something of a miscellany, and do not establish any secondary subgeneric finale type.[40]

The preference for fast duple or quadruple meter is consistent with the tendency of minor-key symphonies to adopt a serious tone. Whereas the time signature 3/8 was the default for the final sections of Italian opera sinfonias, **C** was associated with heroic arias in opera seria, while 2/2 (alla breve) had an old connection with sacred vocal polyphony and thus latterly with Fuxian counterpoint, a connection upheld by eighteenth-century theorists, even if not always by composers.[41] In the 1760s, symphony finales in 2/2 usually belonged to works conceived in a solemn style. Before 1766 Haydn notated only four finales in 2/2 (all of them in fact before early 1763).[42] Three of them are fugal (3/iv, 38/iv, and 40/iv), while the other (5/iv) is from a symphony in sonata da chiesa form (first movement slow). Symphony No. 3 even has a contrapuntal minuet—very rare for a major-key symphony—as well as contrapuntal textures in its first movement.[43] These tendencies can be detected also in Ordonez's symphonic output before 1770: the few finales in 2/2 appear to be either conspicuously contrapuntal or in a minor key.[44]

The notated time signature is not always a reliable guide to a finale's rhythmic character. Some of the finales notated as **C** share characteristic gestures with those in 2/2. Most of them date from after 1770, possibly for no other reason than that the notation 2/2 declined in line with a general standardization of time signatures in the course of the eighteenth century. Haydn 39/iv, in **C**, could be better notated as 2/2, at least for the first twenty-three bars and parallel passages. However, the first

---

[39] The only finales in triple meter are Wagenseil G5/iii (3/4) and G6/iii (3/8) and Vaňhal f1/iii (3/4), none of which could be described as stormy.

[40] Finales notated in meters other than 2/2 or C are as follows. In 3/8: Wagenseil G6/iii. In 6/8: Vaňhal e2 and Gassmann 23. In 2/4: Wagenseil G4/iii, Dittersdorf e1/iv, a2/iv, Vaňhal c3/iv, e3/iv (but effectively 6/8 for much of the movement), Haydn 78/iv, Gassmann 83/iv, and Ordonez B1/iii.

[41] See Wye Jamison Allanbrook, *Rhythmic Gesture in Mozart*, 15–17.

[42] Judging by Gerlach's dating. ("Joseph Haydns Sinfonien bis 1774.") The Mandyczewski chronology is very misleading for Nos. 38 and 40.

[43] Haydn increased his use of 2/2 in both major and minor after 1766. Out of twenty-six symphony finales composed between 1766 and 1774, fourteen are in 2/2. Bernhard Moosbauer, *Tonart und Form in den Finali von Joseph Haydn zwischen 1766 und 1774* (Tutzing: Hans Schneider 1998), 39.

[44] Judging by Table 12 in Young, "The Symphonies of Karl von Ordonez," 65. For Vaňhal, basic problems of dating make these kind of statistics difficult to compile.

TABLE 4.2 Fast sonata-form minor-key finales notated in 2/2 or 4/4

Dittersdorf g1	C	B
Gassmann 45	2/2	A
Gassmann 83	Notated in 2/4	A
Haydn 52	2/2	New version of A
Haydn 44	2/2	A
Haydn 49	2/2	B
Haydn 45	2/2, turning to Adagio 3/8	
Haydn 39	C	B
Hoffmeister e1	C	B
Koželuch I:5	C	B
Mozart K. 183	2/2	Traits of A
Mozart K. 550	2/2	
Ordonez C14	2/2	A, traits of B
Ordonez F12	2/2	A
Ordonez G7	2/2	A
Ordonez G8	2/2	A
Swieten 7	C	
Vaňhal a1	C	B
Vaňhal a2	C	B
Vaňhal c2	2/2	B
Vaňhal d1	2/2	B
Vaňhal d2	2/2	B
Vaňhal e1	2/2	B
Vaňhal g1	2/2	B
Vaňhal g2	2/2	B
Wranitzky 30	C "La tempesta"	New version of B
Wranitzky 43	C	Traits of A and B

half of Haydn 45/iv, in 2/2, could be renotated as a contradance in 2/4. Its slurred eighth notes on beats 1 and 2 are unusual for a minor-key finale, and are shared only by Dittersdorf a2/iv (as slurred eighth-notes in 2/4). Despite its time signature Haydn 45/iv is really a dance finale, not a stormy finale (see chapter 5). Gassmann 83/iv is notated in 2/4 but shares its rhythmic gestures and many other features with Gassmann 45/iv in 2/2. Whatever their notated time signature, many finales can be heard in quadruple meter for long stretches (4/2 in relation to the notated half-note pulse); in other words, there is a consistent two-bar hypermeter relative to the notated bars.

Most finales in 2/2 or C stay in the minor mode to the end, and most recapitulations parallel the exposition closely, with no coda. The exceptions are Vaňhal a2/iii, which changes mode at the start of the recapitulation, and Dittersdorf g1/iv, Wranitzky 30/iii, and Hoffmeister e1/iv, which do so in a coda. Haydn 45/iv, if it is to be counted as 2/2 at all, turns to the tonic major within a two-part, compound finale, the slow second part of which begins in III: an exceptional strategy among eighteenth-century symphonies.[45] Finales of minor-key symphonies that begin in minor but end in major are found disproportionately amongst movements in meters other than 2/2 or **C**, such as Gassmann 23/iv (6/8), Vaňhal e3/iv (2/4), Vaňhal f1/iii (3/4), Haydn 78/iv (2/4), and Dittersdorf e1 (2/4) and a2 (2/4).

On the basis of inductive analysis, stormy finales can be divided into two broad types, which in practice correspond roughly to the distinction between composers associated with the imperial court and those without direct connection to it. The first—Type A in the third column of Table 4.2—deploys an untimely rhetoric appropriate to the ecclesiastical associations of alla breve meter. It may feature contrapuntal textures, either instrumental or vocal in style, fast-moving basslines, allusions to the "Corelli leapfrog" pattern, forceful, ritornello-like unison gestures to open and/or end the movement, and the avoidance of elaborate melodic diminutions. *Trommelbass*, tremolandi, and characteristic violin figuration—unambiguous markers of modern orchestral style—are absent. The mediant tutti is missing too, or is articulated only very faintly. Examples include Gassmann 45/iv (see Ex. 2.6(i)) and 83/iv (Exx. 2.8 and 2.9), Ordonez F12/iv, G8/iii (Ex. 2.11), G7/iii (Ex. 2.14), and C14/iv, and Haydn 44/iv. Haydn 52/iv is recognizable as Type A, although it comes in an original guise (discussed in chapter 5).

The second type of stormy finale—Type B in the third column of Table 4.2—avoids untimely rhetoric and draws instead on the vocabulary of rage arias and theatrical representations of devils or furies. It features *Trommelbass*, tremolandi, homophonic textures, fast violin figuration characteristic of the Italian sinfonia, especially in the second half of expositions, and often a mediant tutti (see, for instance, Exx. 1.2, 1.4, and 1.6). Vaňhal was especially fond of mediant tuttis in finales; Haydn probably has priority with 39/iv, but avoided the mediant tutti in finales thereafter.[46] All of these features are of course shared with a number of first movements around 1770. The overall range of tempi of Type B finales, however, is faster than in first movements. Furthermore, Type B finales are more tightly organized throughout. Phrases and themes tend to be symmetrical and clearly articulated. There is much repetition of units, often literal, at all levels. Although sentential construction of themes is common in both first movements and finales, finales have a tendency to a block-like, additive construction, even in themes. Chromaticism is minimal and modulation is usually abrupt. There is some loosening of the formal organization when the mediant is reached in the exposition, although this is achieved mainly through further repetitive and additive processes. Thematic ideas are bold and simple rather than highly wrought, and tend to be more conventional than those found in the equivalent positions in first movements. Even when motives feature a diversity of rhythmic and intervallic content—normally the criteria for characteristic material—they are usually clichés, as in the violin figures in the

---

[45] Vaňhal d2/iii ends with D major chords, but retains the minor scale degree in the manner of a *tièrce de picardie*. See chapter 6.

[46] Haydn 49/iv has a mediant tutti gesture, but it is preceded by a perfect authentic cadence in the tonic rather than the usual half cadence, placing it on the fringes of this convention.

second half of expositions. Lyricism is generally avoided even when a distinctive subordinate theme is introduced.

In Type B stormy finales, surface rhythm is almost always fast, whereas harmonic rhythm may be slow, especially if the movement is notated as 2/2 but can be heard in 4/2. The result is storm and bustle, a rather static image of movement and energy, without much in the way of motivic ideas to be presented or developed. If this were not a deliberate compositional strategy it could be regarded as bombastic. What is presented is the stormy topic, and what is expressed is simply the markedness of the minor mode. The opening of Vaňhal c2/iv, for instance, eschews characteristic material almost entirely and keeps harmonic change to a bare minimum (Ex. 4.3). Literal repetition is frequent here, with changes of register sometimes providing the only variety. Despite the limitations on compositional resources, however, this main theme has electric energy, and uses contrasts in register and unison textures to great effect (bars 7–9, for instance).

Type B finales are more numerous than Type A (see Table 4.2). Haydn 39/iv appears to be pivotal in the history of this type, and Vaňhal, who wrote seven examples (c2/iv, e1/iv, g1/iv, g2/iv, d1/iv, a2/iii, and a1/iv) certainly knew it well. Its opening is clearly the model for that of Vaňhal d1/iv, while the opening of Vaňhal G8/iv (a major-key movement) is a direct paraphrase of Haydn 39/iv with the mode changed from minor to major and some of the intervals inverted (compare Exx. 4.4 (i), (ii), and (iii)). Also falling under Type B are Dittersdorf g1/iv, Haydn 49/iv, Vaňhal d2/iii, Hoffmeister e1/iv, and Koželuch I:5/iii. These movements show somewhat greater rhythmic or melodic diversity and looser organization than those of Vaňhal. Since several Type A finales have been discussed in chapter 2, and two of the most interesting, Haydn 44/iv and 52/iv, will be dealt with in chapter 5, the rest of this chapter deals mainly with the more numerous, although, from the point of view of compositional strategies, less ambitious, Type B.

The main theme of a Type B finale is usually a tight-knit sentence in which intricate harmonic and melodic shaping is minimized. The presentation phrase may use exact or near-exact repetition. The continuation tends to be based on repetition or alternation of harmonies, or even a pedal rather than sequential progressions (Ex. 4.3). The main theme of Vaňhal g2/iv is sixteen bars in length, but as the meter is really 4/2, this is a standard, tight-knit, eight-bar sentence (Ex. 4.5; compare with Ex. 4.3, where the same dimensions and meter are found). The harmony in the presentation phrase changes once every 4/2 hypermeasure; the basic idea is then the standard two bars in length, the presentation phrase the standard four bars. While surface rhythm is fast, harmonic rhythm is slow and the rate at which phrases and formal functions unfold is even slower, even though the proportions of the theme are conventional and symmetrical. The echo effects in bars 5 and 9 are necessary for this symmetry to be maintained, demonstrating the paradoxical slowness of motion in the theme. It is as though the presentation of material takes place too quickly for the metrical structure, which then needs to be filled out. In the rest of g2/iv the harmonic rhythm seldom accelerates and the 4/2 hypermeter is seldom broken. The main theme of a Type B finale usually begins with direct, accented attacks on first beats without anacruses or appoggiaturas. However, the main theme may begin

Ex. 4.3 Vaňhal c2/iv, bars 1–16 (reduction)

Ex. 4.4

(i) Haydn 39/iv, bars 1–10

(ii) Vaňhal d1/iv, bars 1–8

Ex. 4.4 (Continued)

(iii) Vaňhal G8/iv, bars 1–12

softly (Vaňhal g2/iv, Haydn 49/iv). The rhythmic and melodic gestures of the galant style are avoided; for instance, there are no stresses on second beats in quadruple meters (notated or implied). The wide leaps often claimed to be a characteristic feature of "*Sturm und Drang* style" are sometimes present, and the melody may have a very wide compass (Ex. 4.3 for instance). The approach to the caesura before the mediant tutti is less faltering than in first movements; the decline in energy has more to do with a fall in register than with dynamics or rhythm, the latter usually remaining fast and furious on the surface. As in first movements there may also be some motivic liquidation at this point, but there are usually fewer characteristic features to liquidate. Sometimes conventionality of melodic material and avoidance of embellishment and rhythmic differentiation are pushed to the point of banality, as in the main theme of Vaňhal a1/iii (Ex. 4.6). Here the minimal motivic information being conveyed contrasts markedly with the frequency and force of attacks in the accompaniment. The opening of Dittersdorf g1/iv is a burlesque on the melodic emptiness of the Type B stormy finale. The presentation phrase is again a standard four bars in length if one hears 4/2 hypermeasures (Ex. 4.7), although in this theme it is immediately repeated softly in its entirety, before leading, in the continuation phrase, to the music cited in Ex. 1.6, itself a witty combination (see chapter 1).

Ex. 4.5 Vaňhal g2/iv, bars 1–16

After 1770 the distinctions between the thematic characteristics and the syntactic organization of first movements and finales are sometimes blurred. Hoffmeister
e1/iv starts with a rising motive in half notes on notes of the tonic triad followed by
an eighth-note figure, just like the start of the first movement of the same symphony
(Ex. 4.8 (i) and (ii)). In the finale the eighth-note figure is a contradance-derived
commonplace of Viennese instrumental music of the time, including minor-key
symphony first movements (Haydn 39/i, Vaňhal d1/i), although it is rare in
minor-key finales around 1770, which tend not to break up their beats with complex articulation in this way, and do not include appoggiaturas.[47] At a tempo of
presto assai, the main theme of Hoffmeister e1/iv thus sounds fussier than usual for
a stormy finale. The finale nevertheless distinguishes itself from Hoffmeister e1/i in
certain ways: in addition to the faster tempo, there is far more repetition of short
units, more abrupt phrase endings, and much less textural variety (*Trommelbass*
continues almost throughout). The main theme of Koželuch I:5/iii (1787) likewise
shares its rhythmic profile with the opening of the symphony's first movement, and
again features the contradance-derived figure (Ex. 4.9 (i) and (ii)). The main themes
of both movements use full statement–response repetition in their presentation
phrases (i–X–V–i)—common for a first movement but rare for a stormy minor-key

---

[47] Another exception is Swieten 7/iii.

Ex. 4.6 Vaňhal a1/iii, bars 1–13

finale—and both move into a phase of harmonic and melodic sequence for their continuation phrases. Moreover, both movements have a "second subject," that is, a subordinate theme with a basic idea that contrasts with that of the main theme and begins at a soft dynamic. This type of subordinate theme is otherwise rare in minor-key finales, where the energy of the opening tends to surge onwards uninterruptedly. Koželuch I:5/iii is relatively complex in its formal strategies and diverse in motivic material and rhythmic gestures; in this respect it is roughly comparable to a first movement of the late 1760s. The only recognizable generic distinction from its own first movement is its faster tempo.

Ex. 4.7 Dittersdorf g1/iv, bars 1–8

Ex. 4.8

    (i) Hoffmeister e1/i, bars 1–4

    (ii) Hoffmeister e1/iv, bars 1 -10

Ex. 4.9

(i) Koželuch I:5/i, bars 1–4

(ii) Koželuch I:5/iii, bars 1 -7

In the Type B finale the reprise of the main theme often stands out as a moment of heightened rhetoric or receives unusually careful preparation. This may be because, in a movement that begins with a strong, energetic gesture and maintains a fast surface rhythm and headlong energy, the reprise is potentially anticlimactic. In c2/iv and g1/iv Vaňhal solves the problem by making parallels between the reprise and the mediant tutti by preparing the former with music that parallels, in extended form, the continuation phrase of the exposition's main theme. In both cases the impression of declining energy is exaggerated in the second version by means of motivic liquidation and conspicuous reductions in dynamics, scoring, texture, surface rhythmic activity, melodic contour, and register. In g1/iv the dominant harmony is recaptured and alternates with augmented sixth chords in a manner very reminiscent of the approach to the caesura before a mediant tutti. In Vaňhal g2/iv the end of the

Ex. 4.10 Vaňhal g2/iv, bars 60–76

development features one of the most striking and imaginative passages in any of his compositions (Ex. 4.10). From bar 65 all melodic information ceases and the syncopated accompaniment is left exposed. The dynamic falls to *p* and the wind instruments fall silent. As in c2/iv and g1/iv the melody outlines a descent in pitch, on this occasion a stepwise motion through chromatic harmonies. The development ends almost identically to the continuation of the main theme (compare bars 73–76 in Ex. 4.10 with bars 13–16 in Ex. 4.5), having taken the process of thematic liquidation even further. Although extraordinary, this passage in fact epitomizes the semiotics of the stormy finale, as the turbulent accompaniment explicitly becomes the content of the passage, the emptiness of the melodic material taken to the final extreme. In all three of these Vaňhal finales, the end of the development avoids anticlimax by "clearing the stage" in somewhat exaggerated fashion in preparation for the re-entrance of the main theme. In Haydn 49/iv the reprise is not preceded by a caesura as in the Vaňhal examples, and the main theme is partially stated in the dominant before the tonic is reached, so thematic and tonal returns are non-aligned. Here, anticlimax is avoided by the elimination of the caesura and the reduction of the articulation of the tonic reprise. This strategy is unique for the finale of a minor-key symphony. It is possible because of the soft dynamic of the main theme, but it also reveals a degree of cyclic integration in Haydn 49. The first movement's tonic reprise is preceded by an allusion to the opening of the movement in the dominant (minor) immediately after the dominant (major) chord has been sounded at the end of the development.[48]

Haydn 49/iv aside, Type B finales seldom manipulate formal categories in original ways.[49] Their forms tend to be schematic; their storminess is a surface phenomenon. In this they differ markedly from the eighteenth-century tradition of French operatic storm scenes and the extension of that tradition in Beethoven's "Pastoral" Symphony, in which the "sublimity" of the storm is reflected in its breaching of conventional formal boundaries (see chapter 7). Freer minor-key finales do exist, including Haydn 44/iv (Type A), 45/iv (neither type), and 52/iv (Type A)—all discussed in chapter 5—and Mozart K. 183/iv (leaning to Type A) and K. 550/iv (of neither type). One exception to this rule is worth noting: the *Molleinschub* (a local tonic-minor interpolation within a subordinate theme or group in major)[50] found in the exposition of the Type B Vaňhal e1/iv. The subordinate theme (Ex. 4.11) begins wittily, but with perfectly conventional galant material and organization (clichéd violin figures, continuation phrase beginning as a Prinner riposte). There follows a stereotypical crescendo passage with rising tremolando notes on violins.[51] At the climax of the crescendo comes the disruption: the local tonic chord turns to minor

---

[48] Webster, *Haydn's "Farewell" Symphony*, 262–67.

[49] The discussion of Haydn 44/iv in chapter 5 notes some partial exceptions, including Dittersdorf g1/iv and Hoffmeister e1/iv. But the omission of the reprise of the main theme in the tonic halfway through the second part of the form, as occurs in these movements, is, statistically, not an exceptional event in late eighteenth-century sonatas.

[50] On *Molleinschüben* in eighteenth-century minor-key sonata movements, see Longyear, "The Minor Mode in Eighteenth-Century Sonata Form," 203–8.

[51] The crescendo is stereotypical for the mid-eighteenth-century symphony in general, although not specifically for the Viennese minor-key subgenre, where it very seldom occurs.

Ex. 4.11 Vaňhal e1/iv, bars 27–53

Ex. 4.11 (Continued)

Ex. 4.11 (Continued)

(G minor, iii in relation to the movement's tonic). The dynamic then drops to *piano* with a descent in octave half notes (bars 39–44; compare Ex. 4.3, bars 7–9). A rising figure outlining a diminished seventh—a chord rarely foregrounded in Vaňhal—increases the energy level once more, and thereafter the subordinate theme is back on track: its cadential phrase follows, again with conventional figuration.[52] In the soft G minor passage, the theme is sidetracked; the strong implication of the crescendo is denied realization. It functions like a passing shiver, as the dark, minor-key mood penetrates momentarily into even the major-key subordinate theme.[53]

Stormy finales almost never turn to the tonic major in the recapitulation, and thus do not realize the comic plot. The only exception is Vaňhal a2/iii (Vaňhal f1/iii turns to major but is in triple time and thus dance-like rather than truly "stormy"). Symphonies that end in major either have a different type of minor-key finale or have a finale entirely in major. Type B stormy finales do not realize the tragic plot with any great strength. They tend to be regular and compact in structure and organized on strict rotational principles, the events of the recapitulation corresponding closely with those of the exposition, with minimal rewriting. These finales function primarily to resolve and complete the whole symphony rather than to unfold a narrative. (Rosen sees only a difference in degree between this type of finale and a movement that turns to major; both effect stabilization and decrease tension.)[54] Type A stormy finales may realize the tragic plot more strongly. Gassmann favors closing ritornello effects as much in finales as in first movements. The two Type A finales by court "outsiders," Haydn 44/iv and Mozart K. 183/iv, both have them too—Haydn

---

[52] In the recapitulation this moment is less striking as the mode of the crescendo is already minor. Instead, there is a significant change to the figure used for the presentation phrase, which is now drawn out much longer and taken for twelve bars through a variety of harmonies, beginning what appears to be a transition, not a subordinate theme at all.

[53] This is the only *Molleinschub* in a minor-key symphony finale, although there is one in a first movement (Haydn 44/i, bars 37–39).

[54] Rosen, *The Classical Style*, 276.

44/iv also disrupts normal rotational principles—as do the first movements of those symphonies, meaning that both stand out in the repertory as especially negative.

Several finales are ambiguously positioned in relation to the two regulative types. As noted in chapter 2 and in the present chapter, Ordonez C14 has affinities with the style of Vaňhal that mark it out from other minor-key symphonies by composers associated with the imperial court. The finale is no exception. Although essentially a Type A finale, it alludes unmistakably to Type B as well. As in many outer movements by Wagenseil, Gassmann, and Ordonez, contrasts of dynamics and scoring are coordinated to create the impression of tutti/solo alternations. The first nineteen bars function like a ritornello, but thereafter the *Trommelbass*, tremolando, and melodic syncopations characteristic of the Type B finale appear: the untimely/modern stylistic distinction is thus projected onto tutti/solo form. Later in the movement certain untimely features of the opening are used intensively: the suspensions of bars 11–12 turn into fourth-species counterpoint at bars 95–99 and the opening eighth-note runs in the violins form the basis of a trio-sonata-like texture with suspensions and imitation between the two violin parts in bars 34–39. The movement's second section begins with the (nonliteral) contrapuntal inversion of the parts from the opening bars. On the other hand, the wide leaps of bars 7 and 9—a Type B characteristic—are also highlighted later (bars 123–26).

Two stormy finales by Wranitzky (see chapter 7) stand in contrasting relations to the two subgeneric types. Wranitzky 43/iv is rooted in Viennese traditions, even though its instrumental resources are expanded and many aspects of its technique are different. It is a late example—probably from the late 1780s or even early 1790s[55]—of a finale with characteristics of Type A (Ex. 4.12). The movement opens with a "hammer blow" followed by a powerful, ritornello-like theme in octaves. At bar 10 there is a clear switch to a solo-like passage, just as in Ordonez C14. Despite the greatly expanded orchestra (flute, oboes, bassoons, horns), this type of procedure recalls the first movements of Wagenseil G6 and G5, composed at least twenty-five years earlier in the same key. There are Type B features as well, including the descending leap of a thirteenth in bar 13 and the mediant tutti in bar 18. The rest of the movement, like Mozart K. 183/iv, explores a wide range of rhythmic gestures that exceeds both normative types. Wranitzky 30/iii, on the other hand, is related only superficially to the Viennese tradition. Headed "La tempesta," and containing "tone painting" effects of rain, wind, and thunder, its antecedents lie in representations of tempests in eighteenth-century French opera, conceived under the aesthetic of "verisimilitude." Wranitzky 30/iii shares with the Type B finale the combination of fast surface rhythm and slow harmonic rhythm and the tendency to

---

[55] David Wyn Jones thinks Wranitzky 43 is the earliest of his symphonies in minor keys, and notes that it "looks back to the 1760s and 1770s." He places it alongside earlier G minor symphonies such as Haydn 39, Mozart K. 183, Vaňhal g1 and g2 and Koželuch I:5. See *The Symphony in Beethoven's Vienna* (Cambridge: Cambridge University Press, 2006), 80. This understanding seems correct, but the discussion here is an attempt to specify the symphony's antecedents more precisely.

Ex. 4.12 Wranitzky 42/iv, bars 1–20 (string parts). Biblioteca del Conservatorio Luigi Cherubini, Firenze. I-Fc, fondo Pitti, FPS.111

repeat short units, but on the large scale it is much more loosely organized than the other finales, much longer (338 bars), and it lacks repeat marks.

The two types of stormy finale described in this chapter are formulaic to a degree, especially Type B, and three of the most ambitious minor-key symphonies avoid both types or transcend them. Mozart K. 183/iv (see chapter 8) fits Type A at its outset, the octave melody suggesting an opening ritornello. The closing ritornello effect recalls Gassmann, as does a melodic allusion (see chapter 8). But, as the movement unfolds, its range of topical references turns out to be much wider than that of most minor-key finales composed around 1770. There are no clear signals of Type B. The finales of the two best-known minor-key symphonies of the late eighteenth century—Haydn 45 and Mozart K. 550—belong to neither type. In terms of topic, Mozart 550/iv (chapter 8) shares little with either type aside from driving energy. The main theme is not a sentence but a small binary form, which places the movement closer to sectional, non-sonata-form minor-key finales such as Dittersdorf e1/iv and a2/iv, Vaňhal e3/iv, Ordonez B1/iii, and Haydn 78/iv. Nevertheless, the regularity of the movement's structure at phrase and sectional levels recalls Type B. Haydn 45/iv is deformational, just like the symphony's first movement. The finale responds to the extraordinary conditions set out there and maintained in the next two movements. The understanding of all three finales requires us to take account of a different background: the multi-movement cycle of the particular symphony that they complete.

Studies in Haydn's Minor-Key Symphonies
1763–72

Haydn pursued a distinctive path with his minor-key symphonies of the 1760s and early 1770s. These extraordinary, powerful, and constantly original compositions are more diverse than the minor-key symphonies of any other composer. Haydn relied much less heavily on schematic formal procedures than Vaňhal, and was the only composer in the Habsburg realm to use every well-established convention of the subgenre: the mediant tutti, the contrapuntal minuet, both types of stormy finale, and every kind of untimely rhetoric. The production of these symphonies was spread fairly evenly over nine years, not, as once thought, packed together as a brief, stormy outburst. They most likely date from 1763 (No. 34), 1765 (No. 39), 1768 (Nos. 26 and 49), 1770/71 (No. 44), 1771 (No. 52), and 1772 (No. 45).[1] Remarkably little analytical or critical attention has been paid to them. There are some familiar difficulties for the analyst or interpreter: uncertainties about dating and chronology and lack of evidence for the social function of the works, the identity of patrons, or the composer's intentions. Little remains to us beyond the scores themselves and a few shreds of circumstantial evidence about their performance. The concept of the subgenre is thus indispensable for interpretation, even if, as will become clear, some symphonies respond better to this approach than others.

Few writers have tried to find an overall pattern in Haydn's minor-key symphonies of this period in a way that might make sense of his chronological path and clarify the significance of individual symphonies. The most interesting attempts are those of H. C. Robbins Landon and Daniel Heartz. Both believe that Haydn began from what Landon called the "sonata da chiesa symphony" ("church sonata symphony")—not necessarily in minor—and continued with minor-key symphonies with explicit liturgical associations, before the elements inherited from those works were employed more abstractly after 1770. A church-sonata symphony has a slow first movement, usually an Adagio, which includes wind instruments (internal slow movements in symphonies of the 1760s were almost always Andantes, and

---

[1] Gerlach, "Joseph Haydns Sinfonien bis 1774."

Haydn's are usually scored for strings alone). All the movements of the cycle have a single tonic and some speak with an untimely vocabulary that includes trio-sonata textures, canon, free counterpoint, and slow, chorale-like melodies against faster basslines. The initial slow movements in particular may evoke the serene styles of Corelli or Hasse. Haydn wrote seven such symphonies: Nos. 5, 11, 18, 21, 22, 34, and 49. The first symphony with a minor-key first movement, No. 34 (its other movements are in the tonic major), is of this type, and so is No. 49 (all four movements in F minor). No. 44 begins with a fast movement, but its internal slow movement is an Adagio rather than an Andante and all four of its movements have the same tonic, as in a church-sonata symphony. Two further internal slow movements, 26/ii and 45/ii, are as long, intricate, and expressive as the first movement of a church-sonata symphony.

Despite the more than half a century since its publication, the finest account of Haydn's minor-key symphonies around 1770 remains Landon's *The Symphonies of Joseph Haydn* (1955). For all its obvious faults,[2] which today amount to easy targets for attack, it approaches an adequate verbal response to the extraordinary expressive force of these works. In contrast to his other writings on this period of Haydn's career, in this book Landon relies very little on the concept of "*Sturm und Drang*." His theme instead is Haydn's growth, starting in 1766, to his first "artistic maturity" in 1771–74. The first four minor-key symphonies (Landon's order is 34, 26, 39, 49) are the main path, forming a transitional style.[3] Final maturity is expressed in its "most dramatic and compelling form" in the last three minor-key symphonies (Nos. 52, 44, and 45).[4] The six minor-key symphonies from No. 39 to No. 45 are thus together the "nucleus" of the artistic revival that Haydn undertook in these years.[5] In the face of the prevailing galant style, Haydn revives the artistic legacy of the Renaissance: "art should contain a spiritual message and must breathe it forth with an emotion, so immediate and so powerful that the listener...must perforce grasp its real significance."[6] The idea that music's purpose was more than entertainment can be compared to Donatello's new approach to sculpture.[7] For Landon, each of the transitional minor-key symphonies is imperfect, either carrying weak movements (34/ii, iii, and iv; 39/ii), appearing incomplete or anticlimactic (26), or pushing emotional expression beyond the capabilities of Haydn's current technique (49).[8] But, ironically, his discussion of these works is far longer, more detailed, and

---

[2] These include an imperfect chronology and a liking for evolutionary models of stylistic development. The tone of connoisseurship and the grand analogies between different arts from different centuries will not appeal to everyone.

[3] H. C. Robbins Landon, *The Symphonies of Joseph Haydn* (London: Universal Edition and Rockliff, 1955), 274.

[4] Ibid., 335.

[5] Ibid., 336.

[6] Ibid., 275. Landon attributes this revival to the influence on Haydn of C.P.E. Bach's aesthetics, but without evidence.

[7] Ibid., 275–76.

[8] Ibid., 297.

more eloquent than his accounts of the supposedly more polished Nos. 52, 44, and 45. In the transitional symphonies, Haydn's music is "hesitating" and "experimental," filled with "a nervous questioning, an unhappy, frustrated dissatisfaction," and even at times "an acid bitterness."[9] In particular, Nos. 26 ("Lamentatione") and 49 ("La Passione"), the two symphonies most obviously connected with Holy Week, are the best examples of Haydn trying to "infuse his music with a unifying spiritual and emotional message." Having uncovered the link of No. 26 to a Gregorian melody and a medieval Passion drama (see chapter 4), Landon adds that it is a symphony of "incredibly violent expression," which Haydn never exceeded for tragedy and emotion. With it he turned away from his own present to recollect the "sterner, more severe art forms of the medieval and gothic eras," and with the Passion drama drew on the Reformation spirit too. "The Sinfonia Lamentatione breathes the atmosphere of a Riemenschneider, Grünewald or Adam Krafft."[10] No. 49 is a work of "pathetic, questioning spirit," occasionally sinister, which reaches "a depth of despair and a bleak emotional outlook never again approached, even during the symphonies of 1771–1774."[11] Its very imperfections contribute to "the dark-hued fascination of the F minor Symphony: as we know from the works of many of the Spanish artists, there can be an undeniable strength in something unpolished." The "sombre, majestic beauty" of the first movement has something of Goya in it.[12] It is the first of Haydn's minor-key symphonies with four movements of equal quality, "each driven by the same unifying emotional and spiritual force."[13]

Heartz groups Haydn's church-sonata symphonies and minor-key symphonies under a single heading, charting the transferral of qualities of one to the other. The bridge is No. 34, one of the "last stragglers" of the church-sonata symphony, but at the same time opening with a movement in the minor mode.[14] The next steps are made with the Lenten symphonies Nos. 26 and 49. The final stage is reached with Nos. 44 and 52, where the elements of the church-sonata symphony "have been so sublimated and transformed that only a few devices, mainly in the first movement, remain to remind us of the legacy."[15] Heartz dispenses altogether with the "*Sturm und Drang*" concept. He points out that at this time Haydn was immersed writing serious, large-scale choral music for the church, and he claims that the minor-key symphonies represent a "corollary activity."[16] Landon and Heartz differ on which symphony with normal movement order is the culmination of the series. For Landon it is No. 44, in which "Haydn reached the perfect form that he had so long sought, for the emotional world of the church sonata was successfully transferred

---

[9] Ibid., 274.

[10] Ibid., 292.

[11] Ibid., 298.

[12] Ibid., 299.

[13] Ibid., 297.

[14] Heartz, *Haydn, Mozart and the Viennese School*, 289.

[15] Ibid., 293.

[16] Ibid., 294.

to the almost normal symphonic structure,"[17] the piece being in four movements, all of them serious, with same tonic, the first being fast.[18] For Heartz the culmination is No. 52, in which he finds "a smouldering sense of latent power and unease," "anger and severity…conveyed with unprecedented vehemence."[19] The first movement has the tone of a stern Lenten sermon. Landon and Heartz agree that the last minor-key symphony of the series, No. 45, breaks the pattern. It anticipates Haydn's treatment of the minor mode later in his career, with an emphasis on major keys, in particular the inclusion of more than one entire movement in major. Heartz discusses this symphony in a separate chapter of his book. It bears no trace of the "horrors of hell" that might be the subject of No. 52.[20]

In the Catholic regions of late eighteenth-century Europe, symphonies could be played in church as part of the liturgy. The great Austrian monasteries collected contemporary symphonies in large numbers, including those of Haydn. In Austria, northern Italy, and southern Germany the church-sonata flourished late into the eighteenth century in orchestral guise: trio sonatas performed with several players to a part.[21] Such works contributed a solemn atmosphere, but orchestral symphonies with slow first movements were probably no more likely to be played in church than any other. It appears that almost any symphony could be utilized, its movements dispersed to various positions within the mass, and some movements omitted if necessary, especially the minuet, if there was one.[22] Various Haydn symphonies, minor-key works in particular, have liturgical connections, mainly with Holy Week. Symphony No. 30 in C major ("Alleluia") quotes part of a chant that appeared in the liturgy only once a year, on Holy Saturday. The chants used for the Passion play on which Haydn drew for 26/i were used only on Palm Sunday, Holy Tuesday, Ash Wednesday, and Good Friday, and the Lamentation melody of 26/ii was used only on Maundy Thursday, Good Friday, and Holy Saturday.[23] At Göttweig abbey in Lower Austria between 1774 and 1786, Haydn 49 ("La Passione") was reserved for performance on Passion Sunday (the fifth Sunday in Lent) in the crypt of the abbey church before the exposed holy of holies. Either the first or the second and fourth movements were played (never the minuet), always in combination with the first or second part of Hasse's *Motetto de dolorosa matre "Sparse crino."*[24] Haydn's biographer Giuseppe Carpani, after discussing the

---

[17] Landon, *Symphonies*, 337.

[18] "Almost" normal is because the minuet is placed second.

[19] Heartz, *Haydn, Mozart and the Viennese School*, 292, 293.

[20] Landon, *Symphonies*, 338–39; Heartz, *Haydn, Mozart and the Viennese School*, 354.

[21] Neal Zaslaw, "Mozart, Haydn and the *Sinfonia da Chiesa*," *Journal of Musicology* 1, no. 1 (1982): 102; Kirkendale, *Fugue and Fugato*, 34–35.

[22] Zaslaw, "Mozart, Haydn and the *Sinfonia da Chiesa*," 103–6. See also Friedrich W. Riedel, "Joseph Haydns Sinfonien als liturgische Musik," in *Festschrift Hubert Unverricht zum 65. Geburtstag*, ed. Karlheinz Schlager (Tutzing: Schneider, 1992), 213–20 (p. 216).

[23] According to Neal Zaslaw, in "Mozart, Haydn and the *Sinfonia da Chiesa*," 114.

[24] Riedel, "Joseph Haydns Sinfonien," 216–17. The title "La Passione" is not Haydn's, however; it comes from a source from Schwerin dated 1790. Elaine Sisman draws attention to an alternative title in a Viennese source that refers to a "good-humoured Quaker," and suggests that parts of the work could be heard as lighthearted rather than tragic and that the symphony might have been used for theatrical

Seven Last Words (orchestral sonata-form movements written for performance during Lent in a church in Cádiz), observed:

> Some other of Haydn's symphonies were written for the holy days. They were played in the chapel at Eisenstadt, in the chapel of the Imperial Court, and in other churches on such sacred feast days. They are written in G major, D major, and C minor. In the midst of the sorrow expressed in them, the characteristically Haydnesque vivacity constantly shines through, and here and there are revealed some hints of the anger, with which the author perhaps would take aim at the sinners and the Jews.[25]

Still, if Carpani is to be believed (he is the least reliable of Haydn's contemporary biographers),[26] then from the keys it is clear that symphonies performed on holy days were not restricted to the church-sonata type (none of Haydn's symphonies with slow first movement is in C minor) or to the minor-key subgenre. The symphony in C minor is likely to be No. 52, as it is the most stern of Haydn's three in that key (the others are Nos. 78 and 95, the latter in any case composed for Haydn's first London visit). Given the context (Carpani's account of the *Seven Last Words*), it seems that by "holy days" Carpani means certain days in Lent. It is notable that he counted the seven individual movements of the *Seven Last Words*, all slow, and possibly also the opening *Introduzione* and closing *Il Terremoto*, as "symphonies." The term did not necessarily apply to a four-movement cycle. By "other symphonies" he may thus have been referring to single movements extracted from four-movement cycles.

Instrumental music was formally banned from the liturgy in Holy Week in most Catholic countries, although there was wide variation in local practice.[27] However, not all musical performances in church were part of services. At Melk abbey, for instance, during Holy Week a model of Christ's sepulchre was erected outside the church, where processions took place and instrumental (probably orchestral) music was played.[28] One Viennese minor-key symphony—Vaňhal d2—was performed on Good Friday 1781 in Regensburg Cathedral, presumably not within a service (the specific occasion is not recorded).[29] Neal Zaslaw suggests that Haydn's symphonies for Holy Week may have been composed for the *concerts spirituels* that emerged in Catholic countries to compensate for the lack of opera and other theatrical performances in Lent, and which could have been held within or outside churches.[30]

---

performances. "Haydn's Theater Symphonies," 331–36. It seems unlikely, however, that competent or sensitive musicians of any age could hear this symphony as lighthearted.

[25] Giuseppe Carpani, *Le Haydine, ovvero Lettere sulla vita e le opere del celebre maestro Giuseppe Haydn* (Milan: Buccinelli, 1812), 111; cited and translated in Zaslaw, "Mozart, Haydn and the *Sinfonia da Chiesa*," 113.

[26] Vernon Gotwals, "The Earliest Biographies of Haydn," *Musical Quarterly* 45 (1959): 439–59.

[27] Zaslaw, "Mozart, Haydn and the *Sinfonia da Chiesa*," 115.

[28] Robert N. Freeman, *The Practice of Music at Melk Abbey: Based upon the Documents, 1681–1826* (Vienna: Verlag der Österreichischen Akademie der Wissenschaften, 1989), 178, 463 (Doc. n. 7822a).

[29] According to a note on the Regensburg parts. Bryan, *Johann Wanhal*, 286.

[30] Ibid.

The Parisian model for these concerts mixed sacred vocal music and instrumental music. It thus seems likely that Haydn's minor-key symphonies of the 1760s and 1770s reflect an atmosphere of Lenten sobriety and penitence, even if they were not intended for the liturgy. Perhaps they stood at the periphery of the liturgy as a kind of devotional instrumental music.[31] Their genesis probably had less to do with the composer's midlife crisis or the irrational urges of *Sturm und Drang* than with the steady cycles of the church year and the ingrained behavior patterns of observant Catholics.

The accounts of Landon and Heartz are thus plausible, even if concrete evidence is sparse. They tend to be vague about what exactly was taken from the church-sonata symphony, but their principle of transferral parallels the conclusions of chapter 2 of this book, which showed that the untimely rhetoric of imperial contrapuntal chamber music—much of which consisted of instrumental cycles with slow first movements—was transferred to the symphony precisely in the court composers' works in minor keys. The concept of subgenre allows a more concrete analysis of what exactly was inherited from the church-sonata symphony, how it was combined with other elements, and with what effect. In general, Haydn's music responds well to analysis of this kind. It abounds in allusions to current and past musical styles and conventions, which Haydn manipulates in original ways. The chronological accounts of Landon and Heartz can be refined and updated as follows.

The first symphony by Haydn normally classified as a minor-key work, No. 34, betrays few recognizable subgeneric conventions (it dates from 1763, after all). Three of its movements are in major, including both fast movements, while the slow movement is in minor, in contrast to most slow movements of Viennese minor-key symphonies. At most, that opening slow movement has a distinctive vocabulary of pathos, while the second opens with wide leaps that anticipate those of 49/ii. The next of the series, No. 39, is pivotal in the history of the Viennese minor-key symphony. It has no documented Lenten associations, but it introduces procedures that would become conventions through repetition in the hands of Vaňhal, Haydn himself, and others. Both outer movements are sonata forms that end in minor and avoid closing ritornello effects; both use mediant tuttis; and there is a Type B stormy finale. The minuet is modestly contrapuntal. The outer movements are filled with a nervous energy that Haydn and Vaňhal would continue to exploit, although neither exceeded its effect in 39/i.

In Haydn's next two minor-key symphonies there is evidence of synthesis of the church-sonata and stormy types of symphony represented by Nos. 34 and 39, respectively. Symphonies Nos. 26 and 49, both dating from approximately 1768, carry subtitles with Easter connections in some sources, while both share certain generic conventions with No. 39. The first movement of No. 26 has a mediant tutti (when the violent minor-key syncopations and sighs—representing the scourging of Christ according to Landon—give way to the Passion chant), while the third is

---

[31] Ludwig Finscher, *Joseph Haydn und seine Zeit* (Laaber: Laaber Verlag, 2000), 266.

a contrapuntal minuet. No. 26 is unique among Haydn's minor-key symphonies for its use of chant melodies, dramatic allusions, and three-movement cycle. No. 49 shares with No. 34 the movement order of a church-sonata symphony, but again draws on conventions first used in No. 39. There are two fast sonata-form movements that both gesture towards mediant tuttis, albeit indirectly, a Type B stormy finale, and a contrapuntal minuet. An expressive vocabulary of sigh figures, syncopations, wide leaps, driving rhythms, and dynamic contrasts is deployed extensively.

The three minor-key symphonies Haydn composed between 1770 and 1772 have the standard four-movement cycle, notwithstanding the position of the minuet in No. 44 (second) and the two-part finale of No. 45. None has explicit links with Easter or Lent, but all draw on techniques and conventions established in Nos. 39, 26, and 49. No. 44 has a first-movement mediant tutti, a contrapuntal minuet, and a Type A stormy finale. All its movements have the same tonic and its slow movement is an Adagio, as in a church-sonata symphony. No. 44 encompasses a wide spectrum of musical allusions, both timely and untimely, and Haydn manipulates conventions in complex and subtle ways. The symphony is unique in the extent of its connections with both types of symphony in the subgenre, those cultivated within and outside the imperial court. Of all Viennese minor-key symphonies, this one is most receptive to generic analysis. No. 52 has an oblique gesture to a mediant tutti in the first movement, a contrapuntal minuet, a Type A stormy finale, and, like No. 44, a wide range of allusions to various musical idioms. In comparison with No. 44 it is positioned at a greater distance from the established norms, but the generic approach is still fruitful. Unlike its three immediate precursors (Nos. 26, 49, and 44), however, its slow movement is an Andante. In this respect it returns to the model of No. 39 and moves away from the church-sonata symphony. No. 45 opens in stormy fashion and gestures to a mediant tutti, but after the exposition of the first movement its dialogue with the norms of the subgenre is limited. The work as a whole is exceptional in Haydn's instrumental music. The symphony has no connections with Easter; indeed, as its famous program makes clear, it is a work of the late autumn.

Symphony No. 49 ("La Passione") and the Church-Sonata Symphony

Haydn 49 is one of only three Viennese minor-key symphonies in church-sonata format. All three use the same tonic for all four movements. However, Haydn 34 and Dittersdorf d1 turn to the major mode for their last three movements, whereas Haydn 49 remains in the minor, making it the only Viennese minor-key symphony to have all its movements in the tonic minor. Of Haydn's previous five symphonies with slow first movement, four begin with an Adagio (Nos. 5, 11, 21, and 22), one with an Andante (No. 18). To these can be added the extraordinary No. 15, which opens with a movement in the form Adagio–Presto–Adagio, the third section being a condensed version of the first. The first movements of these symphonies fall into two groups. Those of Nos. 5, 11, 18, and 22 are in duple or quadruple meter and a modern high style: roughly the style of the slow arias of Hasse. The first movements of Nos. 15, 21, 34, and 49

Ex. 5.1

(i) Haydn 21/i, bars 1–4[1]

(ii) Haydn 34/i, bars 1–4

(iii) Haydn 49/i,bars 1–4

are in 3/4 meter. The opening gestures of Nos. 21, 34, and 49 are remarkably similar: groups of quarter notes (or voices moving at quarter-note intervals) in the register
around or just above c[1] (Ex. 5.1).[32] Pedals are also shared, especially inverted.[33] All four
movements have a tendency to break into repeated eighth-note accompaniment figures.
Dittersdorf d1 is from the same stable.

The three minor-key slow first movements, Haydn 34/i, Haydn 49/i, and
Dittersdorf d1/i, avoid characteristic material at the outset and indeed for much of
the movement. This makes for an odd paradox. In the first half of the 1760s, Haydn,
along with most contemporary composers of symphonies, did not follow a long
first movement with an Adagio, presumably because it was thought to require full
concentration. An Adagio was thus available in a symphony only if it was placed
first. But in the first-movement Adagios of Haydn 34/i and Dittersdorf d1/i, the
minimization of characteristic material gives the listener very little to concentrate
on anyway. In this regard the movements anticipate Haydn's later symphonic slow
introductions, which tend to defer characteristic material to the ensuing Allegro.

---

[32] It is tempting to make a link between the turn figure than begins Haydn 49/i (Ex. 5.1(iii)) and
J.S. Bach's melodies for texts that refer to the crucifixion. However, Bach's practice is not found in the
Italian and Austrian sacred music that Haydn is likely to have known.

[33] Compare Haydn 15/i, bars 21–24; 34/i, bars 1–2; and 49/i, bars 1–4 and 7–8[1].

Perhaps in late eighteenth-century terms the markedness of the minor mode against the neutral background of major is enough in itself to give the music shape and significance. There are further parallels between the three movements too (in addition to the similar opening gestures): all deploy a rhetoric of pathos with heavily stressed appoggiaturas, chromatic harmony, weary syncopations near the beginning, the attacks in the treble part coming on offbeats, and a studied approach to a dominant chord to end the first paragraph. In Haydn 34/i and 49/i this dominant occurs early; 34/i repeats it a little later. That repetition, and the parallel passage in Dittersdorf d1/i, resemble the approach to a mediant tutti in a fast movement. Indeed, Haydn 34/i and Dittersdorf d1/i follow the dominant chord with a pause and then a new phrase beginning on III (bars 19 and 14, respectively). In 34/i this new beginning is a sudden forte, just like a mediant tutti, the first forceful gesture of the symphony.[34] All three movements drift into first-violin passagework in sixteenth notes or triplet sixteenth notes over the course of their expositions. Each avoids the combination of initiating function and characteristic motivic shapes, allowing the listener no moment to recognize the entry of a distinctive subordinate theme.

F minor was an unusual key in the late eighteenth century, especially in instrumental music, with very somber associations. In sacred music the key was connected with lamentation for the death of Christ. Vivaldi's *Stabat Mater* has seven of its nine movements in F minor. Pergolesi's *Stabat Mater*, probably the most frequently copied and performed piece of sacred music of the whole eighteenth century, has its first and last movements in F minor, and also its sixth, "Vidit suum," the text of which speaks of Mary watching her son at the moment of his death. This is a pivotal moment in the text, which thereafter turns from descriptions of the scene at Calvary to prayers to the Mother of God. In Haydn's *Stabat Mater* (1767)—his best-known and most widely disseminated work until the 1780s—the "Vidit suum" is in F minor. The dark centerpiece of Haydn's *Seven Last Words*, Sonata V ("Deus meus, Deus meus, utquid dereliquisti me?"), is in F minor too. Vaňhal's *Stabat Mater* begins and ends, like Pergolesi's, with movements in F minor, with one more in the middle ("Fac me vere," not "Vidit suum" in this case, which is omitted in Vaňhal's version of the text). Multi-movement instrumental works in the key include Haydn's String Quartets op. 20, no. 5 (first movement, fugal finale, and minuet), and op. 55, no. 2 (first and second movements and trio), but they are rare. F minor is also the key of Haydn's Variations Hob. XVII/6 and Mozart's two Fantasias for Mechanical Organ, K. 594 and K. 608. At least one and probably both of the Mozart Fantasias were composed for a commercial pseudo-mausoleum dedicated to the deceased Austrian Field Marshall Gideon von Laudon. Both deploy an untimely rhetoric, which in K. 608 includes fugue.[35]

---

[34] It is not a literal tutti, but that is probably simply because in this work the horns are crooked in the tonic, not the mediant.

[35] Aside from Haydn 49 and Vaňhal f1, the only Viennese symphony in F minor from this time is Ordonez F12, but that work is not pathos-filled and seems independent of the F-minor topos.

Eighteenth- and early nineteenth-century writings on "key characteristics" were in closer agreement on F minor than on any other key, their associations with mourning and grief remaining unchanged over several generations. In general, the more flats in a minor-mode key signature, the more negative the associations in the eighteenth century (all the minor-key movements in the works listed above have flat key signatures).[36] Eighteenth-century key signatures almost never carry more than four flats, so F minor was the negative extreme.

The mood of the opening Adagio of Haydn 49 is somber but also highly expressive, full of appoggiaturas and syncopations that evoke sighs and sobbing. The syncopations at the approach to cadences (bars 11–13, 39–42) are stereotypical in eighteenth-century minor-key sacred music, appearing frequently, for instance, at cadences in Pergolesi's *Stabat Mater*. They suggest trudging or stumbling on the *via crucis*.[37] The exposition withholds characteristic material at moments when a phase of initiating function might be expected. The brooding sixteenth-note neighbor-note figures of bars 15–18 and the conventional arpeggio figuration at bars 25–29, the latter just where the presentation phrase of a subordinate theme is expected, direct attention to the mood and mode rather than the motivic shapes presented, as though the minor mode itself were a distinctive "shape." The dramatic pauses (bars 32 and 33) and shifts in register that follow (bars 34–36) are hyper-dramatic, resembling accompanied recitative. The emotional atmosphere arises from the intensive use of a conventional eighteenth-century vocabulary of musical pathos combined with the minimization of any sense of a dramatic succession of events such as thematic "entries." The movement invites a meditative response, a reflection on symbols of suffering presented within a sonata-form framework. For Landon, "In the Adagio of No. 49, we seem to sense the winding line of penitents before the Cross."[38]

In the recapitulation of Haydn 49/i the rhetoric is intensified further by the interpolation of a new passage that extends the final perfect authentic cadential progression. The harmony and melody are far more unstable than is usual in a cadence: there is even a tonicization of VI (bars 87–90). The analogy with accompanied recitative is even closer here. Few slow movements of the time adopt this kind

---

[36] Rita Steblin, *A History of Key Characteristics in the Eighteenth and Early Nineteenth Centuries* 2nd ed. (Rochester, NY: University of Rochester Press, 2002), 154, 262–66. See also the summary table of Steblin's results in Gretchen A. Wheelock, "*Schwarze Gredel* and the Engendered Minor Mode in Mozart's Operas," in *Musicology and Difference: Gender and Sexuality in Music Scholarship*, ed. Ruth A. Solie (Berkeley: University of California Press, 1992), 201–24 (p. 208). Sir William Jones in 1772 wrote that F minor was "pathetic and mournful to the highest degree, for which reason it was chosen by the excellent Pergolesi in his 'Stabat Mater'." For Heinrich Weikert (1828), F minor was the key of "extreme grief, deep depression, funereal lament, misery, and the grave." Steblin, *History of Key Characteristics*, 154, 264.

[37] Rosemary Hughes may be responding to this sign when she observes that "the leaden-footed opening *adagio*...might well depict the *via crucis*." *Haydn*, The Master Musicians, rev. ed. (London: Dent, 1978), 176.

[38] Landon, *Chronicle*, 2:290. Peter Kivy somewhat overemphasizes the variety of moods in the exposition of Haydn 49/i, at least when the movement is heard against the background of other minor-key symphony first movements. Kivy, *Osmin's Rage*, 229.

of strategy in their recapitulations, although Dittersdorf d1/i is a significant exception. Haydn did something similar in several fast movements from symphonies at this time, such as 52/i (see below) and 43/iv (in major).

Haydn 49/i is distinctive for a symphonic slow movement of the time in that its organization resembles that of first movements and of minor-key first movements in particular. The forte tutti on III in bar 25 resembles a mediant tutti (though it is not immediately preceded by a dominant harmony or a pause); the movement's structure is clearly articulated by means of texture, dynamics, and harmonic rhythm; and there are caesuras in the continuation of the subordinate theme, just as, for instance, in the second half of a typical Vaňhal first-movement exposition. The dramatic interjection just after the start of the recapitulation (bars 65–69) follows the principle of secondary development in a fast movement, turning momentarily to the flat side of the tonic for an unstable passage. The general avoidance of lyricism in presentation phrases, the abundance of conventional material, and the focus on process and drama is more typical of fast than slow movements at this time.

A further distinctive—indeed unique—aspect of the form is the treatment of the moment of reprise. The extraordinary, harmonically all but ungrammatical interpolation of two bars that tonicize C minor (v) between the C major chord (V) at the end of the development and the start of the recapitulation (i) is well known to Haydn scholars.[39] What has not been pointed out is that the next five bars are also an interpolation of a kind. If they, along with the preceding C minor phrase, were eliminated, the second half of the movement (development plus recapitulation) would follow exactly the order of materials of the exposition from the start of the main theme at bar 7 (Fig. 5.1). The first six bars of Haydn 49/i function as a kind of introduction (their harmony is simply tonic pedal followed by a pause on the dominant), even though their opening gesture anticipates the one that starts the main theme at bar 7. The five bars at the start of the recapitulation correspond to those first six introductory bars. The main theme itself (bars 7–14), which proceeds through initiating, medial, and concluding functions, is found nowhere in the second half of the movement after the statement in III immediately after the double bar (bars 44–51). Thus, the form has close affinities with what Hepokoski and Darcy call a "Type 2" sonata, that is, a sonata-form movement with only two rotations of its thematic contents, the second rotation starting like a development section with the main theme (they would call it "P") outside the tonic, before the subordinate theme or themes ("S") return in the tonic. In a Type 2 sonata there is no tonic reprise of the main theme, and Hepokoski and Darcy insist that it is wrong to speak of a recapitulation at all.[40] In Haydn 49/i, to be sure, the clearly articulated dominant arrival at bar 59 and the caesura strongly imply an imminent reprise of the main theme in the tonic, and the return of the opening bars, with their motivic link to the main theme, does fulfill this role. The movement is probably best regarded as a Type 2 / Type 3 hybrid (Type 3 being the familiar sonata form with

---

[39] Webster, *Haydn's "Farewell" Symphony*, 262–67.

[40] Hepokoski and Darcy, *Elements of Sonata Theory*, 353–55.

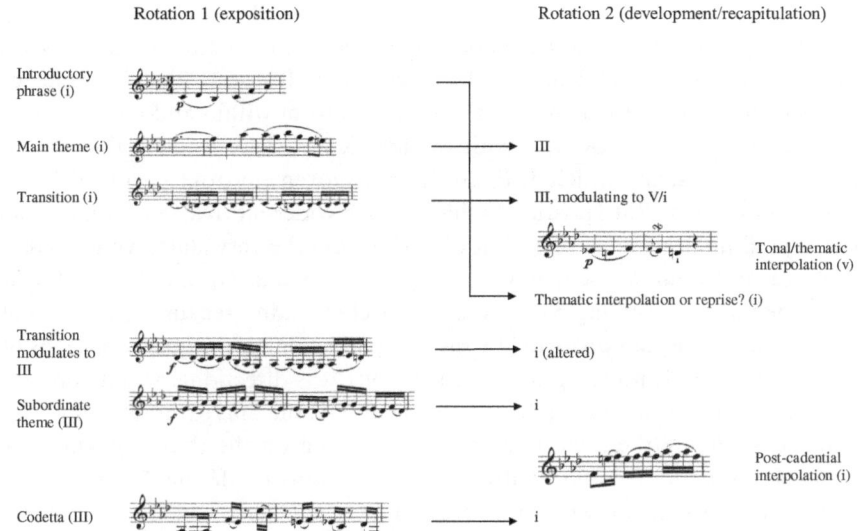

FIGURE. 5.1 Haydn 49/i, rotational structure.

three rotations, including development and tonic recapitulation), that alludes to the standard procedures of both. This unusual strategy reflects the generic ambivalence of Haydn 49/i as an opening slow movement with some formal characteristics of an opening fast movement. The reprise of the movement's opening bars in the tonic sustains the dramatic character and clear formal articulation typical of fast first movements, while the existence of only two thematic rotations sustains momentum that otherwise might be lost given the slow tempo, minimization of characteristic material, and gloomy atmosphere.

The last three movements of Haydn 49, also in F minor, all have a negative emotional character, but otherwise they are quite varied, encompassing anger, frustration, melancholy, and restlessness (the third and fourth were discussed in chapter 4). It is possible to detect motivic links between the start of all four movements and between the treatment of the approach to the recapitulation in the two outer movements,[41] but also easy to overstate the significance of inter-movement unity. These movements still unfold primarily against a background of other symphony movements of their type. From the perspective of generic analysis, then, the second movement of Haydn 49 can be treated as a type of first movement.

Haydn 49/ii is a typical stormy fast movement, as nervous and energetic as 39/i but with an almost relentless *perpetuum-mobile* eighth-note pulse. This dynamism is not reflected on higher levels, however. The form is block-like on the medium scale and even the small, the constructive principle paratactic, and on the large scale the movement is thematically repetitive. The exposition falls into three parts, the development three, and the recapitulation two, all neatly separated by caesuras,

---

[41] See Landon, *Chronicle*, 2:290; and Webster, *Haydn's "Farewell" Symphony*, 262–67.

while there are no caesuras within those paragraphs. The overall structure is quite strictly rotational, the development presenting its materials in the same order as the exposition. Haydn 49/ii shares with Type B stormy finales a tendency to repeat short units rather than expand phrases from within and a fast surface rhythm combined with slow harmonic rhythm. As in a Type B finale, the result is an impression of stasis, which distinguishes the movement from a typical Haydn fast first movement. But Haydn 49/ii has a much wider motivic vocabulary than most Type B finales, and reveals that diversity from the very start, while there is also more contrapuntal independence of parts than is usual in a Type B finale. At the opening, the running bass against the treble minims recalls the textures of Corellian high style, but distorted by the fast tempo and grotesque, wide leaps of the melody. There is no letup to this energy, yet it is directionless and confined within schematic formal units; the movement as a whole thus expresses only frustration. Continuing the line of interpretation taken on the third movement in chapter 4, an analogy could be drawn with the souls of the lustful in Dante's hell: they are eternally blown about here and there in a fierce wind (revealing also their true condition in life).

Symphony No. 44 ("Trauersymphonie")

With the majestic Symphony No. 44 Haydn reverts to a four-movement form with fast outer movements, although with the minuet placed second. However, he retains the monotonal scheme of No. 49 (all movements have the tonic E, the third being in E major). For its time the symphony is exceptionally varied in its vocabulary and generic allusions. No. 44 realizes the tragic plot more strongly than any other Viennese minor-key symphony, with all three of its minor-mode movements contributing. The finale is the only unambiguous Type B finale in a minor-key symphony by a composer not associated with the imperial court. The first movement is a *tour de force* of allusion, implication, and the sophisticated handling of conventions. It is situated more ambiguously within the subgenre, evoking both untimely and modern types—that is, respectively, the symphonies of the imperial court composers and the strand represented by Haydn 39 and Vaňhal's symphonies to the late 1760s—as well as a third type, the Lenten symphony developed by Haydn in Nos. 26 and 49. Both exposition and recapitulation leave it very late to reveal the final direction they will take. The movement's strategy rests on allowing questions to remain open for as long as possible as to the real significance of its materials and of what kind of movement it is. Only in the second half of the recapitulation is the tragic plot realized, unambiguously and irreversibly.

The tonic section of the exposition of Haydn 44/i is itself unusually varied, and leaves the significance of its sharply contrasted materials ambiguous. It has two parts, the first ending with a half cadence (bars 10–11), the second eventually modulating to III and eliding with the mediant tutti (bar 20). Both parts begin with the two-bar figure *a* in octave unison. The opening fits a pattern of unison openings in the symphonies of imperial court composers that suggest ritornellos.[42] The soft semitone figures and chromaticism in bars 2–4 reveal the mode to be minor, but lessen the implication of ritornello. By remaining unharmonized, they allow further ambiguities, such as whether the C on the first beat of bar 3 is an appoggiatura. If it is, then its motive is a sigh figure and the first four bars follow, in highly condensed form, the same order in which materials are presented at the opening of Haydn 26/i (bars 1–12): stark, loud octave gestures followed by soft sighs. The exaggerated internal contrast of the first four bars suggests various possible modes of organization, but the lack of harmony means that none is strongly implied at this stage. The varied repetition of *b* implies sequential procedure that could form the tail of a fugue (*a* being the head) or the continuation of a potential sentence (both presentation and continuation would require some expansion for this implication to be convincingly realized). There is nothing to imply that this is not a bassline, and with only a few modifications it could become a *lamento* bass, from $\hat{8}$ to $\hat{5}$. Which of these implications is realized and how that realization occurs will be significant as the movement unfolds.[43]

Bars 5–8 switch the generic allusion. They present a complete contrast, not just in the concrete terms of melodic figures, articulation, and texture, but in syntactic precision. This is an unambiguous statement-response repetition of the two-bar basic idea *b*. These bars are remarkably close to the lyrical style of Vaňhal—the closest Haydn ever approaches it in a minor-key symphony. Compare the presentations of the main themes of Vaňhal e3/i (Ex. 3.2), e1/i (Ex. 3.3), and c2/i (Ex. 3.5), two of them in the same key as Haydn 44/i. All three of those symphonies were definitely composed earlier than Haydn 44, so in this case there is no question of imitation on Vaňhal's part. In Haydn 44/i the presentation is based on Vaňhal's favorite Do–Re–Mi schema. The repeated-note accompaniment, first-beat appoggiaturas, and above all the anacrusis on the last beat of bar 4 are likewise familiar from Vaňhal. Haydn seldom begins the main theme of the first movement of a symphony with an anacrusis, as here, whereas Vaňhal often did. The approach to the dominant chord in bar 12 with the articulation of the semitones above and below b^1 recalls many outer movements of Vaňhal symphonies of the late 1760s, although also of course Haydn 39/i. The only aspect of Haydn's theme that is uncharacteristic of Vaňhal is the transferral of the repeated-note accompaniment to the horn in bars 6 and 8 (Vaňhal almost never asks even this much from his horn players). At

---

[42] There are, however, other unison openings in Haydn's major-key symphonies around 1770, especially in combination with soft phrases (46/i, 51/i, 52/i, 56/i) as well as other cases of internal contrasts and "double announcement" of the opening idea. Landon's *Symphonies*, 317–19. The rising $\hat{1}$–$\hat{5}$–$\hat{8}$ recalls the *tromba* figure that opens many eighteenth-century symphonies and concerts, but with the third omitted. On the tromba in Haydn 46/i, see Michael Spitzer, "Haydn's Reversals: Style Change, Gesture and the Implication-Realization Model," in *Haydn Studies*, ed. W. Dean Sutcliffe (Cambridge: Cambridge University Press, 1998), 177–217 (pp. 202–6).

[43] A. Peter Brown is alert to the ambiguities of the opening of Haydn 44/i and the need for later clarification. *The Symphonic Repertoire*, vol. 2, *The First Golden Age of the Viennese Symphony: Haydn, Mozart, Beethoven and Schubert* (Bloomington and Indianapolis: Indiana University Press, 2002), 124–26.

bar 12 it would seem that the symphony is not to follow ritornello procedures after all, but will be a modern piece in stormy style. A mediant tutti seems likely to follow the half cadence. Retrospectively, the first four bars now acquire a further potential interpretation: as a short frame for the sonata movement proper like the one that opens Vaňhal e3/i (Ex. 3.1(ii))—another unharmonized phrase in E minor.

Yet this interpretation does not quite fit Haydn 44/i. Bars 1–4 are more rhythmically and dynamically varied than the opening of Vaňhal e3/i, and already have traces of theme-like syntax. Indeed, there are striking parallels between the continuation of Haydn's Vaňhal-like theme (bars 9–12) and bars 3–4: both have the shape c^2–b^1–$a\sharp^1$–b^1, adopt the hesitant approach to the dominant note via semitones and end with a pause. At this stage, retrospectively, one might even notice a parallel between the apparently contrasted initial ideas of the two units: the E–D$\sharp$ motives at the start of the second bars of each (bars 2 and 6). A further interpretation of the relationship between the two units thus becomes plausible: they can be regarded as contrasting "subrotations"—to use the term quite loosely—that move through two phases of materials in the order *ac; bb1c1*, where *a* and *b* are largely, though not entirely, contrasted basic ideas and *c* and *c1* are related continuations (Table 5.1). The significance of this interpretation—still reckoning from the pause in bar 12—is that the statement-response presentation of bars 5–8 seems less likely to have ushered in a Vaňhal-like modern, lyrical movement, and the first four bars seem less like a frame, and more like thematic content.

This interpretation is strengthened by what happens after the pause in bar 12 (Subrotation 3). There is no immediate mediant tutti. Instead, the second part of the tonic section of the exposition begins with an exact repetition of *a* (bars 13–14) followed by sigh figures (bars 15–17; *c2* in Table 5.1), now harmonized and with embellishments similar to those in 26/i (bars 9–12). After a two-bar modulating transition comes the delayed mediant tutti (bar 20); *a*, now in the bass, is followed by a less embellished version of the continuation figure (Subrotation 4). By bar 24 the rotational interpretation of the beginning of the exposition seems still more plausible, and *a* is clearly the central motivic component in the movement's argument, not part of a frame. The short mediant tutti paragraph (bars 20–25^1) is elided

TABLE 5.1 Haydn 44/i, subrotational structure of exposition

Subrotation	Contents	Key / Harmony	Bars	Notes
1	*ac*	i: i–V	1–4^3	frame?
2	*bb1c1*	i: i–V	4^4–12	main theme?
3	*ac2*	i modulating to III	13–19	
4	*ac3*	III: I–I	20–25^1	mediant tutti paragraph
5	*aaak*	III: I–I	25–53	subordinate theme

a: see Ex. 5.2(i).

a: first two notes of a.

b: basic idea of Vaňhal-style statement-response presentation.

c: continuation.

k: alternative continuation.

with the start of Subrotation 5, which is organized as a subordinate theme (in III, a very loosely organized, thirty-one-bar sentence; bars 25–55). There is a good deal of variation here; the presentation consists of three statements of only the first two notes of *a* in various octaves, while the continuation is quite different from all previous versions, being far longer and more varied. The exposition nevertheless consists of five subrotations, four of them beginning with *a*. It thus has much in common with Haydn's "monothematic" expositions that use the same basic idea for main and subordinate themes. From this broader perspective, Subrotation 2—the one with the Vaňhal-like presentation that lacks any reference to *a*—is the exception, not the framed content (see Table 5.1).

The music after the mediant tutti sends conflicting generic signals at first. The rushing sixteenth notes in the first violin part clearly recall the mediant tutti of Haydn 26/i, where eighth-note figuration covers the second violins' statement of the Passion chant (26/ii also has this texture, with much slower figuration, for its Lamentation chant). In Haydn 44/i the texture at the tutti is more like two-part counterpoint with *a* in the bass, starting with *cantus-firmus*-like minims beneath the fast upper part (although the first two leaps amount to a full octave, wider than permitted in the Palestrina style). This texture had many antecedents in grand Viennese concerted sacred music of the mid-eighteenth century—including some of Haydn's early masses—set in what Heartz calls the "Habsburger Prunkstil," evoking the splendor of the ruling dynasty and the Catholic Church at once. In fast movements in this style, a chant melody or vocal parts in pure Palestrina counterpoint could be accompanied by fast violin passagework, known as "rauschende Violinen à la Reutter" after the compositions of Georg Reutter, organist and Kapellmeister at St. Stephen's Cathedral, Kapellmeister to the Imperial court, and the man who plucked Haydn from obscurity as a child and coached him as a cathedral choirboy.[44] There is no doubt, then, that the mediant tutti of Haydn 44/i signifies a sudden turn to celebration. A few bars earlier the sigh version of *c* (*c2*), by evoking parallels with 26/i, had pointed in the direction of a Lenten symphony; now the mediant tutti strengthens these ecclesiastical associations but takes them in a more positive direction. During Subrotation 4 the symphony seems more likely to turn out as a successor to Haydn 26 and 49 than a piece resembling those of Wagenseil, Gassmann, or Ordonez or one similar to Haydn 39 or those of Vaňhal. The turn to the subordinate key (III) seems to be coordinated with this new subgeneric clarification.

In fact, there is a further twist to this exposition, which takes it in yet another direction: away from all untimely and ecclesiastical references to modern style instead. Subrotation 5, which eventually proves to be the exposition's subordinate theme, starts with the two-part counterpoint of the mediant tutti inverted, but proceeds thereafter in a quite different way, turning to modern modes of organization and expression in its expansive continuation (*k* in Table 5.1; bar 28). Although the sixteenth-note surface rhythm and basic two-part texture are retained, the circle of fifths progression that begins *k* signals that this continuation will be longer than

---

[44] Heartz, *Haydn, Mozart and the Viennese School*, 82.

the previous four. The harmonic rhythm slows at this point, and in effect slows even further in bars 35–38, which prolong the local tonic with alternating dominant chords and a two-bar *Molleinschub* in bars 37–38. Despite the local major mode, then, this section in some ways resembles the minor-key style of Vaňhal once again: slow harmonic rhythm coexists with fast surface rhythm and conventional material to the point of a *perpetuum mobile*, while the accompaniment reverts to *Trommelbass* for the first time since the Vaňhal-like Subrotation 2. The movement's untimely rhetoric, first evoked in the second part of the tonic section, thus does not in the end survive the exposition's change of key and mode. There are parallels here with the exposition of Vaňhal g2/i (chapter 3).

The shift to modern style and syntax is paradoxically confirmed when *a* returns at the end of the *perpetuum mobile* (bars 42–43). This is not the start of another subrotation. Instead of a unison statement, this one begins above a suspended dissonance in the bass leading to first inversion tonic harmony, signaling the likely approach of the cadence of the subordinate theme. (Cadential progressions often begin with first inversion tonic harmony, which can act for the listener as a cue.) The initial tonic of the cadential progression is expanded by means of a linear intervallic pattern in parallel tenths (bars 43–46).[45] Within the expansion, the embellished version of *c* that earlier in the exposition (bars 15–17) recalled the sigh figures of 26/i is fragmented, now of course in the major mode rather than the minor (bars 44–46). Residues of the Lenten symphony reappear here but with symbolic corrections comparable to the melodic dips in the continuation of the subordinate theme of Vaňhal e1/i (chapter 3), summarizing in a few bars the overall process of the exposition. Even the caesuras of the tonic section of the exposition return, but integrated into the harmonic flow. When the cadential I^6 is recaptured (bar 47), the accompaniment reverts to *Trommelbass* and the rhythm to the second-beat accents of the galant style that have been absent since the Vaňhal-like *b* of Subrotation 2. This is an unambiguously modern conclusion to the exposition.

At this point the question arises as to whether the shift of rhetoric and organization in the modern direction will be sustained in the recapitulation, which—assuming the movement follows the usual pattern for sonata-form outer movements of minor-key symphonies at this time—will remain in the tonic minor. To this date only Haydn 26/i had turned to major, which, although a potential model for 44/i, is exceptional on account of the liturgical chant used for its subordinate theme, which could hardly have tolerated modal reversal.

The development keeps both modern and untimely elements in play, but places special emphasis on the celebratory ecclesiastical aspect. It is rotationally orthodox, keeping to the order of materials of the exposition, although selectively: *a* (presented twice, in descending sequence, each time with a new version of the continuation *c*); the Vaňhal-like *b* (in statement-response form, but immediately repeated

---

[45] On the initial tonic as a cue and on its expansion, see Caplin, *Classical Form*, 111. Charles Rosen's identification of bar 42 as the start of a new section in a three-part exposition is unconvincing. The subordinate theme continues until the cadential arrival at the start of bar 53. *Sonata Forms*, 100–105.

sequentially); the "rauscheder Violine" from the mediant tutti (initially with *a* in the bass); and a modified version of part of *k*. This scheme allows generous exposure to the "rauschender Violine" figuration, which in the exposition was cut short by the sudden cadence of Subrotation 4.

The recapitulation likewise follows the order of materials of the exposition, and at 57 bars it is, in clock time, the same length as the exposition. But it moves through those materials twice, the second iteration being a decisive reinterpretation of their significance and of the movement. The recapitulation thus has obvious rotational characteristics—*a* appears precisely twice as an initiating function and on each occasion is followed by continuation and cadential functions—although the second iteration begins as an interruption of the cadential progression of the first, which thus in functional terms remains unfinished and is completed only with the perfect authentic cadence at the end of the second. The recapitulation makes a complementary selection of exposition materials to that of the development: it foregrounds materials from the lengthy *k* that were neglected in the development, while, on the other hand, there is no allusion to the "rauschender Violine." Like the development, the recapitulation is more continuous than the exposition, but its materials are more various, with less spinning out. The recapitulation moves through the exposition's materials twice within the same space of time by means of synecdoche, allowing parts to stand for wholes.[46] Conceived as a response to the exposition, the first part of the recapitulation is relatively neutral. The uniform minor mode makes the mood generally somber and the greater continuity is reinforced by gestures of vehemence, but in the continuous sweep of energy neither the untimely nor the modern, and neither pathos nor celebration, is clearly favored.

A crisis occurs that breaks the neutrality and decisively realizes the tragic plot. The cadential progression (corresponding to the one that ends the exposition's subordinate theme) fails to reach a final tonic. The cadence is evaded and a subsequent repetition is blocked by a rising sequence that ends on a half-note diminished seventh chord in strings alone marked with a pause and "tenuto" (bar 140). The reinterpretation now occurs with the second appearance of *a* in initiating guise, presented as a fugato in three parts, the texture moreover saturated with descending chromatic lines and, in the first violin part, sighing appoggiaturas (bars 141–46). The potential of *a* and *c* to form, respectively, the head and tail of a fugue subject is finally realized. This moment combines and intensifies both objective and subjective, fateful and pathetic dimensions of the untimely rhetoric of the exposition: the only un-modern aspect that is altogether omitted is the celebratory "rauschender Violine" of the mediant tutti. The rhetoric is similar to that of the opening of Vaňhal g2/i, although in a quite different formal position and with different strategic significance. This is the critical moment of the first movement, the point at which the various twists and turns finally abate and the movement's generic

---

[46] See Hepokoski and Darcy, *Elements of Sonata Theory*, 233.

affiliations are specified. The recapitulatory rotation is symbolically halted before its completion and an alternative version of the initiating material substituted, as though correcting the first, a version that corresponds to nothing in the exposition. The rest of the recapitulation moves through much of the same materials as the earlier part, though more swiftly, reaching the *perpetuum mobile* in only its seventh bar and restarting the cadential progression only two bars after that. As an answer to the exposition, the recapitulation not only stays in the minor mode—that much could be predicted with reasonable confidence—but coordinates the uniformity of minor mode with a symbolic reversal of the exposition's drift to modern rhetoric and syntax. The recapitulation sets the tone for the rest of the symphony. The second and fourth movements pursue the contrapuntal dimension much further and realize the tragic plot, and the second takes up the rhetoric of lament.[47]

Haydn 44/iv is a spectacular movement, the stormiest of all minor-key finales. Its surface rhythm, however, is not especially fast—tremolando is used sparingly—and even the harmonic rhythm is often relatively slow. Its energy comes from its contrapuntal textures, its sequential processes, and, above all, its formal continuity. The main theme is based on the Do–Re–Mi schema familiar from the first movement,[48] and that underlying stepwise motion later permeates the textures in the guise of ascending and descending sequences. Continuity is found also in the organization of the exposition, in the presence of a retransition at the end of the exposition before the repeat (and a parallel transition at the end of the recapitulation) and in the avoidance of a reprise of the main theme when the tonic key returns halfway through the second half of the movement. The movement only hints at a mediant tutti in the midst of a rising sequence (bar 23), and there is no clear articulation of a medial caesura, making this exposition literally "continuous" in the technical sense of Hepokoski and Darcy.[49] Twice V/III is touched on at the end of a phrase (bars 28 and 37), but medial caesura-type rhetoric is avoided in favor of sequences on both sides of the gaps, which themselves are filled by inner part motion. No new phase of initiating function is articulated after these dominant arrivals. Indeed, there are only two initiating gestures in the exposition, at the very opening and at bar 19, and the latter quickly turns out to be the start of an eight-bar sequence and thus ultimately continuational in function. In the development, an extraordinary storm is blown up by means of extensive stepwise sequences, rising and falling at different rates.

---

[47] Landon notes that "In a way that canonic passage [bars 141–46] is a hint of things to come." *Chronicle*, 2:298.

[48] The pattern is at first obscured by a higher voice in the compound melody moving $\hat{3}$–$\hat{4}$–$\hat{5}$, but the underlying schema is clear when the bass enters in bars 9–12 with its usual $\hat{8}$–$\hat{7}$–$\hat{8}$.

[49] Hepokoski and Darcy, *Elements of Sonata Theory*, 51–52. The central section of the exposition (bars 19–50) is neither a subordinate theme nor even a mediant tutti paragraph, as it begins in the tonic. In English this type of section in Haydn is sometimes called an "expansion section." Jens Peter Larsen's original term was *Entwicklungspartie*; see "Sonata Form Problems," in *Handel, Haydn, and the Viennese Classical Style*, 269–79. On later literature and the English translation of the term, see Hepokoski and Darcy, *Elements of Sonata Theory*, 51–52.

As an unambiguous Type A stormy finale, Haydn 44/iv is all but unique among minor-key-symphony finales of composers not associated with the imperial court. It decisively crosses a boundary in that regard, explicitly evoking a repertory that most symphonies of Haydn, Vaňhal, and Dittersdorf recall only indirectly. Its counterpoint is of instrumental rather than vocal origin, placing it, within Type A, closer to movements such as Ordonez F12/iv and G8/iii (Ex. 2.11) than Wagenseil G5/iii (Ex. 2.2) or Gassmann 45/iv (Ex. 2.6(i)). Like both Ordonez finales, Haydn 44/iv begins with a quarter-note upbeat followed by further quarter notes in its first phrase. The main theme, like Subrotation 1 in the first movement, is first presented in unharmonized octaves. As in the first movement, there is an obvious parallel with the ritornello-like unison openings of minor-key fast movements of the imperial composers (Wagenseil G4/i and G5/i, Gassmann 83/iv, Ordonez G7/iv).

At the end of the finale the untimely rhetoric is heightened in a coda to create an ominous and fateful minor-mode ending. A fragmented version of the opening theme returns loudly in octaves on dominant ninth harmony with pauses between the short melodic snatches (bars 167–74), recalling rhetorically heightened unison or octave endings that use similar techniques in Gassmann 23/i and 83/iv (chapter 2), and, more generally, octave or unison gestures that do not merely parallel the end of the exposition in Gassmann 45/i and 83/i (versions of the main theme), 45/iv (other exposition material), and Ordonez G7/i and F12/iv (entirely new material). In many of these passages the uniformity of texture is complemented by other kinds of uniformity (rhythmic or harmonic) or by liquidation of characteristic features, all emphasizing closure. In Haydn 44/iv a similar principle is followed, and, given the abundant linear motions and stepwise sequences of the movement, it stands out even more. There is a departure from the imperial models, however, for the close of this finale has a final twist. After the unison phrases, the melody of the main theme moves to the bass for a final, stormy, fully harmonized version. Closure is signaled by the omission of the $\hat{3}$ in the original Do–Re–Mi schema. The lowest voice in the compound melody now moves $\hat{1}$–$\hat{2}$–$\hat{1}$ and an alternative pattern emerges: $\hat{3}$–$\hat{4}$–$\hat{5}$–$\hat{1}$ (repeated once). A stepwise model is replaced by a cadential progression, which finally halts the seemingly unstoppable linear motion of the finale, substituting a representation of circling motion. Heightened untimely rhetoric is here combined with exaggerated signals of closure and uniformity.

There is no "double return" of main theme and tonic key midway through the second part of the finale. Allusion to the main theme in the second part of the movement does not occur until the coda. Nevertheless, during the second part there is a clearly articulated return of tonic key and root position tonic harmony, following a long dominant pedal and coordinated with a change of texture and dynamics (bar 119). The emphatic figure played by the violins at that moment, rising through the E minor triad, has not appeared previously in the finale, but recalls the opening of the first movement. Yet, despite this articulation, continuity is still uppermost: there has already been a partial return of exposition material in the tonic key (over a V pedal). This displacement of textural and tonal returns—not to mention the complete absence of a thematic return at this point—obscures section boundaries.

Timothy Jackson has cited Haydn 44/iv as an early example of the "tragic reversed recapitulation" in a Central European tradition extending to Mahler. According to his argument, around 1770 *chiasmus*-like thematic ordering became rare in sonata forms, and recapitulations usually preserved the order of materials of the exposition. At this point the deferral of the tonic presentation of main theme ("first group") until after the subordinate theme materials ("second group"), previously a fairly common procedure, assumed the status of a deformation. Movements that take this course are usually in minor keys, and often have a tragic program or other associations (Haydn 44 is subtitled "Trauersymphonie," although the origin of this name is unclear).[50] Hepokoski and Darcy, by contrast, class Haydn 44/iv as a "Type 2 sonata," a double-rotational form in which the second part begins as a development, but thereafter only the subordinate theme or equivalent returns in the tonic. Because of their emphasis on the order in which thematic materials are presented—an order that cannot be reversed—they maintain that a Type 2 sonata has no recapitulation at all. The second and final rotation begins with the allusion to the main theme at the start of the second part. They regard the basic Type 2 sonata as one without a coda, as found for instance in many keyboard sonatas by Domenico Scarlatti and some by C.P.E. Bach. If, in a movement of this type, a coda appears that alludes to the main theme, then it is an addition to the basic scheme, not an underlying norm. "From the standpoint of midcentury generic practice, at least, there was no widely shared, compelling urge to shore up any 'missing' P [main theme] in the second rotation with a P-based coda."[51]

But the keyboard music of Domenico Scarlatti and C.P.E. Bach is of no immediate relevance to Viennese minor-key symphonies. When the focus is shifted to the subgenre in the 1760s and early 1770s, the background of generic norms changes. The only minor-key outer movements in the subgenre before Haydn 44/iv to adopt Hepokoski and Darcy's basic Type 2 model—two rotations, no return of the main theme in the tonic, no coda—are the outer movements of Vaňhal c3, a work that survives in only one source and was therefore probably not well disseminated, and that, on the evidence of its style, might not even be by Vaňhal. Gassmann was the only Viennese composer before Haydn 44/iv consistently to omit a tonic return for the main theme halfway through the second part of minor-key outer movements. (Neither Wagenseil nor Ordonez ever did it.) Among Gassmann's three minor-key symphonies, four outer movements have no tonic return of the main theme halfway through the second part. But all four allude to the main theme near the end: in a coda after a perfect authentic cadence in the tonic or shortly before. No sonata-form outer movement in the subgenre lacks a tonic allusion to the main

---

[50] Timothy L. Jackson, "The Tragic Reversed Recapitulation in the German Classical Tradition," *Journal of Music Theory 40*, no. 1 (1996): 61–111 (pp. 67–70). There is no evidence to support the claim that Haydn chose the slow movement for performance at his funeral.

[51] Hepokoski and Darcy, *Elements of Sonata Theory*, 382. Their position is delicate, as they reject the theoretical concept of "reversed recapitulation" as a "fallacy," while admitting that the return of the main theme as a coda was an "attractive option" to composers as it fills what may increasingly have been felt as an absence. Ibid., 382, 385.

theme in the recapitulation. For instance—to reiterate points made in chapter 2—in the second half of Gassmann 23/i the main theme returns in the tonic only after the exposition's subordinate-key materials have returned in that key. It is followed by rhetorical dotted chords and finally a variant of the melody of the main theme in octaves. In Hepokoski and Darcy's terms, this movement has only two thematic rotations, but from a more traditional theoretical viewpoint would be said to have a reversed recapitulation. Gassmann 83/iv follows a very similar path. Gassmann 45/i is a little more complicated. In the exposition the subordinate theme begins over a pedal of V/III, and it appears again about halfway through the second half of the movement over a pedal of V/i. The pedal behaves as though it were the preparation for a recapitulation, being followed by a strongly articulated tonic arrival, the movement then remaining in the tonic until the end. However, the melody of the main theme does not appear at this point, only part of the original accompaniment. The violins' double-stopped chords are assertive but thematically neutral gestures. Instead, the main theme's melody returns near the end of the movement in unison. Again, in Hepokoski and Darcy's terms, there are only two thematic rotations. Yet, subordinate key material (their "S") returns, paradoxically, before the tonic arrival that sounds rhetorically like the start of a recapitulation, making a rather different impression from a standard Type 2 sonata. Haydn 44/iv shares with Gassmann 45/iv both the articulation of the tonic return in the absence of the main theme and the use of subordinate-key material over the V/i pedal that prepares that return. Gassmann 83/i is another special case. It too has a dramatic return of the main theme in the tonic at the end of the movement, the first time it has appeared in that key since the beginning of the exposition. Yet it is tri-rotational: the main theme also returns halfway through the second part, first in VI, then moving to a V/i pedal (see chapter 2). Even Hepokoski and Darcy would admit that there is a genuine recapitulation in this movement, despite its beginning in a non-tonic key. In Gassmann, the tonic return of the main theme at the end of a minor-key outer movement is thus a relatively well-consolidated generic norm, and is shared by all movements in which that theme does not return in the tonic midway through the second part, regardless of whether there are two or three rotations in the movement as a whole.

From this perspective Hepokoski and Darcy's background is not right for Haydn 44/iv, for their basic model for Type 2 almost never appears in the Viennese subgenre. Movements that lack a tonic main-theme reprise but compensate with a main-theme-based coda or some other tonic allusion are more common. These late main-theme references take their place within the untimely rhetoric characteristic of Viennese minor-key symphonies, especially those of imperial court composers, which commonly make gestures like closing ritornellos or closing statements of the subject in a fugue. Haydn 44 adopts untimely rhetoric in its first, second, and fourth movements, where it is always of strategic importance. In the Viennese minor-key subgenre, then, the closing return should not be regarded as an optional extra in this type of movement but as a fairly typical procedure. This is underlined by the three further Viennese minor-key symphony outer movements that omit a full return of the main theme midway through the second part. The recapitulation of Dittersdorf g1/iv (a symphony probably composed a few years before Haydn 44) begins with music corresponding to bar 17 of the exposition, omitting the basic idea of the main theme altogether. But that basic idea returns resplendently in a coda in the tonic major. Hoffmeister e1/iv (probably later than Haydn 44) employs a similar strategy. The recapitulation omits the first 17 bars of the exposition, but the return to the tonic is coordinated with the return of an alternative version of the main theme's basic idea (originally from bar 18 of the exposition). That version appears yet again in a coda in the tonic major, now in octaves, a Gassmann-like touch. In Wranitzky 43/i (composed in the 1780s) there is no tonic return for any of the main theme material midway through the second part. After the subordinate theme returns in the tonic, material from the main theme appears within a postcadential closing section. In this regard it parallels the exposition, although at the end of the movement this material receives slightly more rhetorical emphasis and there is a partial statement in unharmonized octaves that brings the movement in line with the Gassmann model. In short, the entire subgenre shows tendencies to rhetorical heightening of the endings of fast outer movements, either by thematic reversal, closing ritornello procedures, octave textures, dramatic pauses, and motivic fragmentation, or a combination of those techniques. Moreover, it even seems reasonable to follow Jackson in interpreting such tendencies, in movements that do not turn to the tonic major at the end, in terms of tragedy. The movement does not just end, but comes full circle; its main theme loses characteristic aspects or becomes, as it were, impersonal; surging energy is terminated through the strenuous assertion of closure.

Haydn 44/iii is an Adagio internal movement, rare for a symphony of the time. But although in this sense a transferral of a church-sonata type of movement into the symphony with standard movement order, it has no further untimely or ecclesiastical associations. Indeed, its syntax is typically galant,[52] and it is best regarded as the sublimation of the galant, major-mode, Andante inner movements common in Viennese minor-key symphonies, perhaps reworked in the manner of a slow aria by Hasse. It may well be Haydn's single best piece in the galant style, but as such it is in dialogue with a quite different set of conventions from the other movements of the symphony.

Symphony No. 52

Of Haydn's last three minor-key symphonies in his phase to 1772, Landon finds No. 52 "the most brutal in the stark power of its outer movements," which, because of their dualistic thematic and dynamic organization respectively "carry to its furthest stage the drama of the first movement of No. 26." The finale's "harsh" coda consists of "a few chords flung out in true Beethovenian spirit."[53] Heartz regards

---

[52] The movement opens with a Romanesca followed by a (nonstandard) Prinner riposte: a typical galant combination for openings. Gjerdingen, *Galant Style*, 45–60.

[53] Landon, *Symphonies*, 336.

No. 52 as the culmination of the series, a transformation of the church-sonata symphony in which the anger and severity of a Lenten sermon are conveyed with "unprecedented vehemence."[54] He thinks it must be the C minor symphony that according to Carpani was played in church. Heartz too hears an anticipation of Beethovenian violence: the main theme of the first movement opens with a "blazing ascent," reaching a "Schrekensakkord" (bar 4) like a shriek. The soft repetition of the opening idea (bars 9–10) conveys "a smouldering sense of latent power and unease."[55]

Yet, the symphony expresses much besides anger, of which, after all, Carpani said there were only "hints" in Haydn's symphonies composed for the church. Otherwise, the main emotion was sorrow, he thought, in the midst of which "the characteristically Haydnesque vivacity constantly shines through." In No. 52 that vivacity takes the form of irony, especially in the first movement: an irony that transforms conventional materials and generic norms and that juxtaposes heterogeneous materials in close succession in a manner that suggests a fast-moving pantomime.[56] No. 52 makes an interesting contrast with No. 44 in this regard. Both works draw on a wide range of topical references and invoke both strands of the minor-key subgenre. But in No. 52 the function of those references is different. The opening of Haydn 44/i presents syntactic ambiguity and later subrotations suggest generic ambiguity, both of which allow subtle strategies of clarification and reinterpretation to take place in the rest of the movement. Haydn 52/i evokes syntactic conventions only to contradict and thus transcend them. The music slips out of the categories it sets up in a manner that, to take up Landon's theme, anticipates Beethoven.

As regards subgeneric types too, the opening paragraphs do not leave a sense of ambiguity so much as total contradiction. It soon becomes clear that this movement will not resemble the models of the imperial court composers, of Vaňhal or of Haydn's own Lenten symphonies, Nos. 26 and 49, even though it momentarily adopts the vocabulary of each. Contrast is fundamental to the organization of the first movement. Unlike Haydn 39/i and 44/i, 52/i uses contrasted basic ideas for the main and subordinate themes of its exposition (as does the finale). The subordinate theme has sharp internal contrasts too. The basic ideas of the respective themes, along with other stormy music from the exposition, are juxtaposed in the development section in rapid alternation, like a dialogue between contrasting characters. The disturbing combination of the irony and the dark undertones of sorrow and anger than run through the work makes No. 52 unique in Haydn's instrumental output. Moreover, the topical diversity and the irony undermine the identity of the minor-key subgenre.

---

[54] Heartz, *Haydn, Mozart and the Viennese School*, 293.

[55] Ibid., 292.

[56] A. Peter Brown thinks that the movement's "rhythmic plan" is "stifled by pauses and spasms of activity" (*The First Golden Age of the Viennese Symphony*, 127), but this is surely a valid compositional strategy and aesthetic effect.

The extraordinary opening of the first movement, so full of anger to the ears of Landon and Heartz, has, paradoxically, a playful dimension too. Its combination of forceful octave gestures followed by a harmonized phrase with galant-style second-beat minims and double-eighth-note upbeats echoes the opening of Haydn 44/i as well as that of Haydn 46/i (in B major, probably composed about one year later than No. 52), but it shifts between topics even more swiftly. First comes an unusual version of the "pathotype" figure, highlighting the diminished fourth b♮–e♭^{1} and raging upwards (bars 1–3); then the galant rhythms, though they are stormy in character, in the minor mode, and accompanied by *Trommelbass* (bars 4–6); and next the trudging figure encountered already in 49/i that might evoke the path to Calvary, here (bar 7) in the cadential position familiar from sorrowful sacred works such as Pergolesi's *Stabat Mater*.

In terms of syntax the opening is paradoxical. The figure in bar 1 is a candidate for the basic idea of a main theme, but the organization is loosened almost immediately, and far more than is usual for a main theme: fragmentation occurs already in bar 3. (The combination of early motivic fragmentation and the semantics of suffering and upward striving could yet again be viewed as proto-Beethovenian.) If bars 1–3 are a presentation phrase, then its length is irregular and it already has continuational characteristics. By bar 7 it would seem nevertheless that this interpretation is the most feasible, as the music appears to be approaching a cadence and bars 4–6 can be regarded as a continuation, albeit one based on exact repetition rather than sequence and stuck around root position tonic harmony—one, in other words, that displays certain presentational characteristics. In fact, the cadence turns out to be deceptive—and thus, functionally speaking, no cadence at all, as it is not followed by an authentic cadence that would adequately express concluding function. Instead, the deceptive cadence is followed by a soft counterstatement (suggesting a double presentation like that of 44/i) that leads to a brief tonicization of VI (bars 12–13)—a curious move at this stage of an exposition—and then turns into a transition that tonicizes III. The first eight bars thus evoke the interthematic function "main theme" but fail to realize it fully. They create a sense of unease and irony at the very start of the symphony.

In the rest of the exposition the topical vocabulary is even wider and changes just as rapidly and abruptly. The formal function of transition is signaled clearly by a stormy texture (bars 14–18) including *Trommelbass* but also cross-hatch figuration in the second violin part rather than the more usual tremolando, which renders the gesture a little bombastic, an arbitrary *perpetuum mobile* that appears from nowhere. On the arrival at a root position chord of III at bar 19 the stormy music gives way to a two-part species counterpoint texture with ecclesiastical overtones signaled by the rising fourths in the cantus-firmus-like whole notes in the treble (bars 20–23). The tripping, exaggeratedly innocent character of the opening of the subordinate theme comes as another complete contrast. It soon turns back to the stormy texture, the melody now inverted, and eventually takes on the character of a very loosely organized period with remarkable internal contrasts, the consequent extended with breathless sighs somewhat in the manner of accompanied recitative, the soft and delicate texture suggesting an aesthetic of sensibility.

The impression of abruptness is attributable not just to the rapid changes of topic and key but also the very rapid rate of liquidation near the ends of paragraphs, especially the transition and the subordinate theme. The five-bar *Molleinschub* within the transition (bars 27–32; the moment when, for Heartz, the anger of the first movement reaches its peak)[57] introduces new characteristic material, but is followed by nothing more than a B♭ major chord and three beats' rest. The consequent of the subordinate theme likewise brings in new shapes during its expanded cadential progression (bars 53–59), but then finishes abruptly. Normally, liquidation of characteristic material takes place during the cadential progression of a theme or even earlier in the continuation. Here even the five-bar closing section cannot compensate for the temporal proximity of characteristic material and cadential arrival. It is as though a whimsical expression of subjective feeling (lingering tenderly on the pre-dominant chord) slows and almost halts the cadential progression, but at the last moment is swept away and dismissed.

In the recapitulation the expansion of the consequent of the subordinate theme, now of course in the minor mode, is even greater. Recitative-like phrases, suggestive of an individual voice of lament, lead the harmony in a new direction and away from anything resembling a cadential progression. The forceful five-bar gesture that ends the movement (bars 159–63) and that corresponds to the exposition's postcadential closing section seems all the more abrupt because it must accomplish the cadence itself. The cadential arrival at the end of the recapitulation thus does not occur until the very final bar of the movement—an extremely unusual phenomenon in a late eighteenth-century sonata movement. Here is an early example of a strategy that later became more frequent in minor-key symphonies: the alteration of detail within a subordinate theme when its mode is changed to minor in the recapitulation. Such alterations are not necessitated syntactically by the change of mode but record a sensitivity to the change of character that results, as though a shadow were cast across the theme and its physiognomy altered.[58] Expressive recomposition or extension of the subordinate theme can be found in several of Haydn's minor-key solo keyboard sonatas of this time.[59]

A similar effect is found in the finale, where the order of the two subordinate themes—both sharply contrasting with the main theme—is reversed so that the soft, lyrical theme comes second, while the stormy, tutti theme based on conventional material—a theme that to some extent resembles a closing section—precedes it. In the recapitulation the tutti theme tails off on a diminished seventh chord and a pause (bars 153–55), while the characteristic theme leads to a deceptive cadence. As in the first movement's recapitulation, the concluding function that completes the theme is supplied by a passage that possesses the rhetoric of a closing section. First

---

[57] Heartz, *Haydn, Mozart and the Viennese School*, 292.

[58] In 1796 Francesco Galeazzi called the subordinate theme of a sonata the "passo caratteristico." Bathia Churgin, "Francesco Galeazzi's Description (1796) of Sonata Form," *Journal of the American Musicological Society* 21, no. 2 (1968): 181–99 (p. 193).

[59] Sonata in G minor, Hob. XVI, no. 44/i; Sonata in C♯ minor, Hob. XVI, no. 36/i.

come the Beethovenian, flung-out chords (Landon; bars 175–9), but the cadence is completed with untimely rhetoric: an eight-bar unison passage of ritornello character (bars 181–88), starting with an allusion to the tutti subordinate theme, but ending, like Ordonez G7/i and F12/iv, with completely new material that strikingly suggests the kind of gesture that might be found in an old-fashioned concerto outer movement. In neither exposition nor recapitulation is there a closing section at the end of a subordinate theme, aside from the odd repeated chord. In the exposition the second subordinate theme was at least vigorous and conventional in its material, partly compensating for the lack of postcadential function. Just as in the first movement, then, the end of the recapitulation is highly abrupt, and the arrival of the final tonic of the cadence is left to the penultimate bar of the movement.

The finale appears to begin as a Type A stormy finale, but, as in the first movement, the category is soon transcended. The opening is in two-part counterpoint but has a nervous character reminiscent of the main theme of Haydn 39/i: the result of small-scale repetitions and metrical displacement dissonance,[60] the upper part consistently stressing quarter-note beats 2 and 4. This metrical displacement means that the texture distantly resembles fourth-species counterpoint in the order of attacks in the two parts, although not in note lengths (mainly quarter notes plus quarter-note rests in the upper part), articulation (staccato, slurs), or contour (repetitive, odd leaps). In the secondary development in the recapitulation (which is almost as long as the development section proper) displacement dissonance is intensified and the short overlapping figures recall similar passages in the symphony's third movement (chapter 4), though now there are at least three overlapping parts, not just two, within a contrapuntal texture (bars 112–17). When these already conflicted signals are combined with the two contrasted subordinate themes, a topical mixture results that approaches that of the first movement, although in the finale the alternations are much less rapid and each topic is confined to a separate large-scale paragraph. With the second subordinate theme in particular the standard Type A finale is left far behind; its homophonic texture with *Trommelbass* and soft, embellished melody is never found in the contrapuntal stormy finales of Gassmann or Ordonez. Although Haydn 52/iv does not convey anger as directly as the first movement, it too transcends generic categories and suggests irony, dialogue, unfulfillment, and the misalignment of form and content. Both outer movements draw on an eclectic range of musical styles and gestures, widening the generic horizon and even threatening the integrity of the subgenre. (The C major second movement, although it does not—and could not—reference subgeneric conventions, furthers the impression or irony and paradox in subtle ways that involve a play with syntax and formal function. It is a typical example of Haydn's "expressive ambivalence" in his slow movements of the 1770s,[61] and provides no respite in its demand for sophisticated listener responses.)

---

[60] On this terminology, see Krebs, *Fantasy Pieces*, 33–38.

[61] Sutcliffe, "Expressive Ambivalence," 98–110.

This chapter has attempted to flesh out the critical accounts of Landon and Heartz with analytical detail, positioning Haydn's first phase of minor-key symphony composition at the periphery of the liturgy as the expression of a Lenten atmosphere of sobriety. Despite lingering uncertainties of exact chronology, it would appear that the diversity and originality of Haydn's compositional strategies enriched the subgenre, allowing unsurpassed cross-fertilization of its various strands (Symphony No. 44), but at the same time undermined its very identity (Symphony No. 52). What is probably Haydn's final minor-key symphony of this period—No. 45—is a unique work, unmatched in his whole output. But it is better regarded as a continuation of the latter process (undermining of identity) than the former (enrichment, cross-fertilization). Despite its fame, it is not so much the culmination of a consistent minor-key practice as a bridge to a predominantly major-key future.

Epilogue: Symphony No. 45 ("Farewell")

No. 45 was Haydn's last minor-key symphony for a decade. It is his best known, largely on account of its program. But it is also an exceptional work that, uniquely, combines its program with a highly unusual key (it is the only known symphony in F♯ minor in the eighteenth century), tonal and gestural links between movements, outer movements that are, in Hepokoski and Darcy's terms, strongly deformational, and of course the spectacle of all but two players leaving the orchestra in the finale. Critics describe it as unusual, experimental, extraordinary, and unorthodox.[62] Brown, for instance, calls the symphony "a remarkable experiment among Haydn's output," with a program and form that "place...it apart from most of the other symphonies."[63] Even among Haydn's minor-key symphonies of the late 1760s and early 1770s, No. 45 stands out. Heartz does not seek its origins in the church-sonata symphony. He deals with No. 45 in a separate section of his book, grouping it with Haydn's major-key symphonies of the time. "The horrors of hell, as they might be depicted in a frightening Lenten sermon, received their most extreme incarnation in the sternly severe Symphony No. 52; they no longer haunt the *Farewell* Symphony, which [Haydn's friend and biographer] Griesinger refers to as 'an extended musical joke'."[64] Landon and Heartz hear in the tonality of No. 45 a foretaste of the future. In contrast to Nos. 49, 44, and 52, No. 45 has a movement in a non-tonic key (the Adagio in A major). Moreover, the minuet is in the tonic major, and the symphony ends in the tonic major as well. By stressing the relative and tonic major keys,

---

[62] Karl Geiringer, *Haydn: A Creative Life in Music* (London: Allen and Unwin, 1947), 233; Landon, *Symphonies*, 338; Antony Hodgson, *The Music of Joseph Haydn: The Symphonies* (London: Tantivy Press, 1976), 74; Webster, *Haydn's "Farewell" Symphony*, 3; Heartz, *Haydn, Mozart and the Viennese School*, 355.

[63] Brown, *The First Golden Age of the Viennese Symphony*, 136.

[64] Heartz, *Haydn, Mozart and the Viennese School*, 354.

Haydn anticipates his later treatment of the minor mode in the 1780s and 1790s in the symphony and other genres. Given the relative fame of the work—or at least of the program, which is probably even better known than the music—it is worth noting that by no means all critics who survey Haydn's minor-key symphonies of this time find it the best. Landon, Brown, and Simon McVeigh consider No. 44 the high point of the series;[65] for Heartz it is No. 52; while Rosemary Hughes deems the latter at least as good as No. 45, which "owes its fame rather to the romantic story of its origins than to any intrinsic superiority over its predecessors."[66]

The unusual form of No. 45 and its restricted use of the minor mode mean that generic analysis is of limited usefulness, and, given the extensive analysis of the work already undertaken elsewhere,[67] only a few observations are needed here. Only the first movement and the first part of the two-part finale—virtually a complete sonata-form movement—are in minor. The minuet has contrapuntal moments and in the view of Landon the trio quotes the Lamentation chant used already in Haydn 26/ii,[68] all of which would seem appropriate to the subgenre, but the entire movement is in major.

The opening of the first movement might seem on first hearing the epitome of Haydn's *Sturm und Drang* style. All the familiar signs are present: minor mode, syncopations, *Trommelbass, forte* dynamic, wide melodic compass, fast surface rhythm and slow harmonic rhythm, the avoidance of characteristic material, and regular phrase rhythm (four consecutive four-bar units, ending with a perfect authentic cadence in the tonic). Nowhere else in the Viennese minor-key subgenre does a composer present the listener so directly with so many conventional signs of the stormy style at the very start of a symphony. In comparison with the openings of Haydn's previous fast minor-key first movements, 39/i, 26/i, 44/i, or 52/i, this is unsubtle. Indeed, the opening may have been intended as a caricature of the style, in line with the jokey quality of the symphony as a whole. It is, as it were, a G minor stormy movement "gone wrong": the key a semitone too low and the meter adjusted to 3/4 (Haydn had never before used triple meter in a fast minor-key symphony outer movement.) The start of Haydn 45/i is in fact reminiscent of the opening of Dittersdorf g1/iv (Ex. 4.7), which is definitely a burlesque, but is at least in the "correct" key and meter.[69]

The finale, by contrast, although energetic, is not conventionally stormy. As indicated in chapter 4, although notated in 2/2, it is really a contradance, and could

---

[65] Landon, *Symphonies*, 337; Simon McVeigh, "Symphony," in Jones, *Haydn*, 381–414 (p. 388); Brown, *The First Golden Age of the Viennese Symphony*, 133. Landon later raised No. 45 at the same level as No. 44 (*Chronicle*, 2:298–99).

[66] Heartz, *Haydn, Mozart and the Viennese School*, 354; Hughes, *Haydn*, 178.

[67] See in particular Judith L. Schwartz, "Periodicity and Passion in the First Movement of Haydn's 'Farewell' Symphony," in *Studies in Musical Sources and Style: Essays in Honor of Jan LaRue*, ed. Eugene K. Wolf and Edward H. Roesner (Madison, WI: A-R Editions, 1990), 339–80; and Webster, *Haydn's "Farewell" Symphony*.

[68] Landon, *Symphonies*, 293.

[69] This opening also recalls the opening of Wagenseil G6/iii, albeit in a frenzied transformation.

easily be renotated in 2/4 with the note values halved. Stormy finales seldom have the mixture of slurs and staccato notes of this main theme. There are no hints of counterpoint at the outset (although a few later), and almost none of the typical features of the Type B finale can be found either. The sixteen-bar main theme resembles the first part (repeated) of a small binary form, the type of form often used in lightweight, sectional, major-key finales. The suddenly loud second phrase of the main theme in unharmonized octaves (bars 5–8) is a gesture that Haydn often used at exactly this position in major-key contradance finales.[70] The only other minor-key finale that deploys such a gesture is Haydn 78/iv,[71] a comic 2/4 Presto in a sectional form that ends in the tonic major (it is also the only symphony finale by Haydn apart from 45/iv to undergo modal reversal). In the second half of the exposition the stamping quarter-note syncopations (bars 31–35) and the first-violin string-crossing display (bars 36–39) and bariolage (bars 45–47) further lighten the mood. In Haydn 45/iv subgeneric definition is fading. He would not write another stormy finale in a symphony.

The deformational features of the outer movements are the minuet-like "D-major interlude"[72] in the first-movement development section and the Adagio that concludes the finale, which starts in A major (the relative major of the overall tonic of the symphony) and ends in F♯ major (the tonic major), finally with only two violins playing softly. No other sonata-form movement in a Viennese minor-key symphony has a development episode like that of Haydn 45/i, and although fade-out endings of finales were not unknown in both major and minor, a full slow section to end a symphony was almost unknown in the eighteenth century. Another feature of the work that, if not a deformation, constitutes at least the replacement of a strong first-order default is the use of v rather than III as the subordinate key of the first-movement exposition. The only sonata-form movements in previous Viennese minor-key symphonies to take this route are Dittersdorf e1/i and Vaňhal e3/i (both of which, like Haydn 45, undergo modal reversal in their finales, ending in major, although neither finale is a sonata form). Vaňhal was using fade-out endings, modal reversal in finales, and i–v exposition schemes about the same time as Haydn 45 or just after. What is unique to Haydn 45/i, however, is the deceptive stabilization of III as the likely subordinate key of the exposition (bars 21–37). There is an oblique but discernable reference to the mediant tutti convention (bars 21–24). After the first four-bar unit of the main theme is repeated *piano* (bars 17–20), the second phrase is played *forte* on V⁷/III–III. The sudden loud dynamic and the entry of III, which in a regular mediant tutti would occur simultaneously, are therefore displaced by two bars. The suggestion of a mediant tutti contributes to the implication that III will

---

[70] See, for instance, String Quartet, op. 64, no. 6/iv, bars 5–8; Symphony No. 63/iv (revised version), bar 6; Symphony No. 97/iv, bars 5–8; Symphony No. 102/iv, bars 7–8; see also Symphony No. 88/iv, bars 20^2–22^1.

[71] Bars 2^2–4^1, 7^2–8^1.

[72] James Webster's phrase; see *Haydn's "Farewell" Symphony*, 39–45.

be the subordinate key.[73] When that implication is finally contradicted, the impression is all the more bleak (the aesthetic qualities of the i–v exposition are discussed further in chapter 6).[74] The emphasis on major keys in the last three movements of the symphony (and already in the development of the first) represents a significant tonal brightening in the wake of the failure of the default i–III exposition.

James Webster has devoted a monograph to the analysis of this symphony and uses it as a lens through which to view Haydn's instrumental output as a whole and call attention to ideological dimensions of twentieth-century musicology in its treatment of Haydn and the idea of "classical style."[75] Webster draws attention to through-composition and cyclic integration (the development of ideas and tonal relationships across and between movements) in Haydn 45 and in Haydn's instrumental music in general. His analytical approach is in one sense the reverse of the one developed in this book, for Webster is not much interested in genre. He begins with intraopus rather than interopus criteria; in other words, the primary background for a musical event is the earlier events in the same movement or in other movements of the same work, not events in movements of the same type in other works. Haydn 45 responds well to that approach. Webster admits that the symphony is an extraordinary work and that systematic through-composition is rare in Haydn, but enumerates inter-movement connections and extra-musical associations in Haydn's instrumental music wherever they exist and examines them at length. In this context it is worth reiterating that the overall strategy found in Haydn 45, which encompasses numerous musical parameters in all four movements, was something quite new for Haydn and that he showed little interest in repeating it. In his previous minor-key symphonies, for instance, one can identify small-scale links between movements—the similar approaches to the recapitulation in 49/i and iv, the notes C–Db–Bb near the start of all four movements of that work, the diminished fourth Eb–B♮ in 52/i, iii, and iv[76]—but they contribute little to inter-movement coherence or narrative. In the more than fifty symphonies, forty string quartets, thirty keyboard trios, and many other multi-movement instrumental works that he was to compose after 1772, Haydn's commitment to the divertimento principle—the instrumental work as a group of discrete, self-contained movements of varied but complementary characters—remained strong. Only in his keyboard sonatas did he regularly write what Webster calls "run-on movements." Only two of his symphonies post-1772 contain a "compound movement" in the manner of 45/iv.[77] The

---

[73] Hepokoski and Darcy call this an example of "delayed tutti affirmation" at the start of a transition, but do not take account of the strong expectation of a mediant tutti at this point of a minor-key outer movement, which is not identical with the start of a transition. See *Elements of Sonata Theory*, 113–14.

[74] See also Ibid., 314–17.

[75] Webster, *Haydn's "Farewell" Symphony*.

[76] See, respectively, Webster, *Haydn's "Farewell" Symphony*, 262–67; Landon, *Chronicle*, 2:290; and Heartz, *Haydn, Mozart and the Viennese School*, 292–93.

[77] Haydn 67/iv and 79/ii. The former may be an adapted opera overture. See Webster, *Haydn's "Farewell" Symphony*, 192.

literal recollection of thematic material from one movement in a later movement occurs only twice in Haydn's entire multi-movement instrumental output, and not at all after 1772.[78] Moreover, in an age when the "characteristic symphony" was rapidly growing in popularity—at least 225 were composed between 1750 and 1815, including seventeen by Haydn's friend Carl Dittersdorf[79]—Haydn's preference for the abstract symphony stands out. Aside from the three programmatic symphonies composed for his first Esterhazy prince, Paul Anton, in the early 1760s (Nos. 6, 7, and 8, "Le midi," "Le matin," and "Le soir"), the "Farewell" is again an exception. As regards tonality, No. 45 did forecast the future of Haydn's writing in minor keys, and, to some extent, the future of the Viennese minor-key symphony. But, as chapter 7 will show, Haydn left the development of explicit programs and narrative effects to other composers.

---

[78] Symphonies No. 31 (1765) and 46 (1772). See Peter A. Hoyt, "Review-Essay: Haydn's New Incoherence," *Music Theory Spectrum* 19, no. 2 (1997): 264–84 (p. 271). This count excludes the baryton divertimenti.

[79] Richard Will, *The Characteristic Symphony in the Age of Haydn and Beethoven* (Cambridge: Cambridge University Press, 2002), 1 and app. 1.

6

Vaňhal's New Paths: Four Later Symphonies

Vaňhal's last four minor-key symphonies, e2, a1, d2, and f1, were probably all composed in the first half of the 1770s in the years after his return from Italy and his likely psychological crisis.[1] Today they are less easily available in score or recorded performance than the earlier minor-key symphonies. The powerful and impressive f1, a rare late eighteenth-century symphony in F minor, has been neither published nor recorded.[2] The four works were probably composed at the same time as, and very shortly after, Haydn 44, 52, and 45, although they appear not to have been influenced by those works. They depart from the subgeneric norms and patterns established in the late 1760s in consistent ways that open new possibilities and widen the range of expression of Vaňhal's minor-key symphonies. The overall results are, however, uneven. Vaňhal appears to have been experimenting, with mixed success. Sometimes the music is repetitious, directionless, or melodically short-winded, and hardly recognizable as the work of the assured composer of e1 or c2. The later minor-key symphonies raise anew a recurrent theme in the reception of Vaňhal's music: the claim that his bright start in the 1760s was followed by a long decline. This chapter evaluates the later minor-key symphonies and argues that the best of them, d2 and f1, do not fit this account. Their first movements can be placed among Vaňhal's finest compositions.

Given the scarcity of source material on Vaňhal aside from the scores of his compositions, very little is known for certain about his activities after his return from Italy, except that he published less in the 1790s than before. By 1772, not long after his breakdown, Vaňhal had fallen on hard times. Burney found it was not easy to track him down, and eventually discovered him living in a garret in an obscure corner of Vienna. In later years he seems to have kept to himself. He continued to enjoy

---

[1] Bryan dates e2 to 1771–72 and d2, f1, and a1 to 1773–74 (all provisional); see *Johann Wanhal*, 150. I am inclined to date a1 a little earlier, as I place it in the same category as e2 as a piece in which Vaňhal's new ideas did not come off well, in contrast to the more successful d2 and f1.

[2] I have been unable to locate a copy of the single recording of a1 (listed in Bryan, *Johann Wanhal*, 340).

the patronage of Count Erdödy, to whose country estates he was invited, but he held no official position, and did not feature prominently in Viennese musical life in later years. He appears nowhere in Mozart's correspondence in the 1780s, for instance. The opera singer Michael Kelly recalled Vaňhal attending a concert by Koželuch and playing in a quartet party with Haydn, Dittersdorf, and Mozart,[3] but these are almost the only records of him in Viennese society. In 1793 the *Wiener Schriftsteller und Künstlerlexicon*, though praising Vaňhal's music, noted that he had not published anything for a long time. In 1796 the *Jahrbuch der Tonkunst von Wien und Prag* made the same point and added that Vaňhal had gone out of fashion in Vienna.[4]

Aside from the declining quantity of music that Vaňhal published in the 1780s and 1790s, the quality of his later work was questioned even during his lifetime. In particular, his later instrumental music was compared unfavorably with his earlier symphonies and quartets.[5] The criticism comes in two strands. In the first, which was expressed by writers in the mid-1770s and was repeated in the early 1790s, Vaňhal is said to have undergone an involuntary change of style after 1770 caused by his personal problems that impoverished all his music, regardless of genre. In the second, dating from the 1790s onwards, it is claimed that Vaňhal turned shallow in the 1780s and 1790s because he cultivated popular genres for commercial profit.

The first strand originates with Burney's report of his meeting with Vaňhal in 1772, not long after his likely psychological crisis during or following his return from Italy. Burney's report of his travels in Germany was widely read and appeared in German translation in the same year as its first English edition (1773). Burney's ingenious argument was that Vaňhal's music had suffered not because of his illness, but because of its cure:

> A little perturbation of the faculties is a promising circumstance in a young musician, and M[r] V[aňhal] began his career very auspiciously, by being somewhat flighty. Enthusiasm seems absolutely necessary in all the arts, but particularly in music, which so much depends upon fancy and imagination. A cold, sedate and wary disposition but ill suits the professor of such an art; however, when enthusiasm is ungovernable, and impels to too frequent and violent efforts, the intellects are endangered. But as insanity in an artist is sometimes nothing more than an ebullition of genius, when that is the case, he may cry out to the physicians who cure him,
> —Pol me occidistis, amici,
> Non servastis.
> M[r] V[anhal] is now so far recovered, and possesses a mind so calm and tranquil, that his last pieces appear to me rather insipid and common, and

---

[3] Michael Kelly, *Reminiscences of Michael Kelly*, 2 vols. (London: Henry Colburn, 1826), 1:222, 237.

[4] *Wiener Schriftsteller und Künstlerlexicon* (Vienna: F.J.J. Reillyschen Verlag, 1793), 147; *Jahrbuch der Tonkunst von Wien und Prag* (Vienna: Im Schönfeldischen Verlag, 1796), 64; facs. repr. ed. Otto Biba (Munich: Katzbichler, 1976); both cited in Bryan, *Johann Wanhal*, 28, 29.

[5] The sacred vocal works that Vaňhal composed in this period have enjoyed a more positive reception, although largely by hearsay: little of it is published.

his former agreeable extravagance seems changed into too great economy of thought.[6]

At a concert in Dresden later the same year, Burney heard "an admirable symphony of Vanhall [sic], produced in those happy moments of effervescence, when his reason was less powerful than his feeling."[7]

Burney's attitudes and his logic have been challenged by Vaňhal's modern champions. Although his account of his search for Vaňhal in Vienna and his judgments on the music are wry and condescending at times,[8] his argument can be read as a defense of the composer, especially if Vaňhal's mental instability was an open secret at the time. Burney makes the best of this circumstance by appealing implicitly to the Platonic doctrine of divine frenzy as the source of artistic creativity, a point of view that would have been familiar to all classically educated readers of his time.

In 1776 the German critic Carl Ludwig Junker concurred, and indeed partly plagiarized Burney:

> The character of his earlier pieces is naivety, flow, melody, easefulness, the character of his later ones fastidiousness, stiffness and lack of melody. Formerly Vaňhal's imagination was inclined to craziness; now his mind is so calm and tranquil that his later pieces seem very shallow and common; his former agreeable enthusiasm [Schwärmerey] seems changed into too great economy of thought.
>
> In his latest symphonies he seems to have taken great trouble to deny his original feeling. His earlier ones are just the opposite: rich, harmonious and splendid. They lack the studied quality that in art is always dull and boring. They are natural outpourings of his heart, whereas in the latest he seems merely to have been thinking.[9]

---

[6] Burney, *The Present State of Music in Germany*, 1:353–54; see also Bryan, *Johann Wanhal*, 4. The quotation is from Horace, Epistle II, 138–39, spoken by a man from Argos who used to sit in an empty theater believing that he was watching great actors. "But friends, you've killed me, not cured me."

[7] Burney, *The Present State of Music in Germany*, 2:46.

[8] Bryan finds Burney "smug" and "self-serving"; Heartz thinks that Burney was "carried away by his own rhetoric." *Johann Wanhal*, 19n47; *Haydn, Mozart and the Viennese School*, 455.

[9] Carl Ludwig Junker, *Zwanzig Componisten, eine Skizze* (Berne: Typographische Gesellschaft, 1776), 102–3, 107. "Der Charakter seiner ersteren Stücke ist Naivetät, Fluß, Melodie, Leichtigkeit;—der Charakter seiner letztern, Aengstlichkeit, Steifigkeit, und Mangel an Melodie. Ehedem war Vanhalls Imagination zum Ueberschnappen geneigt; jetzt ist sein Gemüt so still und ruhig, daß seine letztere Stücke, sehr schaal, und gemein vorkommen; daß seine vorige angenehme Schwärmerey, in eine zu grosse Sparsamkeit der Gedanken verwandelt zu seyn scheint." "Bey seinen letztern Sinfonien Scheint er sich allen Zwang angethan zu haben, seine ursprüngliche Empfindung zu verläugnen, daher das strotzende. Seine ersteren sind just das Gegentheil, voll, harmonisch, plan, und prächlig: es fehlt ihnen das studierte, das in der Kunst allemal matt, und langweilig ist. Sie sind natürlichen Ausgusse seines Herzens; wenn er bey den letztern blos gedacht zu heben scheint." Bryan's transcription of the first passage (*Johann Wanhal*, 23) is inaccurate: it follows the paraphrase in Johann Nikolaus Forkel, *Musikalisch-kritische Bibliothek* (Gotha: Carl Wilhelm Ettinger, 1779), 3:243.

Similarly, in the first edition of his *Historisch-biographisches Lexicon der Tonkünstler* (1792), Ernst Ludwig Gerber praised Vaňhal's early symphonies for their "fire, combined with beautiful singing melodies, and liveliness," but added that "since that time one notices a certain coldness and common tone in his compositions."[10] Gerber reported Burney's meeting with Vaňhal, and he appears to have borrowed the terms "cold" and "common" from Burney's account.[11]

The second strand of criticism was articulated by Gerber in his very next sentence: "Besides this is hardly surprising as his only endeavour is to please the masses and attract as many buyers as he can, and moreover he continues in large quantity without pause."[12] By the 1800s Viennese writers grouped Haydn, Mozart, and Beethoven together as a trio of great masters, superior to most other composers. In the Viennese *Liebhaber Concerte* of 1807–8 this grouping was consolidated in practice around the genre of the symphony.[13] Vaňhal, whose name in the 1770s and 1780s had often been linked with that of Haydn, was now relegated to the second or third rank of composers. In 1805 the Leipzig *Zeitung für die elegante Welt* reported that in Vienna the Sunday morning and Friday concerts usually had "true music," such as the string quartets of Haydn, Mozart, Beethoven, Romberg, and occasionally Wranitzky. "The easier keyboard music of Pleyel, Vaňhall [*sic*] and Koželuch is entirely out of fashion. Compositions of Clementi, Cramer, Beethoven and Dussek have taken its place."[14] It seems that Vaňhal was not even favored in the lighter style in which he had published so copiously. This was an important moment of reconfiguration in the musical values of the leaders of Viennese society.

Recently, Daniel Heartz has mingled the two strands of criticism in his evaluation of Vaňhal's later symphonies. On the basis of the two works then available to

---

[10] "... das mit dem schönen Gesange verbundene Feuer und die Lebhaftigkeit ... Man will aber seit der Zeit eine gewisse Kälte und einen gemeinen Tone in seinen Kompositionen bemerkt haben." Gerber, *Lexicon der Tonkünstler* (1790–92), 2:767.

[11] A point made by Heartz, *Haydn, Mozart and the Viennese School*, 456. See also Bryan, *Johann Wanhal*, 33–34.

[12] "Wunder wäre dies aber auch außerdem nicht, da sein einziges Bestreben ist, dem großen Haufen zu gefallen und so viel Käufer zu locken als möglich, und er überdies in so großer Menge, ohne inne zu halten, fortschreibt." Gerber, *Lexicon der Tonkünstler* (1790–92), 2:767. Bryan makes Gerber into the villain in the story of Vaňhal's reception, but when this sentence is read in context that is hardly justified. *Johann Wanhal*, 28, 30, 32–34. In the second edition of the *Lexicon* Gerber's comments on Vaňhal are positive, even effusive. Ernst Ludwig Gerber, *Neues historisch-biographisches Lexicon der Tonkünstler* (Leipzig: A. Kühnel, 1812–14), 508–9. See also Gerber's comments on Vaňhal in his additions and corrections at the end of the lexicon, 836–39.

[13] Jones, *The Symphony in Beethoven's Vienna*, 123–29.

[14] "Der Sonntagsvormittag, allenfalls auch der Freitag, ist gewöhnlich der eigentlichen Musik gewidmet, die man hier zu keiner Zeit ganz aus den Augen verliert. Man spielt gewöhnlich Violinquartetten von Haydn, Mozart, Beethoven oder Romberg, zuweilen von Wranitzki. Die leichtere Klaviermusik eines Pleyels, Wanhal, Kozeluch ist ganz aus der Mode. Kompositionen von Clementi, Cramer, Beethoven, Dussek sind an ihre Stelle getreten." *Zeitung für die elegante Welt* 1, no. 8 (2 February 1805): 120; cited in Mary Sue Morrow, *Concert Life in Haydn's Vienna: Aspects of a Developing Musical and Social Institution* (Stuyvesant, NY: Pendragon Press, 1989), 9, 447; and in Bryan, *Johann Wanhal*, 29. My translation differs from Morrow's.

him, C11 and d2, he agrees reluctantly with Burney and Junker: "the composer did suffer a falling off in inspiration. These symphonies are less original in their melodic ideas and more mechanical in spinning them out. The *filo* [an allusion to a letter of Leopold Mozart] has been stretched thin and seems in danger of breaking."[15] Heartz then quotes a review of Vaňhal symphonies by Carl Friedrich Cramer from 1783 who hopes that Vaňhal will "not be prevented by a lessening of his faculties as a result of approaching old age from presenting other such symphonies," and points out that, although Vaňhal was only in his forties, he produced no further symphonies thereafter. "During the long twilight of his career he wrote mainly teaching pieces and trifles for keyboard, plus church music."[16]

For present purposes, it is important to keep the two strands separate. The second is irrelevant to the later minor-key symphonies, as it applies to the music Vaňhal composed in the 1780s and 1790s and reflects a changed order in Viennese musical life. The first is the one that must be addressed. On the evidence of e2, a1, d2, and f1, Burney, Junker, and Gerber were right in one respect: these works show changes in style—or, to put it better, new compositional strategies. The mixed results mean that at times it is hard not to follow Heartz in echoing the eighteenth-century criticisms (although not his judgment on d2). But there were gains as well as losses, and they may not have gone unnoticed at the time. An alternative perspective on Vaňhal's work after his illness comes from his biographer Dlabač: "Since the recovery of this excellent artist we have had several great works from him which have been performed by the grandest orchestras to his great fame."[17] This comment can be read—as Bryan does—as referring to the later symphonies.[18] Dlabač had interviewed Vaňhal and thus did not rely on hearsay or recycled excerpts from Burney. Bryan regards him as the most reliable contemporary witness to Vaňhal's life. He is certainly the most sympathetic, even if that is to be expected of a compatriot compiling an encyclopedia of Bohemian artists. The comment about the "grandest orchestras" rings true, as some of Vaňhal's symphonies of the 1770s are scored for orchestras with up to five horn parts.[19] Dlabač's remark offers a starting point for a re-evaluation of Vaňhal's later minor-key symphonies.[20]

Even if Vaňhal's later works in the subgenre vary in quality, from a purely historical perspective they are all significant. He took the minor-key symphony in new directions at about the time, or shortly after, Haydn temporarily ceased his work in this field.

---

[15] Heartz, *Haydn, Mozart and the Viennese School*, 460–61.

[16] Ibid., 461.

[17] "Seit der Herstellung dieses vortrefflichen Künstlers erlebte man verschiedene große Werke von ihm, welche zu seinem größten Ruhm von den zahlreichsten Orchestern aufgeführt wurden." Dlabač, *Allgemeines historisches Künstler-Lexicon*, 326; reprinted in Bryan, *Johann Wanhal*, 6. My translation differs from Bryan's.

[18] Bryan, *Johann Wanhal*, 22.

[19] Bryan, *Johann Wanhal*, 164–65.

[20] Although Bryan points out this comment (n. 19), he is not in a position to construct a strong defense, being too attached to evolutionary concepts to draw up a convincing balance of gain against loss or to make undistracted aesthetic judgments on individual works.

Some accounts of late eighteenth-century Viennese instrumental music have implied that the irrational winds of *Sturm und Drang* blew themselves out suddenly in the early 1770s—Haydn ceased composition of minor-key symphonies that winter and did not recommence for a decade—and were eventually superseded by the more controlled Classical style of the 1780s. Vaňhal too stopped composing minor-key symphonies sometime in the 1770s—in his case for good—but some of his innovations parallel those found in Haydn 45 and, as will become clear in chapter 7, anticipate minor-key symphonies by other composers in the later 1770s and the 1780s, again including Haydn, indicating a degree of continuity rather than a sudden break.

New Paths

Table 6.1 shows some distinctive traits of e2, a1, d2, and f1. One further symphony is included: a2, probably the last minor-key symphony to be composed before those last four. It can be regarded as a transitional work that shares some features with the group of the late 1760s (e1, c2, d1, g1, and g2), mainly in the first movement, and some with the later works, mainly in the finale. Aside from a2, most of the listed traits almost never appear in Vaňhal's earlier minor-key symphonies, with the exception of his very first, e3. Nevertheless, the concept of the subgenre is still essential to an understanding of the last four symphonies: they allude to many of

TABLE 6.1 Distinctive traits of four later Vaňhal minor-key symphonies, plus the transitional symphony a2

	a2	e2	a1	d2	f1
		The Four Later Symphonies			
No minuet-and-trio	✓		✓	✓	✓
No "stormy finale"		✓			✓
Many horns and unusual crooking combinations			✓	✓	✓

	a2 i	a2 iii	e2 i	e2 iii	a1 i	a1 iii	d2 i	d2 iii	f1 i	f1 iii
Long movement				✓			✓		✓	✓
v as subordinate key					✓	✓			✓	
"Monothematicism"				✓		✓			✓	✓
Movement ends in major key / on major chord		✓						✓		✓
"Fade-out" end to movement		✓					✓	✓		
Coda		✓			✓		✓	✓	✓	✓
Development and recapitulation not repeated		✓					✓	✓		✓
Retransition at the end of exposition				✓		✓	✓		✓	

the conventions and norms established in the 1760s and unfold against the horizon of expectations established then, even when they confound some of those expectations. For instance, *Trommelbass* and syncopated accompaniments can be found in e2/i, a1/iii, d2/iii, f1/i, and f1/iii; sudden pauses interrupt strong dynamic currents in the second half of most outer-movement expositions; e2/iii, the single minuet and trio movement, includes a stretch of canon; e2/i and d2/i allude to the mediant tutti convention, albeit indirectly; a1/iii and d2/iii are Type 2 stormy finales; and—a negative correlation—in all four symphonies the slow movements are, as before, of limited interest and do not stand out from slow movements of major-key symphonies. Vaňhal brought off his new strategies most effectively in d2 and f1. But, although e2 and a1 are less successful in outcome, the table shows that they are part of a consistent change of strategy in the writing of minor-key symphonies.

As the table indicates, three of the four later symphonies have no minuet-and-trio movement, and neither does a2. These symphonies have only three movements in total, whereas all Vaňhal's earlier minor-key symphonies have four. However, minuet topic dominates two outer movements: d2/i and f1/iii. This is also unprecedented among Vaňhal's minor-key symphonies; indeed, f1/iii is his first (and only) minor-key finale in 3/4 meter. By definition, then, f1 lacks a stormy finale, as does e2, which has a dance finale in 6/8. Vaňhal's only other minor-key symphony without a stormy finale is his very first, e3, probably composed under the influence of Dittersdorf (see chapter 3), and before Vaňhal had become acquainted with Haydn 39.

Three symphonies are scored for large groups of horns with unusual combinations of crooks. Five horns are required for d2 (two in D, two in F, one in A); four for f1 (two in F, one in C, one in Ab); and three for a1 (one in A, one in C, one in E). After Haydn 39 it was common for composers to call for horns crooked in both tonic and mediant for minor-key symphonies (Vaňhal e1, d1, g1, and a2 and Mozart K. 183 have two of each; in Vaňhal c2 the clarini are in C, the horns in Eb). Vaňhal e2 (one horn in E, one in G) is thus unexceptional. However, the use of three different crooks is unique to Vaňhal a1, d2, and f1, as is the total of five horns in d2.[21] Vaňhal's major-key symphonies never require more than two horns or horns crooked in non-tonic keys. On this evidence, at least, it was precisely his later minor-key symphonies that were destined for "the grandest orchestras." The temporal dimensions of outer movements of the later minor-key symphonies likewise tend to be large. Several are much longer than any previous minor-key outer movement by Vaňhal. These judgments are partly subjective and not easily quantified, but the point is clear with d2/i (351 bars of 3/4 Allegro molto), e2/i (242 bars of 3/4 Allegro moderato), and f1/iii (252 bars of 3/4 Allegro molto). By contrast, Vaňhal's earlier minor-key outer movements are usually between one hundred and 130 bars in length, with the two longest, g2/i and a2/i, just passing 160.[22]

---

[21] See Bryan, *Johann Wanhal*, 164–65.

[22] The lengths for the other movements are, as follows: e2/iii, 157 bars of 6/8 Allegro; a1/i, 227 bars of 2/2 Allegro (but could be heard as 119 bars of 4/2); a1/iii, 191 bars of 4/4 Allegro molto (second part not repeated); d2/iii, 130 bars of 2/2 Allegro (second part not repeated); f1/i, 175 bars of 4/4 Allegro moderato.

Three movements use v as the subordinate key instead of the usual III. Again, Vaňhal had not taken this option since e3/i, which follows the example of Dittersdorf e1/i. Aside from those two, the only other Viennese minor-key symphony sonata movement not to end its exposition in III is Haydn 45/i. For Hepokoski and Darcy, the "i–v exposition" is "minor-mode saturated," "a doggedly negative tonal choice," which, unlike expositions that modulate to III, does not even hold open the possibility of eventual transformation into the tonic major. "The sonata's modal 'fate' is decreed in advance."[23] For a minor-key symphony outer movement of the 1770s this means, in particular, non-optimal realization of the mediant tutti convention, which by that time had become established as a strong subgeneric expectation. Haydn 45/i feints at III with a mediant tutti-type gesture before dramatically reverting to the minor mode and cadencing in v. Vaňhal does not adopt that ploy: in his i–v expositions there is no hint of a mediant tutti at all.

Four expositions are, in standard (but ambiguous) musicological parlance, "monothematic." This does not mean that the main and subordinate themes—conceived as paragraphs expressing a sequence of formal functions (initiating, medial, concluding)—are identical, still less that the exposition spins out only one motive or figure. It means that the basic idea of the subordinate theme is identical or very similar to that of the main theme. (The mode of repetition of the basic idea, the continuation phrase, and the cadential phrase may all be quite different; indeed, they will have to be if the subordinate theme is to be more loosely organized than the main theme, as is almost always the case in Vaňhal and other Viennese composers at this time.) Here Vaňhal may be following the example of Haydn, who used the technique frequently throughout his career, although it was not entirely new to him in either major or minor mode. Vaňhal had already written several two-part minor-key expositions with mediant tuttis in which the tutti begins with the basic idea of the main theme (e1/i, g1/iv, g2/iv). As noted in chapter 1, in the two-part type (Fig. 1.1), the caesura preceding the tutti functions like a medial caesura, and so the mediant tutti paragraph resembles, at least retrospectively, a subordinate theme, and one can speak of monothematicism in the conventional sense. In a1/i and f1/i monothematicism is combined with the choice of v for the subordinate key, resulting in an unusually insistent focus on an idea of starkly negative character.

Two of the four later finales, along with a2/iii, end in major. Once again, Vaňhal had not taken this option since e3/iv, which doubtless emulates the major-mode ending of Dittersdorf e1/iv. The turn to major takes place in two quite different ways, however. In a2/iii and f1/iii it occurs at the start of the recapitulation, the whole of which is in the tonic major. In d2/iii the tonic major chord appears only in the closing bars of the coda, like a *tièrce de picardie*, with the sixth scale degree still minor. This is a striking effect, especially as it is combined with a fade-out ending,

---

[23] Hepokoski and Darcy, *Elements of Sonata Theory*, 315. Their account, however, owes not a little to the character of Beethoven's i–v expositions. "Typically, the remainder of the sonata experience unfolds as something to be endured or struggled against, grimly, determinedly, or stoically." See also Joseph Kerman, "Beethoven's Minority," in *Write All These Down: Essays on Music* (Berkeley and Los Angeles: University of California Press, 1994), 155–72.

marked *perdendosi*, something d2/iii shares with a2/iii (also ending in major, but having reached it much earlier) and a1/iii (but remaining in minor). Again e3/iv is the only finale—in fact, the only movement—in Vaňhal's earlier minor-key symphonies to end quietly. It and Dittersdorf e1/iv combine the fade-out with a turn to major. Unlike the finales of Vaňhal's later minor-key symphonies, however, neither of those movements is a sonata form, as a2/iii, d2/iii, and a1/iii are. They are both sectional, with many short internal repeats.

The outer movements of the later symphonies often end with codas (of widely varying lengths), in contrast to the sonata-form movements of Vaňhal's minor-key symphonies of the late 1760s, in which recapitulations usually end with double "hammer blows" that closely parallel the end of their expositions. As in other ways, a2/iii is an exception among the earlier symphonies: it has a twenty-two-bar coda (which ends with the fade-out). In f1/iii the recapitulation has just one emphatic extra bar in comparison with the exposition. The end of the recapitulation of a1/i is expanded and rhetorically heightened in relation to the exposition, although the interpolated passage is not strictly a coda, as it comes before the perfect authentic cadence in the tonic, and the codetta that follows the cadence parallels that of the exposition. Neither of these movements earns a tick in Table 6.1, although the modest alterations in their recapitulations go further than most of Vaňhal's earlier sonata-form movements. In the (unambiguous) codas of e2/i, d2/iii, and f1/i some or all of the main theme returns in the tonic before the movement ends: a strategy that recalls the closing-ritornello gestures of the minor-key symphonies of imperial court composers and of some Type 1 stormy finales. The twenty-bar coda of d2/i is highly dramatic: after a loud cadence, there is a series of pauses alternating with soft echoes of the final repeated-note figure of the cadential phrase, before stern, tutti dominant and tonic chords end the movement. The coda of d2/iii is anticipated by the eight-bar codetta at the end of the exposition, which is itself a fade-out ending (although not actually marked *perdendosi*, as the end of the movement is). That codetta is entirely in III, without any local change of mode. At the end of the recapitulation it is expanded into an eighteen-bar coda, starting with a loud interpolation of the opening of the main theme, before moving to an extended version of the exposition's fade-out. The effect is heightened in relation to the exposition by starting the diminuendo from a louder dynamic and introducing F♯ into the tonic harmony. According to all currently available editions, the finales that have fade-out endings and/or that turn to major (a2/iii, a1/iii, d2/iii, and f1/iii) have no repeats marked in the second part of the sonata form (development plus recapitulation). The concluding transformation or alteration is heard only once. (The lack of second-part repeat markings is shared by a rare major-turning sonata-form movement of the 1760s: Haydn 26/i.)

Modulating retransitions are found at the end of the expositions of the first movements of all four symphonies, although not in any finales. They are absent from all of Vaňhal's earlier minor-key symphonies (including a2): the standard hammer-blow chords confirming III as local tonic are usually followed immediately by the opening of the movement for the exposition repeat. Retransitions at the end of minor-key sonata expositions are much more likely to be found at this time in chamber music than in symphonies.[24] In the later Vaňhal symphonies it could be argued that the retransitions match the large scale of these movements and the relatively leisurely pace at which the expositions unfold. However, the retransition in f1/i is only one bar in length, features no embellishment at all, and replaces a codetta entirely. In other words, after the tonic arrival in a very long-delayed perfect authentic cadence in the subordinate key, v, the music almost instantly plunges back into i.

Two Problematic Symphonies: e2, a1

Vaňhal's third symphony in E minor, e2, belongs firmly to the subgenre, yet subverts several strong expectations. Familiar subgeneric features include *Trommelbass*, syncopations, and a mediant tutti in the first movement, even though all are withheld longer than usual and the mediant tutti is articulated less clearly than in many previous outer movements by Vaňhal. The minuet uses canon in its second part. On the other hand, the finale is a 6/8, dance-like sonata movement that would be unexceptional if the mode were major, but, in terms of the minor-key subgenre, is all but *sui generis*.

In the first movement Vaňhal's usual virtues of succinctness, directness, and high momentum are absent. The result might well be described as "cold" (Burney, Gerber), "fastidious" or "stiff" (Junker). The structure of the main theme (Ex. 6.1) is the familiar abb', yet the hesitations, appoggiaturas, and repetitions that Vaňhal's earlier minor-key outer movements had left to the end of their b- or even b'-phrases, as part of a process of liquidation just before the mediant tutti, are here brought forward to the a-phrase.[25] The nervous motive *a* (Ex. 6.1) is introduced early and undergoes an extraordinary number of repetitions. The presentation of the main theme, which already contains five successive statements of *a*, recurs, in only modestly varied form, no less than eleven times in the movement (counting the first-time modulating retransition at the end of the recapitulation that leads back to the start of the development, but not the repetitions caused by the repeats marks themselves, which would take the total number of statements to twenty-two). (See Table 6.2.) Whenever it appears, the formal function expressed is always initiation. By the same count the number of iterations of *a* is fifty-nine (102 with repeats), although there are many more in rhythmically varied forms. As well as being highly repetitious, at 242 bars (again discounting repeats) of Allegro moderato, e2/i is very long for Vaňhal. It is remarkable that an experienced and successful composer could have miscalculated so badly. The most plausible explanation is that he had in mind the

---

[24] Haydn 44/i and iv and Mozart K. 183/i and iv are exceptions. See Longyear, "The Minor Mode in Eighteenth-Century Sonata Form," 208–9.

[25] The model for this opening may be the codetta to the minuet of Haydn's String Quartet in D minor, op. 9, no. 4, but there the formal function it articulates is "after-the-end."

Ex. 6.1 Vaňhal e2/i, bars 1–15[1]

TABLE 6.2 Appearances of the main theme's presentation phrase in e2/i

Bar	Key		Number of Iterations of a
Exposition			
1	i	presentation of main theme	5
15	i	second presentation	5
45	III	presentation of subordinate theme	4
76	III–i / III–VI	modulating retransition / transition	3/5
Development			
82	VI	start of development	4
101	i	sequential version	10
119	v	parallel to subordinate theme version	4
Recapitulation			
149	i	reprise of main theme	5
163	i	reprise of second presentation	5
193	i	reprise of subordinate theme	4
224	i–VI	modulating retransition (first-time bars only)	3
228	i	coda (second-time only): reprise of main theme	5

principle of economy of thematic means, one that Haydn often applied successfully and for which he was later commended by French and English critics.

The outer movements of a1 are also longer than usual for Vaňhal. The first is not as repetitious as that of e2—although it too reuses the basic idea of its main theme for the subordinate theme—but the lack of directness is shared. Again Vaňhal's melodic gift is not in evidence. There is much reiteration of short units and conventional motives, but without much overall shape, logic, or flow, as though the piece consisted of building blocks lined up in succession. Although conventional material is abundant in almost all late eighteenth-century Viennese instrumental music—not least that of Haydn and Mozart—it is associated with specific formal functions (especially cadential and postcadential) and the manner of its alternation with characteristic material is carefully handled. Here the conventional material is brought forward to the stage of initiating function, while, on the other hand, when later formal functions are reached liquidation is only partial and new characteristic material is sometimes introduced.

The main theme (Ex. 6.2) has some Vaňhal trademarks: abb' structure and gestures of hesitation in the continuation. The accompaniment's surface rhythm is slower than usual, however, as there is no *Tromemelbass*, tremolandi, or syncopations (in fact, there are none of these in the movement at all). The accompaniment has more linear motion than usual for Vaňhal, who normally foregrounds the treble melody unambiguously. The melody itself is not one of his best: the descent e^2–c^2–$g\sharp^1$–a^1 occurs twice in the space of the first seven bars, while the repeated e^2s in bars 4–5 mean that the melody of the continuation starts blandly. At bar 11 the repetition of two-bar units with alternating tonic and dominant root position harmony suggests a statement-response presentation, but the scales in the bass and oddly unidiomatic, repetitive figures in the violins are too conventional to articulate a new phase of initiating function.

Ex. 6.2 Vaňhal a1/i, bars 1–15 (string parts)

Similar points can be made about the continuation of the subordinate theme and the postcadential closing section that follows it (Ex. 6.3; the first four bars of continuation and fifteen bars of postcadential music are omitted). Again the bass scales appear over tonic root position harmony (here repeated three times in succession). The figuration in the cadential progression is strangely static and repetitive (bars 55–58), while the closing section introduces new, and in context relatively characteristic, material of several types (bars 59–64 and later in the section too, where repetitive eighth-note triplets suddenly appear just before the end of the exposition). The results seem arbitrary and fussy. The trill at the cadence evokes an aria or concerto, but without obvious motivation. In the recapitulation it is extended to two bars (bars 222–23), a gesture that seems still more arbitrary and even tasteless.

There are strange passages in a1/i that appear unintentionally asyntactic. In the development there is a succession of scales and suspensions in the first violins that recall imitative trio-sonata textures (Ex. 6.4). But there is no imitation from the second violins, and no first-beat dissonances for the tied notes. Here an unmistakable rhythmic/melodic gesture has been lifted out of its usual harmonic/contrapuntal context, as though some other music were being half-remembered. In the finale the Corelli leapfrog pattern receives similar treatment (bars 71–74). Together these passages raise questions about Vaňhal's contrapuntal understanding and competence

Ex. 6.3 Vaňhal a1/i, bars 45–64 (string parts)

Ex. 6.4 Vaňhal a1/i, bars 99–106 (string parts)

(see also the discussion of g2/i in chapter 3). Another odd feature is the medial caesura choice in the first movement. A half cadence in the tonic is followed by a caesura and then a subordinate theme in v. In other words, an E major chord leads directly to an E minor chord interpreted as the new tonic.

Junker's remarks about "lack of melody" and "fastidiousness" ring true for a1. Perhaps Vaňhal was copying features of music that he admired or was encouraged to admire without fully understanding the principles behind them. Ideas seem to have been taken from here and there and thrown together so that, out of context, they no longer make sense. The symphony shows that the eclectic combination of contrasting figures and topics so characteristic of Viennese music of the late eighteenth century was not straightforward to bring off. It can hardly be argued that the two outer movements are parody or burlesque, notwithstanding the points made about the opening of the finale in chapter 4 (see esp. Ex. 4.6). The exaggeration of conventional features is not clear or consistent enough and too many new strategies are used.

Tragic Symphonies (1): d2

Some of the same new strategies are found in d2, but here Vaňhal's innovations are much more successful. Heartz's negative judgment about the work is surely misplaced: the first movement is the best movement among Vaňhal's later minor-key symphonies, and opens new expressive possibilities. Although 351 bars in length and repetitive in places, it sustains momentum and interest far better than e2/i or a1/i. The large dimensions are mainly the result of expansion of paragraphs from within rather than additive processes applied to short units. The movement's distant key relationships, the dramatic events of the development, and the recomposition of the recapitulation recall or anticipate much-admired aspects of the best symphonies of Haydn and Mozart. Vaňhal's trademark nervous energy is still present in places, but without the usual *Trommelbass*, tremolandi, or syncopations. Indeed, it is complemented by a degree of rhythmic composure rare for him, which helps to give the movement a tragic character that goes beyond Vaňhal's usual storminess or rest-lessness. The outer movements in Vaňhal's minor-key symphonies of the 1760s could be characterized as stormy, nervous, plaintive, or uneasy, but seldom tragic (with the usual exception of a2; see chapter 3). There are three markings of *perdendosi* (the word also appears at the very end of the finale), and the movement contains many phases of waxing and waning energy, brooding moments, and pauses that recall heroic arias in contemporary opera (see chapter 1).

The main theme instantly evokes tragic sentiment, but in an unusual way. Although its structure (abb') has many precedents in Vaňhal's earlier minor-key symphonies, in terms of topic it is quite new and points to diverse antecedents. Minuet topic is strongly suggested at times, for instance in the cadential bars 7–8 and 11–12.[26] However, the opening rising third progression in bars 1–3 carries a quite different association. The voice leading does not reinforce the galant "Do–Re–Mi" schema that underlies the opening melodies of e3/i, c2/i, and e1/i. Instead, there are untimely allusions, such as the fast-moving bass and the suspension in bar 2 that recalls a Corelli leapfrog with the notes redistributed between the two upper parts.[27] Like the main theme of e2/i, this one introduces its hesitant appoggiaturas early, although with fewer repetitions (Ex. 6.5). The minor mode, Corelli allusion, and minuet gestures indicate formality and objectiv-ity, the hesitant appoggiaturas subjective suffering.

The exposition as a whole is broad and continuous, developing the solemn, pro-cessive aspect of the main theme. Indeed, in terms of its structure it could argu-ably be regarded as a "continuous exposition" in the technical sense, as there is no

Ex. 6.5 Vaňhal d2/i, bars 1–12[1]

---

[26] Vaňhal had already used minuet topic for the main theme of the first movement of a symphony (G11) but there the effect is sweet, lyrical, and slightly humorous.

[27] A real Corelli leapfrog would have one voice moving from the c♯[1] in bar 2[3] to the f[1] in bar 3[1].

clear candidate for medial caesura; at the very least, the caesura is "filled" so elaborately that the division of the exposition into two halves is obscured (bars 44–51).[28]
However, at the local level there are many uncertainties and discontinuities that
make the overall path to the final tonic of the cadence in III highly circuitous and
dramatic, heightening the original element of hesitation in the main theme. The
first of these is the ambiguity about a mediant tutti. Given the precedents in many
earlier minor-key symphonies, the fragmented gestures over a dominant pedal at
bars 38–42 clearly signal that a mediant tutti is likely to follow, albeit rather later in
the exposition than usual. There is no pause, and the mediant tutti does not occur
immediately: instead, a sequential, modulating transition is inserted and the chord
of III is deferred until bar 52. In its local context this arrival of III is not unambiguously articulated as a mediant tutti, but bars 38–43 cue a listener familiar with
the subgeneric conventions to hear it as such. In addition to the hesitancy of bars
38–42, there are three pauses within the continuation that follows the tutti (bars
63, 79–80, and 93–94), which on each occasion coincide with a drop in dynamics
and scoring (the second and third are shown in Ex. 6.6). A low, brooding passage marked *perdendosi* precedes the third pause (bars 91–93). After the second
and third pauses there are sudden, loud tuttis, symbolically putting the exposition
back on course, headed for the perfect authentic cadence in III. These techniques
are familiar from Vaňhal's earlier symphonies (such as e1/i—see chapter 3), but he
never before used them so intensively. The exposition is sparing with characteristic
material—the mediant-tutti-like gesture, for instance, reuses an earlier idea—but
there is no monotony as there was in e2/i. As in a1/i there is plenty of conventional
material in the second half of the exposition, but here it is used more effectively,
supporting continuation or cadential functions, the internal expansion of the paragraph and the delaying of cadential arrival.

The development of d2/i further dramatizes the main theme's original moment
of hesitation and brings the movement to a crisis of continuation. It is one of
Vaňhal's biggest development sections (108 bars), although at the outset the first
thirty bars of the exposition are simply repeated in III, including two statements of
the main theme, the second played by oboes exactly as in the exposition. (Vaňhal
often made complete thematic repetitions at this point in a sonata form: in g2/i,
for instance, the whole of the mediant tutti paragraph is repeated note for note in
III, just as in the exposition.) If these repetitions seem suspiciously mechanical, the
rest of development is highly effective. The music gains momentum in a modulating paragraph before another *perdendosi* and a pause. Now the main theme starts
in E♭ (♭II in relation to the tonic D minor)—a very distant key for Vaňhal—but a
further pause occurs halfway through, and the thematic statement never restarts.
Here, halfway through the development and far from the tonic, is the movement's

---

[28] "Continuous exposition" is Hepokoski and Darcy's term for an exposition that lacks a medial
caesura and thus by definition (in their view) also lacks a "secondary" (subordinate) theme. *Elements
of Sonata Theory*, 51. Hepokoski and Darcy largely neglect the subject of medial caesuras in minor-key
movements.

Ex. 6.6 Vaňhal d2/i, bars 76–99

crisis. The journey back for the start of the recapitulation is begun by a slowly rising sequence, which very gradually accelerates and builds to *f*. Near the climax comes one of Vaňhal's harshest passages (Ex. 6.7, bars 207–10), with diminished seventh harmony (over an implied E pedal in the bass), off-beat *sforzandi* and a high register for all instruments. The final climax of the development is in A minor (v), the only move to a key on the sharp side of the tonic in the whole movement. The material here is the triplets and syncopations from the exposition's codetta: the syncopations, so common in Vaňhal's minor-key style of the 1760s, have been used sparingly to this point in the movement, and so carry a special rhetorical emphasis. No other Vaňhal minor-key sonata movement dramatizes the reprise of the main theme so forcefully.

There are three notable alterations in the recapitulation relative to the exposition, all of which darken the mood and reinforce the minor mode. First, the second statement of the main theme (in oboes and violins) enters in VI (B♭ major); then the next, transition-like section modulates to vii (C minor). An exploration of flat keys at this point in the form is characteristic of "secondary development" in Haydn, Mozart, and Beethoven,[29] but it is rare in the works of other Viennese composers

---

[29] Rosen, *Sonata Forms*, 289–95.

Ex. 6.7 Vaňhal d2/i, bars 202–19[1]

in the 1770s (Ordonez G7/i is an exception; see chapter 2). In Vaňhal d2/i the link with secondary development is purely tonal: no new motivic fragmentation takes place. The second alteration is the use of a Neapolitan sixth chord (♭II6/3) for the *perdendosi* passage (bars 307–10) instead of the diatonic supertonic sixth (ii6/3). Now in D minor, its brooding quality anticipates some of Mozart's music in that key. The third alteration is the addition of the dramatic coda, which reviews the movement's hesitations, pauses, and forceful gestures, all in a context of almost total motivic liquidation.

Despite a few imperfections, d2/i is one of Vaňhal's strongest minor-key movements. The main theme's initial allusions to both formal solemnity and subjective suffering, along with its complex minor-key minuet signals and its combination of steady forward motion and hesitation are developed to create a movement of tragic character that approaches epic dimensions. The development of d2/i is far more ambitious than usual for Vaňhal, and, after a slow start, its architecture is impressive: a moment of discontinuity halfway through in a very distant flat key is followed by a slow, continuous buildup to a violent climax in a sharp key, but one closely related to the tonic. The movement opens new expressive possibilities that were unavailable in Vaňhal's style of the late 1760s and exploits them to the full.

The finale of d2 does not reach the level of the first movement, although it is still of high quality. It has fewer formal manipulations or modulations, and is fairly close to the Type 2 stormy finale of the late 1760s: it is in 2/2 meter, frequently repeats short units, opens with a loud unison gesture followed by *rf* accents, and combines fast surface rhythm with slow harmonic rhythm. On the other hand, the three-bar hypermeter of the main theme is never found in stormy finales of the 1760s. As in several other movements of the later minor-key symphonies, including d2/i, Vaňhal does not introduce *Trommelbass* and tremolandi immediately: in this case he delays them until the middle of the development (bar 58). The *perdendosi* effect of the coda (described above) means the symphony ends with a gesture of diminishing energy that recalls many moments in the first movement.

Tragic Symphonies (2): f1

Vaňhal's interest in the tragic continues with f1/i, although in this case the finale turns to major much earlier than d2/iii and even before it does so it gestures to the comic. Indeed, Vaňhal f1 explores opposite extremes more than any other Viennese minor-key symphony. The first movement is exceptionally dark, yet the finale, beginning also in minor, transforms itself and ends in unambiguous cheerfulness.

The first movement's character matches the uniquely negative associations of the key of F minor in the eighteenth century (see chapter 5). In terms of mode the exposition is uniformly negative. The subordinate key is v, and there is not even a gesture towards III during the transition—indeed, no major keys are touched on at all until the development. The exposition is "monothematic" both in the sense that the basic idea of the main theme is reused in varied form as the basic idea of the subordinate theme and in the looser sense that the figures from that idea are used intensively throughout. At first, direct emotional expression is blocked by the main theme, but it gradually emerges over the course of the exposition until it finally overflows.

The main theme is formal and abrupt: it opens with emphatic tonic and dominant chords, heavily scored, with all instruments playing in low registers, followed by a rest (Ex. 6.8). There is no anacrusis, which is in itself notable for Vaňhal in a minor-key first movement; he seldom starts with a strong downbeat attack. The first two chords sound like a motto, and the melodic figure they accompany (*a* in Ex. 6.8) indeed functions referentially throughout the movement. The customary fast surface rhythm, *Trommelbass*, and syncopations are deferred until the start of the theme's continuation (bar 5). The moderate tempo and silences give the presentation a spacious quality that, as in d2/i, indicates the dimensions of the movement to come. Also highly unusual for Vaňhal is the sharp contrast within the two-bar basic idea: the harsh chords are answered by a soft, descending line for first violins alone with staccato notes and appoggiaturas, beginning on an off-beat eighth note (*b*). The small-scale contrasts and pauses of the presentation phrase block continuity and Vaňhal's usual broad lyricism. The structure of the phrase suggests instead the dialogue of a contemporary operatic ensemble: a peremptory command alternates with a pleading answer. There is nothing like this opening elsewhere in Vaňhal, or even in the minor-key instrumental music of Haydn to this date. But comparisons could be drawn with the openings of the first movements of Mozart's Piano Quartet in G minor, K. 478 (1785), and Piano Sonata in C minor, K. 457 (1784), both composed a decade later than Vaňhal f1.

Ex. 6.8 Vaňhal f1/i, bars 1–12. Fürst Thurn und Taxis Zentralarchiv und Hofbibliothek, Regensburg. D Rtt no. 40

As the exposition progresses the sternness of the presentation of *a* is gradually ameliorated and the expressive qualities of *b* come to the fore. The disjointed opening gives way to greater continuity and mounting waves of energy, and the exposition even acquires a lyrical dimension. The mood is still bleak, but the harshness and stiffness of the opening are softened and the rhetoric of lamentation emerges. The process occurs in three stages, each more expansive than the last. The first is in the continuation of the main theme. As the *Trommelbass* and syncopated accompaniment begins, rests are eliminated, the rate of attacks of *a* accelerate fourfold to half-bar intervals, and rising and falling arpeggios broaden the melodic span (bars 5–8). The cadential progression is accompanied by stereotypical devices for expressing sorrow: a Neapolitan sixth chord with *sf* accent (bar 9), then Lombardic appoggiaturas (bars 10–11). The second stage of the process occurs in the transition.[30]

---

[30] The main theme, although sentential in structure, ends with a half cadence, thus taking the form that Hepokoski and Darcy call "grand antecedent." The transition begins with a reference to the

Like the original continuation, the transition soon introduces *Trommelbass*, syncopations, fragmentation, and rising melodic gestures, but with the melody an octave higher than before and the upward motion more gradual (melodic sequence), while avoiding rests by extending *a* with quarter notes. Sustained wind chords contribute to a sense of broadening span.[31] There is a curious effect halfway through the transition (bar 21), as lyricism and rhythmic steadiness unexpectedly emerge. While the well-spread texture and faster surface rhythm are maintained, there is a sense that the formal function reverts to presentation, with the return of two-bar (instead of one-bar) intervals between the attacks of *a*. This type of process is unusual in transitions, which are more likely to move in the opposite direction (fragmentation and liquidation). In comparison with the movement's opening, though, the mode of presentation is transformed: there are no caesuras and less internal contrast within the basic idea. The figures *a* and *b* are integrated within a smooth melodic line.

The third stage in the softening of expression occurs in the subordinate theme (shown in part in Ex. 6.9), which rehearses the same process, but still more expansively, bringing it to a crisis. The basic idea of the subordinate theme (bars 29–32) is the lyrical idea introduced halfway through the transition, now played by violins rather than in the bass (a similar procedure was noted at the same stage of the exposition in d2/i). The idea now quite comfortably expresses initiating function. At the start of the subordinate theme the repeated-note accompaniment coincides with a presentation phrase for the first time in the movement, bringing the thematic syntax closer to Vaňhal's normal first-movement minor-key style. The continuation is extremely dramatic and leads to the crisis: a tense rising melodic sequence over a *Trommelbass* tonic pedal leads to a cadential progression that begins softly with *a* extended into a lyrical melodic line with appoggiaturas, while—a very striking touch—the *Trommelbass* turns into unbroken minims. But the theme will not be brought to a conclusion so straightforwardly. The cadence is interrupted and the broad continuity of the theme breaks down. A nervous figure related to the second half of *b* is softly and hesitantly repeated in sequence, finally ending in an unaccompanied echo (bar 43). The newfound momentum of the exposition ebbs away into silence. At bar 44, dammed-up energy bursts out in a loud tutti on a diminished seventh chord, the wind re-entering, having been silent since the end of the transition. At last the sternness and formality of *a* in its original guise is combined with the rhetoric of lamentation that has been emerging during the exposition, resulting in a long, climactic outpouring that extends the cadential progression to twenty-four bars (the exposition as a whole is only sixty-one bars in length).

This untrammelled emotional expression is abruptly ended, however. The final tonic chord of the cadential progression is elided with a two-bar retransition and the music plunges back into the main theme for the exposition repeat, immediately

---

opening of the theme, taking the form of "dissolving consequent." Hepokoski and Darcy, *Elements of Sonata Theory*, 77.

[31] John Spitzer and Neal Zaslaw call this the "wind organ" effect. *The Birth of the Orchestra: History of an Institution, 1650–1815* (Oxford: Oxford University Press, 2004), 464–67.

Ex. 6.9 Vaňhal f1/i, bars 29–47. Fürst Thurn und Taxis Zentralarchiv und
Hofbibliothek, Regensburg. D Rtt no. 40

blocking the expression of pain once again. There is, in other words, no pause for
breath with a postcadential closing section, a formal function that is almost always
found in this position in late eighteenth-century Viennese sonata forms, especially
after such a loosely organized subordinate theme. A closing section normally helps
to dissipate energy built up by the drive to the final tonic of a subordinate theme's
cadential progression.

The parallel moment of cadential arrival in the recapitulation of f1/i is almost as
abrupt. A five-bar coda replaces the retransition, likewise elided with the cadential
arrival, which brings back the main theme's presentation phrase in the tonic. The
coda confirms the motto status of *a*, which thus frames the movement at beginning
and end—another effect that Vaňhal, in contrast to the imperial court composers,
had avoided in minor-key outer movements of the 1760s. Otherwise, the recapitulation follows the exposition closely, save for the one moment in the transition. The
exposition's tonal drift to v begins, but is swiftly terminated by a return to the tonic
that is dramatized by a repeated two-bar unit with melodic appoggiatura, the second time with a pause over a V7/i chord (bars 128–31). This gives the impression

that the music has been forcefully pulled back—wrenched—into the tonic through an external intervention. Then the transition picks up again with music that parallels bar 21, now stable in the tonic. These modest alterations enhance the tragic aspect of the movement, lending a fateful quality to the recapitulation's tonal and thematic returns.

The development of f1/i is problematic. Of its three sections, the two outer ones are unstable, the first based on the retransition bars, the other resembling the main theme's continuation and the exposition's transition. The second section of the development is an expanded, but otherwise literal, statement of the main theme in III. If one's way of making sense of the movement is to listen for a narrative (an approach implicit in the forgoing discussion) then this seems an unmotivated event. It can hardly be interpreted as a transformation of the theme in the name of triumph, hope, or rejoicing, as nothing prepares or justifies it and neither does it endure. Instead, the passage seems merely to mark time before the next unstable section of the development. In this way it recalls the excessive repetitions of e2/i and the complete restatement of the main theme in III of d2/i in the development of that movement. The major mode appears nowhere else in the movement, so it could be argued that the restatement provides variety and relief, but in that case Vaňhal's near-literal restatement of his main theme seems a half measure.[32]

The finale of f1 is another long movement, and it shows some striking parallels with the first. *Trommelbass*, for instance, appears only at the start of the continuation of the main theme (Ex. 6.10), and does so on a tonic pedal with climbing sequential repetitions in the melody above: all reminiscent of the early stages of f1/i. As in the first movement, the main theme and transition take on the form Hepokoski and Darcy would call "grand antecedent" / "dissolving consequent,"[33] which Vaňhal had seldom employed before. Again there is no hint of a mediant tutti. The exposition is "monothematic" in that the basic ideas of the main theme and the first of the two subordinate themes are similar. All these similarities mean that the finale unfolds against a background determined to a great extent by the first movement. The differences between them thereby assume particular significance.

Most importantly, perhaps, the tonal and modal plan of the finale is the opposite of the first movement's. The exposition's subordinate key is III and the entire recapitulation is in the tonic major. Moreover, unlike the first movement, the finale begins softly and with fast, continuous motion. There are no sharp internal contrasts within the presentation phrase, and the mood is restless rather than tragic. In fact, the main theme opens as a fast, minor-key minuet, albeit one that is undone by the continuation phrase (staccato repeated notes, pedal, *sforzandi*). The expositions of both movements undertake syntactic and semantic transformations, but that of the finale replaces unease by levity and effects syntactic normalization.

---

[32] Given the tonal parallels with Haydn 45/i (both expositions using v rather than III), it is interesting that Haydn too has a stable major-key section in the development. But Haydn's is totally contrasting in mood, dynamics, scoring, and rhythm (minuet topic).

[33] Hepokoski and Darcy, *Elements of Sonata Theory*, 77, 101–2.

Ex. 6.10 Vaňhal f1/iii, bars 1–13². Fürst Thurn und Taxis Zentralarchiv und Hofbibliothek, Regensburg. D Rtt no. 40

Chapter 4 explored the paradoxes and ambiguities of minor-key minuets. The exposition of f1/iii sets up some of them initially, but resolves them in the first subordinate theme.

In that theme (starting at bar 46³; see Ex. 6.11) normalization takes place on several levels. The mode is major; the four-bar basic idea is now repeated in full (with variation) rather than only in part (compare bars 1–6¹ with bars 46³–54¹); there are no repeated notes or pedal; the harmony is more varied and moves more regularly; four-bar phrases are ubiquitous, as in a danced minuet; and the form is small binary (rather than a sentential grand antecedent) with the repeats written out. The small binary form is normal for a minuet but unusual for a sonata-movement subordinate theme of the 1770s. Moreover, despite its thirty-two-bar length (including repeats) the first subordinate theme is unusually tight-knit in terms of harmony and phrase structure: unusual for a subordinate theme as such, but normal for a minuet.

Along with this normalization, the exposition registers a drift to the comic in two respects. First, the transition engages in some witty play with the listener's expectations of a kind seldom found in Vaňhal. It appears to be making for the

Ex. 6.11 Vaňhal f1/iii, bars 27–54[2]. Fürst Thurn und Taxis Zentralarchiv und
Hofbibliothek, Regensburg. D Rtt no. 40

primary default medial caesura: one preceded by a half cadence in the subordinate
key.[34] But after the dominant chord of III (E♭ major) has been prolonged for five bars
(bars 27–31), the bass falls away to D♭ (bar 32), the harmony moves to an A♭ major 6/3
chord (bar 33), and the transition continues (Ex. 6.11). This tactic is similar to the one

---

[34] For Hepokoski and Darcy in major keys V: HC MC; here III: HC MC.

that Hepokoski and Darcy call "bait-and-switch."[35] Vaňhal eventually makes a medial caesura after a perfect authentic cadence in III (bars 43–46), although only after some further toying with expectations through comic effects such as pauses, abrupt dynamic switches, short staccato phrases, and surprising harmonic twists (for instance bar 37). The second aspect of the comic drift is found in the second of the two subordinate themes, which takes up the passagework and the witty silences of the transition, while the *Trommelbass*, pedal, and rising melodic sequences also re-enter. The bustling combination of rapid surface rhythm with all but trivial harmony (alternating I and V) suggests an allusion to *opera buffa*. The function of this section is to confirm—in a narrative account one might say celebrate—the now-stabilized subordinate key and major mode.

The development begins with a restatement of part of the main theme in III. Given the positive events of the second half of the exposition, this makes more sense than the similar restatements in d2/i and f1/i (as well as being more concise). The main event of the second half of the movement, however, is the reprise of the main theme in the tonic major after a portentous, twelve-bar prolongation of the dominant (bars 134–45) that implies the tonic minor instead (A♭s rather than A♮s). This further positive gesture, aside from dissolving the marked minor mode into the unmarked major, further extends the exposition's process of normalization: there is no combination of minuet topic and minor key at all in the recapitulation. No repeats are marked in the second half of the finale, which encourages the narrative account developed here: the transformation from minor to major occurs only once.

This symphony is impressive, even if it lacks a movement at the level of d2/i. The parallels between the first movement and the finale mean that the latter can be heard as an answer to the former, making a comprehensible narrative through the three-movement cycle. Whether that narrative is convincing is another question. The turn to tonic major in the finale could be felt to trivialize the tragedy of the first movement, presenting a problem similar to that of the finale of Mozart's G minor String Quintet, K. 516. The practice of ending minor-key symphony outer movements in major became common in the 1770s and in the 1780s; indeed, by the time of Vaňhal f1, Haydn had already taken that route in 26/i and 45/iv. In those works the modal reversal is usually accompanied by some other significant alteration—to motivic material, scoring, or form—or occurs in a coda that is quite distinct from the rest of the movement (examples are discussed in chapter 7). In Vaňhal f1/iii (just as in a2/iii) the whole of the recapitulation is presented in the tonic major, with hardly any further alterations. The baldness of this modal reversal is underlined by the fact that, of all the Viennese minor-key symphonies that turn to major by the end of the finale, Vaňhal f1 is the one with the darkest first movement. A belief in

---

[35] Hepokoski and Darcy, *Elements of Sonata Theory*, 54–60. They discuss "bait-and-switch" only in the context of the "continuous exposition"—one in which there is no medial caesura at all. But the principle can apply also to "two-part" expositions that eventually do make a caesura and follow it with a subordinate theme.

providence, the efficacy of divine grace, or simply an amoral outlook on the world may be necessary in order to accept f1 as a satisfying experience.

Vaňhal Questions

Why did Vaňhal make the changes in style and strategy in his later minor-key symphonies, especially as the results were so mixed, and sometimes meant the abandonment of the very qualities—melodic fluency, "fire" (Gerber), succinctness, directness—that had served him so well? Unfortunately, very little is known about the tastes and musical values of his patrons, let alone how they might have changed over time.[36] There is no evidence that in the early 1770s he knew any of Haydn's minor-key symphonies after No. 39,[37] and in any case the direction in which he took the minor-key symphony resembles that taken by Haydn in the 1780s more than the one Haydn pursued c. 1770. One could of course fall back on the tried-and-trusted explanation, and attribute the unsuccessful experimentation in e2/i and a1/i to Vaňhal's recent bout of insanity, or alternatively, following Burney, to his even more recent emergence into sanity.

A more convincing explanation—albeit one that must remain speculative—would account for Vaňhal's insanity and his change of compositional direction as symptoms of the same cause: his humble, provincial origins. They may have caused difficulties of assimilation within the cosmopolitan worlds of aristocratic courts and of professional musicians, and a lack of self-confidence that left Vaňhal over-sensitive to criticism and readily influenced by apparently authoritative judgments and theoretical reasoning. This would account for his turn to monothematicism and sometimes excessive repetition, his three-movement schemes, and his modal reversals. In the 1770s many north German critics adhered to the old-fashioned principle that each movement should contain a single main idea to be developed and repeated in various guises, even if they sometimes justified it with reference to contemporary theories of human sensation.[38] Even Haydn and Mozart were criticized on these grounds.[39] In the 1780s Haydn was commended by French and English critics for the ability to write an interesting movement using only one theme. As noted in chapter 4, north German critics also rejected the inclusion of minuets in symphonies—their targets were Viennese symphonies in particular—and preferred a

---

[36] The multiple horn parts and unusual crook combinations may reflect the large orchestra of the Prince of Thurn und Taxis, who owned copies of these and many other symphonies by Vaňhal. Bryan, *Johann Wanhal*, 157.

[37] He must have known Haydn 44 later. See chapter 3.

[38] See the excerpts quoted in Bellamy Hosler, *Changing Aesthetic Views of Instrumental Music in Eighteenth-Century Germany* (Ann Arbor: UMI Research Press, 1981), chap. 5 (pp. 143–88). Hosler's aim is to show the German writers justifying the modern, contrast-based style of instrumental music with a concept of human emotion as mutable, but in fact what is striking is their adherence to overall unity (it is only a single passion that swells, dies away, and so on).

[39] Zaslaw, *Mozart's Symphonies*, 416, 530–31.

three-movement format. In the 1770s the major mode came to be regarded by intellectuals as more natural than minor, perhaps accounting for Haydn's modal reversals of the 1780s and Vaňhal's as well (chapter 1).

Vaňhal arrived in Vienna still formally a serf with a debt of bondage. His first language was Czech. He must have become proficient in German, but in 1772 Burney thought it noteworthy that he could speak no French. After a long stay in Italy, he had acquired only a little Italian—a hindrance for a musician of the time. Vaňhal never held an official position such as Kapellmeister to a court, and he never composed an opera, still in the late eighteenth century the most prestigious musical genre and the one most likely to lead to fame and fortune. Moreover, Vaňhal felt that he lacked a good teacher, telling Dlabacž that he was forced to study the scores of the greatest masters for himself, so he may have had the psychology of the insecure autodidact. In particular, Vaňhal probably lacked a thorough grounding in counterpoint, and may have felt inadequate in that area of traditional compositional craftsmanship. His attempts at formal counterpoint in his instrumental music are infrequent, brief, often problematic in some way, and sometimes consist of direct paraphrases of contrapuntal passages by Haydn. It has been claimed that Vaňhal proved himself a good contrapuntist in his sacred music, but this is not substantiated by the small fraction of his sacred music that is currently published or recorded.[40] But he paraphrased Haydn in non-contrapuntal passages too, a practice that seems extraordinarily deferential for a composer who had an international reputation of his own and was hardly short of ideas. An anonymous biographer writing after Vaňhal's death in 1812 reported that during his psychological crisis Vaňhal suffered hallucinations during which he was persuaded, among other things, to throw onto the fire some compositions, including a symphony that he had just completed.[41] That might be nothing more than scurrilous gossip, of which there was plenty in Vienna at the time. But in the context of what is known about the rest of Vaňhal's circumstances, it should not be dismissed out of hand. Disregarding the sensational aspect, one could interpret this tale as the symptom of an underlying psychological truth: Vaňhal's lack of confidence in his own abilities.

Vaňhal's situation was less advantageous than those of his Viennese contemporaries. From the older generation, Wagenseil came from a court family and sang in the Empress's chapel as a boy. His pupil Leopold Hofmann, a close contemporary of Vaňhal's and a fellow symphonist, was from a similar background and followed the same route through the Empress's chapel, eventually succeeding Wagenseil as Hofklaviermeister and becoming Kapellmeister at St. Stephen's Cathedral. Gassmann, like Vaňhal, was from Bohemia, but his family was German, and he spent his formative years in Venice. Ordonez was the son of a nobleman and army lieutenant, Dittersdorf the son of a costumier at the imperial court and theater.

---

[40] There is a fugue in the *Stabat Mater*, though not an especially complex one.

[41] Anonymous, "Nekrolog auf das Jahr 1812 [sic]. Johann Wanhall," in *Vaterländische Blätter für den Österreichischen Kaiserstaat 2* (1813): 476–78; cited in full and in translation in Bryan, *Johann Wanhal*, 7–11.

Mozart was the antithesis of Vaňhal in many ways: the son of a court musician, a fluent linguist, well-travelled from an early age, at ease in society, and highly—even excessively—self-assured. Haydn's background was the most similar to Vaňhal's. He was of rural peasant stock, lived in a garret in his youth, probably always regarded himself as an outsider relative to the Viennese establishment, and as a young man was reserved when in polite company. But Haydn was a native speaker of German, carried no debt of bondage, as a chorister sang almost daily in St. Stephen's for a decade, and grew up familiar with imperial ceremony. He later enjoyed the support of a powerful patron, and displayed remarkable energy and resilience. Haydn was irritated by criticism but not swayed by it: he kept to his own course.

Still, in evaluating his overall achievement this aspect of Vaňhal's personality should not be overstressed. After all, he rose from obscurity to win fame and respect in Vienna and abroad and enjoyed a long life. If he imitated Haydn on occasion, then he showed better judgment than many contemporary composers and patrons, especially those around the imperial court, for whom the vocal style of Hasse, the galant style in keyboard and orchestral music, and the pseudo-learned style in chamber music were still the touchstones. His contribution to the minor-key subgenre surpasses all other Viennese composers apart from Haydn and Mozart in quantity and quality.

7

Modal Reversal and Characteristic Symphonies

Vaňhal was not alone in taking the composition of minor-key symphonies in new directions from the mid-1770s. Most composers in the Habsburg monarchy who continued to write such pieces adopted a few distinctive strategies that had not been heard in the first flush of minor-key symphonies in the late 1760s. At this time the overall production rate of symphonies in the monarchy was slowing because of financial pressures on the aristocracy, the consequent disbandment of small court orchestras, and the growth of the music publishing industry and middle-class consumption of music.[1] Those minor-key symphonies that did appear were likely intended for concert audiences abroad or for publication, and often came in sets of three or six, alongside major-key counterparts (Haydn 78, 80, 83, and 95; Hoffmeister e1; Koželuch g1; and possibly Mozart K. 550 are examples). These changes in patronage appear to coincide with changes in musical idioms and compositional choices. Contemporary rationalist thought about music, according to which the minor mode was imperfect and dissatisfying, may have played a role too.[2] Although evidence for the direct influence of philosophical aesthetics is scarce, there was certainly a growing reluctance to end a symphony, or indeed any fast movement, in minor. Moreover, there is a strong narrative thread in these pieces. As Floyd Grave puts it, the modal switch could stand for "adversity overcome, yearnings satisfied or a state of impairment rectified by the restoration of wholeness and stability."[3] There is a tendency to the picturesque, evidenced in tone-painting, subtitles, and extra-musical commentary in the scores. Some minor-key works may be classified as "characteristic" symphonies,[4] while others have oblique connections with works of that type. Many of them invite new forms of judgment and understanding from the listener, replacing the traditional values of compositional craft

---

[1] David Wyn Jones, *The Symphony in Beethoven's Vienna* (Cambridge: Cambridge University Press, 2006), 36–49.

[2] As argued by Grave, "Recuperation, Transformation and Transcendence," 27–32.

[3] Ibid., 33.

[4] Richard Will, *The Characteristic Symphony in the Age of Haydn and Beethoven* (Cambridge: Cambridge University Press, 2002), 1.

with ideas borrowed from the theater, literature, or the visual arts. Some pieces include passages that resemble operatic storm scenes, and at least one was used as incidental music to a play. In the more abstract works, wit and humor are far more prominent than before. This chapter examines later minor-key symphonies that turn to major at some stage and end there. A much smaller group from the 1780s, which remain resolutely in minor, is deferred to chapter 8.

At first glance it might seem that with these major-turning symphonies it is almost meaningless to speak of a subgenre, as by the end the minor-key symphony all but dissolves back into a major-key symphony. Moreover, on the argument of chapter 1, according to which the minor-key symphony stands out as a reaction against the default entertainment function of so much instrumental music of the time, these works would appear relatively shallow in conception. The cheerful major ending trivializes the minor beginning; rationalistic aesthetics leads to generic standardization and the suppression of individuality and personal expression, especially the expression of suffering; and tone-painting indicates a decline in the quality of listening, an inattention to the sonic phenomenon. As Grave puts it, major-key endings can be seen as "a compromise, or perhaps as recompense for the liberty of indulging in minor to begin with."[5] Such arguments may have some validity when a first movement ends in minor and the rest of the symphony is in major, as though the movements were drawn from different sources. In that case there is no narrative of transformation within any movement. Dittersdorf a1 and Wranitzky 11 in particular could be cited here (see Table 7.1; Wranitzky 43 has a special program, while the two other symphonies listed are of the uncommon, monotonal "da chiesa" type). Yet even Dittersdorf a1 hangs together by virtue of the element of humor that is already found in the first movement. There may be further subtleties that ameliorate the sense of trivialization. The choice of keys for the inner movements often betrays the lingering influence of the tonic minor, widening the tonal range of the symphony as a whole far beyond that of most major-key symphonies of the time. This applies to the non-"da chiesa" symphonies in Table 7.1, along with Haydn 80 (d→D, B♭, d, D), Haydn 83 (g→G, E♭, G, G), and Haydn 95 (c→C,

TABLE 7.1 Viennese minor-key symphonies that end in major but without a movement that changes mode

	Movement Keys
Dittersdorf a1	i VI III I
Dittersdorf d1	i I I I
Haydn 34	i I I I
Wranitzky 11	i III i I
Wranitzky 12	i III I V–I
Wranitzky 43	i V I

---

[5] Grave, "Paths from Minor to Major," 41.

Eb, c, C), all of which have chromatic mediant shifts between moveme
of which revert to the tonic minor for their minuets. Haydn 78 has
the tonic major, C major, but soon tonicizes i and bIII (C minor and
unusual moves in a major-key Classical minuet.[6] Moreover, when a movement tur..
from minor to major, the subgenre is not simply cancelled, as the major key has a
special significance; within the context of the movement it becomes "marked" in
relation to the minor.[7] And for the interpretation of these pieces the concept of
subgenre remains useful because in their minor-key sections they evoke the recent
musical past and its techniques, conventions, and movement-level strategies. As
Grave puts it again, Haydn's later minor-key works gave him "an opportunity . . . to
sustain connections with his own past accomplishments in the minor domain, and
they allowed for the persistence of older traditions or otherwise marginal idioms
and styles."[8] Understanding their expressive effects, including the precise significance of each conversion to major, requires knowledge of those traditions.

Table 7.2 lists the movements of the minor-key repertory that convert minor into
major. It shows first that the imperial court composers Wagenseil, Ordonez, and
Gassmann, who were active in the subgenre mainly in the 1760s, largely avoided
modal reversal, with only Gassmann 23/iv bucking the trend. The early minor-key
symphonies of Haydn and Vaňhal are likewise absent, with the exceptions only of
Haydn 26/i (in which the Gregorian Passion melody can hardly be used in minor
in the recapitulation without distortion), the notorious Haydn 45/iv, and Vaňhal
e3 (in this respect as in others the twin to Dittersdorf e1). Most of the movements
in Table 7.2 are either sonata forms or sectional forms with short repeated sections. The latter—always finales—sometimes alternate minor and major sections
(Dittersdorf a2/iv, Haydn 78/iv), or else turn to major for the last (unrepeated)
section (Dittersdorf e1/iv, Vaňhal e3/iv). Wranitzky 30/iii and Gassmann 23/iv are
unusual forms that resemble sonata forms; the first half of the exceptional Haydn
45/iv is a sonata form, but the move to major occurs in the slow second half.

The conventional sonata-form movements may turn to major in one of three
ways. The whole of the recapitulation may be in major (this version is employed
only by Vaňhal in a2/iii and f1/iii, both discussed in chapter 6). The movement
may turn to major only in a coda that follows the end of the recapitulation proper.
Or the movement may turn to major somewhere in the course of the recapitulation, usually at the return of the subordinate theme. The latter is Haydn's favored
minor-key strategy across all instrumental genres after 1780.[9] The moment of
modal reversal is usually rhetorically heightened. Whichever of the three methods
is used, Grave's point about Haydn usually applies: "At a critical moment, often
marked by an emphatic caesura or fermata or a tell-tale hiatus in the texture, minor

---

[6] For a complete list of "remote juxtapositions between movements" in Haydn's minor-mode instrumental cycles, see Webster, *Haydn's "Farewell" Symphony*, 220.

[7] Grave, "Paths from Minor to Major," 18.

[8] Ibid., 40–41.

[9] Grave, "Recuperation, Transformation and Transcendence," 35.

TABLE 7.2 Movements of Viennese minor-key symphonies that turn to major

	Sectional Form With Many Repeats	Turns to Major During Recap	Turns to Major for Final Section / Coda	Entire Recap in Major	Extended Tièrce De Picardie Only
Dittersdorf a2/i		✓			
Dittersdorf a2/iv	✓				
Dittersdorf e1/iv	✓		✓		
Dittersdorf g1/iv			✓		
Gassmann 23/iv			✓		
Haydn 78/iv	✓				
Haydn 95/i		✓			
Haydn 26/i		✓			
Haydn 80/i		✓			
Haydn 45/iv					
Haydn 83/i		✓			
Hoffmeister e1/iv			✓		
Vaňhal a2/iii				✓	
Vaňhal d2/iii					✓
Vaňhal e3/i					✓
Vaňhal e3/iv	✓		✓		
Vaňhal f1/iii				✓	
Wranitzky 10/i		✓			
Wranitzky 30/iii			✓		

will yield to major for the remainder of the form."[10] Thus the moment of thematic reprise at the start of the recapitulation sometimes faces a challenge to its status as the dramatic crux of the second half of the movement, especially, as often happens in Haydn, if it has been rendered ambiguous or problematic in some way.

In these symphonies, recapitulatory modal reversal occurs only in first movements, never, as in Haydn's string quartets, in finales (op. 62, no. 2; op. 74, no. 3; and op. 76, nos. 1 and 3). Nowhere in the repertory can two sonata-form movements be found in a single symphony that undergo modal reversal (as in the Quartet op. 74, no. 3). If the first movement of a symphony turns from minor to major, the finale normally begins in major and remains there. Vaňhal e3 and Dittersdorf a2 have reversals in both outer movements, but only one of those movements is a sonata form and both modal reversals in Vaňhal e3 occur very late in their respective movements. The early Haydn 26 is the only symphony whose finale reverts to minor (and ends there) after the first movement has converted to major. That movement is, exceptionally, a minuet, and in general the finale rule does not apply to minuet third movements, which may revert to minor after a first movement that ends in major (Dittersdorf a2/iii, Haydn 80/iii, and Haydn 95/iii, for instance). Haydn's last three minor-key symphonies, Nos. 80, 83, and 95, make their moves to the major early in the cycle, and there are no dramatic conversions within movements thereafter even

[10] Ibid., 34.

if the minuet is in minor. Judged on formal process and movement keys alone, the balance of minor to major is lightest in Haydn 80 and Wranitzky 10, both of which convert to major in the recapitulations of their first movements and have no further movements in minor.

The movements in Table 7.2 indicate a treatment of the minor mode quite different from the approaches found in instrumental sonata-form movements of Mozart and Beethoven. Mozart remains in minor to the end of almost all his fast minor-key sonata forms, transposing subordinate-key material (usually major) into the tonic and changing the mode to minor, occasionally with small but significant alterations. This applies to the outer movements of his two minor-key symphonies. Beethoven's practice is either to use the dominant (v) for the subordinate key and remain in the tonic minor for the recapitulation, resulting in a minor-saturated movement, or to move to the mediant (III) in the exposition and then touch on the tonic major somewhere in the recapitulation, usually while reprising material first presented in the mediant. The mode then turns back to minor, save perhaps for a *tierce de picardie* ending. The first strategy is typical of Beethoven's sonata-form movements in minor keys other than C minor, the second of sonata-form movements in C minor.[11] Neither Mozart nor Beethoven favors an "escape" from minor within a sonata-form movement (there are of course examples at the level of the whole multi-movement cycle such as Mozart's String Quintet, K. 516, and Beethoven's Fifth and Ninth Symphonies). It would seem that although Haydn's treatment of the minor mode after 1780, especially in sonata forms, was distinctive (he dominates the second column in the table and would do so still more if other genres were included), in general his later strategies were more representative of minor-key symphony writing of the time than Mozart's, while Beethoven took a different path altogether. When Beethoven's minor-key multi-movement cycles end in major, they do so via laborious processes and tortuous routes. Beethoven's sonata-form movements do not readily switch to major. A sudden glimpse of the tonic major during a C-minor sonata-form recapitulation is always swiftly contradicted, as though revealed as a false hope or illusory consolation. The Beethovenian models were influential in the nineteenth century, and knowledge of that repertory may contribute to a modern listener's retrospective interpretation of the late eighteenth-century pieces as shallow. The modal switch is achieved without much toil; it is, as it were, unearned.[12]

---

[11] Joseph Kerman, "Beethoven's Minority," in *Write All These Down* (Berkeley: University of California Press, 1994), 217–37.

[12] On the modern perception of sonata form as labor, see Scott Burnham, "The Second Nature of Sonata Form," in *Music Theory and Natural Order from the Renaissance to the Early Twentieth Century*, ed. Suzannah Clark and Alexander Rehding (Cambridge: Cambridge University Press, 2001), 111–41 (pp. 136–41). For Landon and Jones, the C major minuet of Haydn 78 and the conclusion to the finale are "gratuitously joyful"; see H. C. Robbins Landon and David Wyn Jones, *Haydn: His Life and Music* (Bloomington: Indiana University Press, 1988), 217.

Modal Reversal in the Sonata Recapitulation:
Haydn and Dittersdorf

Haydn's last two instrumental cycles with sonata form outer movements both ending in minor (comparable to most earlier minor-key symphonies) are the String Quartets op. 33, no. 1 (1781), and op. 42 (1784/5). Haydn's final symphony of this type, No. 52, was composed much earlier (1771). The two quartets also have his last finale sonata forms ending in minor, and Op. 42 is his final multi-movement composition to have any kind of finale ending in minor.[13] In the symphonies, the later Haydn minor-key sonata forms are all first movements: 78/i, 80/i, 83/i, and 95/i. The first of these remains in minor to the end, while the other three turn to major during the recapitulation, the strategy for minor-key sonata movements that he favored across all genres at the time. Yet on close examination these movements are not an altogether clean break with past practice. There are unmistakable links with Haydn's own earlier minor-key symphonies far beyond the obvious allusions to the stormy style, and also parallels with compositional strategies used much earlier by Vaňhal.

Although these four first movements betray notable similarities, they are chronologically well spread out, and are independent in other ways too. After 1780 most of Haydn's instrumental compositions were written for the consumption of musicians and audiences beyond the Esterhazy court: publishers, concert societies in Paris and London, connoisseurs in Cádiz (the *Seven Last Words*), and of course purchasers of printed scores. Haydn's symphonies now rapidly reached listeners outside the monasteries and courts of central Europe that assiduously collected his earlier symphonies (many of those earlier symphonies were later published, but without financial gain for Haydn and for distribution only within the Habsburg empire).[14] He now offered symphonies to publishers or concert societies in sets, just as he had always done with quartets, and, as with quartets (with the exception of op. 20), there was exactly one minor-key work in each set. The first such set comprised Nos. 76, 77, and 78, which were originally composed in 1782 for a planned visit to England in 1783 that never came about. Haydn sold them independently to three different publishers. In a letter to the Paris firm Boyer he showed an awareness of the likely demands of the public and publishers and the limitations of orchestras, calling them "three beautiful, magnificent and by no means overly long symphonies…all very easy, and without much concertante," and added "I assure you that these three symphonies will have a huge sale."[15] Haydn's decision to end all four symphonies in major may have had something to do with his pitch for a wide audience. But from the confines of the Esterhazy court, with which he moved only around eastern

---

[13] See Grave, "Recuperation, Transformation and Transcendence," 35.

[14] Landon and Jones, *Haydn*, 215.

[15] July 15, 1783. Published in Armin Raab, "Haydns Briefe an den Verleger Boyer," *Haydn Studien* 8 (2003): 237–52 (pp. 237–38); cited and translated in Daniel Heartz, *Haydn, Mozart and Early Beethoven, 1781–1802* (New York and London: W. W. Norton, 2009), 350–51.

Austria and on the Hungarian borders, Haydn knew little for certain about audiences or orchestras abroad. All the music he produced for European distribution before the "London" symphonies was in this sense composed "blind." Perhaps with Symphony No. 78 in C minor, his first minor-key symphony in a decade, he hoped to win the approval of the connoisseurs in the London audience, while making the concession of a cheerful conclusion, thus widening his appeal across the spread of expert and inexpert listeners, like C.P.E. Bach with his keyboard collections "für Kenner und Liebhaber" or Mozart with his Concertos K. 413, 414, and 415.[16] This would explain the same strategy at the start of his first actual visit to London in 1791, when he again offered a C-minor symphony (No. 95) that ends in major. There is no hard evidence, however, that experts—or anyone—in London especially relished minor-key symphonies; the two leading composers in the city of the preceding decades, J.C. Bach and Carl Friedrich Abel, had produced only one between them,[17] and Haydn 95 was later to prove relatively unpopular.

Haydn 78 unmistakably upholds subgeneric convention at its opening, with its combination of pathos, agitation, and untimely rhetoric: the "pathotype" basic idea (bars 1–2) based around $\hat{1}$–$\natural\hat{7}$–$\hat{6}$,[18] the start of a descending *lamento* bass, and hints of an opening ritornello in the octave texture. There are distinct reminders of the opening pages of Haydn 52 in the same key: the octaves and diminished intervals, the eight-bar opening phrase with only the second half homophonic, the scrubbing accompaniment in second violins. The basic idea seems designed for contrapuntal treatment: Haydn usually needs less excuse to exercise his powers of compositional craft. But these implications are not fully realized until much later. Instead, there is immediate fragmentation. In bar 3 the descending chromatic line $\hat{8}$–$\natural\hat{7}$ is broken and in bar 4 the dynamic drops suddenly to *piano* and the phrase falters rhythmically. The expected chromatic harmonic progression is blocked by the parallel sixths ab^1–f^2, g^1–eb^2. The next phase of the chromatic descent would have required Bb with G and either Db or D♮: compare the opening of Vaňhal g2/i, for instance, or the opening of Mozart's Fantasia in C minor, K. 475. The ab–f figure might still be part of a diminished seventh harmony from the end of the pathotype idea, but its progression to g–eb makes little sense on the terms of the usual schema, implying a pair of parallel 6/3s. The drop to piano articulates this ambiguity. After the hesitation of bar 4 the theme recovers its coherence, finds a homophonic texture and harmonic clarity, and makes for its cadence, resulting overall in a theme of standard, eight-bar length, rounded off with a minuet-derived cadential formula (bars 7–8).

This main theme has been called "the most unstable... of any Haydn symphony to date,"[19] but this could be expressed more precisely: the main theme starts with one type of syntax and ends with another, first evoking old practices and preparing for compositional artifice, before switching tack and converting to galant gestures.

---

[16] Mozart, letter to his father, December 28, 1782. Anderson, *The Letters of Mozart*, 833.

[17] Landon and Jones, *Haydn*, 217.

[18] Brown, *The Symphonic Repertoire*, 2:200.

[19] Ibid., 201.

The wide prospects opened in the first two bars are closed down within the span of the main theme itself, which turns out to be of regular dimensions overall.[20] At this point the movement already seems to be trying to throw off its minor-mode associations, shifting early to a "galant minor."[21] The question arises as to which implication will eventually be realized: will the contrapuntal possibilities later be allowed to unfold freely and the *lamento* to sing forth, or will the piece trim itself neatly and fashionably? The immediate varied repetition of the main theme (bars 9–15) sends conflicting signals and keeps both possibilities open. The homophonic, repeated-note accompaniment reduces any sense of an opening ritornello and clarifies the phrase structure, yet the imitation between treble and bass already brings some contrapuntal techniques into play.

Later in the exposition, when the mode changes to major, modern syntax dominates. Regularity and conventional organization are conspicuously restored; continuity and even rhythmic flow replace fragmentation; increasing harmonic stability, diatonicism, and homophonic texture banish the ambiguity of the movement's opening bars; minuet topic replaces untimely rhetoric; the combination of busy surface rhythm with a relative lack of characteristic material aids the discharge of tension. The long transition, which is drawn out by the evasion of two possible medial caesuras (bars 31–34, 41–42), helps to stabilize the key of the mediant as the tonal goal of the exposition when it is finally confirmed. The subordinate theme (bars 55^2–61^1, repeated in bars 61^2–67^1) is unusually tight-knit, and stands in complete contrast to the ambiguous main theme: it is fully diatonic, and its presentation phrase uses exact repetition and only tonic and dominant chords. Indeed, after the true medial caesura all the harmony is either tonic or dominant, with the exception of only one chord: the pre-dominant ii^6 that defines the cadential progression of the subordinate theme. Without that chord one could hardly speak of a theme at all in functional terms, so closely fixed is the music to the tonic. The subordinate theme even lacks an independent stage of continuation, moving immediately from the presentation to the start of its cadential progression, and lasting only six bars.[22] In the main theme, by contrast, it is the presentation phrase that is hard to identify, as the theme turns swiftly to motivic fragmentation, and thus the expression of continuation function. In the closing section that follows the subordinate theme, the untimely associations of the opening have been entirely superseded. A stereotypical galant rhythm emerges with an appoggiatura on the first beat of a bar and a longer note on the second (bar 71). The exposition thus proposes a straightforward solution to the movement's initial ambiguity by moving decisively to the major

---

[20] This approach can be found elsewhere in Haydn, for instance in the main theme of the String Quartet, op. 50, no. 2. Matthew Riley, Review of Metric Manipulations *in Haydn and Mozart*, by Danuta Mirka, *Music Analysis*, 31, no. 2 (2012): 251–58.

[21] On this concept, see Grave, "Paths from Minor to Major," 11–15.

[22] On this type of theme see Matthew Riley, "Haydn's Missing Middles," *Music Analysis* 30, no. 1 (2011): 37–57.

mode and the galant style at once, at the same time stressing regularity, closure, and stability.

The development and recapitulation take the opposite path. The contrapuntal implications of the main theme are realized near the start of the development with a harmonically unstable passage that verges on eight-part counterpoint with inversion and stretto-like imitation on the opening figure of the main theme in seven of the parts and the opening figure of the subordinate theme in the other (bars 88–93; see also bars 124–29). The opening of the recapitulation picks up the contrapuntal textures (bars 134–51) and presents an array of contrapuntal techniques: imitation and inversion (bars 134–38); more imitation with the suggestions of fugato (bars 142–45); and the combination of the opening figures from main and subordinate themes (bars 142–51). Most significantly of all, the reprise of the main theme also realizes at last the *lamento* topic by extending the descending first-violin line from c^2–b^1♮ through b^1♭ and a^1♭ (in violas, bars 136–37, doubled an octave below by second violins) and finally to the dominant, at the correct harmonic pace. There are two further allusions to the descending chromatic line, first in the tonic (142–45), then in the dominant (146–49), each based on the main theme's opening figure. This procedure references not just the harmonic progression of the *lamento*, but its repetitive formal organization too. By continuing and intensifying the stretto-like procedures of the development and by rewriting the main theme to bring out its sequential tendencies, this reprise heightens the instability of the main theme and further strengthens its expression of continuation function rather than presentation. Brown even finds it difficult to decide whether the music has yet reached the recapitulation at all, and regards Haydn 78/i as a rare Haydn sonata movement that is "more bipartite in orientation than tripartite."[23]

The sharp contrast between the main and subordinate themes in the exposition is eroded in the recapitulation. The scrubbing accompaniment to the subordinate theme is used for the main theme too, while the subordinate theme recurs in the minor mode (for the last time in a Haydn symphony) with its registral range widened for rhetorical emphasis (bars 171–74, 177–80).[24] The melody of the closing section is altered to stress the characteristic $b\hat{6}$ degree of the minor scale (bars 186–87), the same note that featured in the opening pathotype figure. In retrospect, then, the reprise of the main theme comes to seem the decisive dramatic event of the movement, confirming the change of direction begun in the development, and rejecting the proposed solution of the exposition. The second half of the movement could be heard as a casting off of the fetters imposed on the main theme in the second half of the first phrase, allowing the implications of its opening figure full, even luxurious, realization. The composer indulges his own imagination, allowing it to devise a host of ingenious contrapuntal combinations.

In this light Haydn 78/i reveals many strategies found in minor-key symphonies composed around 1770, as described in chapters 3 and 5. The contrast of untimely

---

[23] Brown, *The Symphonic Repertoire*, 2:201.

[24] Grave, "Paths from Minor to Major," 16–17.

and modern idioms, the former challenged by the latter but finally winning out in the "untimely returns" of the recapitulation, can be found in Vaňhal c2/i and g2/i, and Haydn 44/i. Complications at the moment of recapitulation are found in Haydn 39/i, Vaňhal e1/i, Haydn 49/i, and Haydn 49/iv.[25] As in Ordonez G7/i and Vaňhal c2/i the recapitulation of Haydn 78/i seems more expansive than the exposition, regardless of its literal length. The later movements too, although more lightweight than the first, are not wholly out of line with earlier practice. The major-key minuet is unusual, but the choice of the mediant of the tonic minor (E♭ major) for the slow movement is standard and the sectional finale that turns to major by the end echoes Dittersdorf e1/iv and Vaňhal e3/iv. The same type of "galant minor" finale, albeit remaining in minor to the end, is found in Ordonez B1/iii.

The next set of three symphonies, Nos. 79, 80, and 81, appears to have been composed for the traditional pair of Lenten concerts of the Vienna Tonkünstler-Societät in March 1785, organized that year by Mozart. In the end only two were played, along with Mozart's contrafacta oratorio *Davidde penitente*, K. 469, the storm chorus from Haydn's oratorio *Il ritorno di Tobia*, and other, lighter pieces.[26] In comparison with Haydn's efforts of the 1760s and early 1770s, No. 80 seems uncannily inappropriate for a Lenten concert, despite the contrapuntal minor-key minuet and the appearance of the Lamentation chant in the trio, which Haydn had used already in two earlier minor-key symphonies (26/ii and 45/ii).[27] Not only does the first movement turn dramatically and cheerfully to major during the recapitulation, but the finale is entirely in major and plays a cunning metrical joke throughout. Perhaps the attitude to religious festivals at the Tonkünstler-Societät was different from that of the provincial courts and monasteries.

Haydn 80/i has attracted more critical attention than 78/i, and is noted for its originality and its new tone of irony: the combination of themes based on highly contrasted topics (one ultra-stormy, the other a humorous Ländler that appears very late in the exposition); the switch to major for the second half of the recapitulation (Haydn 80/i is his first symphony movement to do this since 26/i); the way the Ländler comes to dominate the development section after its humble beginnings; and the ambiguity of the opening of the recapitulation.[28] The last of these points obviously recalls the movement's immediate minor-key precursor, 78/i, and close examination reveals further connections with 78/i, although the movements' respective outcomes are quite different.

The opening of 80/i, like that of 78/i, is turbulent and unstable and offers possibilities for contrapuntal writing. It too stops for a dramatic pause. The movement begins, as it were, *in medias res*; the signals of continuation function are strong.

---

[25] As Brown says, citing 44/i, 78/i, and 80i, "the recapitulation in minor-mode works can be unusually irregular and/or unconvincingly articulated." Brown, *The Symphonic Repertoire*, 2:201.

[26] Heartz, *Haydn, Mozart and Early Beethoven*, 105–6; McVeigh, "Symphony," 397.

[27] Landon, *Chronicle*, 2:566.

[28] See for instance Brown, *The Symphonic Repertoire*, 2:203–6; Heartz, *Haydn, Mozart and Early Beethoven*, 354–55; Webster, *Haydn's "Farewell" Symphony*, 167.

The first nine bars sound as though they undertake the fragmentation of material that has already—in some imaginary earlier beginning—been presented in more complete form. If they belong at all in a late eighteenth-century piece, then they sound as though they have been lifted out of a development section, although the fast-moving, sturdy bass suggests a texture from an earlier instrumental style. The even, stepwise-rising motive of three quarter notes promises imitation, inversion, or stretto. Inversion of the motive against itself indeed occurs as early as bars 13–14. Implicit suspensions and the literal tied note across the barline of bar 20 reinforce the sense of a contrapuntal texture. Again like its predecessor, 80/i has a strong stabilizing tendency later in its exposition. The mediant is established early, and the subordinate theme (from bar 25) starts with the same motive that began the main theme but smooths out some of the instability, normalizing the syntax to some extent with a sentence initially of default, eight-bar dimensions (four-bar presentation, four-bar continuation, although the cadence is evaded and the cadential arrival deferred). The continuation is even a sort-of Prinner riposte (bars 29–31): there could hardly be a more conventionally galant gesture. The parallels with the transition and subordinate theme of 78/i are again clear.

In the critical literature, the Ländler tune at the end of the exposition (starting at bar 57^2) is usually called the "second theme" or "second subject," but in functional terms this section does not express the interthematic function "subordinate theme": it is far too short, and it uses only tonic and dominant harmony, thus never moving through the succession of intrathematic functions necessary to be regarded as a "theme" at all. Rather, it is a "closing section" that follows the cadential progression of the true subordinate theme. There is of course an irony here in the way Haydn withholds new, characteristic material until after the point of true closure of the theme. Moreover, the presentation phrase of the true subordinate theme, which is based on sequence and has very short units, is not altogether stable: there is some sense of continuous flow through the medial caesura and on to the cadence of the subordinate theme, so the start of the closing section sounds momentarily like the best candidate of the whole exposition for an initiating gesture and thus for the start of a theme. The Ländler seems to be trying to be a proper theme, but has arrived too late, and perhaps, given its incongruous topical associations, even in the wrong movement. Its later recurrences in the development thwart any sustained treatment of the main theme, and add to the humor. There are few precedents for this type of humor in minor-key symphonies of the late 1760s and around 1770: the end of the first section of Haydn 26/iii is a rare example, and even that turns serious in the second half (chapter 4).

The beginning of the recapitulation closely parallels that of 78/i. A new version of the main theme (starting at bar 128) brings out its untimely aspects with various inversions of the three-note motive (compare the inversion in 78/i, bars 134–37) and a dense texture of multiple independent parts. A descending chromatic bass progression (bars 128–31) realizes the *lamento* progression at the same formal juncture as in 78/i. This reprise is still unstable, just as in the earlier movement. The main theme is not prepared with dominant harmony and does not even begin with root position tonic harmony; it now sounds even more like the continuation of something rather than a new start. The tension quickly dissipates, however, through descending melodic gestures as the music reaches a long dominant pedal (bars 136–46) that ends softly with a pause. This prepares the return of the subordinate theme, now in the tonic major. The status of the preceding allusion to the main theme now becomes, retrospectively, even more ambiguous: like the reprise of 78/i it might well be regarded as a continuation of the development, which finally exhausts itself only at the pause before the change of mode. Grave speaks of a "dramatized approach that highlights the change to tonic major as an event of the greatest importance," in which Haydn "undermines the point of recapitulation" and then turns the reprise of the main theme into a "long anacrusis."[29] After the pause the mode remains major to the end of the movement, which concludes with the Ländler. Haydn 80/i thus reaches a completely different outcome from 78/i, and, significantly, the second part of the movement is not marked to be repeated, so the dramatic turn to major is heard only once. On the face of it, the end of this movement seems a clean break with Haydn's earlier minor-key practice, yet it sets up its recapitulatory modal reversal by means of very similar techniques, gestures, and formal strategies. Haydn did not use any of those distinctive techniques or strategies—untimely/galant equivocation, *lamento* realization, recapitulatory ambiguity—in the major-key symphonies of the two three-work groups: Nos. 76, 77, 79, and 81.

The next two movements of the symphony stay in touch with the work's minor-mode opening while progressively emphasizing major. The Adagio is in B♭, the submediant of D minor, a relationship often found between first and second movements of minor-key symphonies. It is much more distant in relation to the immediately preceding D major—an unheard-of ♭VI—suggesting that the tonic minor still exerts a tonal pull. The Adagio is itself minor-inflected, turning dramatically to B♭ minor at the start of the second part and to G minor thereafter. The freely contrapuntal D-minor minuet begins with an allusion to the opening of the first movement. The trio, which uses the Lamentation chant, is in D major, revisiting the modal reversal in the recapitulation of the first movement, and dramatizes the modal opposition through sharp contrasts with the minuet proper (homophony/counterpoint; legato/staccato; soft/loud; conjunct, embellished melody/disjunct, unembellished melody).[30] The lighthearted D-major finale is thus not gratuitous: the minor/major opposition has been kept in play during all three preceding movements, and the finale represents an intensification of the solution reached at the end of the first movement. Nevertheless, in this symphony, as Grave points out, "The unsettled state of tonic minor now serves mainly as a point of departure at the head of the first movement, to be retrieved in earnest only within the relatively small proportions and restrictive formal conventions of the dance movement." He notes a "tendency to channel minor discourse into increasingly narrow spaces."[31]

---

[29] Grave, "Paths from Minor to Major," 19.

[30] Ibid., 20.

[31] Ibid.

The contrasts and irony of 80/i, along with the recapitulatory modal reversal, are pushed further in 83/i (1785), a symphony that, moreover, has no later movement even starting in minor. It is the only minor-key symphony of the six "Paris" symphonies written for a commission from the *Concert de la Loge Olympique*, and, as Bernard Harrison points out, it stands out in other ways. While the other "Paris" Symphonies always keep their bold strokes within limits that ensure general intelligibility, No. 83 is "challenging," "bizarre in the extreme," full of strange contrasts, "the most willful and eccentric of the set," in which Haydn seems "at times to be careless of his listeners." It lacks the "decorum" of the others.[32] From this perspective it might appear that the minor key and the stormy style are no longer controlling or defining features of the work, but merely aspects of this bizarreness, a form of extremity against which contrasts can be defined. In other ways, however, the symphony is highly unified. The consistent use of contrast and juxtaposition across all four movements amounts to a paradoxical kind of cyclic coherence. In the first movement, moreover, sharp contrasts in topic and mood are underpinned by motivic unity in a manner that one encounters more frequently in nineteenth-century music. Harrison even speaks of "thematic transformation" without fear of anachronism.[33] Brown finds that "The surface and intellectual brilliance, the wit, and the endless facile skill which converge in Symphony No. 83 . . . reach a height not achieved in any previous Haydn symphony."[34] Nevertheless, Haydn 83/i maintains some of the characteristic features and strategies found already in 78/i and 80/i, and to this extent the concept of a minor-key subgenre is still useful.

As in 78/i and 80/i the exposition of 83/i conspicuously abandons the minor-mode complex in its second half. The main theme could not evoke the stormy style more clearly, with the *ff* dynamic, repeated-note accompaniment, *forzando* accents, and the prominent C♯ on the first beat of bar 2. Its untimely rhetoric is subtler. The fast repeated-note dotted rhythms combined with slow harmonic rhythm are the most obvious factor (this combination can be found in other Haydn minor-key movements with untimely rhetoric such as String Quartet, op. 55, no. 2/ii), especially when the melodic chromaticism of bars 10–11 appears as well. The first four bars hint once again at a *lamento* progression with their harmonic progression i–V⁶. Just as in the main theme of 83/i, however, it is cut off before it can unfold fully: the second four-bar unit turns the opening into a statement-response presentation phrase with a four-bar, compound basic idea. Again, possible harmonic and melodic fluidity is replaced by stability and symmetry. In the end, after five bars of standing on the dominant, the main theme lasts sixteen bars: longer, but no less regular, than that of 78/i (eight bars). Haydn 83/i does not draw on galant gestures at this point, but the long phase of standing on the dominant and the liquidation of most of the characteristic motivic features (all save the dotted rhythm), neutralize any sense

---

[32] Bernard Harrison, *Haydn: The "Paris" Symphonies* (Cambridge: Cambridge University Press, 1998), 81.

[33] Ibid., 83.

[34] Brown, *The Symphonic Repertoire*, 2:216.

of instability and express closure and regularity unambiguously. As in 80/i, the stormy style is answered with humor, in this case in the clucking "hen" theme in the mediant (the source of the symphony's nickname, "La poule"; starting at bar 45³). The contrast of topics is extreme: light scoring replaces heavy, diatonicism replaces chromaticism, short units replace long ones.[35] This soft, quirky theme is preceded and followed by forceful gestures, making a region of relative calm in the exposition that is new for Haydn in a minor-key symphony.

Yet this new contrast disguises a new kind of unity. Basic materials are shared by the two themes: the repeated-note dotted rhythm, which now becomes the clucking of the oboe, and the rising chromatic appoggiatura, which saturates the "hen" theme. The first figure of the main theme's basic idea is used in diminution and inversion in the closing section of the subordinate theme (bars 59–61). Moreover, the same essential principles of construction are found in both themes and indeed throughout the movement. The clarity and symmetry of the phrase structure and the "block" construction is shared with the main theme, as is the relatively slow harmonic rhythm. The development adheres to the same principles: slow harmonic rhythm, clarity of phrase structure and block construction, sometimes with contrasting topics for adjacent blocks. This is a development as conceived in modern textbook fashion: contrasted materials from the exposition are brought into dialogue and even conflict.

In the second half of 83/i, just as in 78/i and 80/i, the main theme is significantly altered and its untimely implications are realized. But the strategy and the unfolding narrative are again new. By the end of the recapitulation the movement makes a conspicuous point of breaking free from minor-key vocabulary. The untimely rhetoric emerges clearly only in the development. Materials from the main theme and the first subordinate theme are used there in the manner of third-species counterpoint. At the same time the *lamento* implications are brought out in the harmonic setting (bars 83–86, and, even more, 92–97, where the underlying descending fourth in the bass is C–B♭–A♭–G). In the recapitulation untimely rhetoric is put aside. A transformation is undertaken, but of a different kind from those of 80/i and 83/i. There is no ambiguity here about where the recapitulation starts; the stormy energy of the development falls away over a long dominant pedal (bars 120–29), clearly marking the end of that section, and the main theme is not rewritten this time. The moment of modal reversal is deemphasized in comparison with 80/i: the half cadence at the end of the main theme is followed directly by the first subordinate theme, now in the tonic major (with change of key signature), which is retained until the end of the movement. The move is abrupt but quite in keeping with the block construction of the movement. The climactic moment in the recapitulation comes when the closing section at the end of the second subordinate theme is expanded into an elaborate coda-like section. It includes a tonic-major version of the main theme's presentation phrase (from bar 176), now symbolically divested of its minor-mode rhetoric. It is linked plainly to the "hen" theme: its dotted rhythm turns into the familiar

---

[35] Harrison, *Haydn: The "Paris" Symphonies*, 83.

clucking figure (bars 184–87). It concludes with a stereotypical galant cadence (bars 188–89[1]) that is entirely new in the movement and thus corresponds to nothing in the exposition. This takes the rhetoric of modal reversal still further than 80/i. There the stormy gestures had simply dropped out in the recapitulation. Now Haydn's minor-mode materials are highly malleable: not only can their untimely implications be realized, but they can be transformed in the opposite way, converted into celebratory major-mode gestures. Haydn is unconstrained in his treatment of materials by convention or symphonic type.[36]

Haydn's last minor-key symphony was No. 95, one of the first two symphonies he composed in England in early 1791, the other being No. 96 in D. It is the odd one out among the twelve "London" Symphonies: the only one in a minor key, and the only one that does not begin with a slow introduction. Haydn may have been testing out his audience with these two symphonies, perhaps attempting to appeal to connoisseurs with No. 95 and the larger public with No. 96; if so, then the latter was a more successful strategy. He wrote three more D-major symphonies for England with slow introductions similar to that of No. 96. No. 95, by contrast, was one of the slowest sellers of the twelve symphonies in the edition for piano trio brought out by Haydn's London concert impresario Johann Peter Salomon. Landon calls it "an experiment that Haydn took great care never to repeat."[37] Even so, the symphony is hardly tragic. Jones and Landon call No. 95 "a fusion of the minor-key and the C major symphonic traditions."[38] The first movement reverses its mode in the recapitulation, and the finale is a brilliant C-major contrapuntal movement reminiscent of the finale of Mozart's "Jupiter" Symphony. Yet there is a stormy minor-key outburst in that finale, and the minuet is also in minor, even though it is not contrapuntal and would work nicely (give or take some modulations) if the mode were changed to major. The horns are crooked in C and E♭ (two in each key), but the latter are asked to change to C crooks for the C major portions of the work, including halfway through the first movement.

In some respects the opening of Haydn 95/i re-establishes links with his earlier minor-key practices that had been suppressed in his two previous minor-key symphonies. The octaves with which the work begins unmistakably recall the earlier C-minor openings of Haydn 52/i and 78/i. The internal contrasts of the main theme (bold octaves followed by soft, sighing appoggiaturas) hark back to Haydn 26/i and 44/i. And there is a mediant tutti (bar 16). In its overall construction, however, the exposition of 95/i closely resembles that of the more recent 83/i. Like the "hen"

---

[36] For Grave, this is "a revelatory transformation that reconfigures the opening idea as an agent of harmonious accord rather than conflict while nevertheless retaining its core identity." "Paths from Minor to Major," 23. David P. Schroeder regards the passage as evidence of parallels between Haydn's compositional approach and Enlightenment thought on tolerance and the coexistence of opposing forces. This view is plausible in principle, although it downplays the significance of the transformative modal reversal. *Haydn and the Enlightenment: The Late Symphonies and Their Audience* (Oxford: Clarendon Press, 1990), 84–88.

[37] Landon, *Chronicle*, 2:516.

[38] Landon and Jones, *Haydn*, 245.

theme of 83/i, the first subordinate theme of 95/i (bars 29–44) is a jaunty interlude contained within more energetic sections. Again the basic idea of the main theme returns near the end of the exposition (bars 54–55), in this case at the end of the second subordinate theme, which is noisier and more conventional in material than the first. Just as in 83/i, this allusion is expanded in the recapitulation into a continuous phrase, a transformation of the main theme into major, now symbolically linked with the triplets that belong to the second subordinate theme, a gesture of reconciliation between the two thematic areas and at the same time a rejection of minor-mode rhetoric (bars 151–59[1]). Grave points out that whereas in the exposition this thematic recall functions to destabilize the subordinate key, in the recapitulation it aids tonal stability and contributes phrase-structural symmetry (two four-bar phrases) and melodic completion in its path through a descending octave.[39]

Other techniques from the later minor-key symphonies are apparent too. The contrapuntal potential of the octave opening of the main theme is realized in the development, first in stretto (bars 62–74), then by putting it in combination with the triplets (bars 98–103) and with running eighth notes in the bass (bars 110–12). The beginning of the recapitulation is as ambiguous as that of 80/i. After sequential statements of the octave figure, one of which starts on C minor, the recapitulation gets underway clearly only with the soft second idea of the main theme (bar 119[2]). This reprise lasts only nine bars before the change of key signature and the return of the first subordinate theme in C major.

Symphony No. 95 has puzzled critics, especially the first movement. Landon complains of "the constant attempt to escape the basic minor tonality with its attendant emotional responsibilities."[40] He finds "something unsatisfactory about [the first] movement as an aesthetic whole."[41] For Simon McVeigh, "This symphony does not attempt to work out the drama implied by its stern unison opening gesture and the challenging uncertainties that follow: indeed Haydn immediately undermines these tragic implications, rapidly escaping to E♭ major for a charming second-subject melody of luxuriant length."[42] For Heartz, "The marriage of dour lessons in counterpoint with luxuriant sonorous beauty is not entirely happy."[43] For David P. Schroeder, "The elaborate process which gives rise to intelligibility in No. 83 simply does not happen in No. 95."[44] Aside from the single episode in the finale, the symphony lacks any music in the stormy style. There is no fast surface rhythm at the start of the first movement, and the energy dissipates early. The music seems hasty to leave the minor mode: the main theme does not even cadence, the mediant is reached at bar 16 in an exposition of sixty-one bars, and the transition ends abruptly. In terms of its topics and gestures and their combination, and especially

---

[39] Grave, "Paths from Minor to Major," 27–28.

[40] Landon, *Symphonies*, 553.

[41] Landon, *Chronicle*, 2:517.

[42] McVeigh, "Symphony," 408.

[43] Heartz, *Haydn, Mozart and Early Beethoven*, 449.

[44] Schroeder, *Haydn and the Enlightenment*, 163.

in post-Beethoven hindsight, Haydn 95 may seem tame, casting off the minor mode with even less fuss than 80/i and 83/i. Scott Burnham, reflecting on the tendency of modern critics to treat sonata form as a mythic archetype and to hear its tonal return and resolution as the fruit of hard work, says "But sonata form can be so much less! Haydn reminds us that return is not always a return from the underworld, that we do not have to keep working so hard to hear it that way."[45] With Haydn 95/i that argument must be taken a stage further: even the turn to major at the end of a sonata movement need not be hard work.

Two further sonata-form movements in the repertory turn to major during the recapitulation: Dittersdorf a2/i and Wranitzky 10/i. The Wranitzky movement has little else in common with the Haydn pieces, and will be considered below alongside his other minor-key symphonies. The Dittersdorf is more relevant here. A friend of Haydn from their youth in Vienna, Dittersdorf had always shown traits that a modern listener would presume to be Haydnesque, and pioneered them himself, at least in tandem with Haydn and sometimes probably in advance. Dittersdorf a2/i turns to major in the recapitulation and uses humor and irony, yet its date is no later than 1779, when it was advertised in the Breitkopf catalog, and may be considerably earlier. It certainly predates all the Haydn movements discussed in this chapter. The ironic title "Il delirio delli compositori, ossia Il gusto d'oggidi" ("The delirium of composers, or modern taste") suggests a satire on the stormy style and on the minor-key symphony in general. This is confirmed by the first movement and is continued in the quirky, mock-serious contrapuntal minuet (see chapter 4). But the satire is not overplayed, and the work is carefully crafted.

The main theme hardly deserves the name insofar as there is almost no melodic content, just syncopated throbbing. To a modern ear, the voice exchanges within diminished-seventh chords seem a remarkable anticipation of Tchaikovsky (Ex. 7.1, bars 10–13). All four phrases at the start end with half cadences, prolonging the uncertainty. Thereafter, a mediant tutti begins a long and complex transition that appears to be moving to the dominant (E minor) before switching to the mediant for the true medial caesura (bar 73).[46] The subordinate theme (Ex. 7.2(i)) is a rustic Ländler, with tonic drones, anticipating in its character and incongruousness the closing section at the end of the subordinate theme in Haydn 80/i. In the recapitulation there is a bizarre surprise. The transition confuses the meter and ends with four chords of V in the tonic major but on the wrong beats (beat 4 to beat 3, not beat 1 to beat 1). When triple meter and periodic phrase structure are regained, the correct topic for the subordinate theme is present—a Ländler with a drone in the lower parts, the tune above played in octaves, sometimes with two-eighth-note anacruses or groups of six eighth notes in a bar—but the tune itself is completely different (Ex. 7.2(ii)). This theme is new in the movement, while the subordinate theme of

---

[45] Burnham, "The Second Nature of Sonata Form," 140.

[46] The accepted medial caesura is of the dominant perfect authentic cadence type, consistent with Hepokoski and Darcy's theory about the default deployment order of medial caesura options. See *Elements of Sonata Theory*, 36–40.

Ex. 7.1 Dittersdorf a2/i, bars 1–16

Ex. 7.2

(i) Dittersdorf a2/i, bars 73³–81

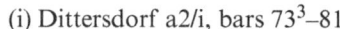

(ii) Dittersdorf a2/i, bars 179–86

the exposition does not recur in the recapitulation at all: an amusing b\
the "sonata principle," by any standards. The movement ends softly and at\
with no closing-section rhetoric or conventional material to indicate impendi\
sure. It is unclear how this strange, topic-preserving substitution of one theme for
another relates to the movement's subtitle or to the subgenre.

The Characteristic Minor-Key Symphony

The rest of the modally reversing symphonies in the repertory—those in which the
turn to major does not occur during the recapitulation or which are not in sonata
form at all—approach the status of "characteristic symphony" at some level, revealing connections with the theater and the visual arts. Some of these works recall
orchestral storm scenes from French opera. They seem to presuppose of the listener
not just different expectations but different types of understanding and interpretation, drawing on the French aesthetic of "tone painting" and the principle of "verisimilitude"—both controversial in German-speaking central Europe at the time,
and condemned by some as a sign of declining taste and a betrayal of the true
nature of music.[47] The tendency may be slight (Hoffmeister e1/iv) or pronounced
(Wranitzky 43). At the furthest extreme, the symphonies approach sound-effects
music, perhaps for the purpose of theatrical or outdoor spectacle, just as French
opera aimed for "le merveilleux." Most often, such effects appear only for a while
or just momentarily, usually at the very end of the symphony, thus introducing an
explicit narrative dimension into an otherwise largely abstract piece. Nevertheless,
minor-key symphonies that reverse mode and end in major are much more likely
to have explicit extra-musical associations or programmatic commentaries in their
scores than those that stay in minor to the end of their outer movements.

According to Richard Will, characteristic symphonies (his phrase, but derived
from eighteenth-century usage) make up about 225 of the over 16,000 symphonies
composed during the period.[48] Some come with merely a subtitle, some with a more
detailed program. Forty-four of the 225 tell a story, rather than being just illustra-
tive. By far the most common subject for characteristic symphonies was the pastoral (over seventy works), followed by national character (thirty), military themes
(fifteen), hunts (fifteen), and storms (ten).[49] Often two subjects are used in combination. Beethoven's "Pastoral" Symphony, of course, has storm as well as pastoral,

---

[47] See, for instance, the article "Tone Painting" ("Gemähld in Musik") from Johann Georg Sulzer's
Allgemeine Theorie der schönen Künste (1771–74), translated in *Aesthetics and the Art of Musical
Composition in the German Enlightenment*, ed. Nancy Kovaleff Baker and Thomas Christensen
(Cambridge: Cambridge University Press, 1995), 90–91. Even Handel often came in for sharp criticism
in this respect. Haydn was uneasy about some of the sound effects in *Die Jahreszeiten* (see Heartz, *Haydn,
Mozart and Early Beethoven*, 637–38), and Beethoven famously described his "Pastoral" Symphony on
the handbill for the first performance as "mehr Ausdruck der Empfindung als Malerei," 1.

[48] Will, *Characteristic Symphony*, 1.

[49] Ibid.

and this is also the implicit combination in a number of characteristic minor-key symphonies, although the proportions and location of these topics within the cycle are different. (This common pairing crops up in other genres besides symphonies, such as Haydn's *Die Jahreszeiten* and, later, Rossini's *Guillaume Tell* overture.) Wranitzky 30 ("La tempesta") has a pastoral slow movement as well as a storm; Wranitkzy 43 ("con temporale e caccia") combines storm and hunt even in its subtitle, while Wranitzky 12 ("Grande sinfonie caracteristique pour la paix avec la Republique francoise") has a battle in its third movement, as well as touching on national characteristics in its marches for the English, Austrians, and Prussians.

Storm scenes ("tempests") were popular with audiences of the French *tragédie en musique* from the late seventeenth century and through most of the eighteenth. Along with sleep scenes, earthquakes, battles, oracle scenes, and the portrayal of hellish furies, tempests offered the composer the chance to deploy spectacular orchestral effects.[50] The most famous operatic tempest was from Marin Marais's *Alcyone* (1706), which was often played outside the theater. At least eleven further tempest scenes can be found in French opera in the following decade.[51] The vocabulary of tempest scenes was highly conventionalized. They shared with later Viennese minor-key symphonies a tendency to slow harmonic rhythm and fast surface rhythm, as well as repeated notes low in the texture and tremolandi. But much of the syntax was quite distinct from the later instrumental repertory. The mode was usually major and the organization very loose and episodic, though with literal repetition and sometimes without any modulation to non-tonic keys. Characteristic features include rapid scales in the violins, sometimes up to two octaves, timpani rolls, crescendos, and diminuendos. Regular phrase rhythm and conventional melodic structures are avoided, placing the emphasis on sound effects to represent thunder, lightening, driving rain, and whistling wind. Tempest scenes represent the temporal course of the storm literally, imitating the sound of its buildup, climax, and abatement.[52] In order to achieve these literalistic effects they could spill across the traditional formal boundaries between operatic numbers (recitatives, arias, choruses). The impression of the sheer force of nature overriding the conventional structure of the opera is the phenomenon that later in the eighteenth century would be called "sublime." The tempest usually dies down and is followed by a slumber scene or some other calming music. Tempests could represent divine rage, a catastrophe, or a reversal of fortune for the hero. In the second half of the eighteenth-century opera the tradition was still alive: Rameau's *Les Boréades*

---

[50] Michele Cabrini, "Breaking Form through Sound: Instrumental Aesthetics, *Tempête*, and Temporality in the French Baroque Cantata," *Journal of Musicology* 26, no. 3 (2009): 327–78 (p. 336).

[51] Caroline Wood, "Orchestra and Spectacle in the *Tragédie en musique* 1673–1715: Oracle, Sommeil and Tempête," *Proceedings of the Royal Musical Association* 108 (1981–82): 25–45 (p. 43).

[52] See Cabrini, "Breaking Form through Sound," 331; Wood, "Orchestra and Spectacle"; 40–46; Elke Lang-Becker, *Szenentypus und Musik in Rameaus tragédie lyrique* (Munich: Katzbichler München, 1977), 69–83; and John Spitzer and Neal Zaslaw, *The Birth of the Orchestra: History of an Institution, 1650–1815* (Oxford: Oxford University Press, 2004), 488.

(1763), Gluck's *Iphigénie en Tauride* (1779), Niccolò Piccinni's *Iphigénie en Tauride* (1781), and Mozart's *Idomeneo* (1781) have tempest scenes, all of which run across the boundaries between conventional numbers.

Tempest music transferred easily to performance outside the theater, starting with the French Baroque cantata,[53] and even much later works such as Haydn's London cantata *The Storm* (1792). In instrumental music it can be found already in Vivaldi and Telemann, and later in characteristic symphonies (see Table 7.3), most famously of course Beethoven's "Pastoral." Hard and fast distinctions between abstract and characteristic symphonies are difficult to sustain, and many early minor-key symphonies may have been understood to evoke storms. One early manuscript copy of Haydn 39 carries the words "Il maro turbito."[54] The typical "stormy finale" of the Viennese minor-key symphony (see chapter 4) is at the abstract end of the spectrum, with only the most basic vocabulary shared with the operatic type of tempest and no explicit programmatic indications. The syntactic organization of these movements is rather similar to that of major-key symphonies. Run-on movements such as those found in Beethoven's "Pastoral" are unusual in the minor-key symphonies. This aspect of the sublime, common in tempest scenes and rather typical of characteristic symphonies in general,[55] did not transfer directly to the storms of instrumental music. The finale was a common position for symphonic storms, and often a programmatic indication for the work is given only above the finale. The rest of the symphony may have no obvious programmatic associations.

In Viennese minor-key symphonies the combination of storm and pastoral was especially common. The pairing had a long cultural history beyond music and had become something of a visual and literary topos, notably in two paintings by Poussin and the critical writings they generated.[56] In Justin Heinrich Knecht's *Le Portrait musical de la nature* (1785), called a "symphony" despite being in five movements and lacking a sonata-form movement, an idyllic pastoral calm is disrupted by a storm and afterwards restored. The course of events is described in detail on the title page.[57] Louis Massonneau's Symphony *La Tempête et le calme* (1794) represents storm and calm in its first and second movements respectively. But in Viennese minor-key symphonies the change of topics usually appears only at the very end of the finale, in the order storm–calm, and is coordinated with the minor–major modal reversal. Finales that switch to major in this way may suggest that there is a last-minute providential intervention, or the major-key section may sound like a cheerful addendum, as though the whole symphony were made the object of

---

[53] Cabrini, "Breaking Form through Sound," 333–35, 350–71.

[54] Joseph Haydn, *Kritischer Ausgabe sämtliche Symphonien*, ed. H. C. Robbins Landon, 12 vols. (Vienna: Universal, 1967), 3:xl; cited in Sisman, "Haydn's Theater Symphonies," 338–39n121.

[55] Will, *Characteristic Symphony*, 167–69.

[56] Cabrini, "Breaking Form through Sound," 327–31.

[57] For a summary, see David Wyn Jones, *Beethoven: Pastoral Symphony* (Cambridge: Cambridge University Press, 1995), 18–19.

TABLE 7.3 Late eighteenth-century symphonies with storms (adapted from Will, "Time, Morality and Beethoven's *Pastoral* Symphony" and *The Characteristic Symphony*); overtures excluded

Croubelis, S	Symphony in C, No. 7	c. 1780
Haydn, J	Symphony in G, No. 8, Le Soir	1761
Holzbauer, I	Symphony in E♭, No. E♭ 3b	–1768
Klöffler, JF	Simphonia l'orage et tempête, No. 15	–1777
	Simphonia tempête No. 16	–1777
Knecht, JH	Le Portrait musical de la nature	1785
Massonneau, L	La Tempête et le calme	1794
Raimondi, I	Les Aventures de Télémaque dans l'isle de Calypso	1777
Richter, FX	La tempesta del mare	c. 1744–52
Rosetti, FA	Calypso et Télémaque (lost)	1791?
Ruge, F	Symphony in G, No. 5	1756
	La nova tempesta	1757
Stamitz, C	Le Jour variable or La Promenade royale	1772
Vaňhal, JB	E♭12 "La tempesta"	1763–65?
Wranitzky, A	Aphrodite	1792
Wranitzky, P	Grande sinfonie caracteristique … (P12)	1797
	La tempesta (P30)	–1795
	… Sinfonia … con temporale e caccia (P43)	–1790

gentle humor. In sonata-form movements, the major-mode coda therefore cannot be interpreted as the outcome of a struggle or as a human achievement within the temporal span of the movement. One might infer that, just as in the *tragédie en musique*, human destiny is in the hands of the gods, although the results here are not tragic but benign. The material used in the pastoral major-mode section, at least at the start, is usually hymn-like or suggests a folk song—perhaps, to anticipate Beethoven, a country song of thanksgiving. Melodies feature predominantly conjunct motion and even rhythmic values, and usually parallel thirds or sixths. The harmony emphasizes the subdominant, especially with the rocking motion 5/3–6/4–5/3 over a bass tonic pedal. The material is always new within the movement and in comparison with most of the preceding material is less highly wrought and contrasted in character. The final bars may fade out with a diminuendo.

The first clear examples date from the 1760s: the twin symphonies Dittersdorf e1 and Vaňhal e3 (see Exx. 7.3 and 7.4). Both finales end softly with a rocking motion in a narrow texture that, in notation, spans only the octave e–e^1. These major-mode conclusions come at the end of sectional forms with short internal repeated units without obvious reference to the stormy style. Dittersdorf g1/iv, a sonata movement, turns to major in a coda that follows full, emphatic closure in G minor at the end of the recapitulation (bar 133). The music picks up again softly before a G major hymn appears, in complete contrast to everything else in the movement (Ex. 7.5). This is followed by a major-mode version of the beginning of the movement's main theme, a similar move to Haydn's in the later 83/i and 95/i. In Dittersdorf g1/iv, however, this is the very first allusion to the opening of the main theme in the tonic in the

Ex. 7.3 Dittersdorf e1/iv, bars 56–63, string parts

Ex. 7.4 Vaňhal e3/iv, bars 83–90

Ex. 7.5 Dittersdorf g1/iv, bars 145–54, reduction

second half of the movement. The recapitulation picks up from the exposition's bar 17, omitting its first sixteen bars. The sudden reversal of mode and mood is in keeping with the antics of the exposition and indeed those of the first movement (see, respectively, chapter 4 and chapter 1).

Hoffmeister e1/iv is another sonata-form movement in a stormy vein (marked Presto assai). The major-mode coda begins in a galant idiom (Ex. 7.6), but with relatively straightforward texture and rhythmic values in comparison with the rest of the movement. The accompaniment is an eighteenth-century stereotype that represents gentle breezes or the rustling of foliage by a pair of inner voices moving gently in thirds. (A famous example is "Soave sia il vento" from Mozart's *Così fan tutte*, also in E major). As in Dittersdorf g1/iv, in Hoffmeister e1/iv the start of the main theme returns at the end of the coda, *forte*, in a transformed, major-mode version (bar 106). Like the main themes of Haydn 83/i and 95/i it is in octaves. As

Ex. 7.6 Hoffmeister e1/iv, bars 93–103

in Dittersdorf g1/iv the original version of the main theme is omitted from the recapitulation, which alludes instead to an unstable, sequential version that first appeared in the exposition only at the mediant tutti, after which the recapitulation parallels the exposition exactly (compare bars 18 and 65; this is also the version used in the coda). The tradition of the contrapuntal finale is invoked in this movement: sequences and chains of suspensions are common. The openings of both outer movements of Hoffmeister e1 recall the opening of Haydn 44/i, in the same key, and another movement that alludes to its main theme near the end. But the celebratory, major-key ending of Hoffmeister e1/iv would be almost unthinkable in that imperial-court tradition. There seems to be crossover here between different subgeneric strands as a moment of narrative tone-painting is briefly set against an old-fashioned aesthetic of craftsmanship.

Towards the end of Wranitzky 30/iii (the finale, marked "La tempesta"), the storm gradually abates during a diminuendo and a passage marked *perdendosi*. There follows a change of key signature from D minor to D major and a hymn-like passage for wind only, with fanfare figures in the horns (Ex. 7.7). The main theme of the movement then re-enters in D major, at first softly but then building strongly to end the symphony in a tone of celebration, the storm material transformed and combined with fanfares. At the turn to D major for the hymn, the phrase "es heitert sich auf" ("it clears up") is written in the score. In Wranitzky 43/i the music at the turn to major following the dying down of a storm is a hymn for strings almost entirely in whole notes (Ex. 7.8). Eventually, the opening music of the movement returns, now in major, to end the movement, but not before a snatch of piping (the melody doubled by wind instruments; bar 317). This idea anticipates in its rhythm

Ex. 7.7 Wranitzky 30/iii, bars 291–308 (reduction)

Ex. 7.8 Wranitzky 43/i, bars 301–24. Biblioteca del Conservatorio Luigi Cherubini, Firenze. I-Fc, fondo Pitti, FPS.119

and contour the introduction to the finale (the shepherd's song of thanksgiving) that follows the storm in Beethoven's "Pastoral" Symphony.[58] Both refer to the *ranz des vaches* melody of the Swiss Alpine herdsmen, which at the time was a theme in Romantic literature.

The most overtly "characteristic" Viennese minor-key symphonies are by Paul Wranitzky (1756–1808), a Moravian who won the favor of the Habsburg imperial family and became a central figure in Viennese musical life in the 1790s. He was director of the orchestra at the court theaters, the Burgtheater and later the Kärntnertortheater, secretary to the Tonkünstler-Societät, a performance director and orchestral leader, and the composer of at least forty-five symphonies, half of which were published, along with numerous stage works and much chamber music. Some of Wranitzky's minor-key symphonies fully absorb the operatic type of tempest.[59] All three movements of 30 were used as incidental music for a play. The movement headings and score indications in 30 and 43 (in the keyboard part), which describe the building and waning of a storm, suggest the possible use of sound effects or lighting, perhaps in the theater or even outdoors, recapturing the original purpose of the operatic tempest: lavish display, entertainment, and stunning, literalistic effects (see Table 7.4). The pragmatic construction of much of these storms, in which a fixed block of figuration is shifted from one harmony to another at a steady rate, suggests an essentially improvisatory approach, inviting comparisons with, for instance, the spectacular contemporaneous organ improvisations of Abbé Vogler, which drew on startling sound effects and sometimes evoked storms.[60] But overall, Wranitzky's minor-key symphonies are varied in type: some movements resemble the traditional Viennese instrumental minor-key symphony in their tight construction and musical argument, and some symphonies mix different types of stormy movement.

Most and perhaps all Wranitzky's minor-key symphonies probably date from the 1790s, and all but one ends in the tonic major. Wranitzky's orchestra is, unsurprisingly, slightly larger and more varied than those of most earlier minor-key symphonies: flutes and trumpets are standard, No. 33 has a bass drum, Nos. 10, 12, and 43 clarinets, No. 12 a piccolo, and No. 43 a prominent keyboard part. In their length, these works reflect an overall growth in symphonic dimensions at the time. All apart from No. 30 have some kind of slow introduction at the start. The keys are unadventurous: three symphonies are in C minor, two in G minor, and one in D minor, the three most common minor keys in the eighteenth century.

Table 7.5 arranges the Wranitzky minor-key symphonies on a spectrum from abstract, where most of the traditional generic and subgeneric markers are in place, to characteristic, where the program dictates that the form and the style is more theatrical. The tonic major becomes more significant on the right-hand side of the table, whereas No. 42, on the left, has both outer movements beginning in minor and remaining there to the end. The works on the left have no subtitle, whereas,

---

[58] Compare also a passage from near the start of "Sommer" from Haydn's *Die Jahreszeiten*, a section which later contains a storm. Jones, *Beethoven: Pastoral Symphony*, 12–13.

[59] Jones, *The Symphony in Beethoven's Vienna*, 74–78.

[60] For instance, "Die Spazierfahrt auf dem Rhein vom Donnerwetter unterbrochen." Margaret Grave, "Vogler, Georg Joseph," in *The New Grove Dictionary of Music and Musicians*, 2nd ed., ed. Stanley Sadie, 29 vols. (London: Macmillan, 2001), 26:863–68 (p. 865).

TABLE 7.4 Characteristic subtitles, title-page explanations, and score annotations in Wranitzky's minor-key symphonies

Wranitzky 12
"Grande sinfonie caracteristique pour la paix avec la Republique francoise"

No. 1

La Revolution	The Revolution
Marche des Anglois	March of the English
March des Autrchiens et Prussions	March of the Austrians and Prussians

No. 2

Le sort et la mort de Louis XVI	The fate and death of Louis XVI
Marche funebre	Funeral march

No. 3

March des Anglois	March of the English
Marche des Alliés	March of the allies
Tumulte d'une bataille	The turmoil of a battle

No. 4

Negociations de paix	Peace negotiations
Cris de joie pour la paix réstituée	Shouts of joy for restored peace

Wranitzky 30
Finale "La tempesta"

[ein Blitz] schlägt ein	a lightning strike
stiller Regen	quiet rain
[ein Blitz] schlägt ein	a lightning strike
Das Wetter verliehrt sich	the [stormy] weather wanes
es heitert sich auf	it clears up

Wranitzky 43
"Gran Sinfonia in G min. con temporale e caccia"

I Allegro con spirito	
Ein Donnerwetter	A thunderstorm
das Wetter beginnt von ferne	the storm begins in the distance
Furcht der Einwohner	fear of the inhabitants
das Wetter nähert sich	the storm approaches
Sausen der Winde	whistling of the winds
das Blitzen	lightening
Es donnert stark	loud thunder
Es fliegt ein	it closes in
der Regen	rain
II Adagio 2/2 Eine Jagd	a hunt
Allegro 6/8 La Caccia	the chase

in the three right-hand columns, increasing numbers of movements are explicitly programmatic. The three symphonies on the left have the traditional Viennese four movements with minuet; Nos. 30 and 43 lack a minuet; while No. 12, on the far right, is the least orthodox in the arrangement of its movements. Although it has four on paper, each is subdivided into various sections with subheadings and music of diverse character and, in the fourth movement, even of different keys

TABLE 7.5 Paul Wranitzky's minor-key symphonies on a scale from abstract to characteristic

Symphony	42	11	10	30	43	12
			Abstract ⟶ Characteristic			
Explicitly programmatic mvts	No subtitle			Programmatic subtitle; Only finale	First two	All
No. of mvts	4	4	4	3	3	4 with internal subdivisions
Minuet	Minor (contrapuntal)	Minor (not contrapuntal)	Major	N/A		
Manner of storm	Mediant tutti in both outer movements; Symphonic	Mediant tutti in first movement	Theatrical		No mediant tutti	Symphonic
Mode	Outer mvts remain in minor (slow mvt: I–i–I)	No modal reversal within mvts; finale in major	Modal reversal in first mvt; rest of symphony in major	Modal reversal in finale	No modal reversal within mvts; finale in major	No modal reversal within mvts; only first movement in minor
Repeats in minor-key sonata-form movements	i: second part; iv: none	i: first part	None	i: both parts; iii: none	N/A	N/A

(see Table 7.4). Subgeneric definition is greater on the left: No. 42 has a contrapuntal minor-key minuet, whereas, moving to the right, No. 11 has a non-contrapuntal minuet in minor and No. 10 has one in major, like Haydn 78 and 83. By the same token, mediant tuttis are most common on the left, but become gradually less frequent moving to the right. Minor-key sonata forms are nonexistent in the two right-hand columns. The storminess of minor-key fast movements in Nos. 42 and 11 stands in the symphonic tradition, with coherently formed themes, transitions, development sections, and so on. Further to the right, Nos. 10, 30, and 43 have storms of the theatrical type. The symphonic storms are in sonata form and tend to have repeats, whereas the theatrical storms have no repeats and usually no double bars to mark the end of an exposition and the start of a development or even a clear cadence in the mediant. The arrangement in Table 7.5 may reflect a rough chronology: No. 42 is typical of Wranitzky's symphonic approach of the 1780s,[61] while No. 12 certainly dates from 1797 and was probably the last to be composed. Symphonies Nos. 12, 20, and 43 clearly deserve the name "characteristic"; it could be applied cautiously to No. 10 as well. When Will says that "The characteristic symphony is first and foremost a genre of pastoral idylls, thunderstorms, military conflicts, hunts and political identities" he could have been speaking precisely of Wranitzky 12, 20, and 42: they contain all those programmatic themes and no others.[62]

At the start of the Allegro non troppo of Wranitzky 10/i there is no "theme" in the conventional sense, but scales, passagework, sequences, forzandos, *fp*s, tremolandos (Ex. 7.9), and later, syncopation. The material is conventional to a greater extent even than in the typical stormy finale of earlier Viennese minor-key symphonies (chapter 4).

Ex. 7.9 Wranitzky 10/i, bars 10–21, first violin part. Biblioteca del Conservatorio Luigi Cherubini, Firenze. I-Fc, fondo Pitti, FPS.117.

---

[61] Jones, *The Symphony in Beethoven's Vienna*, 78.

[62] Will, *Characteristic Symphony*, 2.

The rate of harmonic change is slow and steady, with conventional passagework often repeated studiously over different slow-moving harmonies. Something that resembles a subordinate theme eventually appears in the mediant, but not until bar 76. Although the movement is in a kind of sonata form, no repeats are marked for the exposition or for the development and recapitulation; indeed, locating the exact end of the exposition is difficult as there is no double bar and the music just moves seamlessly into developmental processes. The development itself is likewise unconventional: it contains a good deal of music in the tonic (minor) with stormy material from the first half of the exposition. The form of the movement could thus be described as: slow introduction, storm (i), calm interlude (III), storm (mainly i), interlude (I), triumphant conclusion (I). Both phases of storm are mainly sound effects. In its avoidance of characteristic melodic material in the minor mode in favor of anonymous scales and syncopated repeated notes, it resembles the first movement of Massonneau's *La Tempête et le calme* more than any previous Viennese minor-key symphony. However, unlike French operatic tempests it can hardly be called sublime in any strong sense, as the storm is neatly contained within a sonata form, and does not even last to the end of that, after which the rest of the symphony is in major.

Wranitzky 30 is his only minor-key symphony that includes both types of stormy movement. The first movement (without any subtitle) is more symphonic than 10/i. Both first and second parts of the sonata form are repeated. The material at the opening of the work is far more characteristic than in 10/i, with a rhythmic gesture of four eighth notes that was a hallmark of Viennese instrumental music (Ex. 7.10; see bars 4 and 7), a mediant tutti (bar 38) with conventional statement-response presentation, and a lyrical subordinate theme. The recapitulation goes through these materials in order, all in the tonic minor. The slow movement is an Andante in D major in 6/8 meter, with strings muted; it signifies pastoral, though it is not labeled as such. The finale ("La tempesta") is a storm of the theatrical type. Much of its figuration and orchestral effects are shared with 10/i, as is the lack of repeats within what is approximately a sonata form, the lack of a mediant tutti, the modal reversal near the end, the slow harmonic rhythm, and the unsubtle, block-like construction. But 30/iii extends the stormy effect even further than 10/i through the range of its figuration (Ex. 7.11), its duration, and its sheer loudness. In

Ex. 7.10 Wranitzky 30/i, bars 1–8 (strings)

Ex. 7.11

(i) Wranitzky 30/iii, bars 1–6

(ii) Wranitzky 30/iii, Bars 15–16

Ex. 7.11 (Continued)

(iii) Wranitzky 30/iii, Bars 36–37

addition, it features a long, gradual crescendo and a thunder roll and clap on the bass drum. All these features distinguish the movement in type from the first movement of the same symphony and from Wranitzky's other symphonic-style fast minor-key movements, 42/i and iv and 11/i. The two bars of score given in Ex. 7.11(ii) reveal some distinctive features. The texture is deliberately confused, indicating turmoil, the harmony is static, the score is heavily marked, and there is a sudden doubling of first violin and bass. All this contrasts sharply with the clarity and economy of the design and notation of earlier Viennese minor-key symphonies, and of the Viennese instrumental-music tradition in general. In Ex. 7.11(iii) fine adjustments of (full) texture and (loud) dynamics—compare the timpani and bass drum parts—are made, while, harmonically, the passage prolongs nothing more than a D-minor triad. The two bars are immediately repeated with further adjustments before the whole four-bar unit is shifted to a B♭ triad. The indications on the score give explicit and banal interpretations of the effects (Table 7.4). All three movements were used in slightly altered form and in a different order as part of the incidental music for a play entitled "Die Rache" (1795).[63] The score indications in the finale might therefore have to do with stage directions or instructions for the "machinist" or the lighting crew. It is unclear, however, whether the stage version or the concert version came first. Such adaptations of instrumental pieces for the theater and vice versa were common. (It is possible that 10/i had a theatrical function as well.) Nevertheless, the fact that all the movements of Wranitzky 30—including the symphonic storm—were used in the theatrical version illustrates the pragmatism of such adaptations: one should not assume a direct correspondence between movement types and functions or performance venues.

While Wranitzky 10/i and 30/iii maintain residual links with the instrumental type of stormy movement by sticking to a kind of sonata form and allowing the occasional theme-like structure to emerge, 43/i is almost pure sound effect and

---

[63] James A. Ackerman and Daniel Bernhardssohn, Introduction to *Paul Wranitzky, Symphony in D minor, "La Tempesta,"* http://www.wranitzky.com.

in-time imitation of the progress of a storm, the stages of which are indicated in the keyboard part (see Table 7.4). "Rain" is illustrated by staccato eighth-note scales in the strings, and "fear of the inhabitants" with diminished seventh chords and wide leaps in register, indicating oppressed, heavy breathing. The latter is the sonic equivalent of the images of the people fleeing the storm in Poussin's *L'orage*; comparable figures could be found also in many representations of sublime nature in late eighteenth-century painting. Wranitzky 43/ii portrays a hunt, another popular topic for characteristic symphonies. Its key, D major, as V of the first movement's i, is very unusual for a minor-key symphony of the time, and represents perhaps the boldest tonal relationship between movements in the repertory, given that the first movement ended in minor. The G-major finale is not obviously programmatic, and is cast in a conventional sonata form.

Wranitzky 12/i (1797) has a metaphorical storm—more symphonic than theatrical this time—which portrays the spirit of the French revolution. It is presumably a negative portrait, as the symphony celebrates the Treaty of Campo Formio (1797) between Napoleon and Austria from an Austrian perspective. The other movements are mainly in major, as are the two interpolated march episodes in the first movement, representing respectively the English and the Austrians and Prussians. The symphony is one of four that Wranitzky wrote for the purpose of commemoration and celebration of the Habsburg dynasty, at the time embattled in the face of Revolutionary France. The occasions for the other three were the coronation of Leopold II as king of Hungary (1790), the coronation of the emperor Franz II (1792), and the wedding of the Archduke Joseph to the daughter of the Russian Tsar (1799), all events of political significance in the revolutionary era.[64] Will points out that the symphony offers a dubious, Habsburg-biased account of the events leading to the treaty, which in reality were hardly glorious for the Austrians.[65] Even so, the censors refused permission for the work's performance two days before its planned premiere, a decision that more likely indicates either incompetence or irrational fear than any subversive message in the music.

There are four movements, corresponding loosely to the traditional four movements of Viennese symphonies. Each carries a programmatic heading (see Table 7.4; given in the published score in French on the title page and in German in the orchestral parts). The movements are formally unconventional and are split into contrasted sections. Unusually for a symphony at the time, material is shared between the first and third movements. The first movement is a kind of sonata form with strange interpolations: after the slow introduction there is a prolonged stormy section, with the subordinate theme in the mediant beginning only at bar 99. The march for the English then enters in the tonic major (C major); this soft, perky, and lightly scored music is incongruous and counter-generic. After further stormy music ending on V/i, there is a double bar and a repeat sign, apparently the end of the exposition (bar 182). At this point the mediant key has long ago

---

[64] Jones, *The Symphony in Beethoven's Vienna*, 91–92.

[65] Will, *Characteristic Symphony*, 205–9.

been left behind, and the repetition of the whole fast section makes little sense in terms of a sonata-form exposition or a narrative. In the "development"—if a sonata-form account still makes sense—the march for the Austrians and Prussians appears as a second interpolation, this time in the mediant (E♭). The recapitulation remains largely in the tonic minor. The symphony's second movement is slow and galant in style in its outer sections, representing the nobility of Louis XVI; the central section is a funeral march in C minor. The third movement, in C major, is fast, but is not a minuet or scherzo, being in common time and lacking any ternary or binary structures. The two marches are brought back before a battle commences, still in C major, without any hint of the Revolutionary minor-key music. The finale begins with a slow section in G major representing peace negotiations, which is followed by a celebratory C-major sonata form. Thus, the stormy music of Wranitzky 12 is localized and contained within the first movement, and, even there, tamer, major-mode music obtrudes. Again the storm is hardly sublime, as befits a counter-revolutionary symphony.

Conclusion

The preponderance of major-mode endings to Viennese minor-key symphonies after the early 1770s is the only occasion in the history of the subgenre when one "primary default" (Hepokoski and Darcy's phrase) is replaced by a new one that is in turn well consolidated. As usual with the minor-key symphony, hard evidence about aesthetics and poetics is lacking. But it seems clear that the process reflects changes in patronage, as symphonies were written for publication and public concerts rather than princely salons and monasteries, and that composers opened up to some intellectual dimension, which could crudely be termed "Enlightenment," and also to models derived from the theater and the visual arts. Haydn created a new kind of minor-key first movement. The turn to major in the recapitulation functions within a movement-length strategy in which the music equivocates between old-fashioned and modern syntax and expression. Just as in the large majority of his major-key symphonies of the time, Haydn avoided programmatic hints in these pieces. Since other composers at the time were doing the opposite, and since Haydn himself had composed programmatic symphonies for his first Esterhazy prince, Paul Anton, in the early 1760s (Nos. 6, 7, and 8, "Le midi," "Le matin," and "Le soir"), and the minor-key "Farewell" Symphony in 1772, the fact that he took that approach no further seems a significant decision. Paul Wranitzky, on the other hand, took the major-turning minor-key symphony firmly into the realm of the characteristic symphony. Thus, as the minor-key symphony turned to face outwards, the final result was an odd cultural reconfiguration. A composer associated with the imperial court pursued a modern, populist agenda, whereas Haydn stayed in touch with traditional values and procedures, alluding to the untimely rhetoric so favored by the earlier imperial composers. In this way, the situation of the 1760s was turned back to front.

8

Mozart and the Minor-Key Symphony

At first glance Mozart seems a special case in the history of the Viennese minor-key symphony. He wrote only two minor-key concert symphonies, which, despite his short life, are widely spaced in time, providing two isolated snapshots of different practices. Today K. 550 is better known than any of the other works discussed in this book, with K. 183 not far behind. The works have entered popular culture and Mozart industry kitsch: K. 183 was used at the opening of the film *Amadeus* (1984), while the opening of K. 550 was at one time commonly heard as a mobile phone ringtone. The literature on the Mozart works is vast, especially K. 550. In particular, it is an analyst's warhorse that has been called on to illustrate theoretical principles by Heinrich Schenker, Rudolf Reti, Leonard Meyer, Jan LaRue, Jean-Jacques Nattiez, Fred Lerdahl and Ray Jackendoff, Richard Cohn, and others.[1]

It might seem idle to write still more on these pieces, even from the perspective of a minor-key subgenre. Can any new insight be brought to them and is any needed? Does not their interest lie precisely in what distinguishes them from the works of composers such as Dittersdorf and Vaňhal? A masterpiece like K. 550, it may be argued, transcends its background and context. My contention here is that new insight can indeed by brought by means of generic analysis. Although these two symphonies are extraordinary in many ways, it would be wrong to place them only in the context of Mozart's own oeuvre, as stages in his unfolding genius. Other composers' minor-key symphonies were extraordinary in their own, different, ways, and that hardly precludes generic analysis for them. Without knowledge of the minor-key traditions that Mozart evokes there can be only limited understanding of what he was transcending or precisely how he was being original. That point has already been recognized by some musicologists and attempts have been made to address it, even if they have not been altogether satisfactory. In particular, K. 550, despite its familiarity, remains in many respects a mysterious work and one ripe for a fresh perspective. Finally, if the customary tight focus on Mozart's two minor-key

---

[1] For discussion of some of these, see Jean-Jacques Nattiez, "A Comparison of Analyses from the Semiological Point of View (The Theme of Mozart's Symphony in G Minor, K. 550)," *Contemporary Music Review 17*, no. 1 (1998): 1–38.

concert symphonies is loosened to encompass all his fast minor-key sonata-form orchestral or pseudo-orchestral movements, then it emerges that Mozart was much more closely involved with the vocabulary and conventions of the Viennese minor-key symphony, and more consistently over several decades, than has hitherto been thought. K. 550 was the culmination of that involvement.

There is already a long scholarly tradition that contextualizes K. 183 with reference to other minor-key symphonies, starting with the Mozart scholars Theodor de Wyzewa and Georges de Saint-Foix and continuing with Larsen, Landon, and, latterly, A. Peter Brown. In fact, K. 183 was the focus for the studies that anticipate this book's approach to the whole minor-key repertory. By contrast, K. 550 has seldom been studied in this way, save for general allusions to a putative "G-minor symphony" tradition. In one sense this is unsurprising, for while K. 183 clearly belongs to the subgenre, alluding unmistakably to minor-key conventions and differing markedly from the major-key symphonies that Mozart was writing at the same time, K. 550 is a deeply original and synthetic work with a broad network of influences and allusions. Whereas K. 183 applies the rules and conventions of the subgenre intensively (arguably to excess), K. 550 does so subtly and in new ways. Nevertheless, it has a contrapuntal (partly canonic) minuet and shares with K. 183 a mediant tutti in its first movement and a tendency to untimely rhetoric, especially in codas. The subgeneric method is not irrelevant to K. 550, though it must be used flexibly.

There is plenty about K. 550 that such an approach might help to clarify. Its basic content has been disputed in a way that is extraordinary for a work so central to our experience of classical music. Critics have disagreed, for instance, about whether the symphony is essentially tragic or comic. Historical understanding of the work is limited, and sources of information about it few. For many years the theory that Mozart wrote K. 550 without any practical purpose in mind went unchallenged, and even today claims about its exact purpose must remain speculative. Its likely meaning and significance to contemporaneous audiences is obscure. In 1984 Gary Tomlinson, at the start of a programmatic essay for the cultural turn in musicology at that time, chose K. 550 to illustrate his thesis that a piece of music should be understood essentially as an artifact of the culture that produced it, a choice that doubtless reflected its central status as an aesthetic experience of the Western musical canon.[2] But he did not follow up that idea, and neither has anyone else. Even Brown, who has the most penetrating historical account of K. 183, all but despairs over K. 550. "From whatever perspective one hears K. 550 it remains an elusive work. Its character seems undefinable and its musical skill unfathomable. . . . Even its Menuetto resists classification, as does the symphony as a whole."[3] Yet elsewhere he does the job convincingly for the "Jupiter" Symphony K. 551, and holds open the possibility that K. 550 too could, in theory, be grasped in a

---

[2] Gary Tomlinson, "The Web of Culture: A Context for Musicology," *19th-Century Music 7*, no. 3 (1984): 350–62 (pp. 350–51).

[3] Brown, *Symphonic Repertoire*, 2:423.

meaningful historical context: "one can also argue that the G minor Symphony and the 'Jupiter' are works that reflect strong contexts from both the immediate and distant past: composers still alive during the 1780s, revered figures from earlier generations, as well as their collective traditions."[4]

The present chapter will by no means solve the mysteries of K. 550, but will bring some new insights. At a concrete level, the data assembled in this book shows that Mozart used some familiar conventions and that he avoided some. But more importantly, at a broader cultural level, interpretation can reveal something of the stance that K. 550 represents, the statement that Mozart was making by writing this work in this way in Vienna in 1788. Despite its originality, the symphony is striking for the way it reconnects with a Viennese tradition that had all but died out by the late 1780s. In this sense it parallels the "Jupiter," which, on Brown's account, revives the C-major "trumpet symphony" that was cultivated by Fux and Caldara. Mozart chose to end all the minor-mode movements of the symphony in minor, unlike most other composers of the 1770s and 1780s, including his friend Haydn, but in line with his own minor-key keyboard and chamber music of the 1780s. With its mediant tutti, canonic minuet, minor-mode endings, and untimely rhetoric, K. 550 was itself a deliberately untimely work. In this way, it may be argued, the symphony contributed to Mozart's unfashionable investment in musical tradition in his three symphonies of 1788 and his aim to extend that tradition and pass it on to a new public.

Mozart's Minor-Key Symphonic Movements

As Table 8.1 shows, Mozart's production of fast minor-key symphonic movements was more voluminous and more evenly spread across his career than is usually thought, at least if we apply the concept "symphonic" a little more broadly than is usual today (but in accordance with the eighteenth-century meanings of "symphony"). In this his output resembles in miniature the repertory of the Viennese minor-key symphony as a whole, which is also more evenly spread than was once thought. The works listed here illustrate overall a deep and sustained engagement with minor-key symphonic practice, and, moreover, a concern with almost all types of minor-key movement. Mozart prided himself on his ability to assimilate and reproduce any style, and here we find movements in the imperial court style and those more in the manner of the "outsiders"; movements that turn to major as well as those that stay in minor; a "characteristic" movement (with an explicit program) as well as his more customary abstract movements; movements with mediant tuttis and movements without. Mozart even invented a one-off new type of minor-key

---

[4] A. Peter Brown, "Eighteenth-Century Traditions and Mozart's 'Jupiter' Symphony K. 551," *Journal of Musicology* 20, no. 2 (2003): 157–95 (p. 159). Mozart drew on old Viennese and south German traditions also in his Requiem (1791). See Simon P. Keefe, *Mozart's Requiem: Reception, Work, Completion* (Cambridge: Cambridge University Press, 2012), 4–5, 118.

TABLE 8.1 Fast minor-key symphonic movements by Mozart

	Year	Key	Imperial Court Style	Mediant Tutti	Ends in Major	Characteristic
Overture, *La Betulia liberata* K. 118, first section	1771	d	✓			
Overture, *La Betulia liberata* K. 118, third section	1771	d	✓			
Symphony K.183/i	1773	g				
Symphony K.183/iv	1773	g	✓			
Thamos, König in Ägypten K. 345, entr'acte between Acts I and II (NMA No. 2)	1776?	c		✓		
Thamos, König in Ägypten K. 345, entr'acte between Acts IV and V (NMA No. 5)	1776?	d			✓	
Thamos, König in Ägypten K. 345, music to follow the end of Act V (NMA No. 7a)	1776?	d				✓
Wind Serenade K.388/i	1782/3	c				
Wind Serenade K.388/iv	1782/3	c			✓	
Symphony K.550/i	1788	g		✓		
Symphony K.550/iv	1788	g		✓		

symphony for wind ensemble. K. 388 is quite unlike any other wind serenade of the time: it is stern and serious, has only four movements, which are in conventional symphonic order (slow movement second, minuet third), opens with lavish untimely rhetoric, and has a canonic minuet (and, as if to outdo all other minor-key symphonies, a canonic trio as well). The spread of keys among these movements is more even than might be expected, given the fame of Mozart's "G minor mood." D minor (four), G minor (four), and C minor (three) are roughly equally represented, in line with general eighteenth-century practice. Mozart emerges from this survey as the most versatile composer of minor-key symphonic movements in the Habsburg realm.

Nevertheless, this very versatility highlights the existence of a set of minor-key practices favored by, and largely unique to, Mozart. In his orchestral and chamber music over the 15 years between K. 183 and K. 550 we can discern a subset of minor-key movements that display family resemblances and reveal a characteristic approach to minor-key fast movements (Table 8.2). In this group a greater proportion of movements are in G minor and all the movements end in the tonic minor. The selection includes precisely those movements from Table 8.1 that are in sonata form and have repeated expositions. All have at least two of the four characteristic features listed on the right of the table. The last two of these features specify Mozart's preferred version of the "tragic plot" available to the composer of a minor-key symphony.

TABLE 8.2 Characteristic features in certain fast minor-key sonata-form instrumental movements by Mozart

	Date	Key	Buffa-style ST	Modulating link back to tonic at end of (repeated) exposition	Significant melodic alterations to ST on return in tonic minor	Coda in which untimely rhetoric is heightened
Symphony K.183/i	1773	g	✓	✓		✓
Symphony K.183/iv	1773	g		✓		✓
Thamos, König in Ägypten K. 345, No. 2	1776?	c	✓	✓	✓	✓
Wind Serenade K.388/i	1782/3	c	✓		✓	
Piano Quartet K.478/i	1785	g	✓	✓	✓	✓
String Quintet K.516/i	1787	g		✓		✓
Symphony K.550/i	1788	g	✓	✓	✓	✓
Symphony K.550/iv	1788	g		✓		

"Buffa-style ST" means that the subordinate theme has a lively character with short, even phrases that could support syllabic patter. This type of subordinate theme is likely to contrast sharply with a stormy main theme. Arias and ensembles in minor keys are uncommon in opera buffa, so the clouding of cheerful buffa-style tunes by transposition into minor has no obvious precedent outside the recapitulations of minor-key symphonies: it is a phenomenon of the symphonic subgenre. The buffa-style subordinate theme is an extreme case of Mozart's preference for contrast between the basic ideas of main and subordinate themes. He seldom brings back the basic idea of his main theme for his first subordinate theme when he writes in minor keys.[5] In K. 550 the buffa theme occurs only as the second subordinate theme and has the character of a buffa ensemble, specifically a quartet (bars 72–80).

Mozart's consistent use of modulating retransitions at the end of expositions stands out. They are uncommon in the minor-key repertory as a whole. Haydn avoided them, with the exception of the outer movements of 44, while Vaňhal has them only in the first movements of his four later minor-key symphonies.

Significant melodic alterations to the subordinate theme on its return in the recapitulation are especially characteristic of Mozart in minor-key movements (although see also Vaňhal a2/i), and the result might be termed "altered physiognomy." These changes are sometimes necessitated by transposition to the minor mode, especially in chromatic themes, but sometimes Mozart makes gratuitous alterations when an exact transposition would have been possible.[6] In both cases the alterations underline the change of mode. They are especially interesting when the

---

[5] K. 478/i is an exception, although the construction of its exposition is unique and it has no fewer than five subordinate themes. K. 550/i brings back the basic idea of the main theme for a second subordinate theme. The Piano Concerto in C minor, K. 491, does likewise, but in the local minor (E♭ minor), a bold "minor-key insertion" (*Molleinschub*) within the subordinate-key region.

[6] Brian Newbould, "Mozart's Lost Melody," *Musical Times* 132, no. 1785 (1991): 552–53.

subordinate theme is in buffa style. There is a sense of fateful irony as a fragment of a bright world of life and comedy is drawn into minor and, as it were, distorted. There may be an echo here of the *vanitas* tradition in the visual arts (still lifes that portray beautiful things at a moment of incipient decay).

The heightening of untimely rhetoric in a coda of course recalls the symphonies of the imperial court composers, especially Gassmann, and also Haydn 44/iv. In K. 183/iv and K. 478/i the sense of a closing ritornello is conveyed with a loud melody in octaves, the provenance of which, as in Gassmann, varies (in K. 183/iv the material is from the retransition, in K. 478/i it is from the main theme but with an additional old-fashioned fast dotted rhythm). In general, codas are rare in Viennese minor-key symphonies, which are more likely to end with abrupt hammer blows that parallel the end of the exposition. A different technique, and one unique to Mozart, is found in K. 183/i, K. 345 no. 2, K. 516/i, and K. 550/i, in which the coda begins with imitative treatment of the melody of the main theme.

It seems that Mozart had a set of distinctive procedures for minor-key movements that he tended to deploy together, producing movements that are internally contrasted but ultimately serious and even tragic. Movements that lack them tend to occupy quite different categories. For instance, neither the second nor third *Thamos* entr'acte (K. 345 nos. 2 and 3) appears in Table 8.2. The second turns to major during the recapitulation, an unusual decision for Mozart, and lacks an exposition repeat, while the third is a non-sonata-form movement that directly represents a storm with "tone painting." Both belong in the company of the symphonies surveyed in chapter 7. The first entr'acte, by contrast, which displays all four of Mozart's characteristic features, also has a mediant tutti, placing it at the center of Mozart's minor-key instrumental practice and squarely in the Viennese abstract minor-key symphony tradition. To take two further examples from Mozart's chamber music, the first movement of the D minor Piano Trio, K. 442, lacks all the distinctive features and turns to major in the recapitulation. The first movement of the E minor Violin Sonata, K. 304, aside from a touch of untimely rhetoric in the coda, again has a quite different set of compositional strategies, including a transformed version of the main theme in the recapitulation that has parallels nowhere else in Mozart's fast minor-key movements.

After K. 550, Mozart composed no further fast minor-key sonata movements, orchestral or otherwise. It is worth noting, however, that he did continue a different, though equally personal, type of minor-key instrumental movement, which deepened still further the association between minor mode and untimely rhetoric, drawing on fugue, pathotype themes, lamento bass progressions, in one case Gregorian chant (tonus peregrinus), and often intensive chromaticism. This separate but parallel development from the last decade of his life begins with a sequence of C minor pieces: the Fugue, K. 426 (1783), arranged for strings as K. 546 (1788); *Mauerische Trauermusik*, K. 477 (1785); the Fantasia, K. 475 (1785); and the first movement of the Piano Concerto, K. 491 (1786). After K. 550 it continues with two F minor pieces for mechanical clock: the Adagio and Allegro, K. 594 (1790), and—the final culmination—the Fantasia, K. 608 (1791).

Mozart in the 1770s: Minor-Key "Symphonies" from *Betulia* and *Thamos*

The overture to the oratorio *La Betulia liberata* (D minor; 1771) was written when Mozart was fifteen for a projected performance in Padua, which may or may not have taken place.[7] In its construction it is typical of an Italian opera *sinfonia*. It is in three succinct parts without repeats, all in D minor, which run into one another. The opening of the third echoes that of the first. The overture was cited by Barry S. Brook as the earliest example of *"Sturm und Drang"* style in Mozart.[8] It is certainly stormy but lacks some of the features typical of stormy movements in the Viennese subgenre. There are tremolandi but no *Trommelbass* or mediant tutti in either of the outer parts. Syncopation appears but supports chains of suspensions rather than a stormy accompaniment. The use of the same key and mode for all the movements, as here, is not found in Viennese minor-key symphonies that begin with a fast movement (Haydn 49 begins with an Adagio). The dimensions are small and there is no minuet. Moreover, the overture lacks the characteristic features that Mozart would later favor (Table 8.2). On the other hand, the chains of suspensions and, especially, the fast, running bass in the first part of the overture place the work closer to the imperial court tradition of minor-key symphonies than the Italian *sinfonia*. In short, Mozart seems to have known something of the "stormy style" that was common in orchestral music of the time, and perhaps was aware of the association between the minor mode and old-fashioned compositional techniques, but at this stage does not adopt the manner of the concert symphony as practiced at the time by Vaňhal and Haydn.

Mozart's only incidental music was written for the play *Thamos, König in Ägypten* by Baron Tobias Philipp von Gebler about a conspiracy to overthrow a pharaoh. The music consists of choruses and instrumental entr'actes, including one melodrama. The play premiered in Pressburg in 1773 and was performed in Salzburg by the Karl Wahr troupe in 1776.[9] The *Thamos* music has, for Mozart, an unusually complex compositional history. Studies of the autographs suggest that work was done in three stages: two choruses were written in 1773–74, a further chorus and the instrumental pieces in 1775–77, and in 1779 Mozart rewrote the earlier choruses.[10] The three minor-key symphonic movements therefore date from around 1776, about three years after K. 183. They contrast with the grand choruses, which anticipate *Die Zauberflöte* in tone and subject matter. The play appears to have had alternative musical endings. The third minor-key orchestral piece has a

---

[7] Stanley Sadie, *Mozart: The Early Years 1756–1781* (New York: Norton, 2006), 246.

[8] Brook, *"Sturm und Drang,"* 281.

[9] Sadie, *Mozart: The Early Years*, 316, 513–14.

[10] Ibid., 513–14 and 575n21; Alan Tyson, *Mozart: Studies of the Autograph Scores* (Cambridge, MA, and London: Harvard University Press, 1987), 24. See also Wolfgang Plath, "Beiträge zur Mozart-Autobiographie II: Schriftchronologie 1770–1780," *Mozart-Jahrbuch* (1976–77): 131–73 (p. 172).

note in Mozart's hand "After the fifth and last act," but it was probably replaced by the new chorus. It may have gone instead at the end of the second scene of the last act. It appears that at some stage Mozart separated its pages from the rest of the score.[11] In the *Neue Mozart Ausgabe* it is given as "7a" in an appendix (No. 7 itself being the new final chorus). Each entr'acte has a note in Leopold Mozart's hand explaining briefly its purpose in the drama (those for the minor-key movements are given in Table 8.3).

Of the three minor-key movements, the first (NMA No. 2, C minor) is the closest to the stormy type of minor-key concert symphony being composed by Haydn, Vaňhal, and others around 1770. The movement is in an unambiguous sonata form and ends in the tonic minor; the main theme is accompanied by *Trommelbass* and *tremolandi*; there is a mediant tutti; both first and second parts are marked to be repeated; and there are familiar melodic figures. It also shares all four of the distinctive features of Mozart's minor-key symphony movements indicated in Table 8.2. The melodic alterations to the subordinate theme are gratuitous and clearly serve an expressive purpose. Like K. 183/i, the main theme (Ex. 8.1) packs much information into a short space and makes multiple signals of pathos and agitation. There are dynamic contrasts and *fp*s, staccato and legato markings, falling and rising arpeggios, throbbing *tremolandi* on alternate beats (bars 9–10), Neapolitan harmony, a descending chromatic scale (atypical in the subgenre outside characteristic symphonies), a moment of silence, and rhythmic snaps at the approach to the cadence. No other fast minor-key movement in the repertory begins with a short introduction like this one or starts its Allegro on dominant harmony. The coda begins with the opening of the main theme in imitation at the octave in mock fugato that lasts only three bars (Ex. 8.2): a clear gesture of untimely rhetoric in an otherwise homophonic movement. As in K. 183/i, the possibility of a positive resolution held out by the mediant tutti and the subordinate theme's hint of comedy are decisively rejected by the recapitulation and coda.

TABLE 8.3 Leopold Mozart's written comments on the autograph of the *Thamos* entr'actes

K. 345 No. 2 "Der erste Aufzug schließt mit dem genommenen Entschluß zwischen Pheron und Mirza, den Pheron auf den Thron zu setzen" [The first act closes with the resolution of Pheron and Mirza to put Pheron on the throne]
K. 345 No. 5 "Der vierte Akt schließt mit der allgemeine Verwirrung" [The Fourth Act closes with general confusion]
K. 345 No. 7a "Pherons Verzweiflung. Gotteslästerung und Tod" [Pheron's despair. Blasphemy and death]
At bar 18: "Anfang des Donnerwetters" [Beginning of the thunderstorm]

[11] Harald Heckmann, "Vorwort," in *Chöre und Zwischenaktmusiken zu "Thamos, König in Ägypten"*, series II, group 6, vol. 1 of *Neue Mozart Ausgabe* (Kassel and Basel: Bärenreiter, 1956), vi–ix.

Ex. 8.1 Mozart, *Thamos, König in Ägypten*, K. 345, no. 2, bars 1–14[1]

Ex. 8.2 Mozart, *Thamos, König in Ägypten*, K. 345, no. 2, bars 115–20

The second minor-key movement (NMA No. 5, D minor) shares some features with the first, but takes them in a different direction, ending rather like an operatic ensemble to reflect the "general confusion" that Leopold Mozart noted. The main theme shares with that of No. 2 a diversity of materials, dynamic contrasts and *fp*s, staccato and legato markings, tremolandi, and Neapolitan harmony, although it begins on tonic harmony and with much more conventional melodic material. Fragmentation and sequence appear from the outset, as though the piece had begun in the middle, perhaps reflecting the tumult and confusion of the dramatic situation. It is interesting that the octaves with violins playing tremolando and lower strings playing single notes (from bar 10) is a texture unique to Mozart; K.

183/i is the only other minor-key symphony movement in which it is found. Unlike in No. 2, there are no repeats in this movement, again making it less like a movement from a concert symphony and more theatrical. The tutti that follows the subordinate theme at the end of the exposition modules to v, where it makes a half cadence, rather than confirming III as a normal concert symphony would. The movement ends, very unusually for Mozart, in the tonic major, but there are many modal twists before the final chords. Even in the exposition the subordinate theme is modally unstable, touching twice on the minor third. The recapitulation first presents an unambiguous minor version of the complete subordinate theme, but this is followed by the turn to major and an extended version of the theme but with heightened modal instability. The dimensions of the movement are thus thoroughly unlike those of a conventional sonata (no repeats, double recapitulation of the subordinate theme). Near the end the alternations between soft hints of minor and major-mode tuttis anticipate the expressive ambivalence found near the end of Mozart's later operatic ensembles, for instance the sextet "Riconosci in questo amplesso" from Act III of *Figaro*.

The third minor-key movement (NMA No. 7a, D minor) also begins as though in the middle, with diverse yet minimally characteristic material and early fragmentation. Here, though, dissociation and disorder are taken much further than before. Although the movement's dimensions are similar to the others, this is not a sonata form at all, hardly leaves the tonic, and has no cadences save for an unharmonized octave $\hat{4}$–$\hat{5}$–$\hat{1}$ gesture near the end. Without cadences, this is thus a movement without sections—as strictly defined in functional terms—and in that sense formless. The music that (according to Leopold Mozart) represents the thunderstorm consists simply of sound effects in the French tradition, so perhaps no modulation is needed. The chromatic scales, crescendos, "tirades," and ominous repeated notes are straight from the vocabulary of operatic tempests. Such effects are very uncharacteristic of Mozart in instrumental music, who steered clear of verisimilitude and the characteristic symphony throughout his career and disparaged French taste. The closest piece composed within the Habsburg sphere would be *Il terremoto* from Haydn's *Die sieben letzten Worte* (1786/87), given its position at the end of the work. The two movements use similar sound effects, are continuous, and avoid the confirmation of alternative tonics.

K. 183

Attempts to understand K. 183 in a Viennese tradition stretch back a century and have gradually been refined to the present day. The work has attracted this attention mainly because its sudden outburst of passion and its seriousness of purpose are isolated in Mozart's instrumental music of the early 1770s. It is generally regarded as the most interesting and important of Mozart's instrumental works to that date and for some time thereafter.

Wyzewa and Saint-Foix applied to K. 183 their general method, which meant establishing an elaborate network of "influences." While sometimes speculative and lacking a precise understanding of style and genre, this approach at least started to position Mozart in historical and compositional context. For K. 183 they thought the direct influences were Haydn 44 and Vaňhal d1.[12] They were aware of Vaňhal's significance and speak of "the thrilling allure of his melody, his syncopated rhythms and the whole of his instrumental realization,"[13] but of his minor-key symphonies they appear to have known only d1 and g1. They mention Gassmann, but none of his works. They think Mozart got to know Haydn's minor-key symphonies while in Vienna, specifically 44 and 45, although without evidence. Wyzewa and Saint-Foix were hindered by their adherence to an evolutionary model of compositional development that made them try to divide Mozart's work into discrete "periods." Mozart was "a true composer of the Viennese school"[14] from the summer of 1773 to his arrival in Mannheim at the end of 1777, during which time he conceived music as a grand, noble, and serious art. Development sections grow in length, codas are weightier, finales rival first movements in scale and form, workmanship is more elaborate, and counterpoint more prominent. But without a conception of a minor-key subgenre, the explanations of Wyzewa and Saint-Foix lead in the end to disappointment, as Mozart fails in his later works of the 1770s to follow through on K. 183 and resist "the increasingly universal contagion of the 'galanterie'."[15]

Later musicologists cast the net wider to include Haydn 39 and Vaňhal g1 (Landon), J.C. Bach's G minor Symphony, op. 6, no. 6 (Sadie), and the minor-key numbers in Mozart's own recent operas *Lucio Silla* and *Mitridate* (Sadie).[16] Larsen, provocatively for his time but significantly for the present study, maintained that Mozart was simply "trying his hand" at a minor-key symphony.[17] This has the virtue of explaining why he did not build its expressive vocabulary into his later works in a seamless process of "compositional development," and puts the lid on "romantic crisis" theories, but treats the work as a compositional exercise. Later Mozart scholars have emphasized that he almost never composed without a practical purpose.[18]

The tradition of contextualization of K. 183 culminated in the writings of A. Peter Brown, who knew more Viennese music of the early 1770s than previous writers and was more judicious in establishing connections. He has an explanation

---

[12] Théodor de Wyzewa and Georges de Saint-Foix, *W.A. Mozart: sa vie musicale et son œuvre* (Paris: Perrin, 1912), 2:121.

[13] Ibid., 122. "…l'allure frémissante de son chant, ses rythmes syncopés, et tout l'ensemble de sa réalisation instrumentale."

[14] Ibid., 45.

[15] Ibid., 123.

[16] Landon, "La crise romantique," 37; Stanley Sadie, *Mozart Symphonies* (London: BBC Publications, 1986), 46.

[17] Jens Peter Larsen, "The Symphonies," in *The Mozart Companion*, ed. H. C. Robbins Landon and Donald Mitchell (London: Rockliff, 1956), 156–99 (p. 173).

[18] Sadie, *Mozart Symphonies*, 80; Zaslaw, *Mozart's Symphonies*, 421, 431; see also Neal Zaslaw, "Mozart as a Working Stiff," in *On Mozart*, ed. James M. Morris (New York: Woodrow Wilson Center Press; Cambridge: Cambridge University Press, 1994), 102–12.

of the purpose of K. 183 and the reasons why Mozart did not repeat it. The symphony was completed on October 5, 1773, shortly after the return of Mozart and his father to Salzburg following a two-month stay in Vienna. It is usually assumed that by visiting Vienna in the summer of 1773 the Mozarts were angling for positions at court, given the rumors of the likely death of Gassmann, then imperial Kapellmeister, which might have resulted in vacancies. Their correspondence is discreet on this subject, as letters could be intercepted in Salzburg. In the event Gassmann survived until early 1774 and the Viennese plan was a failure. Brown has argued convincingly that the works composed or begun during Mozart's stay in Vienna, including K. 183 and the six string quartets K. 168–173, reflect the taste of Joseph II. Leopold may have made Wolfgang study the works of the current imperial composers, including Gassmann and Ordonez, in order to master their combination of solemn affects, contrapuntal idioms, and galant touches. Mozart K. 168/ii (an F minor canonic minuet) appears to be modeled on the first movement of Ordonez's String Quartet in C minor, op. 1, no. 3.[19] K. 183 too was "a product of this environment" even though it was completed only on Mozart's return to Salzburg and so was probably not actually played in Vienna.[20] Brown finds an allusion to Gassmann's G minor String Quartet, H. 476/2, in the striking new idea that opens the development of K. 183/i and then becomes the opening theme of the finale.[21] The syncopations that begin the work are uncharacteristic of Mozart but highly characteristic of the openings of Gassmann's chamber works.[22] The start of the finale's development too "seems to be plucked out of an episode of a contrapuntally oriented chamber work."[23] The specific task that the symphony was presumably created to fulfill "probably accounts for the unexpected shock of this work in the context of Mozart's symphonic output."[24] It also explains why the completion of K. 183 on October 5 is immediately preceded and succeeded by "business as usual" in major keys, that is, the completion of the Symphony in B♭, K. 182, ("an unremarkable work of high craftsmanship")[25] on October 3, and then in December the String Quintet in B♭, K. 174, the Piano Concerto in D, K. 175, and a set of Minuets, K. 176, none of which unleash stormy passions.

Conscious of Mozart's untimely rhetoric in K. 183, Brown convincingly turns the evolutionary account of Wyzewa and Saint-Foix on its head: "An eighteenth-century connoisseur would certainly not hear [the opening pages of K. 183/i] as music of the future, maybe as music of the present, but most likely as music of the past."[26] He also overcomes the customary Mozart hagiography surrounding the symphony

---

[19] Brown, "Weeding a Musicological Garden," 203–9.

[20] Brown, *Symphonic Repertoire*, 2:373.

[21] Brown, "Weeding a Musicological Garden," 224–29.

[22] Ibid., 223.

[23] Ibid., 224.

[24] Ibid., 223.

[25] Ibid.

[26] Brown, *Symphonic Repertoire*, 2:373–74.

(Zaslaw calls it a "haze of adjectives"[27]), pointing out that Mozart's assimilation of the imperial style may have been imperfect. The opening of the first movement is "an overwrought panoply of Josephinian taste": syncopations; Fuxian cantus-firmus or fugue subject when the theme is given to the oboe in long notes; diminished sevenths hinting at a "pathotype" theme; octaves suggesting a ritornello in a *seria* aria. "Perhaps Mozart packed the beginning with too many signals, a complaint [about his music in general] voiced by a number of contemporary critics including the Emperor himself."[28] Like the *Thamos* entr'actes, this opening section in minor—in form-functional terms it is more than a single "theme"—is long and extremely diverse in texture, scoring, and material by eighteenth-century standards. Oboe solos such as the ones at bars 13–28 are not found elsewhere in the minor-key repertory at the time.

The information gathered and perspectives developed in this book suggest that Brown's interpretation is sound, but can be supplemented and refined. He does not point out that both outer movements work their way out of the imperial style to something more "modern" at the point in the exposition when they turn to major. It is all the more significant, then, that both underline their return to the tonic minor in the recapitulation with heightened untimely rhetoric in the coda. (Codas as such are not uncommon in Mozart's symphonies at this time, but the rhetoric certainly is.) Moreover, in addition to its allusions to the imperial style, K. 183 has strong theatrical elements and at time verges on the melodramatic. As Sadie puts it, K. 183 is distinctive not for the use of the minor mode as such—Mozart had done that before in opera, oratorio, and the Viennese string quartets—but for "the application to instrumental music, and particularly to the symphony, of techniques and styles more usually reserved for operatic heroines *in extremis*."[29]

The first movement has a mediant tutti—a convention almost entirely confined to symphonies by imperial-court "outsiders" and hardly evidence of "Josephinian taste"—with typical galant-style "snaps" that can be found in countless major-key symphony movements of the time. Brown calls this the first assertion in the movement of a "fully symphonic idiom,"[30] which captures something of the usual effect of mediant tuttis: restarting the movement on new terms. In both outer movements of K. 183, the first subordinate theme is in buffa style. The material that follows the theme's cadence is likewise very operatic: fast and bustling on the surface but repetitive and harmonically static, like a phase of frozen action near the end of a buffa ensemble. In the last four bars of the first movement the low, "boiling" sixteenth notes in the violins are also theatrical, and the texture as a whole at that

---

[27] Zaslaw, *Mozart's Symphonies*, 261–63.

[28] Brown, "Weeding a Musicological Garden," 223. Brown cites Carl Ditters von Dittersdorf, *Autobiography*, trans. by A. D. Coleridge (London, 1986), 251–52, where the Emperor seems to agree with Dittersdorf's critical comments on Mozart. These may have been received wisdom.

[29] Sadie, *Mozart: The Early Years*, 328.

[30] Brown, *Symphonic Repertoire*, 2:374.

point—descending arpeggios in the lower strings—is quite unlike the ending of any symphonic fast movement of the time, in either major or minor. A more conventional ending would have come with the hammer blows immediately before this passage (bar 210), which Mozart instead downplays (they are given only to violins in unison). The coda of the finale likewise mixes untimely rhetoric with melodramatic touches: the arpeggiated diminished seventh (bars 189–90) is as distant from the instrumental style of the imperial composers as it is from the minor-key symphonies of Haydn and Vaňhal. Both outer movements are heterogeneous in textures, melodic materials, and allusions to subgeneric types, but both realize the tragic plot in exceptionally dramatic ways.

In a sense K. 183 is paradoxical. Its tragic character, which is pronounced even among minor-key symphonies composed around 1770, seems at odds with the symphony's likely practical purpose. The symphony raises anew the sociological issues discussed in chapter 1. Can it really be said that Mozart was composing against the grain if he was copying the style of establishment figures in order to appeal to official taste? Given the usual dearth of information it is hard to answer this question. There is no doubt, though, that the symphony is exceptional for Mozart's instrumental music of the early 1770s in style and intensity of expression. Moreover, if Brown's account is accepted, then it would seem that Mozart was following the logic of his own abundant imagination to create something that, in the first movement at least, exceeded the boundaries of good taste and took "the music of pathos" further than, in the imperial salon, it was ever meant to go.

K. 550

According to a familiar romantic point of view, the three great symphonies that Mozart composed in 1788 (K. 543, K. 550, and K. 551) transcend their context and environment: they were written without specific purpose in an exceptionally short time, and Mozart died without hearing them.[31] Recent scholarship has sought to put these works back into Mozart's everyday world.[32] He probably intended them for some planned subscription concerts, which according to Mozart were scheduled for June and July 1788 but are more likely to have taken place in the autumn or even at Advent. Mozart may also have hoped to publish the symphonies as a single opus, although in practice that did not happen during his lifetime. The publication of symphonies in threes was standard practice at the time. Mozart's last three appear together in contemporaneous catalogs, although not in any manuscript. He may have been paying tribute to, or responding to, Haydn, whose six "Paris" symphonies had recently been published in Vienna by Artaria in two sets of three, one

---

[31] See, for instance, Alfred Einstein, *Mozart, His Character, His Work*, trans. Arthur Mendel and Nathan Broder (New York: Oxford University Press, 1945), 234.

[32] Zaslaw, *Mozart's Symphonies*, 421–31; H. C. Robbins Landon, *1791: Mozart's Last Year* (London and New York: Thames and Hudson, 1988), 31–33; David Wyn Jones, "Why Did Mozart Compose His Last Three Symphonies? Some New Hypotheses," *Music Review* 51 (1990): 280–89.

of which contained works in E♭, G minor, and C major, the same keys as Mozart's three. Mozart might also have had in mind a planned visit to London that never happened. He probably used them on a German tour he made in 1789, and there were almost certainly further performances in his lifetime, including in Vienna. It is very unlikely that Mozart wrote the symphonies in the space of six weeks in the summer of 1788, as legend would have it. He may even have been planning them at the end of 1787.[33]

There seems no reason to deny that in composing K. 550 Mozart was addressing an audience and was fully engaged with the musical and social worlds around him. The symphony is part of music history and the history of Mozart's times. That does not mean that it would have been easily digested by contemporary listeners or that its place in the minor-key subgenre is uncomplicated. In his time Mozart had a reputation as a difficult and learned composer, and there are many passages in K. 550, most obviously the abrupt, distant modulations at the start of the development sections of both outer movements, that would probably have been found disconcerting. The first movement has all four of Mozart's characteristic features in fast minor-key movements (Table 8.2), so to some extent he appears to have been pursuing still further a path of his own that he had taken consistently in several genres over the previous fifteen years, regardless of the audience he was writing for. As usual there are no surviving reactions to the symphony—not, at least, until well after Mozart's death. It seems fair to say, though, that in contrast to K. 183 it is unlikely anyone would have heard this as "music of the past," even as it brings in untimely rhetoric and reaches back to an almost-lost minor-key tradition. Viewed as part of the history of the Viennese minor-key symphony, K. 550 is striking for its deep originality. Mozart draws on certain conventions of the minor-key subgenre, as well as rules and conventions from elsewhere, but applies and combines them in quite new ways that were never to be repeated.

K. 550 has emerged from two centuries of criticism with a reputation for inscrutability. Its centrality in the performed and recorded canon and the vast literature devoted to it have yielded no consensus as to its meaning. For Brown, "perhaps no work of Western classical music has so confused critical opinion of its essential character."[34] Some have heard it as a model of the Classical style, others as the first stirrings of Romanticism, still others as the last echo of the rhetorical figures of the Baroque;[35] some have called it chamber music,[36] whereas others hear it as essentially orchestral and public; some have deemed it comic, others tragic.

---

[33] Jones, "Why Did Mozart Compose His Last Three Symphonies?," 282.

[34] Brown, *Symphonic Repertoire*, 2:419. See also Stefan Kunze, *Wolfgang Amadeus Mozart, Sinfonie g-moll, KV 550* (Munich: Fink, 1968), 4. See also Nattiez, "A Comparison of Analyses," 6; and Zaslaw, *Mozart's Symphonies*, 436.

[35] For the latter, see F. J. Smith, "Mozart Revisited, K.550: The Problem of the Survival of Baroque Figures in the Classical Era," *Music Review* 31 (1970): 201–14.

[36] Einstein, *Mozart*, 235, quoted in Nathan Broder, ed., *Wolfgang Amadeus Mozart, Symphony in G Minor K. 550, The Score of the New Mozart Edition* (New York: Norton, 1967), 112.

In the mid-nineteenth century, Schumann thought it the expression of "Grecian lightness and grace" and Berlioz a "model of delicacy and naivete," whereas Oulibicheff heard in it "the desires and regrets of unhappy love." In the twentieth century, Charles Rosen heard "passion, violence and grief" and Hermann Abert "deep, fatalistic pessimism." Landon regarded it as a sign of the manic depression he attributed to the composer.[37] All this must mean that there is something unusual about its semantics.

A consistent theme of British criticism of K. 550 has been to downplay its passion. George Grove wrote: "I cannot find in this beautiful movement the distress which some critics have discovered... Pathetic it is, no doubt, but there is something in the definite regularity with which its various sections and even the sentences of its themes are laid out, that gives a more formal character to the music than we now associate with grief."[38] For Donald Francis Tovey, "The G minor symphony shows poignant feeling, but its pathos is not that of a tragedy; it is there from first to last as a result, not a foreboding nor an embodiment, of sad experiences."[39] Tovey in fact denied that Mozart's music was ever tragic (not that he thought it any the worse for that).[40] According to Stanley Sadie, "The symphony exists, as Mozart did, in a stylised, conventional world, where the expression of emotion in art takes particular, accepted forms that make it coherent and meaningful to listeners. The G minor symphony may be an outburst, but only within well understood limits."[41] Jack Westrup placed the opening of K. 550/i in the world of opera buffa, pointing out the close similarities of rhythmic figures, accompaniment, and agitated mood with the opening of Cherubino's *aria agitata* "Non so più cosa son" from *Le nozze di Figaro*, and speculating that the main theme was an instrumental version of a (lost) aria on a similar text used in place of "Non so più" for a performance of *Figaro* in Florence in spring 1788.[42] These writers and their readers were trying to make sense of Mozart's compositional decisions with the legacy of nineteenth-century minor-key music in their ears. But they do a useful service in drawing attention to the symphony's deep roots in eighteenth-century practices, some of them from

---

[37] Hector Berlioz, *Gazette musicale*, March 6, 1836, quoted in Georges de Saint-Foix, *The Symphonies of Mozart*, trans. Leslie Orrey (London: Denis Dobson, 1947), 142; Alexandre Oulibicheff, *Nouvelle biographie de Mozart*, 3 vols. (Moscow: A. Semen, 1843), 3:255, quoted in Broder, *Symphony in G Minor*, 106; Rosen, *The Classical Style*, 324; Hermann Abert, *W.A. Mozart*, trans. Stewart Spencer, ed. Cliff Eisen (New Haven and London: Yale University Press, 2007), 1132, quoted in Broder, *Symphony in G Minor*, 82; Landon, *Golden Years*, 197.

[38] George Grove, "Mozart's Symphony in G minor," *Musical Times* 48 (1907): 26; quoted in Broder, *Symphony in G Minor*, 110.

[39] Donald Francis Tovey, "Sonata Forms," in *Encyclopedia Britannica*, 11th ed. (Cambridge and New York: Cambridge University Press, 1910–11), 25:396. Quoted in Broder, *Symphony in G Minor*, 110–11.

[40] Donald Francis Tovey, "Symphony in G Minor," in *Essays in Musical Analysis*, vol. 1, *Symphonies* (London: Oxford University Press, 1935), 191–95 (pp. 191–92).

[41] Sadie, *Mozart Symphonies*, 86.

[42] J. A. Westrup, "Cherubino and the G Minor Symphony," in *Fanfare for Ernest Newman*, ed. Herbert van Thal (London: Arthur Baker, 1955), 181–91.

earlier minor-key symphonies, some not. K. 550 is certainly in some ways quite restrained. The layout of the outer movements is unambiguous: sectional boundaries are abundantly clear. There is no hint of Sadie's distressed opera-seria soprano that is suggested by some of its minor-key predecessors, such as K. 183 at its opening. At the same time, the argument that the symphony does not convey tragic feelings at all must be contested. The presence of a minor-key contrapuntal minuet is almost enough in itself to refute it. Moreover, in the first movement Mozart realizes the minor-key tragic plot and even invents new strategies in order to do so.

Although familiar to modern ears, the opening of K. 550/i sounds different from that of any earlier minor-key symphony. Pinning down exactly what makes it unusual is not straightforward, for its innovations are subtle and it leaves some conventions unaltered. To begin a first-movement Allegro softly was rare in any symphony when there was no slow introduction, but it was far from unprecedented. Vaňhal in particular favored soft, cantabile openings in both major and minor. There are significant precursors even in G minor: Haydn 39/i (no less agitated, although much more discontinuous), Ordonez G7/i, and Vaňhal g2/i. All these movements acquire a narrative dimension in the recapitulation by means of significant new events or the alteration of old ones, and this is true also of K. 550. The opening bar of accompaniment figuration is typical of an aria agitata but not the opening of a symphony, yet even this is not altogether unprecedented: Dittersdorf a2/i begins with syncopated accompaniment figuration without a melody. The structure of the main theme is not unusual: it takes the form "grand antecedent / dissolving consequent," the antecedent being a sentence (bars 1–20) with an eight-bar presentation with statement-response repetition. In this structure it is identical to the main theme of Haydn 83/i. In both cases, the antecedent is prolonged by five bars of loud standing on the dominant at the half cadence with similar rhythmic figures.

There are three genuinely distinctive aspects of the opening of K. 550/i: topic, accompaniment figuration, and rhythmic and metrical organization. The first is the buffa idiom of the aria agitata. A short rhythmic motive is repeated continually, as though breathlessly, in a way that would support a fast, syllabic text setting. There is thus far more motivic repetition within the presentation phrase than is usual in the Classical style: the four-bar basic idea is compound, with its two-bar unit repeated with variation, while that unit is itself made up of three statements of the motive, which is thus played no less than twelve times within the presentation. Buffa allusions in minor-key symphonies are much more likely to occur in the subordinate theme or themes than in the main theme. The style of the main theme, if it is operatic at all, is likely to be seria. One could speak of a general stylistic drift in fast minor-key expositions from seria to buffa, which may be realized more or less concretely in any given movement. Mozart K. 183/i gives it highly concrete realization, as does Haydn 83. Obviously, not all fast minor-key movements begin with explicit seria allusions, but to start with an explicitly buffa idiom is countergeneric and means that later conventions may take on a different meaning. In Haydn 83/i, for instance, the buffa-style subordinate theme (ironically, a kind of gavotte) is something new and incongruous, whereas Mozart's buffa-ensemble subordinate theme extends this aspect of his main theme, even drawing on the same short motive.

The second new feature of the opening is the accompaniment figuration (violas). Although its high surface rhythmic activity is of course typical of the stormy style, the standard repeated notes or tremolando on a single note per harmony are abandoned and eighth notes are grouped in pairs that arpeggiate the harmony, thus articulating quarter-note beats as well. *Trommelbass* is absent too, and the bass notes articulate half notes by their attacks and whole notes by their register. Each "layer" of pulses from eighth note to whole note is thus articulated, each in a different way. This gives the theme a unique energy profile, and the accompaniment's eighth-note pulse is maintained through most of the movement, subsiding only for the first subordinate theme before it restarts again halfway through and continues in the second subordinate theme and through the development, which is based entirely on material from the main theme.

The (notated) eight-bar length of the presentation gives a clue to the peculiar metrical organization of the main theme. Most eight-bar presentations in the Classical style are really standard four-bar presentations with the meter renotated. Caplin calls this R=2N, where R is the "real" bar and N is the notated bar. With the notated note-values retained, then, the opening of K. 550/i is really in 2/1, not 2/2, which is underlined by the greater articulation of the half-note pulse (with the bass notes) than the minim pulse. There is, however, yet another twist. Although the presentation stretches from the notated bar 2 to the notated bar 9, the real bars are not the notated bars 2–3, 4–5, and so on, but bars 1–2, 3–4, and so on. The downbeats are articulated by the low bass notes. The key to hearing this theme correctly is to realize that it has the essential rhythm of a gavotte in 2/1, but with utterly non-gavotte-like buzzing surface rhythmic activity and nervous repeated motives. The gavotte is a slow, formal, aristocratic dance, beginning with a double upbeat halfway through a bar, but K. 550/i actually begins at the start of a "real" gavotte bar (notated bar 1); the double upbeat in the second half of that "real" bar occurs only in the notated bar 2 (see Ex. 8.3). From a metrical and topical perspective this explains the empty notated bar 1 and the positioning of the first bass note in the low octave, the second in the higher octave.[43] Most stormy minor-key movements begin with a strongly articulated downbeat—Haydn 83/i is a good example. Vaňhal sometimes begins with an upbeat figure, but only a short one. Mozart K. 550/i begins on a downbeat but the melody starts only later with an elaborate double-upbeat (real, not notated). The idea that this opening is a sped-up gavotte that has been overlaid with the breathless repetitions of an aria agitata and then squeezed into the form of the main theme of a fast symphony movement (statement-response presentation) accounts for the sense of something strange in a recognizable guise. It also goes some way to accounting for the differences of opinion about the character of this movement. If one hears groups of minims as the primary metrical layer, the agitation of the theme is pronounced; if one hears groups of whole notes as the primary layer then it is more serene.[44]

---

[43] On the historical significance of this first bar, see Glen Carruthers, "Strangeness and Beauty: The Opening Measure of Mozart's Symphony in G Minor, K.550," *Journal of Musicology* 16, no. 2 (1998): 283–99.

[44] Terminology of Krebs, *Fantasy Pieces*.

Ex. 8.3 Mozart K. 550/i, bars 1–5, gavotte rhythm at hypermetrical level

Ex. 8.4 Mozart K. 550/i, Sol-Fa-Mi schema at hypermetrical level unfolding over notated bars 3–9

The presentation phrase is based on the galant schema that Gjerdingen calls "Sol-Fa-Mi." It unfolds in the typical four stages with two harmonies on "Fa" and two pairs of events (Ex. 8.4). This schema was popular between the 1750s and 1790s, but was common in movements of slow or moderate tempo, especially Adagios in minor, and was sometimes used for subordinate themes in fast movements.[45] In the slow aria "Dies Bildnis ist bezaubernd schön" from *Die Zauberflöte*, which, as has often been pointed out, begins with the same melodic and harmonic patterns as the main theme of K. 550/i, Mozart applies the "Sol-Fa-Mi" in more conventional fashion and spreads it over four notated bars rather than eight. This reinforces the feeling that the underlying pulse of the theme is whole notes and that events move rather slowly in relation to the fast surface activity. The Sol-Fa-Mi schema had never before been used for the main theme of a fast minor-key symphony movement, and there are no obvious candidates in major either. The most common schemata for the opening of fast minor-key movements—all by court outsiders plus Ordonez C14 which follows Vaňhal rather than the imperial style—were the pathotype (Haydn 26/i, 49/ii, 44/i, 78/i, Vaňhal c2/iv, d2/i, a1/i, Mozart K. 183/i) and the Do-Re-Mi (Haydn 44/iv, Vaňhal e3/i, c2/i, e1/i, a2/i, d2/i, Ordonez C14/i). Variants of Gjerdingen's "Meyer" schema can also be found (Dittersdorf g1/i, Vaňhal g1/i, Ordonez G8/i).

This is a kind of originality that we have not yet encountered in this study of the minor-key symphony: a specifically Mozartian kind. It explains why a search for direct antecedents for the opening of K. 550/i in the composed repertory of minor-key symphonies proves fruitless, even though a number of abstract qualities are preserved. Mozart extracts some rules from different sources and follows

---

[45] Gjerdingen, *Music in the Galant Style*, 253–62, 463.

all of them at the same time as far as he can take them: the rhythm of a gavotte, the short motives of an aria agitata, the fast surface rhythm of the stormy style, statement-response presentation, and the Sol-Fa-Mi schema. Mozart does not generate a piece of the type usually specified by any of these rules: the main theme is not a gavotte or a stormy theme or a buffa aria or a slow Sol-Fa-Mi theme. Neither does the music sound as though he has broken any of the rules by adding others. Haydn's favorite strategy of conspicuously breaking a rule in order to set up a "problem" that is later "solved" is a quite different practice. The question posed by the opening of K. 550 is not whether by the end of the movement the theme will be turned into, say, a proper gavotte. Mozart is working with rules at a more abstract level: applying them in unusual ways and combining them in order to create new rules, which are then followed only in this piece. Mozart's application of the schemata of the galant style in the second movement of the symphony, which has been analyzed by Gjerdingen, shows a similar approach.[46]

The ebb and flow of energy had always been important in fast minor-key symphony movements, but the main theme of K. 550/i establishes a unique energy profile, and the movement sustains a driving eighth-note pulse almost throughout.[47] The grand antecedent / dissolving consequent structure transfers the momentum straight into the transition, and there is no decrease in energy before the mediant tutti (bar 28), which is absorbed into the flow. The eighth-note pulse is suspended at the start of the first subordinate theme, but reappears halfway through (bar 58) and then continues in the second subordinate theme, with the agitated motive again prominent. The development is based entirely on the main theme, and thus sustains the eighth-note pulse still further. Nevertheless, against the background of this driving force can be discerned what Abert called "the two fundamental contrasts of the movement, wild outbreaks and resigned ebbing of feeling."[48] In particular, section boundaries are approached with descending melodic lines and ebbing energy, such as the consequent of the main theme (bars 20–21), the reprise of the main theme (bars 160–65), and the cadence of the second subordinate theme in the recapitulation (bars 285–92). This note of resignation transfers the unease of the main theme to higher levels as tension is never fully discharged by the drive to a climax at an important section boundary. The first movement's energy profile is uniquely colored by the combination of wind scoring and chromatic harmony, for instance at bars 14–16 (where the eighth-note pulse briefly stops) and in the first subordinate theme at bars 58–61 (where it restarts). This kind of scoring has no precedents in the subgenre.

For the 1780s, K. 550 stands out for ending both outer movements in minor, something that Haydn by this time never did in a multi-movement instrumental work (apart from the exceptional *Sieben letzte Worte*). Indeed, Haydn's last three

---

[46] Ibid., 122–28.

[47] Larsen, "The Symphonies," 193.

[48] Cited in Broder, *Symphony in G Minor*, 75.

minor-key symphonies turn to major in their first movements and the finales are entirely in major. Mozart realizes the tragic plot clearly in the first movement, something that Haydn had not done since 44 (1770/71), but a strategy that Mozart had been pursuing more recently in his chamber music. Like Haydn in the 1780s, Mozart has contrasted topics for main and subordinate themes, but there is no symbolic synthesis of untimely and modern idioms represented by those themes in the recapitulation as found in Haydn 83/i and 95/i.

The most obvious evidence of the tragic plot is the use of the basic idea of the main theme in imitation at the end of the second subordinate theme in the recapitulation. The untimely rhetoric is not strictly part of a coda this time (the theme has not completed a cadence), although it enters at a dramatic moment after a pause that initiates a new phase of initiating function at a hushed dynamic level in a fashion similar to the other movements listed in Table 8.2. In fact, given the sudden drop in dynamics after the pause, the halting of the drive to a cadence, the use of a chromatic chord before the silence, and the imitative texture that follows, this moment might well be modeled on the events of Haydn 44/i. But Mozart invents some further, novel techniques. The recapitulation is substantially longer than the exposition (136 bars to ninety-nine), and the additional events there help to dramatize the switch to minor of the subordinate-key materials. The main theme's grand consequent is massively extended in the manner of a secondary development. This section follows the model of the equally impressive secondary development in K. 516/i, with prominent imitation and circle-of-fifths harmony. The move to VI (the submediant) for the equivalent of the mediant tutti is unique in the minor-key repertory, and likewise the snuffing out of the alternative major key by a second restatement of the tutti, now in the tonic minor, "as if forcing us to face a harsh reality."[49] Even Tovey would have to admit that this is a moment of tragic expression. The extension of the second subordinate theme seems about to build to a shattering climax when it suddenly subsides (an example of Abert's resigned ebbing of energy) and switches to the imitation of the main theme. As Sadie says, "at the very end there is a moment of threatened drama, from which, however, [Mozart] seems to draw back, offering instead a few bars of imitation around the opening theme before the movement closes."[50] A knowledge of other Viennese minor-key symphonies and Mozart's other minor-key instrumental music tells us that these bars of imitation represent a strategy peculiar to Mozart (Table. 8.2).

The finale too is original. In terms of topic this is not a stormy finale of either Type A (its essential texture is not contrapuntal) or Type B (there are no repeated notes or tremolando). The "rocket" figure with which it opens was favored by Mozart in minor-key instrumental music (Piano Concerto in D minor, K. 466/iii, Piano Sonata, K. 457/i), but not by composers of symphonies in the Habsburg realm. As regards the subgenre, the binary-form of the main theme—seldom used for themes in sonata movements—and the upbeat at the start mean that the

---

[49] Sadie, *Mozart Symphonies*, 88.

[50] Ibid., 89.

finale most resembles the sectional dance finales in minor-key symphonies such as Dittersdorf e1/iv and a2/iv, Vaňhal e3/iv, Ordonez B1/iii, and Haydn 78/iv. But K. 550/iv has much greater energy than any of those movements and the main theme is much more internally contrasted: a characteristic feature of Mozart's instrumental writing of the 1780s in both major and minor. The finale does share two basic principles with its Type B predecessors: the regular phrase structure over which its storm breaks, and the continuity of its energy, which subsides only for the subordinate theme in the exposition and the recapitulation. The application of these principles, however, takes place with new means and in new ways. Also like most earlier Type B stormy finales, K. 550/iv does not strongly realize the tragic plot. To be sure, the subordinate theme is rescored and its melody rewritten in the recapitulation, but it is not dramatized any further. The final pages of the movement, while forceful, do not bring in distinctive contrapuntal devices or any sense of a final ritornello. For Rosen, despite Mozart's decision to remain in minor throughout, this finale is fully in line with the fine sense for resolution that he and Haydn cultivated in the 1780s: "essentially it resolves, grounds, and settles."[51]

The second half of the finale, especially the contrapuntal development section, which as in the first movement is based only on material from the main theme, has called forth much of the symphony's "haze of adjectives," but some penetrating insights alongside. Georges de Saint-Foix found the "demonic" Mozart in this passage:

> The development is perhaps of all his work the one wherein Mozart shows the highest degree of passion and even fury. All the resources of his art, rhythm, harmony, counterpoint, are carried to extremes; a contorted, demonic force has seized him … Such boldnesses indicate a paroxysm of exaltation, and not free artistic creation. There is no more liberty here, but a mad constraint that seems to leave the composer with not an atom of air to breathe.[52]

These remarks touch on a distinctive feature of Type B minor-key stormy finales that is inherited by K. 550/iv: the contrast of surface-level storm and underlying regularity. Oulibicheff likewise spoke of Mozart's "frenzied yet classic inspiration" in this passage and remarked on the paradox of overflowing passion and refined compositional craft.[53] For Rosen, the finale is "despairing and impassioned" yet also "rhythmically one of the simplest and squarest pieces that Mozart ever wrote."[54]

For the Viennese minor-key symphony, that counterpoint is of a new kind, and can hardly be grasped merely as subgeneric untimely rhetoric. The finale opens with homophonic textures, but the counterpoint has no frame-breaking or narrative function as at the end of the first movement. Instead, it seems like an intensification

---

[51] Rosen, *The Classical Style*, 276.

[52] Georges de Saint-Foix, *The Symphonies of Mozart*, 138.

[53] Quoted in ibid., 147. See also Broder, *Symphony in G Minor*, 108.

[54] Rosen, *The Classical Style*, 275.

of the driving energy of the main theme. Again Saint-Foix touches on an important point: "the way the general mood of the movement—of fury and almost delirious exaltation—is strengthened and fortified by its audacious freedom seems to me a transmutation of the technique of the older music to the most 'modern' ends."[55] That transmutation of technique from old to modern—and highly original modern music at that—parallels the first movement in the way that familiar rules are applied in new ways.

In the absence of texts that might offer clues to Mozart's intentions or the contemporary reception of K. 550, Mozart's strategies can be clarified a little by comparison with the G minor Symphony of 1787 (Poštolka I:5) by his sometime Viennese neighbor Leopold Koželuch (1747–1818). Koželuch, who composed eleven symphonies, was trained as a musician and lawyer in Prague before moving to Vienna in 1778 where he worked as a pianist, teacher, and composer. In 1781 he refused an offer from the Archbishop of Salzburg to succeed Mozart as court organist. In 1784 Koželuch began a music publishing business and in 1792 was appointed imperial *Kammer Kapellmeister* and *Hofmusik Compositor*. His G minor Symphony is unusual in lacking a minuet. Like K. 550, though, it looks back to earlier practices and it shares a remarkable number of distinctive features with the symphony that Mozart composed the following year. The works are scored for similar orchestras (before Mozart added clarinets) with one horn in G and one in B♭, and have their respective second movements in E♭. In both symphonies the outer movements end in minor; the first-movements' main themes begin with statement-response presentation and have a long, loud phase of standing on the dominant at the end; the first movements have a mediant tutti (Koželuch's finale has one too); and the first movements have a buffa-style subordinate theme which undergoes melodic alterations in the recapitulation. Like K. 550, the outer movements of Koželuch I:5 are longer than most comparable movements of the 1760s and 1770s, and the first movement has a long development section and a long secondary development in the recapitulation. The latter is in two parts, both of which make the customary move to the subdominant. The second part begins with the mediant tutti now transposed to the tonic minor, an important expressive event that also occurs in K. 550, but in very few other movements in the subgenre (Vaňhal g2/i is an exception).

Where the two symphonies differ is the degree to which their common vocabulary functions to exemplify the subgenre or to formulate a different kind of minor-key musical experience. Koželuch makes abundant subgeneric signals, often with quite disparate materials. In the first movement especially, he lays on the untimely rhetoric with a trowel: the fast bass in bars 5–7; the very conspicuous Corelli leapfrog pattern (bars 13–18; Ex. 8.5 (i)) with imitative entries thrown in, starting softly in the tonic minor like a second attempt at a main theme at the point when a mediant tutti would have been expected; the octave passage at the end of the exposition and recapitulation like a closing ritornello (bars 62–66 and 177–82; Ex. 8.5 (ii)); sequences in the recapitulation that embellish descending chains of suspensions,

---

[55] Ibid., 139.

Ex. 8.5 Koželuch I:5

(i) Bars 13–18

(ii) Bars 177–82

(iii) Bars 140–441

(iv) Bars 171–74

one over a long dominant pedal (bars 130–35 and 140–43; Ex. 8.5 (iii)); and, most unsubtly of all, a sudden switch near the end of the recapitulation (bars 171–74; Ex. 8.5 (iv)) to the "trudging to Calvary" style found in Haydn 49/i (see chapter 5) and in sacred music for Easter such as Pergolesi's *Stabat Mater*. The latter is a complete surprise and shares no material with the rest of the movement; it is simply a piece of standard eighteenth-century minor-key vocabulary inserted gratuitously near the end of a movement of the relevant subgeneric type. The finale too has a chain of descending sequences over a dominant pedal in the recapitulation (bars 108–12) and a ritornello-like return of the main theme at the end of the movement mainly in octaves in imperial-court style (bars 155–64). Neither suspension chain sounds the note of resignation found in the famous retransition of Mozart K. 550/i; they much more explicitly allude to the tradition of a dominant pedal near the end of a fugue. In this light, Mozart's application of untimely rhetoric in K. 550 is sparing.

Even when Koželuch's materials are not heterogeneous, the same principle applies. In the first movement the basic ideas of the main theme and the subordinate theme are variants (brought into even closer relation in the recapitulation; bars 147–48), but their different modes of presentation clearly convey the typical drift from a stormy, broadly seria style to buffa over the course of the exposition. This is precisely the default arrangement that Mozart avoids in K. 550/i. In short, Koželuch's symphony, just like Mozart's, is a deliberate revival of an old type of symphony, and the two even share many techniques and much rhetoric, but Koželuch's, especially in the first movement, is much more concerned with the intensive application of old rules rather than their application in new ways. In this sense it resembles K. 183.

The conclusions advanced here about K. 550 in the light of the Viennese minor-key repertory as a whole harmonize with the suggestions of Rose Rosengard Subotnik, who finds evidence of a "critical worldview" in Mozart's last three symphonies.[56] She sees them running parallel with wider developments in intellectual culture in that meaning does not rest on abstract, universal principles and cannot be separated from its particular manifestation as perceived by the senses. This modern worldview records a move away from metaphysics and rational justifications of the world to an understanding based on concrete and individual human experience. The analytical approach of the present book, drawing as it does on the theories of Caplin (formal function) and Gjerdingen (schemata) is especially sensitive to such questions. Does a musical event exist primarily to fulfill a standard function, to ensure the correct execution of a rule that has been deployed in countless other pieces, or does it exist first and foremost for the sake of its immediate effect? Clearly the shift is a matter of degree. Mozart still adheres to the four-movement divertimento principle for the symphony: he does not change the number or order of movements, allow them

---

[56] Rose Rosengard Subotnik, "Evidence of a Critical Worldview in Mozart's Last Three Symphonies," chap.6 in *Developing Variations: Style and Ideology in Western Music* (Minneapolis: University of Minnesota Press, 1991), 98–111. For an interesting comparison, see Peter Gülke, *"Triumph der neuen Tonkunst": Mozarts letzte Sinfonien und ihr Umfeld* (Kassel and Stuttgart: Metzler-Bärenreiter, 1998), 138–58.

to share characteristic material, or obscure their boundaries. On the large scale the parts of each sonata or rounded-binary form are clear, and each movement is monotonal. Even at a more local level there is no conspicuous breaking of rules, but rules are applied in new contexts, sometimes incongruously and simultaneously, producing a piece that follows its own principles. Scoring, instrumental color, and, in the outer movements, relentless rhythmic momentum have crucial roles to play in defining those principles. Along the way the music alludes to familiar generic and subgeneric conventions but maintains its own unique energy profile. In the first movement that energy does not subside before the mediant tutti, which instead is absorbed into its flow. Even within the lyrical first subordinate theme the energy wells up again at a mysterious chromatic shift in the harmony, before resuming in full in the second. The tonal disjunctions at the start of the development sections of both outer movements do not submit to logical "explanation"—at least, not convincingly.[57] In the first movement, the note of "resignation," as Abert would put it, that is sounded as formal boundaries are approached—the consequent of the main theme, the reprise of the main theme, the cadence of second subordinate theme in the recapitulation with its imitative texture—points to the conventionality of those boundaries and thus their dissociation from the symphony as a here-and-now temporal-sensory experience, even as it accepts them in practice.

A comparison with Haydn makes the point clearer. Haydn liked to start a movement with a "problem" to be worked through later, suggesting a strong implication that needs to be realized or an error that has to be corrected. Realization or correction almost always occurs eventually within the same movement. For instance, a movement may begin with a harmonic progression like a cadence, or may begin *in medias res* with the expression of continuation function.[58] Later this material will be given its correct formal function of conclusion or middle within a larger paragraph. Elsewhere in a movement, cadences are frequently delayed by sudden disruptive events or distant modulations, yet they do eventually occur, the final tonic chord is reached, and conventional syntax is upheld. Haydn's conspicuous rule-breaking almost always results in the confirmation of the rules in the end.[59] What emerges strongly from the process is an awareness of the controlling rational mind of the composer, which is in agreement with the rational minds of listeners about what constitutes correctness. Musical events thus participate in a kind of logic. As regards minor-key symphonies, this type of compositional process has been discussed in chapter 7 in relation to Haydn 78/i, 80/i, 83/i, and 95/i. It applies also to 44/i (chapter 5). It is not clear how the initial ambiguities of that movement will be

---

[57] Subotnik, "Evidence of a Critical Worldview," 106.

[58] For instance, the first movements String Quartets, op. 30, no. 5, and op. 50, no. 6, and the fast sections of the first movements of the Vivace assai section of Symphony No. 94/i. For other problematic first-movement openings that call forth "solutions" later in the movement, see String Quartets op. 33, no. 1, op. 50, nos. 1 and 2, Symphonies Nos. 81, 86, 92, among others.

[59] One notable exception is the second movement of Symphony No. 64 ("Tempura mutandur"), but against the background of Haydn's vast oeuvre it proves the rule.

clarified, but in the end they are, and a single outcome emerges unchallenged. In Haydn's minor-key instrumental compositions of the 1780s (not just symphonies) the minor mode itself is treated a problem, which he solves by turning to major. Mozart sometimes played Haydnesque syntactic games—the trio of the "Jupiter" Symphony's minuet is an example—but there is nothing of them in K. 550.

What kind of statement did K. 550 make in the Vienna of 1788? Mozart's three great symphonies of that year may be seen as a significant investment in the abstract concert symphony at a time when the fortunes of that genre were at a low ebb. The works reconnect with symphonic music of the recent and more distant past, uphold certain subgeneric types, extend and refine the range of expression, reach for grandeur of concept and dimensions, and pass on the symphonic inheritance to the broadening public that attended contemporary concerts. Mozart had already begun this approach with the "Prague" Symphony, K. 504; he now formalized it with a set of three. Unlike many of his contemporaries, Mozart showed no interest in characteristic symphonies for the concert hall, then growing in popularity, but chose to preserve the multi-movement symphony without program, building on the public, international success of Haydn's "Paris" symphonies. Like that set and the sets of three symphonies published in Vienna by Hoffmeister and Koželuch, Mozart's contained a single minor-key work. As in the "Jupiter" Symphony, K. 551, in K. 550 Mozart is self-conscious about Viennese tradition. The "Jupiter" revives the Viennese C major "trumpet symphony," a tradition that stretches back to Fux and Caldara and recalls the magnificent court of Charles VI,[60] but at the same time extends the fugal finale to unheard-of complexity. That applies also to K. 550, even though its symphonic subgenre is different.

In the single minor-key work of the three, Mozart looked back to a specifically Viennese tradition of the late 1760s and early 1770s, choosing to employ a mediant tutti, a contrapuntal minuet, minor-mode endings for both outer movements, and touches of untimely rhetoric. But he also stuck to his own distinctive version of the fast minor-key movement. For a composer who was conversant with a wide range of eighteenth-century minor-key practices and compositional options and who put them all into practice on occasion, Mozart's consistency in returning to that conception over fifteen years is striking, as is its intensification in the 1780s with the first movements of the three great G minor instrumental works, K. 478, K. 516, and K. 550. In the latter, Mozart was demonstrating his skills, perhaps making an appeal to connoisseurs and aiming to equal and even surpass his peers in writing the finest minor-key symphony of their times. He came up with extraordinary new ideas and combinations, but in the end preserved conventional symphonic forms and the principle of abstraction. To the eighteenth-century connoisseur with a knowledge of the subgeneric tradition, the results would probably have seemed familiar and apparently comprehensible, yet also in some ways deeply original and even strange.

---

[60] Brown, "Eighteenth-Century Traditions and Mozart's 'Jupiter' Symphony."

{ APPENDIX 1 }

Thematic Catalogs Consulted for the Information in Table 1.1

Brook, Barry S., ed. *The Symphony, 1720–1840*. New York and London: Garland Publishing, 1986.

Reference Volume: Contents of the Set and Collected Thematic Indexes (1986)

VOLUMES IN SERIES B

1. Grave, Margaret G. *Thematic Index*. In Karl Ditters von Dittersdorf, *Six Symphonies*, edited by Eva Badura-Skoda. With Georg Matthias Monn, *Five Symphonies*, Johann Christoph Mann, *One Symphony*, edited by Kenneth E. Rudolf. New York and London: Garland, 1985.

3. Kucaba, John. *Thematic Index*. In Georg Christoph Wagenseil, *Fifteen Symphonies*, edited by John Kucaba. New York and London: Garland, 1981.

4. Brown, A. Peter. *Thematic Index*. In Carlos d'Ordoñez, *Seven Symphonies*, edited by A. Peter Brown with the assistance of Peter M. Alexander. New York and London: Garland, 1979.

5. Hickman, Roger. *Thematic Index*. In Franz Anton Hoffmeister, *Two Symphonies*, edited by Roger Hickman. With Joseph Leopold Eybler, *One Symphony*; Johann Baptist Gänsbacher, *One Symphony*, edited by Hildegard Herrmann-Schneider. New York and London: Garland, 1984.

7. Kimball, G. Cook. *Thematic Index*. In Franz Asplmayr, *Three Symphonies*, edited by Dennis C. Monk; Leopold Hofmann, *Four Symphonies*, edited by G. Cook Kimball; Wenzel Pichl, *Three Symphonies*, edited by Anita Zakin; Leopold Mozart, *Three Symphonies*, edited by Cliff Eisen. New York and London: Garland, 1984.

10. Hill, George R. *Thematic Index* (Gassmann) and Paul R. Bryan, *Thematic Index* (Vaňhal). In Florian Leopold Gassmann, *Seven Symphonies*, edited by George R. Hill; Jan Křtitel Vaňhal, *Five Symphonies*, edited by Paul Bryan. New York and London: Garland, 1981.

OTHER CATALOGS

Brown, A. Peter. "The Symphonies of Carlo d'Ordonez: A Contribution to the History of Viennese Instrumental Music during the Second Half of the Eighteenth Century." *Haydn Yearbook* 12 (1981): 5–121.

Bryan, Paul. *Johann Wanhal, Viennese Symphonist: His Life and His Musical Environment*. Stuyvesant, NY: Pendragon Press, 1997.

Grave, Margaret G. "First-Movement Form as a Measure of Dittersdorf's Symphonic Development." PhD diss., New York University, 1977.

Hill, George R. "The Concert Symphonies of Florian Leopold Gassmann (1729–1774)." PhD diss., New York University, 1975.

Kimball, G. Cook. "The Symphonies of Leopold Hofmann (1738–1793)." PhD diss., Columbia University, 1985.

Kucaba, John. "The Symphonies of Georg Christoph Wagenseil." PhD diss., Boston University, 1967.

Poštolka, Milan. *Leopold Koželuh: Život a dílo*, 161–365. Prague: Státní hudební vydavatelství, 1964.

———. "Thematisches Verzeichnis der Sinfonien Pavel Vranickýs." *Miscellanea musicologica* 20 (1967): 101–27.

Schmidt, Ernst Fritz. "Gottfried van Swieten als Komponist." *Mozart Jahrbuch 1953* (1954): 15–31.

Young, David. "The Symphonies of Karl von Ordonez (1734–1786): A Biographical, Bibliographical and Stylistic Study." PhD diss., University of Liverpool, 1980.

Sources of the Symphonies Used for Analysis; CD Recordings

Abbreviations

RR: Recent Researches in the Music of the Classical Era (Madison: A-R Editions).

AM: Accademia Musicale (Universal Edition: Mainz).

Artaria: Artaria Editions, Wellington, New Zealand.

Bryan, Vanhal: Paul Bryan, "The Symphonies of Johann Vanhal." PhD diss., University of Michigan, 1956.

DM: Diletto Musicale (Munich and Vienna: Doblinger).

DTÖ: Denkmäler der Tonkunst in Österreich (Vienna, Graz: various publishers).

Symphony B: The Symphony, Series B (New York and London: Garland Publishing).

MAB: Musica Antiqua Bohemica (Prague: Supraphon).

CHF: Český hudební fond, Prague.

WP: The Wranitzky Project (www.wranitzky.com).

RE: Ries & Erler, Berlin.

RISM sigla

D Bds: Berlin, Deutsche Staatsbibliothek, Musikabteilung.

CZ Bm: Brno, Moravské zemské muzeum, Hudebné historické oddělení.

I Fc: Florence, Conservatorio di musica "Luigi Cherubini," Biblioteca.

DK Kk: Copenhagen, Det kongelige Bibliotek Slotsholmen.

CZ Pnm: Prague, Narodní muzeum, Hudebněhistorické oddělení.

D Rtt: Regensburg, Fürst Thurn und Taxis Hofbibliothek und Zentralbibliothek.

		Modern ed.	18th-century ed.	Manuscript
Dittersdorf, C.	a1	DTÖ lxxxi		
	a2	Artaria 033		
	d1	Artaria 037		
	e1	*Symphony* B, i		
	g1	Artaria 038		
Gassmann, F. L.	83	Vienna: Universal, 1933		
	23	*Symphony* B, x		
	45			CZ Bm A 16 700a
Hoffmeister, F. A.	e1		Lyon: Guera, 1778	
Koželuch, L.	I:5	MAB 72		
Ordonez, C.	B1	Artaria 118		
	C14	*Symphony* B, iv		
	F12	Artaria 059		
	G7	Artaria 116		
	G8	Artaria 060		
Swieten, G. B.	7		London: Forster, 1785?	
Vaňhal, J. B.	a1	DM 328		
	a2	Bryan, *Vanhal*		
	c2	*Symphony* B, x		
	c3			CZ Pnm IX C5
	d1	RR 17		
	d2	*Symphony* B, x		
	e1	*Symphony* B, x		
	e2	RR 18		
	e3	Artaria 290		
	f1			D Rtt no. 40; CZ Pnm XXXIV B287
	g1	DM 38		
	g2	RR 17		
Wranitzky, P.	10			I Fc FPS 117
	11	CHF 324.53 S		
	12	RE 51125		
	30	WP		
	42			I Fc FPS 111
	43			I Fc FPS 119
Wagenseil, G. C.	G5			D Bds KHM 5547
	G6	AM 19		
	G4			DK Kk A2

{ GLOSSARY OF ANALYTICAL TERMS }

Most definitions are borrowed word-for-word from one of the following sources. A few are original to this study.

Caplin, William E. *Classical Form: A Theory of Formal Functions for the Instrumental Music of Haydn, Mozart and Beethoven.* **New York: Oxford University Press, 1998.**Gjerdingen, Robert O. *Music in the Galant Style.* **New York: Oxford University Press, 2007.**Hepokoski, James, and Warren Darcy. *Elements of Sonata Theory: Norms, Types and Deformations in the Late-Eighteenth-Century Sonata.* **New York: Oxford University Press, 2006.**bait-and-switch (Hepokoski / Darcy) The creation of the expectation of an imminent medial caesura that is not realized.

basic idea (Caplin) An initiating function consisting of a two-bar idea that usually contains several melodic or rhythmic motives constituting the primary material of a theme.

cadential (Caplin) A concluding intrathematic function that produces the requisite conditions for thematic closure. It is supported exclusively by one or more cadential progressions.

cadential arrival (Caplin) A moment in time marking the structural end of a theme or themelike unit.

cadential idea (Caplin) A concluding function consisting of a two-bar (or shorter) unit, supported exclusively by a cadential progression, that effects (or implies) a cadence.

cadential phrase (Caplin) A phrase supported exclusively by an expanded cadential progression. It does not usually exhibit continuational characteristics.

cadential progression (Caplin) A progression that confirms a tonality by bringing its fundamental harmonic functions.

characteristic material (Caplin) Melodic and rhythmic configurations used to define a theme as unique (compare **conventional material**).

closing section (Caplin) A postcadential intrathematic function following a perfect authentic cadence. It consists of a group of codettas, often featuring fragmentation and a recessive dynamic.

codetta (Caplin) A postcadential function following a perfect authentic cadence and ranging in length from a single chord to a four-bar phrase. It is supported by a tonic prolongational (occasionally a cadential) progression (compare **closing section**).

concluding function (Caplin) Any number of functions at various hierarchical levels that express the temporal quality of "ending" (compare **initiating function; medial function**).

continuation (Caplin) A medial intrathematic function that destabilizes the prevailing formal context by means of fragmentation, harmonic acceleration, faster surface rhythm, and harmonic sequence.

continuation phrase (Caplin) The second phrase of the sentence. It fuses continuation and cadential functions.

continuation=>cadential (phrase) (Caplin) A phrase supported exclusively by an expanded cadential progression. It fuses continuation and cadential function.

continuous exposition (Hepokoski / Darcy) An exposition that lacks a clearly articulated medial caesura followed by a successfully launched secondary (subordinate) theme.

deformation (Hepokoski / Darcy) A rejection of all default choices; a stretching or distortion of a norm beyond its understood limits; a pointed overriding of a standard option; a surprising or innovative departure from the constellation of habitual practices.

dissolving consequent (Hepokoski / Darcy) The apparent consequent to a grand antecedent that dissolves into a transition (compare grand antecedent).

exact repetition (Caplin) A unit (usually a basic idea) immediately restated in the same harmonic context (although the melody may be altered or transposed to different scale-degrees).

formal function (Caplin) The specific role played by a particular musical passage in the formal organization of a work. It generally expresses a temporal sense of beginning, middle end, before-the-beginning, or after-the-end. More specifically, it can express a wide variety of formal characteristic and relationships.

grand antecedent (Hepokoski / Darcy) A lengthy, multimodular antecedent that constitutes the first extended limb of P (the main theme) (compare **dissolving consequent**).

half cadence (Caplin) A cadential arrival articulated by the final dominant of a half-cadential progression.

imperfect authentic cadence (Caplin) An authentic cadence in which the soprano voice ends on the third (or, rarely, the fifth) scale-degree (compare **perfect authentic cadence**).

initiating function (Caplin) Any number of functions at various hierarchical levels that express the temporal quality of "beginning" (compare **medial function**; **concluding function**).

loose (Caplin) A formal organization characterized by the use of non-conventional thematic structures, harmonic-tonal instability (modulation, chromaticism), an asymmetrical grouping structure, phrase-structural extension and expansion, form-functional redundancy, and a diversity of melodic-motivic material (compare **tight-knit**).

main theme (Caplin) An initiating interthematic function that brings the main melodic-motivic ideas of the movement, establishes and confirms the home key, and defines the standard of tight-knit organization.

medial caesura (Hepokoski / Darcy) The brief, rhetorically reinforced break that serves to divide an exposition into two parts, tonic and subordinate key. The medial caesura follows a transition and a gain in energy. It marks the end of the first part of the exposition, "makes available" the second, and defines the type of exposition. The default types of medial caesuras are: (1) dominant half cadence; (2) tonic half cadence; (3) dominant perfect authentic cadence.

medial function (Caplin) Any number of functions at various hierarchical levels that expression the temporal quality of "being-in-the-middle" (compare **initiating function**; **concluding function**).

mediant tutti (MR) An energetic gesture (not always a literal tutti) on III at or soon after the start of the second paragraph of a minor-key symphony fast movement, the first having ended with a half cadence. The second paragraph continues in the key of III.

paragraph (MR) A section of a piece of medium size, beginning after one concluding function and stretching until the next. It typically expresses the functions initiating–medial–concluding in that order. A paragraph may be a theme, a transition, a developmental "core," the A section of a minuet, or some other type.

perfect authentic cadence (Caplin) An authentic cadence in which the soprano voice ends on the tonic scale-degree (compare **imperfect authentic cadence**).

postcadential (Caplin) One of several framing functions that express the sense of "after-the-end." It follows a cadence and prolongs its final harmony, usually with a recessive dynamic.

presentation (Caplin) An initiating intrathematic function consisting of a unit (usually a basic idea) and its repetition, supported by a prolongation of tonic harmony.

rotation (Hepokoski / Darcy) A principle of large-scale recurrence by means of the recycling of a referential thematic pattern established as an ordered succession at the outset of a piece. It underpins a variety of forms that are conventionally distinguished, such as theme and variations, strophic songs, strophic variation, rondos, ostinato-grounded pieces, but also movements conventionally described as in "sonata form."

sentence (Caplin) A theme consisting of a presentation phrase and a continuation (or continuation=>cadential) phrase.

sequential repetition (Caplin) A unit that is followed by a restatement transposed to a different scale-degree.

standing on the dominant (Caplin) A postcadential intrathematic function following a half cadence. It may also follow a perfect authentic cadence at the end of a small ternary exposition to initiate a contrasting middle. It consists of one or more ideas supported exclusively by a dominant prolongation.

statement-response repetition (Caplin) A tonic version of a unit (usually a basic idea) immediately restated by a dominant version.

schema (Gjerdingen) A mental representation or category of "galant" musical utterances.

subordinate key (Caplin) A closely related tonal region confirmed by a perfect authentic cadence as the principal contrasting key to the home key.

subordinate theme (Caplin) An interthematic function that confirms a subordinate key by closing with a perfect authentic cadence. It loosens the formal organization in order to solidify the new key in relation to the home key.

theme (Caplin) A unit consisting of conventional set of initiating, medial, and ending intrathematic functions. It must close with a cadence.

tight knit (Caplin) A formal organization characterized by the use of conventional theme-types, harmonic-tonal stability, a symmetrical grouping structure, form-functional efficiency, and a unity of melodic-motivic material (compare **loose**).

untimely rhetoric (MR) A compositional strategy that evokes unfashionable idioms preserved from before the triumph of "galant" style and aesthetics at mid-century but still current in sacred music. They include fugato, imitative textures, canon, species counterpoint textures, ritornello gestures, Corellian trio-sonata textures, and fast-moving bass lines.

{ BIBLIOGRAPHY }

Abert, Hermann. *W.A. Mozart*. Translated by Stewart Spencer. Edited by Cliff Eisen. New Haven and London: Yale University Press, 2007.

Ackerman, James A., and Daniel Bernhardssohn. Introduction to *Paul Wranitzky, Symphony in D minor, "La Tempesta."* http://www.wranitzky.com.

Allanbrook, Wye Jamison. "Mozart's Tunes and the Comedy of Closure." In *On Mozart*, edited by James M. Morris, 169–86. Cambridge: Woodrow Wilson Center Press and Cambridge University Press, 1994.

Allanbrook, Wye Jamison. *Rhythmic Gesture in Mozart: "Le nozze di Figaro" and "Don Giovanni."* Chicago: University of Chicago Press, 1983.

Anderson, Emily, ed. and trans. *The Letters of Mozart and His Family*. 3rd ed. London and Houndsmills: Macmillan, 1985.

Anonymous. "Nekrolog auf das Jahr 1812 [*sic*]. Johann Wanhall." *Vaterländische Blätter für den Österreichischen Kaiserstaat* 2 (1813): 476–78.

Arneth, Alfred Ritter von, ed. *Briefe der Kaiserin Maria Theresia an ihre Kinder und Freunde*. 4 vols. Vienna: Wilhelm Braumüller, 1881.

Alexander, Peter M. "Karl von Ordonez." In *The Symphonic Repertoire*. Vol. 2, *The Eighteenth-Century Symphony*, edited by Mary Sue Morrow and Bathia Churgin, 516–28. Bloomington and Indianapolis: Indiana University Press, 2012.

Badley, Allan. "Georg Christoph Wagensil." In *The Symphonic Repertoire*. Vol. 2, *The Eighteenth-Century Symphony*, edited by Mary Sue Morrow and Bathia Churgin, 472–82. Bloomington and Indianapolis: Indiana University Press, 2012.

Badura-Skoda, Eva, ed. Introduction to Karl Ditters von Dittersdorf, *Six Symphonies*. Series B, vol. 1 of *The Symphony, 1720–1840*. New York and London: Garland, 1985.

Baker, Nancy Kovaleff, and Thomas Christensen, eds. *Aesthetics and the Art of Musical Composition in the German Enlightenment*. Cambridge: Cambridge University Press, 1995.

Bey, Henning. *Haydns und Mozarts Symphonik nach 1782: Konzeptionelle Perspektiven*. Neurid: Ars Una, 2005.

Bonds, Mark Evan. "Haydn's 'Cours complet de la composition' and the *Sturm und Drang.*" In *Haydn Studies*, edited by W. Dean Sutcliffe, 152–76. Cambridge: Cambridge University Press, 1998.

Bonds, Mark Evan. *Wordless Rhetoric: Musical Form and the Metaphor of the Oration*. Cambridge, MA: Harvard University Press, 1991.

Bouissou, Sylvie. "Les fonctions dramatiques de la tempête et de l'orage dans l'opéra français (1674–1774)." In *Penser l'opéra français de l'âge classique*, edited by Catherine Kintzler, 89–103. Paris: Collège international de philosophie, 1993.

Bouissou, Sylvie. "Mécanismes dramatiques de la tempête et de l'orage dans l'opéra français à l'âge baroque." In *D'un opéra l'autre: Hommage à Jean Mongrédien*, edited by Jean Gribenski, Marie-Claire Mussat, and Herbert Schneider, 218–30. Paris: Presses de l'Université de Paris-Sorbonne, 1996.

Boyce, William. *Cathedral Music*. 2nd ed. London: John Ashley, 1788.

Broder, Nathan, ed. *Wolfgang Amadeus Mozart, Symphony in G Minor K. 550, The Score of the New Mozart Edition*. New York: Norton, 1967.

Brofsky, Howard. "The Symphonies of Padre Martini." *Musical Quarterly* 51, no. 4 (1965): 649–73.

Brook, Barry S. *La symphonie française dans la seconde moitié du XVIIIe siècle*. Vol. 1, *Étude historique*. Paris: Université de Paris, Institut de Musicologie, 1962.

Brook, Barry S. "Simon Le Duc 'l'aine', a French Symphonist at the Time of Mozart." *Musical Quarterly* 48, no. 4 (1962): 498–513.

Brook, Barry S. "*Sturm und Drang* and the Romantic Period in Music." *Studies in Romanticism* 9 (1970): 269–84.

Brown, A. Peter, ed. *Carlo d'Ordonez, String Quartets, Opus 1*. Madison, WI: A-R Editions, 1980.

Brown, A. Peter. "The Chamber Music with Strings of Carlos d'Ordoñez: A Bibliographic and Stylistic Study." *Acta Musicologica* 46, no. 2 (1974): 222–72.

Brown, A. Peter. "The Earliest English Biography of Haydn." *Musical Quarterly* 59 (1973): 343.

Brown, A. Peter. "Eighteenth-Century Traditions and Mozart's 'Jupiter' Symphony K. 551." *Journal of Musicology* 20, no. 2 (2003): 157–95.

Brown, A. Peter. "Haydn and Mozart's Stay in Vienna: Weeding a Musicological Garden." *Journal of Musicology* 10, no. 2 (1992): 192–230.

Brown, A. Peter, ed. Introduction to Carlo d'Ordondez, *Seven Symphonies*. Series B, vol. 3 of *The Symphony, 1720–1840*. New York and London: Garland, 1979.

Brown, A. Peter. "The Symphonies of Carlo d'Ordonez: A Contribution to the History of Viennese Instrumental Music during the Second Half of the Eighteenth Century." *Haydn Yearbook* 12 (1981): 5–121.

Brown, A. Peter. "The Trumpet Overture and Sinfonia in Vienna (1715–1822): Rise, Decline and Reformulation." In *Music in Eighteenth-Century Austria*, edited by David Wyn Jones, 13–69. Cambridge: Cambridge University Press, 1996.

Bryan, Paul. "Johann Baptist Wanhal." In *The Symphonic Repertoire*. Vol. 2, *The Eighteenth-Century Symphony*, edited by Mary Sue Morrow and Bathia Churgin, 529–41. Bloomington and Indianapolis: Indiana University Press, 2012.

Bryan, Paul. *Johann Wanhal, Viennese Symphonist: His Life and His Musical Environment*. Stuyvesant, NY: Pendragon Press, 1997.

Burney, Charles. *A General History of Music from the Earliest Ages to the Present Period*. 4 vols. London: Payne and Son, 1776–89.

Burney, Charles. *The Present State of Music in Germany, the Netherlands and the United Provinces*. 2 vols. London: T. Beckett and Co., 1773.

Burney, Charles. "VAŇHALL." In *The Cyclopaedia; or Universal Dictionary of Arts, Sciences, and Literature*, edited by Abraham Rees. 39 vols. London: Longman, Hurst, Rees Orme, and Brown, 1802–19.

Burnham, Scott. "The Second Nature of Sonata Form." In *Music Theory and Natural Order from the Renaissance to the Early Twentieth Century*, edited by Suzannah Clark and Alexander Rehding, 111–41. Cambridge: Cambridge University Press, 2001.

Cabrini, Michele. "Breaking Form through Sound: Instrumental Aesthetics, *Tempête*, and Temporality in the French Baroque Cantata." *Journal of Musicology* 26, no. 3 (2009): 327–78.

Caplin, William E. *Classical Form: A Theory of Formal Functions for the Instrumental Music of Haydn, Mozart and Beethoven.* New York: Oxford University Press, 1998.

Caplin, William E. "The Classical Cadence: Conceptions and Misconceptions." *Journal of the American Musicological Society* 57, no. 1 (2004): 51–117.

Carpani, Giuseppe. *Le Haydine, ovvero Lettere sulla vita e le opere del celebre maestro Giuseppe Haydn.* Milan: Buccinelli, 1812.

Carruthers, Glen. "Strangeness and Beauty: The Opening Measure of Mozart's Symphony in G Minor, K.550." *Journal of Musicology* 16, no. 2 (1998): 283–99.

Carse, Adam. *The Orchestra in the XVIIIth Century.* Cambridge: W. Heffer, 1940.

Chantler, Abigail. "The *Sturm und Drang* Style Revisited." *International Review of the Aesthetics and Sociology of Music* 34, no. 1 (2003): 17–31.

Churgin, Bathia. "Francesco Galeazzi's Description (1796) of Sonata Form." *Journal of the American Musicological Society* 21, no. 2 (1968): 181–99.

Churgin, Bathia. "Stormy Interlude: Sammartini's Middle Symphonies and Overtures in Minor." In *Giovanni Battista Sammartini and His Musical Environment*, edited by Anna Cattoretti, 37–62. Turnhout: Brepols, 2004.

Clarke, Stephen L., ed. and trans. *The Letters of C.P.E. Bach.* Oxford: Clarendon Press, 1997.

Cohn, Richard. "Metric and Hypermetric Dissonance in the Menuetto of Mozart's Symphony in G Minor, K. 550." *Intégral* 6 (1992): 1–33.

Danckwardt, Marianne. "Zu zwei Haydnschen Sinfoniesätzen mit liturgischer Melodie (Sinfonien Nr. 30, 1. Satz, und Nr. 26, 2. Satz.)." In *Festschrift Rudolf Bockholdt zum 60. Geburtstag*, edited by Norbert Dubowy and Sören Meyer-Eller, 193–200. Pfaffenhofen: Ludwig, 1990.

Dearling, Robert. *The Music of Wolfgang Amadeus Mozart: The Symphonies.* Rutherford, NJ: Fairleigh Dickinson University Press; London: Associated University Presses, 1982.

Diergarten, Felix. "'Auch Homere schlafen bisweilen': Heinrich Christoph Kochs Polemik gegen Joseph Haydn." *Haydn-Studien* 10 (2010): 78–92.

Dittersdorf, Carl Ditters von. *Lebensbeschreibung, seinem Sohne in die Feder diktiert.* 1801; Regensburg: Gustav Bosse, 1940.

Dlabacž, Gottfried Johann. *Allgemeines historisches Künstler-Lexicon für Böhmen und zum Theil auch für Mähren und Schlesien.* 3 vols. Prague: Gottlieb Haase, 1815.

Einstein, Alfred. *Mozart, His Character, His Work.* Translated by Arthur Mendel and Nathan Broder. New York: Oxford University Press, 1945.

Fertonani, Cesare. "'Vo Solcando un mar crudele': Per una tipologia dell'aria di tempesta nella prima metà del Settecento." *Musica e storia* 5 (1997): 67–110.

Floros, Constantin. "Mozarts letzte Sinfonien." In *Mozart, Klassik für die Gegenwart*, edited by Hartmut Heinicke, 80–84. Hamburg: Vereins- und Westbank, 1978.

Finscher, Ludwig. *Joseph Haydn und seine Zeit.* Laaber: Laaber Verlag, 2000.

Fischer, Wilhelm. "Zur Entwicklungsgeschichte des Wiener klassischen Stils." *Studien zur Musikwissenschaft* 3 (1915): 25–84.

Forkel, Johann Nikolaus. *Musikalisch-kritische Bibliothek.* 3 vols. Gotha: Carl Wilhelm Ettinger, 1778–79.

Freeman, Robert N. *The Practice of Music at Melk Abbey: Based upon the Documents, 1681–1826.* Vienna: Verlag der Österreichischen Akademie der Wissenschaften, 1989.

Frisch, Walter. *Brahms and the Principle of Developing Variation.* Berkeley and London: University of California Press, 1984.

Geiringer, Karl. *Haydn: A Creative Life in Music*. London: Allen and Unwin, 1947.

Geiringer, Karl. "Haydn and His Viennese Background." In *Haydn Studies*, edited by Jens Peter Larsen, Howard Serwer, and James Webster, 19–40. New York: Norton, 1981.

Gerber, Ernst Ludwig. *Historisch-biographisches Lexicon der Tonkünstler*. 2 vols. Leipzig: Breitkopf, 1790–92.

Gerber, Ernst Ludwig. *Neues historisch-biographisches Lexicon der Tonkünstler*. Leipzig: A. Kühnel, 1812–14.

Gerlach, Sonia. "Joseph Haydns Sinfonien bis 1774: Studien zur Chronologie." *Haydn-Studien* 7, no. 1–2 (1996): 1–287.

Gjerdingen, Robert O. *Music in the Galant Style*. New York: Oxford University Press, 2007.

Gotwals, Vernon. "The Earliest Biographies of Haydn." *Musical Quarterly* 45 (1959): 439–59.

Gotwals, Vernon. *Joseph Haydn: Eighteenth-Century Gentleman and Genius*. Madison: University of Wisconsin Press, 1963.

Grave, Floyd. "Galant Style, Enlightenment, and the Paths from Minor to Major in Later Instrumental Works by Haydn." *Ad Parnassum* 7 (2009): 9–41.

Grave, Floyd. "Metrical Dissonance in Haydn." *Journal of Musicology* 13, no. 2 (1995): 168–202.

Grave, Floyd. "Recuperation, Transformation and the Transcendence of Major over Minor in the Finale of Haydn's String Quartet Op. 76 No. 1." *Eighteenth-Century Music* 5, no. 1 (2008): 27–50.

Grave, Margaret. "First-Movement Form as a Measure of Dittersdorf's Symphonic Development." PhD diss., New York University, 1977.

Grave, Margaret. "Vogler, Georg Joseph." In *The New Grove Dictionary of Music and Musicians*, 2nd ed., edited by Stanley Sadie, 26:863–68. 29 vols. London: Macmillan, 2001.

Gresham, Carolyn. "Stylistic Features of Haydn's Symphonies from 1768 to 1772." In *Haydn Studies*, edited by Jens Peter Larsen, Howard Server, and James Webster, 431–34. New York: Norton, 1981.

Grim, William E. *Haydn's Sturm und Drang Symphonies: Form and Meaning*. Lewiston, NY, and Lampeter: Edwin Mellen Press, 1990.

Grove, George. "Mozart's Symphony in G minor." *Musical Times* 48 (1907): 25–28.

Gülke, Peter. *"Triumph der neuen Tonkunst": Mozarts letzte Sinfonien und ihr Umfeld*. Kassel and Stuttgart: Metzler-Bärenreiter, 1998.

Harrison, Bernard. *Haydn: The "Paris" Symphonies*. Cambridge: Cambridge University Press, 1998.

Harriss, Ernest. "Johan Adolf Hasse and the *Sturm und Drang* in Vienna." *Revista de Musicologia* 16, no. 5 (1993): 10–21.

Harpster, Richard W. "Genius in the Eighteenth Century: C. F. D. Schubart's 'Vom musikalischen Genie'." *Current Musicology* 15 (1973): 73–80.

Hatten, Robert S. *Musical Meaning in Beethoven: Markedness, Correlation and Interpretation*. Bloomington and Indianapolis: Indiana University Press, 1994.

Haydn, Joseph. *Kritischer Ausgabe sämtliche Symphonien*, edited by H. C. Robbins Landon. 12 vols. Vienna: Universal, 1967.

Heartz, Daniel. *Haydn, Mozart and Early Beethoven, 1781–1802*. New York and London W. W. Norton, 2009.

Heartz, Daniel. *Haydn, Mozart and the Viennese School, 1740–1780*. New York and London: W. W. Norton, 1995.

Heartz, Daniel. *Music in European Capitals: The Galant Style, 1720–1780*. New York: W. W. Norton, 2003.

Heartz, Daniel. "Sturm und Drang im Musikdrama." In *Bericht über den internationalen Musikwissenschaftlichen Kongress, Bonn, 1970*, edited by Carl Dahlhaus et al., 432–35. Kassel: Bärenreiter, 1971.

Heckmann, Harald. "Vorwort." In *Chöre und Zwischenaktmusiken zu "Thamos, König in Ägypten."* Series II, group 6, vol. 1 of *Neue Mozart Ausgabe*. Kassel and Basel: Bärenreiter, 1956.

Hepokoski, James, and Warren Darcy. *Elements of Sonata Theory: Norms, Types and Deformations in the Late-Eighteenth-Century Sonata*. New York: Oxford University Press, 2006.

Heuss, Alfred. "Die kleine Sekunde in Mozarts g-moll Sinfonie." *Jahrbuch der Musikbibliothek Peters* 40 (1934): 54–66.

Hill, George R. "The Concert Symphonies of Florian Leopold Gassmann (1729–1774)." PhD diss., New York University, 1975.

Hill, George R., ed. Introduction to Florian Leopold Gassmann, *Seven Symphonies*. Series B, vol. 10 of *The Symphony, 1720–1840*. New York and London: Garland, 1981.

Hill, George R. *A Thematic Catalogue of the Instrumental Music of Florian Leopold Gassmann*. Hackensack: Boonin, 1976.

Hodgson, Antony. *The Music of Joseph Haydn: The Symphonies*. London: Tantivy Press, 1976.

Hogwood, Christopher. "In Defence of the Minuet and Trio." *Early Music* 30, no. 2 (2002): 237–51.

Hortschansky, Klaus. "Die g-moll-Sinfonie zur Zeit der Wiener Klassik." In *Traditionen–Neuansätze: Für Anna Amalie Abert (1906-1996)*, edited by Klaus Hortschansky, 329–48. Tutzing: Schneider, 1997.

Hosler, Bellamy. *Changing Aesthetic Views of Instrumental Music in Eighteenth-Century Germany*. Ann Arbor: UMI Research Press, 1981.

Hoyt, Peter A. "Review-Essay: Haydn's New Incoherence." *Music Theory Spectrum* 19, no. 2 (1997): 264–84.

Hughes, Rosemary. *Haydn*. The Master Musicians. Rev. ed. London: Dent, 1978.

Hunter, Mary. *The Culture of Opera Buffa in Mozart's Vienna: A Poetics of Entertainment*. Princeton, NJ: Princeton University Press, 1999.

Irving, John. "The Viennese Symphony 1750–1827." In *The Cambridge Companion to the Symphony*, edited by Julian Horton, 15–28. Cambridge: Cambridge University Press, 2013.

Ivanovitch, Roman. "Mozart's Art of Retransition." *Music Analysis* 30, no. 1 (2011): 1–36.

Jackson, Timothy L. "The Tragic Reversed Recapitulation in the German Classical Tradition." *Journal of Music Theory* 40, no. 1 (1996): 61–111.

Jan, Steven. *Aspects of Mozart's Music in G Minor: Toward the Identification of Common Structural and Compositional Features*. New York and London: Garland, 1995.

Johnson, James H. *Listening in Paris: A Cultural History*. Berkeley and Los Angeles: University of California Press, 1995.

Jones, David Wyn. *Beethoven: Pastoral Symphony*. Cambridge: Cambridge University Press, 1995.

Jones, David Wyn, ed. *Haydn*. Oxford Composer Companions. 2nd ed. New York: Oxford University Press, 2009.

Jones, David Wyn, ed. Introduction to Johann Baptist Vaňhal, *Six Quartets: An Edition and Commentary*. Cardiff: University College Cardiff Press, 1980.

Jones, David Wyn. *The Life of Haydn*. Cambridge: Cambridge University Press, 2009.

Jones, David Wyn, ed. *Music in Eighteenth-Century Austria*. Cambridge: Cambridge University Press, 1996.

Jones, David Wyn. "The String Quartets of Vanhal." 3 vols. PhD diss., University of Wales, 1977.

Jones, David Wyn. *The Symphony in Beethoven's Vienna*. Cambridge: Cambridge University Press, 2006.

Jones, David Wyn. "Why Did Mozart Compose His Last Three Symphonies? Some New Hypotheses." *Music Review* 51 (1990): 280–89.

Junker, Carl Ludwig. *Tonkunst*. Bern: Typographische Gesellschaft, 1777.

Junker, Carl Ludwig. *Zwanzig Componisten, eine Skizze*. Berne: Typographische Gesellschaft, 1776.

Kamien, Roger. "Style Change in the Mid-18th-Century Keyboard Sonata." *Journal of the American Musicological Society* 19, no. 1 (1966): 37–58.

Keefe, Simon P. *Mozart's Requiem: Reception, Work, Completion*. Cambridge: Cambridge University Press, 2012.

Keller, Hans. "Wolfgang Amadeus Mozart." In *The Symphony. Vol. 1, Haydn to Dvořák*, edited by Robert Simpson, 50–103. Harmondsworth: Penguin, 1966.

Kelly, Michael. *Reminiscences of Michael Kelly*. 2 vols. London: Henry Colburn, 1826.

Kerman, Joseph. *Write All These Down: Essays on Music*. Berkeley and London: University of California Press, 1994.

Kimball, G. Cook. "The Symphonies of Leopold Hofmann (1738–1793)." PhD diss., Columbia University, 1985.

Kirkendale, Warren. *Die Kunst des reinen Satzes in der Musik*. 2 vols. Berlin and Königsberg: G. J. Decker, 1776–79.

Kirkendale, Warren. *Fuge und Fugato in der Kammermusik des Rokoko und der Klassik*. Tutzing: Hans Schneider, 1966.

Kirkendale, Warren. *Fugue and Fugato in Rococo and Classical Chamber Music*. Translated by Margaret Bent and the author. Rev. ed. Durham, NC: Duke University Press, 1979.

Kirnberger, Johann Philipp. *Die Kunst des reinen Satzes in der Musik*. 2 vols. Berlin and Königsberg: G. J. Decker, 1776–79.

Kivy, Peter. *Osmin's Rage: Reflections of Music, Drama and Text*. 2nd ed. Ithaca, NY, and London: Cornell University Press, 1999.

Koch, Heinrich Christoph. *Versuch einer Anleitung zur Komposition*. 3 vols. Leipzig: Adam F. Böhme, 1782–93. Reprint, Hildesheim: Olms, 1969.

Köchel, Ludwig Ritter von. *Johann Joseph Fux: Hofcompositor und Hofkapellmeister der Kaiser Leopold I., Josef I. und Karl VI. von 1698 bis 1740*. Vienna: A. Hölder, 1872. Reprint, Hildesheim: Georg Olms, 1974.

Kolk, Joel. "*Sturm und Drang* and Haydn's Opera." In *Haydn Studies*, edited by Jens Peter Larsen, Howard Serwer, and James Webster, 440–45. New York: W. W. Norton, 1981.

Krebs, Harald. *Fantasy Pieces: Metrical Dissonance in the Music of Robert Schumann*. New York and Oxford: Oxford University Press, 1999.

Krones, Hartmut. "Die Sonatenhauptsatzform in Werken bohmischer und mahrischer Komponisten um 1800." *Musikgeschichte zwischen Ost- und Westeuropa: Symphonik,*

Musiksammlungen, edited by Helmut Loos, 29–47. Sankt Augustin: Academia Verlag, 1997.

Kucaba, John, ed. Introduction to Georg Christoph Wagenseil, *Fifteen Symphonies*. Series B, vol. 3 of *The Symphony, 1720–1840*. New York and London: Garland, 1981.

Kucaba, John. "The Symphonies of Georg Christoph Wagenseil." PhD diss., Boston University, 1967.

Kunze, Stefan. *Wolfgang Amadeus Mozart, Sinfonie g-moll, KV 550*. Munich: Fink, 1968.

Lacépède, Bernard Germain de. *La poétique de la musique*. 2 vols. Paris, 1785. Reprint, Geneva: Slatkine, 1970.

La Gorce, Jérôme de. "Tempêtes et tremblements de terre dans l'opéra français sous le règne de Louis XIV." In *Le mouvement en musique à l'époque baroque*, edited by Hervé Lacombe, 171–88. Metz: Éditions Serpenoise, 1996.

Landon, H. C. Robbins. *1791: Mozart's Last Year*. London and New York: Thames and Hudson, 1988.

Landon, H. C. Robbins. *Haydn: Chronicle and Works. Vol. 2, Haydn at Eszterháza, 1766–1790*. London: Thames and Hudson, 1978.

Landon, H. C. Robbins. "La crise romantique dans la musique autrichienne vers 1770. Quelques précurseurs inconnus de la Symphonie en sol mineur (KV 183) de Mozart." In *Les influences étrangers dans l'oeuvre de W. A. Mozart*, edited by André Verchaly, 27–47. Paris: Centre nationale de la récherche scientifique, 1958.

Landon, H. C. Robbins. *The Symphonies of Joseph Haydn*. London: Universal Edition and Rockliff, 1955.

Landon, H. C. Robbins, and David Wyn Jones. *Haydn: His Life and Music*. Bloomington: Indiana University Press, 1988.

Lang-Becker, Elke. *Szenentypus und Musik in Rameaus tragédie lyrique*. Munich: Katzbichler München, 1977.

Larsen, Jens Peter. *Handel, Haydn, and the Viennese Classical Style*. Ann Arbor: UMI Research Press, 1988.

Larsen, Jens Peter. "The Symphonies." In *The Mozart Companion*, edited by H. C. Robbins Landon and Donald Mitchell, 156–99. London: Rockliff, 1956.

Larsen, Jens Peter. "The Viennese Classical School: A Challenge to Musicology." *Current Musicology* 9 (1969): 105–12.

LaRue, Jan. "Bifocal Tonality: An Explanation for Ambiguous Baroque Cadences." In *Essays on Music in Honor of Archibald Thompson Davison*, 173–84. Cambridge, MA: Department of Music, Harvard University, 1957.

LaRue, Jan. *A Catalogue of 18th-Century Symphonies. Vol.1, Thematic Identifier*. Bloomington: Indiana University Press, 1988.

LaRue, Jan. "A Haydn Speciality: Multistage Variance." In *Joseph Haydn: Bericht ueber den internationalen Joseph Haydn Kongress*, edited by Eva Badura-Skoda, 142–46. Munich: Henle, 1986.

LaRue, Jan. "Major and Minor Mysteries of Identification in the 18th-Century Symphony." *Journal of Musicology* 18, no. 2 (2001): 249–67.

LaRue, Jan. "Multistage Variance: Haydn's Legacy to Beethoven." *Journal of Musicology* 1, no. 3 (1982): 265–74.

Le Huray, Peter, and James Day. *Music and Aesthetics in the Eighteenth and Early-Nineteenth Centuries*. Cambridge: Cambridge University Press, 1981.

Leister, Reiner. *Das Finale in der Sinfonik Joseph Haydns*. Stuttgart: Ibidem-Verlag, 1999.

Longyear, R. M. "The Minor Mode in Eighteenth-Century Sonata Form." *Journal of Music Theory* 15, no. 1–2 (1971): 182–229.

Longyear, R. M. "The Minor Mode in the Classic Period." *Music Review* 32, no. 1 (1971): 27–35.

Lowe, Melanie. *Pleasure and Meaning in the Classical Symphony*. Bloomington: Indiana University Press, 2007.

MacIntyre, Bruce C. "Johann Baptist Vanhal and the Pastoral Mass Tradition." In *Music in Eighteenth-Century Austria*, edited by David Wyn Jones, 112–32. Cambridge: Cambridge University Press, 1996.

McClelland, Clive. *Ombra: Supernatural Music in the Eighteenth Century*. Lanham, MD, and Plymouth: Lexington Books, 2013.

McVeigh, Simon, and Jehoash Hirschberg. *The Italian Solo Concerto, 1700–1760: Rhetorical Strategies and Style History*. Woodbridge: Boydell Press, 2004.

McVeigh, Simon, and Jehoash Hirschberg. "Symphony." In *Haydn*, edited by David Wyn Jones, 381–414. Oxford Composer Companions. 2nd ed. New York: Oxford University Press, 2009.

Meyer, Eve R., ed. Introduction to Florian Leopold Gassmann, *Selected Divertimenti a tre and a quattro*. Madison, WI: A-R Editions, 1983.

Mirka, Danuta, and Kofi Agawu, eds. Introduction to *Communication in Eighteenth-Century Music*. Cambridge: Cambridge University Press, 2008.

Moosbauer, Bernhard. *Tonart und Form in den Finali von Joseph Haydn zwischen 1766 und 1774*. Tutzing: Hans Schneider 1998.

Morrow, Mary Sue. *Concert Life in Haydn's Vienna: Aspects of a Developing Musical and Social Institution*. Stuyvesant, NY: Pendragon Press, 1989.

Morrow, Mary Sue. "Reception: The Netherlands and North Germany." In *Haydn*, edited by David Wyn Jones, 330–32. Oxford Composer Companions. 2nd ed. New York: Oxford University Press, 2009.

Morrow, Mary Sue. "Other Classical Repertoires." In *The Cambridge Companion to the Symphony*, edited by Julian Horton, 29–60. Cambridge: Cambridge University Press, 2013.

Morrow, Mary Sue. "Reclaiming the Eighteenth-Century Symphony." In *The Symphonic Repertoire. Vol. 2, The Eighteenth-Century Symphony*, edited by Mary Sue Morrow and Bathia Churgin, 3–17. Bloomington and Indianapolis: Indiana University Press, 2012.

Morrow, Mary Sue. "The Symphony in the Austrian Monarchy." In *The Symphonic Repertoire. Vol. 2, The Eighteenth-Century Symphony*, edited by Mary Sue Morrow and Bathia Churgin, 411–71. Bloomington and Indianapolis: Indiana University Press, 2012.

Nattiez, Jean-Jacques. "A Comparison of Analyses from the Semiological Point of View (The Theme of Mozart's Symphony in G Minor, K. 550)." *Contemporary Music Review* 17, no. 1 (1998): 1–38.

Nettl, Paul, ed. and trans. *Forgotten Musicians*. New York: Philosophical Library, 1951.

Newbould, Brian. "Mozart's Lost Melody." *Musical Times* 132, no. 1785 (1991): 552–53.

Nicolai, Friedrich. *Beschreibung einer Reise durch Deutschland und die Schweiz*. 4 vols. Berlin: Stettin, 1783–95.

Oulibicheff, Alexandre. *Nouvelle biographie de Mozart*. 3 vols. Moscow: A. Semen, 1843.

Plath, Wolfgang. "Beiträge zur Mozart-Autobiographie II: Schriftchronologie 1770–1780." *Mozart-Jahrbuch* (1976–77): 131–73.

Polth, Michael. "Sinfonieexpositionen und musikalischer Zusammenhang im 18. Johrhundert." In *Musikkonzepte–Konzepte der Musikwissenschaft*, edited by Kathrin Eberl and Wolfgang Ruf, 394–403. Kassel and New York: Bärenreiter, 2000.

Poštolka, Milan. *Leopold Koželuh: Život a dílo*, 161–365. Prague: Státní hudební vydavatelství, 1964.

Poštolka, Milan. "Thematisches Verzeichnis der Sinfonien Pavel Vranickýs." *Miscellanea musicologica* 20 (1967): 101–27.

Raab, Armin. "Haydns Briefe an den Verleger Boyer." *Haydn Studien* 8 (2003): 237–52.

Ratner, Leonard. "Ars Combinatoria, Chance and Choice in Eighteenth-Century Music." In *Studies in Eighteenth-Century Music: A Tribute to Karl Geiringer on His Seventieth Birthday*, edited by H. C. Robbins Landon, 343–63. London: Allen and Unwin, 1970.

Ratner, Leonard. *Classic Music: Expression, Form and Style*. New York: Schirmer, 1980.

Ratner, Leonard. "Eighteenth-Century Theories of Musical Period Structure." *Musical Quarterly* 42, no. 4 (1956): 439–54.

Riedel, Friedrich W. "Joseph Haydns Sinfonien als liturgische Musik." In *Festschrift Hubert Unverricht zum 65. Geburtstag*, edited by Karlheinz Schlager, 213–20. Tutzing: Schneider, 1992.

Riepel, Joseph. *Anfangsgründe zur musikalischen Setzkunst. Vol. 4, 1752–68*. Augsburg: Lotter, 1765.

Riley, Matthew. "Haydn's Missing Middles." *Music Analysis* 30, no. 1 (2011): 37–57.

Riley, Matthew. *Musical Listening in the German Enlightenment: Attention, Wonder and Astonishment*. Aldershot: Ashgate, 2004.

Riley, Matthew. Review of *Metric Manipulations in Haydn and Mozart*, by Danuta Mirka. *Music Analysis* 31, no. 2 (2012): 251–58.

Rosand, Ellen. "The Descending Tetrachord: An Emblem of Lament." *Musical Quarterly* 65, no. 3 (1979): 346–59.

Rosen, Charles. *The Classical Style: Haydn, Mozart, Beethoven*. New ed. London: Faber, 1997.

Rosen, Charles. *Sonata Forms*. Rev. ed. New York: Norton, 1988.

Rousseau, Jean-Jacques. *Dictionnaire de Musique*. Paris: Duchesne, 1768.

Rudolf, Kenneth E., ed. *Georg Matthias Monn: Five Symphonies*. Series B, vol. 1 of *The Symphony, 1720–1840*. New York and London: Garland, 1985.

Ruhling, Michael. "Johann Michael Haydn." In *The Symphonic Repertoire. Vol. 2, The Eighteenth-Century Symphony*, edited by Mary Sue Morrow and Bathia Churgin, 498–515. Bloomington and Indianapolis: Indiana University Press, 2012.

Rywosch, Bernhard. *Beiträge zur Entwicklung ini Joseph Haydns Symphonik, 1759–1780*. Turbenthal: Buchdruckerei R. Furrers Erben, 1934.

Saint-Foix, Georges de. *The Symphonies of Mozart*. Translated by Leslie Orrey. London: Denis Dobson, 1947.

Sadie, Stanley. *Mozart Symphonies*. London: BBC Publications, 1986.

Sadie, Stanley. *Mozart: The Early Years 1756–1781*. New York: Norton, 2006.

Schenker, Heinrich. *Harmony*. Edited by Oswald Jonas. Translated by Elisabeth Mann Borghese. Cambridge, MA: MIT Press, 1973.

Schleuning, Peter. "Sturm und Drang in der Musik: Sturm im Wasserglas oder Drang der Forschung?" In *Sturm und Drang in Literatur und Musik*, edited by Bert Siegmund, 31–50. Blankenburg (Harz): Stiftung Kloster Michaelstein, 2004.

Schmidt, Ernst Fritz. "Gottfried van Swieten als Komponist." *Mozart Jahrbuch 1953* (1954): 15–31.

Schroeder, David P. *Haydn and the Enlightenment: The Late Symphonies and Their Audience*. Oxford: Clarendon Press, 1990.

Schwartz, Judith L. "Periodicity and Passion in the First Movement of Haydn's 'Farewell' Symphony." In *Studies in Musical Sources and Style: Essays in Honor of Jan LaRue*, edited by Eugene K. Wolf and Edward H. Roesner, 293–388. Madison, WI: A-R Editions, 1990.

Sisman, Elaine. *Haydn and the Classical Variation*. Cambridge, MA: Harvard University Press, 1993.

Sisman, Elaine. "Haydn's Theater Symphonies." *Journal of the American Musicological Society* 43, no. 2 (1990): 292–352.

Smith, F. J. "Mozart Revisited, K.550: The Problem of the Survival of Baroque Figures in the Classical Era." *Music Review* 31 (1970): 201–14.

Spazier, Johann Gottlieb Carl. "Über Menuetten in Sinfonien." *Musikalisches Wochenblatt* (1791–92): 91–92.

Spitzer, John, and Neal Zaslaw. *The Birth of the Orchestra: History of an Institution, 1650–1815*. Oxford: Oxford University Press, 2004.

Spitzer, Michael. "Emotions and Meaning in Music." *Musica humana* 1, no. 2 (2009): 155–96.

Spitzer, Michael. "Haydn's Reversals: Style Change, Gesture and the Implication-Realization Model." In *Haydn Studies*, edited by W. Dean Sutcliffe, 177–217. Cambridge: Cambridge University Press, 1998.

Spitzer, Michael. "Six Great Early Symphonists." In *The Cambridge Companion to the Symphony*, edited by Julian Horton, 133–54. Cambridge: Cambridge University Press, 2013.

Steblin, Rita. *A History of Key Characteristics in the Eighteenth and Early Nineteenth Centuries*. 2nd ed. Rochester, NY: University of Rochester Press, 2002.

Steinbeck, Wolfram. "Das Menuett in der Instrumentalmusik Joseph Haydns." PhD diss., Albert-Ludwigs-Universität Freiburg, 1972.

Steptoe, Andrew. "Mozart and His Last Three Symphonies—a Myth Laid to Rest?" *Musical Times* 132 (1991): 550–51.

Subotnik, Rose Rosengard. *Developing Variations: Style and Ideology in Western Music*. Minneapolis: University of Minnesota Press, 1991.

Sutcliffe, W. Dean. "Expressive Ambivalence in Haydn's Symphonic Slow Movements of the 1770s." *Journal of Musicology* 27, no. 1 (2010): 84–134.

Tenschert, Roland. "Die G-moll-Tonart bei Mozart." *Mozart-Jahrbuch 1951* (1953): 112–22.

Todd, R. Larry. "Joseph Haydn and the Sturm und Drang: A Revaluation." *Music Review* 41 (1980): 172–96.

Tomlinson, Gary. "The Web of Culture: A Context for Musicology." *19th-Century Music* 7, no. 3 (1984): 350–62.

Tovey, Donald Francis. "Sonata Forms." In *Encyclopedia Britannica*. 11th ed. Cambridge and New York: Cambridge University Press, 1910–11.

Tovey, Donald Francis. "Symphony in G Minor." In *Essays in Musical Analysis. Vol. 1, Symphonies*, 191–95. London: Oxford University Press, 1935.

Treitler, Leo. *Music and the Historical Imagination*. Cambridge, MA: Harvard University Press, 1990.

Tyson, Alan. *Mozart: Studies of the Autograph Scores*. Cambridge, MA, and London: Harvard University Press, 1987.

Unverricht, Hubert. *Geschichte des Streichtrios*. Tutzing: Hans Schneider, 1969.

Waldoff, Jessica. "Does Haydn Have a 'C Minor Mood'?" In *Engaging Haydn*, edited by Mary Hunter and Richard Will, 158–86. Cambridge: Cambridge University Press, 2012.

Weber, William. "The Contemporaneity of Eighteenth-Century Musical Taste." *Musical Quarterly* 70, no. 2 (1984): 175–94.

Weber, William. "*La musique ancienne* in the Waning of the Ancien Régime." *Journal of Modern History* 56, no. 1 (1984): 58–88.

Webster, James. "The Analysis of Mozart's Arias." In *Mozart Studies*, edited by Cliff Eisen, 101–99. Oxford: Clarendon Press, 1991.

Webster, James. *Haydn's "Farewell" Symphony and the Idea of Classical Style: Through-Composition and Cyclic Integration in His Instrumental Music.* Cambridge: Cambridge University Press, 1991.

Webster, James. "Haydn's Symphonies between *Sturm und Drang* and 'Classical Style': Art and Entertainment." In *Haydn Studies*, edited by W. Dean Sutcliffe, 218–45. Cambridge: Cambridge University Press, 1998.

Wellbury, David. *Lessing's "Laocoon": Semiotics and Aesthetics in the Age of Reason.* Cambridge: Cambridge University Press, 1984.

Wen, Eric. "A Disguised Reminiscence in the First Movement of Mozart's G Minor Symphony." *Music Analysis* 1, no. 1 (1982): 55–71.

Westrup, J. A. "Cherubino and the G Minor Symphony." In *Fanfare for Ernest Newman*, edited by Herbert van Thal, 181–91. London: Arthur Baker, 1955.

Wheelock, Gretchen A. "*Schwarze Gredel* and the Engendered Minor Mode in Mozart's Operas." In *Musicology and Difference: Gender and Sexuality in Music Scholarship*, edited by Ruth A. Solie, 201–24. Berkeley: University of California Press, 1992.

Will, Richard. "Carl Ditters von Dittersdorf." In *The Symphonic Repertoire. Vol. 2, The Eighteenth-Century Symphony*, edited by Mary Sue Morrow and Bathia Churgin, 483–97. Bloomington and Indianapolis: Indiana University Press, 2012.

Will, Richard. *The Characteristic Symphony in the Age of Haydn and Beethoven.* Cambridge: Cambridge University Press, 2002.

Will, Richard. "Time, Morality, and Humanity in Beethoven's Pastoral Symphony." *Journal of the American Musicological Society* 50, no. 1–2 (1997): 271–330.

Williams, Peter. *The Chromatic Fourth during Four Centuries of Music.* Oxford: Clarendon, 1997.

Winter, Robert S. "The Bifocal Close and the Evolution of the Viennese Classical Style." *Journal of the American Musicological Society* 42, no. 2 (1989): 318–19.

Wolf, Eugene K. *The Symphonies of Johann Stamitz: A Study in the Formation of the Classic Style.* Utrecht and Antwerp: Bohn, Scheltma and Holkema, 1981.

Wollenberg, Susan. "Vienna under Joseph I and Charles VI." In *The Late Baroque Era: From the 1680s to 1740*, edited by George J. Buelow, 324–54. Englewood Cliffs, NJ: Prentice Hall, 1994.

Wood, Caroline. "Orchestra and Spectacle in the *Tragédie en musique* 1673–1715: Oracle, Sommeil and Tempête." *Proceedings of the Royal Musical Association* 108 (1981–82): 25–45.

Wyzewa, Théodore de. "Apropos du centenaire de la mort de Joseph Haydn." *Revue des deux mondes* 79 (June 15, 1909): 935–46.

Wyzewa, Théodore de, and Georges de Saint-Foix. *W.-A. Mozart: sa vie musicale et son œuvre de l'enfance à la pleine maturité (1756-1777): essai de biographie critique, suivi d'un nouveau catalogue chronologique de l'œuvre complète du maitre.* 5 vols. Paris: Perrin, 1912.

Young, David. "Karl von Ordonez (1734–1786): A Biographical Study." *Royal Musical Association Research Chronicle* 19 (1983–85): 31–56.

Young, David. "The Symphonies of Karl von Ordonez (1734–1786): A Biographical, Bibliographical and Stylistic Study." PhD diss., University of Liverpool, 1980.

Young, Percy. *A History of British Music*. London: Benn, 1963.

Zaslaw, Neal. "Mozart as a Working Stiff." In *On Mozart*, edited by James M. Morris, 102–12. New York: Woodrow Wilson Center Press; Cambridge: Cambridge University Press, 1994.

Zaslaw, Neal. "Mozart, Haydn and the *Sinfonia da Chiesa*." *Journal of Musicology* 1, no. 1 (1982): 95–124.

Zaslaw, Neal. *Mozart's Symphonies: Context, Performance Reception*. Oxford: Clarendon, 1989.

Zenck, Claudia Maurer. *Vom Takt: Untersuchungen zur Theorie und kompositorischen Praxis im ausgehenden 18. und beginnenden 19. Jahrhundert*. Vienna: Böhlau, 2001.

{ INDEX }